Singapore – Two Hundred Years of the Lion City

Two hundred years after Singapore's foundation by Stamford Raffles in 1819, this book reflects on the historical development of the city, putting forward much new research and new thinking. It discusses Singapore's emergence as a regional economic hub, explores its strategic importance and considers its place in the development of the British Empire. Subjects covered include the city's initial role as a strategic centre to limit the resurgence of Dutch power in Southeast Asia after the Napoleonic Wars, the impact of the Japanese occupation and the reasons for Singapore's exit from the Malaysian Federation in 1965. The book concludes by examining how Singapore's history is commemorated at present, reinforcing the image of the city as prosperous, peaceful and forward-looking, and draws out the lessons which history can provide concerning the city's likely future development.

Anthony Webster is Professor of History at Northumbria University, UK.

Nicholas J. White is Professor of Imperial and Commonwealth History at Liverpool John Moores University, UK.

Routledge Studies in the Modern History of Asia

For a full list of available titles please visit: www.routledge.com/Routledge-Studies-in-the-Modern-History-of-Asia/book-series/MODHISTASIA

Singapore – Two Hundred Years of the Lion City

Edited by Anthony Webster and Nicholas J. White

Routledge
Taylor & Francis Group

LONDON AND NEW YORK

First published 2020
by Routledge
2 Park Square, Milton Park, Abingdon, Oxon OX14 4RN

and by Routledge
52 Vanderbilt Avenue, New York, NY 10017

Routledge is an imprint of the Taylor & Francis Group, an informa business

British Library Cataloguing-in-Publication Data
A catalogue record for this book is available from the British Library

Library of Congress Cataloging-in-Publication Data
A catalog record for this book has been requested

ISBN: 978-1-138-49682-8 (hbk)
ISBN: 978-1-351-02046-6 (ebk)

Typeset in Times New Roman
by Apex CoVantage, LLC

Contents

Illustrations

Contributors

Donna Brunero is Senior Lecturer in the Department of History at the National University of Singapore. She researches the intersections between maritime and imperial history with particular reference to the British presence in the port cities of Asia in the nineteenth and twentieth centuries. Her previous works include *Empire in Asia: A New Global History, Vol 2, The Long Nineteenth Century* (2018) (ed. with Brian P. Farrell), and *Britain's Imperial Cornerstone in China: the Chinese maritime customs service, 1854–1949* (2006).

Tim Bunnell is Professor of Human Geography at the National University of Singapore. He is an urban geographer who works on the development of cities in Southeast Asia and their global connections. His most recent books are *From World City to the World in One City: Liverpool through Malay Lives* (2016) and *Urban Asias: Essays on Futurity Past and Present* (2018) (ed. with Daniel P.S. Goh).

Valeria Giacomin is Founder Fellow at Founder Central, Lloyd Greif Center for Entrepreneurial Studies, Marshall School of Business, University of Southern California, and worked as Assistant Professor of Business History at Copenhagen Business School. Valeria wrote her thesis on the evolution of the rubber and palm oil cluster in Southeast Asia (2016). Her articles have been published in *Management & Organizational History* (2017), *Enterprise & Society* (2018) and the *Journal of Global History* (2018). She received the European Business History Association prize for best doctoral thesis in business history in 2018, and her article 'The Emergence of an Export Cluster: Traders and Palm Oil in Early Twentieth-Century Southeast Asia' received the Mira Wilkins prize for best article in international business history in 2019.

Gillian Huff is with the History Faculty, University of Oxford. She is the author of *Lonrho: Portrait of a Multinational* (with Suzanne Cronje and Margaret Ling), *SWAPO Information on Namibian Political Prisoners* and *The Workers of Namibia* (with Suzanne Cronje). Gillian has authored numerous economic history journal articles.

Gregg Huff is Senior Research Fellow at Pembroke College, University of Oxford. He is the author of *The Economic Growth of Singapore: Trade and*

Development in the Twentieth Century (1994) and *World War II and Southeast Asia: the Economic and Social Consequences of Japanese Occupation* (2019), and has co-edited with Shinobu Majima and contributed to *World War II Singapore: The Chōsabu Reports on Syonan* (2018). Gregg has authored numerous journal articles in economic history and economics journals.

Tomotaka Kawamura is a member of the Academic Support Staff at the Humanities Center, University of Tokyo. His publications include chapters in *Maritime Trade and the Hinterland in Asia* (2015) (eds. Tsukasa Mizushima, George Souza and Denis Flynn) and *Commodities, Ports and Asian Maritime Trade since 1750* (2015) (eds. Ulbe Bosma and Anthony Webster) and *The British Empire beyond the Closed Door: Early History of the British Eastern Exchange Banks* (2019).

G. Roger Knight is Research Fellow of the University of Adelaide, South Australia. His most recent publications include *Trade and Empire in Early Nineteenth Century Southeast Asia: Gillian Maclaine and his Business Network, 1816–1840* (2015); 'Family Firms, Global Networks and Transnational Actors: The Case of Alexander Fraser (1816–1904), Merchant and Entrepreneur in the Netherlands Indies, Low Countries and London', (2018); and (with Alexander Claver) 'A European Role in Intra-Asian Commercial Development: The Maclaine Watson Network and the Java Sugar Trade c.1840–1942', (2018).

Atsushi Kobayashi is Assistant Professor at Center for Southeast Asian Studies, Kyoto University. His previous publications include 'The Role of Singapore in the Growth of Intra-Southeast Asian Trade, c.1820s–1852', (2013), 'Price Fluctuations and Growth Patterns in Singapore's Trade, 1831–1913', (2017) and 'International Bimetallism and Silver Absorption in Singapore, 1840–73', (2019).

Kah Seng Loh is a historian of Singapore and an Honorary Research Fellow at the University of Western Australia. He is the author of the award-nominated *Squatters into Citizens: The 1961 Bukit Ho Swee Fire and the Making of Modern Singapore* (2013) and a forthcoming book (co-authored) on the history of tuberculosis in Singapore. He also runs a research consultancy on the rich and varied heritages of Singapore – housing, industrial, medical, and culinary.

John N. Miksic is Professor in the Southeast Asian Studies department at the National University of Singapore. His publications include *Singapore and the Silk Road of the Sea* (2013), *Between Two Oceans. A Military History of Singapore from 1275 to 1971* (2010) (with Malcolm Murfett, Brian Farrell and Chiang Ming Shun) and 'York Fort, Bengkulu, and the archaeology of southwest Sumatra' (1990).

Stan Neal is the John Springhall Post-Doctoral Lecturer in Modern British/ Imperial History at Ulster University. He has published articles on Chinese migration and British opium trading networks in *Modern Asian Studies* and the *Journal of World History*. His first monograph, *Singapore, Chinese Migration* *and the Making of the British Empire, 1819–67* (2019), places early colonial Singapore in an imperial context.

A. J. Stockwell is Emeritus Professor of Modern History, Royal Holloway, University of London and currently President of the Royal Asiatic Society. He was joint editor of the *Journal of Imperial and Commonwealth History*, 1989–2007. His publications include *Malaya* and *Malaysia* in the series British Documents on End of Empire (London, HMSO/TSO) and 'In search of regional authority in Southeast Asia: The improbable partnership of Lord Killearn and Malcolm MacDonald, 1946–8' (2017).

Anthony Webster is Professor in History at Northumbria University. He specialises in business history, especially in relation to the British Empire in Asia and the international cooperative movement. His key publications are *The Richest East India Merchant* (2007) and *The Twilight of the East India Company* (2009). He recently published *Co-operation and Globalisation* (2019).

Nicholas J. White is Professor of Imperial and Commonwealth History at Liverpool John Moores University and Co-Director of Liverpool's Centre for Port and Maritime History. His previous books include *Business, Government, and the End of Empire: Malaya, 1942–1957* (1996), *British Business in Post-Colonial Malaysia, 1957–70: 'Disengagement' or 'Neo-Colonialism'?* (2004) and *The International Order of Asia in the 1930s and 1950s* (2010) (ed. with Shigeru Akita).

Editors' acknowledgements

This volume has its origins in a workshop held in Liverpool in September 2018. The generous support of Liverpool John Moores University (LJMU), the Centre for Port & Maritime History (a joint enterprise between LJMU, the University of Liverpool and Merseyside |Maritime History), and the Economic History Society in facilitating this workshop and the subsequent collection of essays which has eventuated is gratefully acknowledged. Special thanks are due to James Brocklesby and Dan Feather, who provided invaluable organisational help at the workshop. We would also like to take this opportunity to record our gratitude to Peter Sowden (our editor at Routledge who graciously attended the Singapore 200 workshop), not only for his work in the production of this volume but in his tireless efforts on behalf of imperial, maritime and Asian history over many years. Our better halves – Lesley Webster and Jan Barwise – have, as ever, been crucial sources of support and tolerance and this volume is dedicated to them both.

1 Introduction

Situating Singapore's success

Anthony Webster and Nicholas J. White

Looking to Asia for answers to domestic economic questions has been a recurring theme in British political and economic history. During the economic difficulties of the 1880s and 1890s, the potential of China as a market for British manufactures was regularly touted around the chambers of commerce of provincial Britain as a way out of depression. From the 1960s, commentators aggrieved at British economic decline, became fascinated by the Japanese economic 'miracle' as a potential model for the UK to follow. In the last decade or so, China has once again moved centre stage, arguably with much more justification, as a promising market for British manufactures. The fascination with Asia has been heightened by the proliferation of Asian companies setting up or acquiring manufacturing plants, prestigious property and even football clubs in the UK, including Nissan, Honda, Toyota, Tata, Sime Darby and Air Asia. The prospect of Brexit has sent cabinet ministers to the Pacific Rim in search not only of trading and investment partners but new economic models for Britain after its departure from its European harbour.

In this volume of essays, Tim Bunnell's comparative analysis of the postcolonial reversal of fortunes affecting Liverpool and Singapore points to precisely why emulating Singapore has found favour in the UK: by the 1990s, residents of Liverpool, once one of the world's leading port cities, were talking gloomily of being reduced to 'Third World' status while simultaneously Singaporean leaders, presiding over the world's busiest port, boasted of joining the 'First World'. For 2018, Singapore was ranked ninth in the world in the UN's Human Development Index (HDI) compared to the United Kingdom at 14th.[1] Singapore has been seen, especially by the more zealous supporters of a 'free market' Brexit, almost as a blueprint for post-2019 British political economy. Visiting Singapore in January 2019, Jeremy Hunt, Britain's foreign secretary, ruled out copying the city-state's structures in total, but he did see Singapore – an island nation of, but not entirely integrated with, its immediate region – as an exemplar from which much could be learned. Hunt cited specifically the 'excellence of [Singapore's] education system, the long-term investment in infrastructure and a strategic approach to how a nation sustains competitive advantage in the world.'[2] The vacuum cleaner entrepreneur and vocal pro-Brexit supporter, James Dyson, went a stage further by announcing the relocation of his company's headquarters to Singapore. The island's low taxes, access to growing Asian markets and the recent trade agreement with the EU were cited by observers as possible reasons for Dyson's move.[3]

It is ironic that exactly 200 years after Raffles claimed the island for the English East India Company interest in Singapore has been rekindled in the UK, highlighting this once iconic British colonial possession as a model for the future. The present volume therefore has an unexpected contemporary resonance in Britain, as well as being a timely reflection upon a major example of imperial 'place-making'– of the creation (or revival, in view of the much earlier existence of Temasek-Singapura) of a major entrepôt within Britain's Asian network of imperial city-ports, including Calcutta, Bombay, Madras, Colombo, Rangoon, Penang, Melaka and Hong Kong. Unlike so many former European-controlled cities, Singapore has enjoyed a glittering postcolonial career, rising to become perhaps the most impressive economic and social success story of Southeast Asia. In Singapore itself, this has produced some measure of ambivalence about the colonial origins of modern Singapore, as Donna Brunero emphasises in her chapter in this collection. While the ruling post-independence regime in Singapore is robustly critical of colonialism, Thomas Stamford Raffles, the primary imperial agent of 1819, remains a celebrated figure, not least for his commitment to free trade and enterprise, principles which remain firmly at the heart of modern Singaporean economic policy and national identity. This ambiguity is evident in commemoration or celebration of the bicentennial in Singapore itself. The website of the body organising the bicentennial celebrations refers to 1819 as a 'milestone' in Singapore's development but not in fact the origins of the city, which are firmly placed 700 years ago, as Temasek.[4] In this way, the potentially embarrassing identification of Singapore as a purely imperial creation, which might owe its success to the legacy of colonial rule, is averted. John Miksic's chapter in the present volume certainly confirms that Raffles's acquisition of Singapore was not an act of 'pure' creation but rather one of revival; of re-establishment of what had once been a major centre of trade and political authority. That said, the spectacular and rapid growth of Singapore's population and trade in the two decades after 1819 was unprecedented and justifies the assumption encompassed in the present volume that the port's bicentennial year marks a very significant milestone in the island's development.[5]

Singapore's success since independence is thus a matter of contemporary political attention, though its historical roots have attracted less interest or proper appreciation beyond academia. In part, this reflects that, as a former British possession, Singapore's historical rise to prominence may reveal some uncomfortable truths about the contribution of colonial rule to that success, and this is certainly suggested in some of the chapters in this book. Bunnell's study of Malay seafaring networks, for example, points to the commercial and cultural influence of Liverpool, the so-called 'Second City of the Empire', from the 1860s to the 1960s in the making of global Singapore. A controversial recent reinterpretation of the history of Hong Kong (ranked equal as seventh with Sweden in the UN's HDI for 2018), meanwhile, has placed the offshore city-state alongside Singapore and the Gulf States in Britain's 'Asian city cluster' in which the imperial power promoted free trade and provided institutional frameworks that encouraged private enterprise, while also empowering a cooperative Asian intermediary class. This benevolent colonial legacy left the post-British entrepôts as 'engines of modernisation' in their respective regions.[6] As Stan Neal discusses in his essay in the present collection, educated and inquisitive Singaporeans recognise today how the English language and British-style institutions and law have contributed positively to the nature of the contemporary city-state. But, equally for Singapore as in Hong Kong, racial and class hierarchies, and the resulting income disparities and political upheavals, take the gilding off British colonialism.[7] Moreover, irrespective of the rights, wrongs and wherefores of colonial rule vis-à-vis the postcolonial nation state, the history of Singapore's growth should also give pause to those who seek to find in it a model which can be easily copied or transferred to other contexts. Indeed, it should become clear by reading the chapters in this volume that while Singapore has become seen as an exemplar which might be imitated elsewhere, its relative success was in many ways the interaction of a range of factors not easily replicated. It is worth spelling these out, not only to identify some of the unique reasons for Singapore's spectacular growth (with the important caveat that this has been achieved at the expense of personal liberty) but also to bring out both elements of continuity which span the transition from imperial rule to independence and innovations post-independence which mark a break with the colonial past.

Perhaps the most striking aspect of modern Singapore from its very earliest days after 1819 was both the multi-ethnic composition of its population and its position as a gateway for the inward migration of social (and to a lesser extent financial) capital and people into the city itself and further 'Up Country' into the Malay peninsula. G. Roger Knight reminds us of the importance of the Scottish entrepreneurial diaspora which formed the backbone of the expatriate import-export firms – known as agency houses – which came to dominate the top echelons of Singapore's commerce during the nineteenth century. But the European population was always tiny and itinerant, and the considerable wealth accumulation by the expatriate merchant princes was down to the lure of Singapore for more permanent Asian settlers. Singapore's trade and population grew rapidly from the 1820s as a result of the revitalised port's success in attracting traders from all over the Malay world eager to sell Southeast Asian produce in demand in the Chinese market (to which it was re-exported by both European and Chinese merchants) and to purchase imports from India and later from Britain, especially cotton goods.

Yet a crucial aspect of Chinese immigration into Singapore was its nature. The rapidity of the growth of the port's Chinese population was facilitated by relocation of pre-existing Chinese communities from ports such as Melaka to Singapore, taking with them their own networks of finance and partnerships as well as their connections with China and across Southeast Asia. Recent work in regional studies demonstrates that immigration involving 'Communities-on-the-Move' frequently boosts economic growth most effectively when whole communities relocate, transferring with them business connections and social and familial bonds built up over time. This enables such communities to 'hit the ground running' in economic terms, providing a speedy and lasting boost to the local economy.[8] This certainly seems to have been the case for Singapore, as Chinese merchants provided an invaluable link with traders across the region, rapidly opening markets and sources of Southeast Asian produce not only for the Chinese but for the European agency houses who came to depend on them (as stressed also in Knight's chapter). Added to this, the later large inflow of Chinese labourers for the tin mines of the Malay states was not only facilitated by this Singaporean Chinese community, it also in doing so, furnished the imperial authorities with a means to fund government without resorting to higher taxes or trade tariffs, through the infamous system of opium farming and other exclusive retailing rights, which the Chinese *kongsis* (syndicates) purchased and ran. Even newcomers to Singapore from China such as Seah Eu Chin, who arrived in 1823, were able to quickly find a place within what was already a well-ordered Chinese community (as emphasised in Neal's essay in this collection). This all amounted to the rapid installation in Singapore of a highly organised and effective Chinese community able to deliver well-established and unparalleled business services and regional linkages. Indeed, the relative openness of Singapore to inward migration remained both a feature of official policy into the post-independence period and a source of economic vibrancy. Anti-immigration British Brexiteers seeking to imitate Singapore should take note.

A second key feature of Singapore's success was its embedded role in the commerce of Southeast Asia, and how this helped provide a platform for launching the port as a 'global' city. Singapore quickly became the focal point for intra-regional commerce by the late 1830s, notwithstanding efforts by the Dutch to curb its growth through protectionist tariffs. Knight shows how the Fraser brothers were 'made in Singapore' between the 1830s and the 1850s partly by trades that originated outside Southeast Asia – cotton textiles and opium – but simultaneously by tapping into and piggy-backing on wider intra-regional networks (notably in the rice trade). Tomotaka Kawamura's chapter shows how this intra-Asian dimension was strengthened later in the century with the establishment of major branches for a range of Exchange Banks in Singapore and elsewhere in the region. The port's pivotal role in facilitating mass Chinese immigration further boosted its regional centrality, and as Valeria Giacomin shows in her essay, the development of a highly effective cluster of interests linked with the rubber industry, early in the twentieth century, enabled Singapore to expand the range of its services into other nascent industries, including palm-oil production. From its earliest days, Singapore also developed commerce outside the region (as Knight's discussion of opium reveals). Atsushi Kobayashi's chapter examines how Singapore in the 1820s and 1830s became an important entrée to the Southeast Asia market for Indian cotton goods at a time when the subcontinent's producers were under severe competitive pressure from British industrially produced textiles. In due course, British cottons also displaced Indian cloth from the Southeast Asian market, though local preference for South Asian textiles slowed this process. Singapore also provided the financial and labour provision services which enabled Southeast Asia to become a major supplier of raw materials to the global economy, including tin and later rubber from mainland Malaya, as well as rice and teak from Burma and Siam. It was Singapore's integrated connections within the region which provided the platform for its global 'career' especially after 1900, a point emphatically made by Giacomin.

In their discussion of the Japanese Occupation of 1942–1945 in this collection, Gregg and Gillian Huff show that de-regionalisation through loss of food supplies and de-globalisation (through shutting off world markets for rubber and tin exports and imports of consumer and capital goods) led to severe economic dislocation. This commercial collapse during the Pacific War cannot have been helped by a lack of knowledge and severe repression of the overseas Chinese on the part of Japan's administrators. As such, Huff & Huff view the post-1965 export-oriented industrialisation (EOI) of independent Singapore as a far more significant break point in the city's economic development than the ill-fated era of Japanese rule. As Kah Seng Loh's chapter reveals, however, the EOI strategy – targeted at both regional and wider world markets – had been anticipated as early as 1960–1961, and as Nicholas J. White's essay suggests, this was reinforced by the negative experiences of incorporation into and separation from Malaysia between 1963 and 1965. Inter alia, White's chapter shows how economic tensions between Singapore and Kuala Lumpur were engendered by the island's embroilment in confrontation with Indonesia, which shut off long-established regional exchanges, and by disagreements over the formation of a common market in which Singapore's globalised free-port status was threatened. In the post-independence era, as Loh's chapter elucidates further, Singapore's policy of rapid industrialisation was predicated on attracting foreign investment and selling to the global market rather than simply relying on regional interconnections. The key policy adviser, Albert Winsemius, was especially heeded in this policy, which very much aligned with the strong commercial lobby. Would-be exponents of a British 'Singapore' would do well to ponder the importance of regional interests for global projection in the history of Singapore's rise. The early success of Singapore's containerisation, for example, was linked to the technologically upgraded port's role as a centre for regional transhipment.[9] In similar vein, the coastal feeder services of, for example, the Straits Steamship Company played a key role during the colonial era in the rise of the Southeast Asian hub linked in turn to global ocean-going shipping (as addressed by both Bunnell and Giacomin).

A third factor in Singapore's success, before and after independence, was its creation of a political and institutional framework and culture which privileged (and still privileges) commerce and international openness. The latter, as Loh stresses, was represented not just in economic exchanges but also in the willingness of successive Singapore governments (colonial and postcolonial) to take advice from overseas consultants on social and economic policy from the 1900s. That's not to forget the important geo-strategic role which Singapore came to take on as the outer defence of Australasia as A. J. Stockwell's chapter demonstrates. As noted in White's essay, the British defence complex in Singapore was reckoned to account for 20–25 per cent of Singapore's GDP in the 1960s: it was no surprise, therefore, that Lee Kuan Yew was distraught at Britain's accelerated military withdrawal 'east of Suez' from 1968. But, as Stockwell shows, Singapore was late to the party of fortress colonies compared to Gibraltar, Bermuda and Malta, with the former's naval base completed as late as 1938. Even then, Singapore continued to be valued in London primarily in economic terms as a regional commercial hub and in its facilitation of Malaya's supplies of commodities to world markets (and the resultant dollar earnings from massive sales of rubber and tin to the US especially). This absence of a longer term 'defence culture,' and a lack of integration between civil and military administrations, explains the lack of preparedness for the Japanese onslaught (although Britain's imperial overstretch in fighting a war on two fronts was necessarily a big factor in the fall of Singapore in February 1942).

Back in the early nineteenth century, Anthony Webster's chapter shows, alienation from the East India Company's rule and its priorities for the Straits Settlements mobilised merchants in defence of such policies as free trade and the use of the dollar, and ultimately to campaign for the Colonial Office to take over jurisdiction of the Straits. This was achieved in the late 1860s. Webster shows how Straits' interests, led by the Singapore Chamber of Commerce, built alliances in Britain amongst the East India and China Associations of London, Glasgow and Liverpool as part of their campaign against East India Company policies, and these were continued later into the century with the formation in London of the Straits Settlements Association at the end of the 1860s. Kawamura analyses how the Eastern Exchange Banks moved into the Straits – especially Singapore – partly out of recognition of the congenial political environment there. Giacomin demonstrates how in the twentieth century the rise of a sophisticated cluster of businesses based on rubber production maintained and developed this strong culture of commercial influence. Even after independence, Loh shows that the success of Winsemius in influencing the semi-colonial and post-independence governments of Lee Kuan Yew was built on his willingness to side with multinational business interests against the trade unions, which were roundly condemned by Lee as communist. Symbolically, in terms of the continuities between colonial and postcolonial eras, that pro-business policy included not pulling down Raffles's statue (an issue which is also addressed in the chapters by Miksic and Brunero). Moreover, the policy of repression of the radical left, involving the internment of its leadership during 1963, was endorsed both by Winsemius and the international business community in Singapore. In its Annual Report for 1961, the Singapore Chamber of Commerce, still dominated by European (and especially British) trading and investment groups, reported that a major obstacle to inward capital investment continued to be 'the orgy of strikes, go-slows, sit-downs, etc., which are currently termed "industrial unrest"'. In May 1966, however, the chairman of the restyled Singapore International Chamber of Commerce reported contentedly that labour troubles had 'paled into insignificance compared with five years ago'.[10]

Indeed, the de-globalisation and de-radicalisation of the labour movement under the People's Action Party governments from the late 1950s illustrates the central role of the interventionist 'muscular' nation state in refashioning Singaporean economy and society (notwithstanding the internationalisation of capital beyond the traditional imperial supplier, Britain, that characterised the island's postcolonial globalisation).[11] This semi-authoritarianism has been apparent in attempts to forge a state-led national history, identity and purpose (pointed to in the chapters in this collection by Brunero, Miksic and Neal in their discussions of the commemoration and memorialisation of Singapore's past plus Stockwell's discussion of the Total Defence concept as one of the 'lessons' of the fall of Singapore to the Japanese).[12] Although not explicitly addressed in this volume, authoritarian tendencies and a culture of control have their roots in the era of colonial rule and especially British attempts to manage decolonisation and preserve UK influence in postcolonial Southeast Asia.[13] While right-wing Brexiteers might welcome Singapore-style restrictions on trade unions, the Singapore sociopolitical model, paradoxically drawing its initial inspiration from Britain's welfare state as Loh reminds us, fits uncomfortably with the 'liberal' political traditions of the UK or recent scepticism about the state's role in economic management and social provision. Again, this emphasises that the Singapore experience is not a one-size-fits-all model.

✳ ✳

While there have been various edited volumes and histories of Singapore, this book, *Singapore – Two Hundred Years of the Lion City* (herein *Singapore 200*), comes at a crucial moment in the international history of globalisation (when many are questioning the virtues of free trade and labour flows), and following a long period of Asian economic growth of which Singapore has been at the forefront. This volume is distinguished from the existing literature in a number of ways. *Singapore: A Biography* by Mark Ravinder Frost and Yu-Mei Balasingamchow (Singapore: Editions Didier Millet, 2009) is a marvellous, beautifully illustrated compendium, but, while incorporating a large body of scholarship, it remains a work of public rather than academic history. Edwin Lee's *Singapore: The Unexpected Nation* (Singapore: ISEAS, 2008) is focussed on the post-World War Two period and on nation-building, whereas the present collection has a much longer trajectory, from precolonial to postcolonial eras, and a wider consideration of continuities and changes in Singapore's modern history. The edited collection, *Paths Not Taken: Political Pluralism in Post-War Singapore* (Singapore: NUS Press, 2008; ed. Michael D. Barr and Carl A. Trocki) also has a much shorter chronological focus (from the 1950s to the 1970s) and concentrates primarily on Singapore's political history compared to our wider economic, political and sociocultural coverage. Trocki's *Singapore: Wealth, Power and the Culture of Control* (London: Routledge, 2006) does recognise the colonial inheritance, but most of the text deals with the development of a quasi-authoritarian state under Lee Kuan Yew's premiership from 1959–1990. C. Mary Turnbull's classic overview, *A History of Modern Singapore, 1819–2005* (Revised edition, Singapore: NUS Press 2009; first edition 1977; second edition 1990), has the depth of chronology represented in the present volume, but the last iteration is now a decade old. Turnbull obviously did not have access to the more recent historiography and archival unearthings which have informed *Singapore 200*. Ernest Chew's and Edwin Lee's edited collection, *A History of Singapore* (Singapore: Oxford University Press, 1996), represents another comprehensive overview but again was published some time ago. Turnbull and Chew & Lee, it should be added, are also works of synthesis rather than new research-led explorations. Likewise, the seminal economic history, Gregg Huff's *The Economic Growth of Singapore* (Cambridge: Cambridge University Press, 1994), is now over two decades old, and *Singapore 200* provides a timely opportunity to re-explore some of the ideas developed by Huff in explaining the island's economic trajectory (as indeed is undertaken in the chapters by Giacomin and White, for example). With their historiographical foci, Karl Hack and Jean-Louis Margolin, with Karine Delaye (ed.), *Singapore from Temasek to the 21st Century: Reinventing the Global City* (Singapore: NUS Press, 2010) and Nicholas Tarling (ed.) *Studying Singapore's Past: C.M. Turnbull and the History of Modern Singapore* (NUS Press, 2012) are the closest comparator volumes to this collection. Even so, *Singapore from Temasek to the 21st Century* has more stress on reinventions and discontinuities than the subtle continuities that are addressed in many of the chapters in the present volume. *Singapore 200* also considers Singapore's history from wider intra-Asian, imperial and global history approaches and influences than was the concern of the scholars who contributed to *Studying Singapore's Past* (or indeed most of the other studies mentioned earlier in this paragraph).

The book is divided into two parts: 'Growth, Trade and Economy' and 'Politics, Culture and Identity'. All the essays in the volume have been specially commissioned with a view to revising or synthesising the existing literature and/or adding new insights into Singapore's history from wider comparative and interdisciplinary perspectives. The chapters are frequently informed by original research in previously untapped primary sources and are alive to both 'turning points' and continuities in the city-state's historical development. The transnational (including the intra-Asian) dimension is fully in evidence in the contributions by Kobayashi, Giacomin, Kawamura, Miksic, Knight and Loh. The imperial factor, meanwhile, is reassessed by Bunnell, Huff & Huff, Webster, Knight, Kawamura, Stockwell and Brunero. Neal, Bunnell, White, Knight and Miksic, on the other hand, are highly cognisant of non-European agency in the making of Singapore. Comparative analysis is provided in the studies by Stockwell, White, Brunero, Giacomin, Bunnell, Loh and Webster. At the same time, there is plenty of historiographical reconsideration of key issues and juncture's in Singapore's history – both Kobayashi and Miksic (and, to a lesser extent, Brunero) reinstate the precolonial history of Singapore; Huff & Huff deconstruct the so-called Japanese Occupation 'watershed'; White provides a new take on the reasons for Singapore's exit from Malaysia, and the Republic's subsequent economic development; while, Webster reanalyses the governmental changes of the nineteenth century. There are also highly original contributions on Singapore's historical and contemporary 'sense of itself' in the chapters by Brunero, Bunnell, Miksic and Neal. Indeed, above all in marking 200 years of the Lion City, all the essays in this volume address the present in the past, stressing that Singapore's relative success is not just a phenomenon for historians to pontificate about but represents an evolving and dynamic continuum.

Notes

1 http://data.un.org/DocumentData.aspx?q=human+development+index&id=392, accessed 11 April 2019. The UN's annual HDI scores are based upon an amalgam of health, knowledge and standard of living measures.
2 'UK May Draw Strength from Singapore Independence: British Foreign Secretary Jeremy Hunt,' *Straits Times*, 3 January 2019, available at: www.straitstimes.com/singapore/uk-may-draw-strength-from-spore-independence-hunt.
3 'Dyson to Move Company HQ to Singapore,' *The Guardian*, 22 January 2019, available at: www.theguardian.com/technology/2019/jan/22/dyson-to-move-company-hq-to-singapore.
4 ' "About the Singapore Centennial" SG Bicentennial: From Singapore to Singaporean,' available at: www.bicentennial.sg/about/.
5 As Peter Borschberg argues in his recent re-examination of Singapore's development over the *longue durée*, Raffles 'did not step into a political and economic vacuum' since the island 'had pre-existing settlements as well as a port and harbour.' The '(re)surgent port and regions controlled by the Temenggong [of Johor] offered a platform and an opportunity, and the British vastly expanded activity there by founding a colonial settlement and cultivating a symbiotic relationship with regional and transregional trading networks.' The British settlement was founded 'at an early stage of economic revitalization.' Nevertheless, for Borschberg, this 'does not deny or erase the significant role the British played in boosting Singapore's role as a port of call after 1819.' 'Singapore in the Cycles of the Longue Durée,' *Journal of the Malaysian Branch of the Royal Asiatic Society*, vol. 90, no. 1 (312), 2017, p. 51.
6 Wan-Kan Chin, *Hong Kong as a City-State*, Hong Kong: Enrich Publishing, 2012 cited in Xin Liu, ' "Too Simple and Sometimes Naïve": Hong Kong, Between China and the West,' in R. Shilliam and O. Rutazibwa (eds.), *Routledge Handbook of Post-Colonial Politics*, Abingdon: Routledge, 2018, p. 256.
7 Liu, 'Too Simple and Sometimes Naïve,' pp. 259–260.
8 M.D. Parrili, S. Montresor, and M. Trippi, 'A New Approach to Migrations: Communities-on-the-Move as Assets,' *Regional Studies*, vol. 53, no. 1, 2019, pp. 1–5.
9 Marc Levinson, *The Box: How the Shipping Container Made the World Smaller and the World Economy Bigger*, Princeton: Princeton University Press, 2006, p. 211.
10 Singapore International Chamber of Commerce, Singapore, *Annual Report 1961*, Chairman's Address, 9 April 1962, p. 38; *Annual Report 1965*, Chairman's Address, 20 May 1966, p. 58. A particular collaboration between the postcolonial government and ex-colonial capital was in attempts to prolong the British military presence 'East of Suez' in the late-1960s. In contrast, and demonstrating the instinctive global reflex of the Singaporean state, there were frosty relations with the local Chinese business community as evidenced by the recollections of the Hongkong and Shanghai Banking Corporation's general manager for Singapore and Malaysia in the 1960s. Tan Chin Tuan, the head of the Oversea-Chinese Banking Corporation, the 'most powerful bank in Singapore and Malaysia' and 'the biggest . . . the most influential Chinese' on the island, could not 'bear Lee Kuan Yew'. Tan distrusted Singaporean officials and refused to invest in the Jurong scheme (the massive industrial and infrastructure project which was central to the postcolonial government's development strategy and which is discussed further in this volume in the chapters by Loh and White). HSBC Group Archives, London, 1641/036, S.F.T.B. Lever interview, 20 August 1980.
11 Gareth Curless, ' "The People Need Civil Liberties": Trade Unions and Contested Decolonisation in Singapore,' *Labor History*, vol. 51, no. 1, 2016, pp. 53–70; Gareth

Curless, 'The Triumph of the State: Singapore's Dockworkers and the Limits of Global History, c. 1920–1965,' *Historical Journal*, vol. 60, no. 4, 2017, pp. 1097–1123.

12 For more on the development of national histories and myth-making, see Hong Lysa and Huang Jianli, *The Scripting of a National History: Singapore and Its Pasts*, Singapore: NUS Press, 2008; Loh Kah Seng, Thum Ping Tjin, and Jack Meng-Tat Chia (eds.), *Living with Myths in Singapore*, Singapore: Ethos Books, 2017.

13 See, for example, Carl A. Trocki, *Singapore: Wealth, Power and the Culture of Control*, London: Routledge, 2006; Matthew Jones, 'Creating Malaysia: Singapore Security, the Borneo Territories and the Contours of British Policy, 1961–63,' *Journal of Imperial and Commonwealth History*, vol. 28, no. 2, 2000.

Part I

Singapore – growth, trade & economy

2 The origins of Singapore's economic prosperity, c. 1800–1874

Atsushi Kobayashi

Introduction

So-called 'export-oriented industrialisation' has driven the recent economic growth of Southeast Asian economies. Taking advantage of exports to and foreign investments from developed countries, some Southeast Asian countries have succeeded in expanding their manufacturing industry and have attained the status of middle- or high-income nations. Moreover, with the introduction of free trade agreements in the 1990s, the Association of Southeast Asian Nations (ASEAN) began to promote greater regional economic integration. The ASEAN Economic Community was established at the end of 2015 with the aim of securing greater unity of regional markets. The ASEAN region has a population of 600 million and is characterised by the free movements of goods, capital and people across national boundaries. Notably, Singapore has played a key role in regional economic integration by achieving diplomatic and economic progress and becoming an iconic example of economic liberalisation. How did Singapore, a tiny urban community, survive the turmoil in the move towards post-war independence by Southeast Asian countries and end up as a leading player in the region? What were the determinants of Singapore's success in the context of the development of the region? This chapter addresses the historical roots of the emergence of Singapore as a trade hub and the rise of its economy in the context of the economic development of the region.

To help readers understand the origin of Singapore's foundation and its economic prosperity, this chapter addresses the development of Southeast Asian trade before the establishment of Singapore. From the late eighteenth century, British economic and political influence spread from the Indian colonies to Southeast Asia. Besides securing the route to the Chinese seas, British merchants became involved in intra-Asian trade by controlling the circulation of Southeast Asian produce. Penang was acquired by the English East India Company (EIC) in 1786. Dutch territories in Southeast Asia were temporarily seized by the British during the Napoleonic wars (1793–1815). The establishment of Singapore in 1819 was a result of these extensions of British power in the Eastern seas. This chapter investigates this subject further by focusing on the development of multilateral commercial relations in Southeast Asian trade. In particular, it analyses Singapore's imports of consumer goods from India and Britain using new information on British India between 1800 and 1874.

First, the chapter will examine how intra-Asian trade developed during the eighteenth century. Research on Asian trade in the early modern era suggests that, in the eighteenth century, the explosive population growth in China, which increased from approximately 150 million to 400 million, and the lifting of bans on trade by the Qing government induced a boom in Chinese overseas trade.[1] Southeast Asia exported a variety of regional products, such as pepper, rice and seafood to China on a large scale for mass consumption. Native traders in Southeast Asia collected these commodities and brought them to trade centres, from which they were shipped on Chinese *junks*. Thriving ports such as Riau, Malacca and Siak emerged around the Malacca Straits, which provide an accessible route connecting neighbouring Southeast Asian countries with China.[2] Riau was particularly prosperous. Native Bugis traders collected produce from across the archipelago and transported it to that port. Chinese junks visited Riau with the seasonal monsoon and took back commodities to southern Chinese ports. Looking for lucrative trade, Western merchants also gathered at Riau, and the port prospered as an entrepôt until the attack by the Dutch military in 1784. In exchange for exports of native produce, Southeast Asia imported not only Chinese commodities and Spanish silver coins but also Indian cotton goods that had been circulating worldwide since the sixteenth century.[3] The rise of the Chinese economy generated new demand for Southeast Asian products, and the trade boom between these areas revitalised the exports of Indian textiles to Southeast Asia. Simultaneously, in Britain, the reduction of duty on tea imports increased demand in British society.[4] In Asia, British free merchants – the so-called 'country traders' – were eager to participate in the intra-Asian trade to obtain Chinese products by trading them for Indian goods at Southeast Asian ports.[5]

The momentum of trade development persisted until the early nineteenth century. Southeast Asian exports of native produce to the Chinese market survived the fall of Riau in 1784 and the rampant piracy that followed until Singapore took over the role of a trading centre.[6] One of the driving forces for the initial development of Singapore was the export of Southeast Asian produce to the Chinese market.[7] With respect to the imports of foreign goods into Southeast Asia, the influx of manufactured cotton goods from Britain has been highlighted as a major factor for the development of Singapore as a trade hub.[8] British cloth reached Southeast Asia via Singapore, contributing to the integration of the region into the global economy. However, some studies contend that British cotton goods did not immediately capture the Southeast Asian market since Indian cloth dominated the regional circulation of consumer goods.[9] However, from the 1840s, British products overtook Indian goods in terms of trade volume. The persistence of Indian textiles in the Asian trade and their progressive replacement by British products must have affected the initial growth of Singapore. However, while the significance of the exports of tropical products to the Chinese market has been already discussed in depth, only a few studies traced the trajectory of cotton goods' trade in the eighteenth century. This chapter addresses this subject by focusing on the emergence of Singapore as a trade centre in the period marking the transition from the early modern era to the modern era over the period 1800 to 1874.

In addition, the chapter focuses on the role of imports into Southeast Asia. It has been argued that changes in consumer goods' imports became the driving force for the initial stage of modern trade growth in the peripheral regions of the global economy.[10] From the beginning of the nineteenth century, the overseas trade of the Middle East, Latin America and Southeast Asia increased significantly owing to the remarkable improvement in their terms of trade. The favourable terms of trade, or an increase in the goods that can be imported for every unit of export, was primarily caused by the inflow of manufactured cotton goods from the West. The massive supply of low-priced consumer goods gave local populations an incentive to purchase such items. The rising terms of trade promoted the shift of local livelihoods from subsistence to commercial production in those countries. As a result, international trade with Western industrial countries rapidly grew during the nineteenth century. Some parts of Southeast Asia underwent the same pattern of trade growth, and Singapore became the primary trade hub for importing industrial products from Britain and re-exporting them to neighbouring countries.[11] The imports of low-priced cotton goods via Singapore prompted local people to engage in the production of primary goods to supply Western industries, fostering the integration of the region into the modern global economy. From this point of view, the foundation of Singapore's early economic prosperity depended on its role as a trade hub for the distribution of consumer goods in Southeast Asia.

Hence, this chapter analyses changes in imports into Southeast Asia in the early nineteenth century in order to understand the origin of Singapore's trade growth. The next section of the chapter provides an overview of trade development between India and Southeast Asia between 1800 and 1874. Then the third section deals with the competition between Indian and British cotton goods in Singapore. The fourth section sheds light on local responses to the arrival of new consumer goods, and the final section summarises Singapore's trade development pattern.

The evolving pattern of trade between India and Southeast Asia

Scholars have collected historical trade data on Southeast Asia and have constructed a long-term data series of the main Southeast Asian exports since the fourteenth century.[12] Based on this dataset, Anthony Reid argues that the rapid growth of key commodities' exports from Southeast Asia began in the late eighteenth century, and its growth rate was higher than in the period of full-fledged colonialism after 1850.[13] This suggests that modern economic growth may have begun earlier than previously assumed. In addition, Nordin Hussin argues that Penang's trade expanded in the first two decades after its foundation in 1786, based on the close trade relations with the ports located along the Bay of Bengal.[14] A number of Malay traders' ships arrived in Penang with large quantities of native produce and exported Indian textiles and local foodstuff. Chinese *junks* also visited Penang for trading of tropical produce.

While these studies suggest that the long-term growth pattern of regional trade began in the late eighteenth century, they admit that the statistical data for the period 1790–1820 are not sufficiently reliable.[15] The original data sources of this period may not have collected consistent information owing to disruptive events, such as the failure of the Dutch East India Company (VOC), the Napoleonic Wars, and the rampant piracy around the Malacca Straits. The continuity of historical sources of data on Southeast Asian trade was affected, and reliable data for the first quarter of the nineteenth century are hard to find. However, we addressed this gap in the data by resorting to the networks of intra-Asian trade partners. Because imports of Indian goods facilitated the trade expansion of eighteenth-century Southeast Asia and remained in circulation until the 1820s, the data sources for India's trade, particularly trade statistics, may reinforce the analysis of Southeast Asian trade during that period and partly compensate for the lack of reliable data. Thus, using trade statistics of British colonies in India, this section analyses India's trade with Southeast Asia.

Figure 2.1 describes the aggregated data of British India's trade with Southeast Asia from the first to third quarters of the nineteenth century. After the battle of Plassey in 1757, the EIC progressively expanded its ruling territory in India and established Bengal, Bombay and Madras presidencies. Each presidency began issuing trade statistics around 1800, but there was no uniformity in the format. We

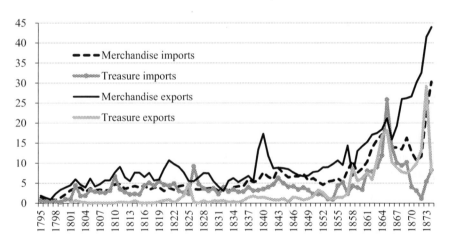

Figure 2.1 British India's trade with Southeast Asia, 1795–1874 (million EIC rupees).

Sources: *Bengal Commercial Reports*, 1795–1847; *Bengal Trade and Navigation*, 1848–1874; *Bombay Commercial Reports*, 1801–47; *Bombay Trade and Navigation*, 1848–1874; *Madras Commercial Reports*, 1802–1850; *Madras Trade and Navigation*, 1851–74.

Notes: Trade statistics differ for each presidency. The statistics for Bengal concern trade in Calcutta. The statistics for Bombay comprise all trade in the port of Bombay. The statistics for Madras include trade in the entire presidency. Data from 1795–1800 include only trade in Calcutta. Bombay's and Madras's trade activities began to be incorporated in the statistics after 1801 and 1802, respectively. The trade values in Sicca, Bombay, Arcot and Madras rupees before 1835 were converted to EIC rupees.

derived trade data for Southeast Asian countries from these sources and arranged them into a consistent dataset. Figure 2.1 shows that India's merchandise exports were large and increased during the first two decades of the century but remained stagnant during the 1820s and 1830s. A rapid increase occurred in the late 1840s. This shows that India's exports to Southeast Asia had a significant upward trend during the first quarter of the century, suggesting growth of Southeast Asian trade in that controversial period. The volume of merchandise imports from Southeast Asia was consistently smaller than the size of exports, so India had a trade surplus and imported 'treasures', such as bullion, ingots and coins as a form of payment until the early 1850s. India's treasure exports to Southeast Asia remained limited until the 1840s.

The primary sector for the trade between India and Southeast Asia was India's merchandise exports. Figure 2.2 breaks down India's exports to Southeast Asia by region and shows the shares of India's three presidencies in merchandise exports to Southeast Asia. Throughout the period studied, Bengal was the most important trading partner for Southeast Asia. Its ratio was over 50 per cent, and after the 1830s, increased to more than 80 per cent. While Bombay remained a minor trading partner for Southeast Asia, Madras presidency continued to have a significant share of around 30 per cent until the mid-1830s. In other words, Bengal and Madras were the principal regions exporting commodities to Southeast Asia until the 1830s, but Bengal became the dominant export region after 1840.

Figure 2.3 shows the Southeast Asian destinations of India's exports. In the trade statistics of each presidency, a variety of Southeast Asian areas appears in the list of trading partners. Southeast Asian trade partners have been grouped by four main sub-regions: the Straits Settlements, the Dutch-ruled islands, the Philippines, and Burma. The Straits Settlements were the primary destination of India's

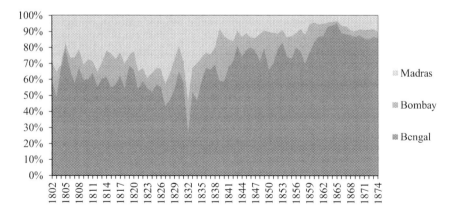

Figure 2.2 British Indian presidencies' exports in merchandise to Southeast Asia, 1802–1874 (in EIC rupees).

Sources: See Figure 2.1.

Notes: See Figure 2.1.

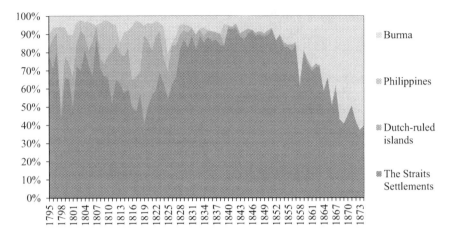

Figure 2.3 British India's merchandise exports to Southeast Asia, by regions, 1795–1874 (in EIC rupees).

Sources: See Figure 2.1.

Notes: See Figure 2.1.

exports. After the 1850s, the increase in the share of exports to Burma reflects the effects of the British colonisation of lower Burma. Figure 2.3 also indicates that the Dutch-ruled islands and the Philippines received significant shares of imports before 1830. In particular, during the 1810s, when the British influence expanded rapidly through its rule over Dutch territories, their shares of imports increased. This suggests that Indian goods were shipped not only to adjacent Penang but also to islands further east through the trade route passing through Malacca and Java. However, in line with the role of Singapore as an entrepôt after the 1820s, we contend that exports of Indian articles to the Dutch-ruled islands and the Philippines may have begun to be traded via its transit trade.

Bengal's exports to the Straits Settlements were the most significant commercial relationship between India and Southeast Asia. Figure 2.4 presents the commodity composition of such trades and indicates a dramatic increase in the trade in opium. The ratio of cotton piece goods, which accounted for about 40 per cent of the trade in the first part of the century, gradually decreased and became negligible after the 1840s. This suggests the decline of India's cotton industry owing to the influx of British manufactured goods and colonial tariff policies. Concerning other commodities, the share of grain increased at times. In the grain trade, Bengal rice was temporarily exported to Penang and Singapore for local consumption. The predominance of cotton piece goods exports characterised the exports from Madras to Southeast Asia in the first quarter of the century, and their ratio remained over 90 per cent.[16] Not only Bengal, but also Madras was exporting significant amounts of Indian cotton goods to Southeast Asia. However, the share

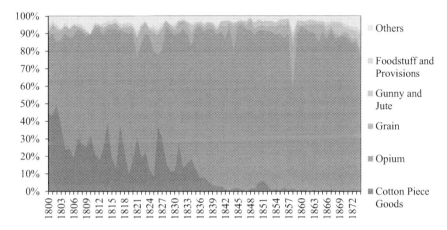

Figure 2.4 Bengal's exports to the Straits Settlements, 1800–1874 (in EIC rupees).

Sources: *Bengal Commercial Reports*, 1795–1847; *Bengal Trade and Navigation*, 1848–1874.

Note: Trade values in Sicca rupees before 1835 were converted to Company's rupees.

of cotton piece goods in Madras exports began falling after the 1820s and finally dropped to approximately 70 per cent in the 1840s. In contrast, other commodities, such as raw cotton, tobacco, and grains, significantly increased their share in Madras exports to Southeast Asia.

The significance of Indian opium for the rise of Singapore's economy has been discussed in prominent studies.[17] Opium offered lucrative opportunities for Chinese business. It was mainly sold to Chinese coolies working in the service sector in Singapore and the mines in the Malay Peninsula. The sale of opium was profitable for Chinese merchants, and the significance of opium for Singapore's trade was comparable to that of cotton goods in terms of trade value. While opium was intensively re-exported from Singapore to China and the Malay Peninsula, cotton piece goods, both Indian and British products, were sent to all parts of Southeast Asia. Owing to this difference in the geographical distribution of traded goods, we argue that cotton piece goods are a more suitable commodity for achieving a comprehensive understanding of the role of Singapore as a regional trading centre. Therefore, the next sections will focus on the development of the trade in cotton goods.

Competition between Indian and British cotton piece goods

Figure 2.5 indicates the trend of Indian cotton goods' exports to Southeast Asia by showing the annual average value and quantity of cotton goods exported from Bengal and Madras every ten years after 1802–1804. Their export value and quantity expanded during the first two decades of the century. After 1820–1822,

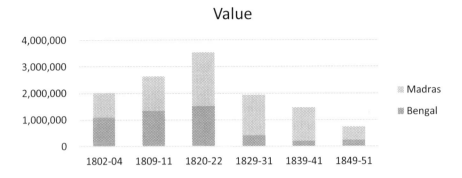

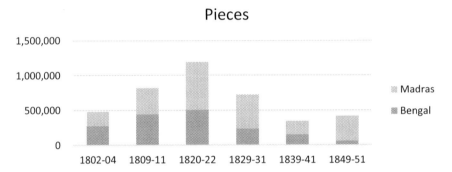

Figure 2.5 Exports of cotton goods from Bengal and Madras by value and pieces, 1802–
1851 (in EIC rupees).

Sources: *Bengal Commercial Reports*, 1795–1847; *Bengal Trade and Navigation*, 1848–1874; *Madras Commercial Reports*, 1802–1850; *Madras Trade and Navigation*, 1851–74.

Notes: This figure reports data on Calcutta's exports of 'Cotton Piece Goods', Madras presidency's exports of items reported in Figure 2.6, and 'Piece Goods of Sorts'. Inconsistent data for various cotton goods recorded in the trade statistics of the Madras presidency were eliminated. Trade values expressed in Sicca and Madras rupees before 1835 were converted to EIC rupees.

Bengal's exports plummeted in both value and quantity, and in the next decade exports from Madras withstood a rapid decline; however, they had begun to shrink gradually by the end of the 1840s.

Anthony Reid estimates the volume of exports of Indian cotton goods to Southeast Asia during the early modern era.[18] According to his estimates, Southeast Asia's imports of Indian textiles reached a peak of around 1.76 million pieces during the mid-seventeenth century, and the volume rapidly decreased to 0.4 million pieces by the early eighteenth century owing to the VOC's (Dutch East India Company's) commercial monopoly. The author argues that the scale of Indian textiles' exports to Southeast Asia was restored after the late eighteenth century and had expanded further by the early nineteenth century, in line with the regional export growth.[19] Although the exports of cotton goods did not reach the record peak of the sixteenth century, Figure 2.5 shows a sustained increase in cotton goods' exports in the first two decades of the century.

During the first half of the nineteenth century, while exports of Indian textiles underwent fluctuations, the type of export products also began to change. The trade statistics of the Madras presidency recorded trade of various sorts of cotton goods (a maximum of 62 items during the period 1809–1811). We organised these data into a consistent data set. Figure 2.6 shows that, during this period of growing exports, the primary products exported were chintz, comboys (sarongs), handkerchiefs and morees. We classify those goods as luxurious fabrics, as detailed in Table 2.1. This suggests that the supply of fine cotton goods drove the growth of exports from Madras to Southeast Asia. After the 1820s, however, other products, such as blue cloth, punjum and long cloth, increased their export shares. Table 2.1 indicates that these products were mainly coarse and durable products suitable for ordinary clothing. The Madras cotton industry barely survived the influx of British industrial products by specialising in the production of cheap and coarse textiles, and such products, particularly blue cloth, were sent to Southeast Asia.[20] Madras's declining exports were characterised by a shift from luxurious to ordinary items after the 1820s. Unfortunately, the trade statistics regarding Bengal's cotton exports do not distinguish between different types of goods.

In Southeast Asia, Indian cotton goods were distributed via the British ports in the Malacca Straits. Singapore became the entry point for foreign cotton goods into the regional market owing to its extensive trade relations with neighbouring countries. There was a notable increase in the competition between Indian and British cotton goods in the area. Figure 2.7 exhibits the secular trends of three kinds of cotton goods' exports from Singapore. Most exports of cotton goods from

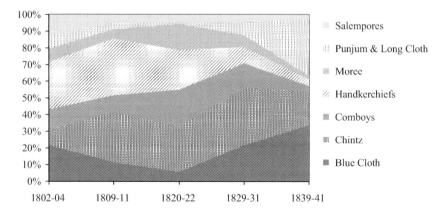

Figure 2.6 Export products of cotton goods from Madras to Southeast Asia, 1802–1841 (in EIC rupees).

Sources: *Madras Commercial Reports*, 1802–1850; *Madras Trade and Navigation*, 1851–74.
Note: This figure only includes data for cotton goods that appeared regularly in the statistics.

Table 2.1 Property of cotton goods in Figure 2.6.

Blue Cloth	Coarse cotton cloth produced chiefly on the Coromandel Coast and mainly supplied to coastal Africa.
Chintz	Artistically hand-drawn and dyed fine cotton cloth produced in an area extending from Western India to the Coromandel Coast.
Comboy	Superior-quality cotton cloth or robe named after the thriving port of Cambay in Gujarat that had extensive exports of luxurious fabrics in the sixteenth and seventeenth centuries.
Handkerchief	Madras handkerchiefs, 0.75 yard square.
Morees	Superior cotton cloth used for making chintz.
Punjum	Cloth with peculiar strong texture, manufactured in the Northern Circars, on the Coromandel Coast.
Long Cloth	Ordinary staple cotton cloth of the Coromandel Coast, mainly exported to the European market.
Salempore	Staple cotton cloth produced on the Coromandel Coast, ranging from coarse to very fine, and white, blue, or brown in colour.

Sources: Milburn, W., *Oriental Commerce; containing a geographical description of the principal places in the East Indies, China, and Japan, with their produce, manufactures, and trade*, London, Black Parry & Co., 1813, pp. 45, 47, 55; Sarada, *Economic Conditions*, p. 205; V. Ramaswamy, *Textiles and Weavers in South India*, Second Edition, New Delhi, Oxford University Press, 2006, pp. 236–238; Riello and Roy, *How India Clothed the World*, pp. 437–441.

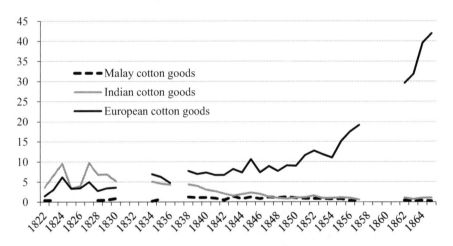

Figure 2.7 Exports of European, Indian and Malay cotton goods from Singapore, 1822–1865 (100,000 Spanish Mexican dollars).

Sources: 1822 from *SFR* G/35/51; 1823 from T.S. Raffles, *Singapore Local Laws and Regulations 1823*, London, Cox and Bylis, 1824; 1824–28 from *SSFR* G/34/160; 1829–36 from *SFP*, Showing the Annual, Commercial Tables; 1837 from *ST*, 27 Aug. 1850; 1838–1865 from *Tabular Statements Singapore*, 1839–1865.

Singapore were destined for Southeast Asian countries. Figure 2.7 shows that the value of Indian products was always greater than that of European (primarily British) goods during the 1820s. Although British textiles began to be imported into the Malay Archipelago from the 1810s, they did not immediately replace

Indian goods. In the 1830s, the exports of European cotton goods increased and they began competing with the exports of Indian textiles. While exports of Indian textiles were decreasing, European cotton's exports progressively rose during the 1840s and soared after the late 1850s, significantly surpassing Indian and Malay goods. Two factors underlay the persistence of Indian cotton goods and gradual shift towards new British manufactured goods. One factor was the activity of Asian merchants, who operated the local trade between Singapore and neighbouring countries. Another factor was the contest in colonial tariff policies between British and Dutch authorities in Southeast Asia. Let us consider briefly their impact on the circulation of cotton goods in Singapore.

As soon as the British port was opened in Singapore in 1819, merchants from various backgrounds began conducting business there. The British agency houses dealt in British manufactured cotton goods in the market of Singapore. However, most of them had limited experience in the business with native traders who visited Singapore from remote islands.[21] To sell their articles, British merchants required intermediaries who could relate to native traders. Chinese merchants who moved from Malacca to Singapore operated the intermediary business. Chinese merchants were accustomed to the local commerce and could speak both English and the vernacular spoken in the Malay Archipelago.[22] Some of them held positions in Singapore's government; therefore, they were perceived as respectable Chinese by the Western community.[23] Chinese intermediaries sold a variety of commodities to Malay and Bugis traders in exchange for their local produce, and native traders carried their purchases, including cotton goods, back to their home ports. In these initial transactions, native traders appeared to prefer Indian textiles to British products in exchange for their produce.[24] British cotton goods were regarded as being of poor quality, and most local consumers preferred conventional Indian textiles. Hence, most native traders refrained from purchasing British cloth. Indian cloth sustained its sales and exports to Singapore until the 1820s.

Colonial trade policies also affected cotton goods' trade in Singapore. After regaining their Southeast Asian territories in 1816, the Netherlands introduced protectionist tariff policies against the import of British cotton goods.[25] During British rule, a massive amount of British cloth flowed to Java, and their influx continued even after the return of the Dutch owing to its direct shipment from Britain and transit trade through Singapore. To better link the domestic cotton industry to the colonial market, the Dutch government set discriminative tariffs on British products; in particular, the imports from Singapore were subject to a considerably higher tariff. The peak tariff rate on imports from Singapore reached 70 per cent between 1834 and 1839. The high tariff hindered re-exports of British cloth from Singapore to Dutch-ruled ports. Meanwhile, because the Dutch tariff on Indian textiles was relatively lower – ranging from 6–12 per cent – the exports of Indian textiles from Singapore to Dutch-ruled ports in Sumatra, Borneo and Celebes was not affected significantly. The Dutch tariff on imports from Singapore was reduced in the early 1840s due to British diplomatic efforts, and this led to the rapid expansion of British textiles' exports to unexplored regions under the Dutch control.

As long as Indian cloth continued to be exported to Singapore in sufficient quantity, local traders were eager to trade it in pursuit of good sales. After the drop in the supply of Indian fabrics, merchants switched to British textiles. In addition, owing to the deregulation of Dutch protectionist tariff in the 1840s, exports of British goods became more lucrative in terms of net return. Thus, the trade of British cotton goods increased in Singapore. The next section will address how the natives reacted to the emergence of this new commodity.

Native reactions to the changes in consumer goods

In the early nineteenth century, in response to the influx of British cotton manufactured goods, Southeast Asian consumers had different reactions. Some continued wearing conventional Indian clothing. Others augmented the domestic production of native textiles. Native consumers only accepted certain types of British cotton goods. These reactions induced a change in the consumer goods market in Southeast Asia, leading to the growth of trade in Singapore. This section will examine the traits of native consumption.

By the beginning of the nineteenth century, British industry succeeded in substituting imports of Indian textiles and began exporting industrial cotton goods worldwide. In Southeast Asia, to expand British textile's circulation, the mercantile community requested the British cotton industry to adapt the dyeing techniques and patterns to the local tastes.[26] In Penang, the colonial authority also mentioned the possible profit on sale of British cotton goods if cloths with the right colours and patterns were to be supplied to the local Malays. Fine textile products with patterns on dark background and large figures were in high demand in the Malay market, while plain and coarse fabrics appeared to be unpopular.[27] Furthermore, when Britain ruled Java between 1811 and 1815, British merchants attempted to export British cotton goods to its market. Samples of local cotton cloth that suited the Javanese tastes were sent to the home industry for the manufacture of British imitations.[28] Thus, British cotton goods began circulating in the Malay Archipelago in the form of patterned and dyed cloth adapted to local consumers' tastes.

However, British textiles had poor sales in Southeast Asia in the beginning. While the intense competition with Indian cotton goods hindered the distribution of British cloth, the primary cause of this lack of success was the unsuitable appearance and poor quality of British fabrics. The Malay traders did not buy any textiles that deviated even a little from natives' tastes. As a result, a large number of British cotton products of colours that were less preferred by Malays remained unsold and accumulated at the warehouse in Penang.[29] In both Penang and Java, British textiles fetched a lower rate than anticipated; the British merchants had no choice but to sell at a loss. The bad reputation of British cloth helped sustain the sale of Indian cotton goods in Southeast Asia. As a contemporary publication reported, 'Indian cloths have met with better sales, in consequence of the Natives beginning to find out that they are far more durable than the English'.[30] Native consumers preferred conventional Indian textiles, which had reliable quality and were well suited to their tastes. In Singapore, native traders preferred to purchase Indian textiles that were more familiar to them than the British goods, whose sale potential was hard to predict. Even though British industrial products could be more lucrative, they could not adequately meet the demand of native consumers during the early nineteenth century. As long as there was a sufficient supply of cotton textiles from India, they maintained a dominant position in the Southeast Asian market. However, after the 1820s, India's exports of cotton goods to Southeast Asia decreased, and their circulation in Southeast Asia also declined. Under these circumstances, local inhabitants faced difficulties in obtaining cloth that suited their tastes. Hence, the domestic production of cotton goods increased.

From the late seventeenth century, the local production of textiles grew in Southeast Asia by developing unique techniques, such as the Javanese dyeing technique known as *batik*.[31] Domestic textile industries developed in Java, Celebes and Sumatra, and their products began circulating across insular Southeast Asia. Until the early nineteenth century, the Javanese textile industry grew by engaging in the whole process from cotton cultivation, spinning and weaving to dyeing. In response to the decline in Indian textiles' trade, the domestic production of clothing increased after the 1820s.[32] To increase production, besides spinning from home-grown cotton, the native industries purchased British manufactured yarn and wove textiles using it. Furthermore, to enhance productivity, the domestic industries bought plain British cloth and then applied dyes and patterns on it.[33] This type of production was observed in southern Celebes, as the following excerpt[34] shows:

> The chief manufacture of the Bugis land is the cloth for sarongs; and on the product of this cloth the families generally obtain what little money they require . . . the stock in trade for purchasing cotton thread for their manufacture is the chief outlay. The thread procured at Singapore is far cheaper, though less durable than the Bugis cotton. Sarongs made of the latter are more expensive and far more durable; and the manufacture is chiefly carried on by females; in every house a number of hand-looms being at work. The staples of Bugis land are sarongs and coffee. . . . The export of sarongs is very unprofitable, as they usually cost more than they sell for at Singapore.

Singapore's exports of cotton yarn to the archipelago grew significantly from the 1820s onwards. Moreover, Singapore's imports of Malay cotton textiles began increasing, and a share of those domestic textiles was re-exported to neighbouring islands. Eventually, the revitalisation of native textile production to complement the falling supply of Indian textile contributed to the growth of Singapore's regional trade.

Following the expansion of British cotton goods' trade, plain textiles became the product of choice in the Southeast Asian market. Figure 2.8 accounts for the large share of plain textiles in the rising exports of British cotton goods from Singapore to Southeast Asia. While the export volumes of dyed and printed textiles increased in the late 1840s, the share of plain items did not significantly decrease.

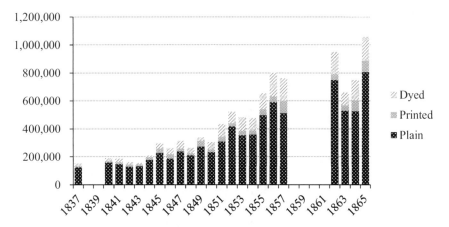

Figure 2.8 Export quantity of British cotton goods from Singapore to Southeast Asia, 1837–1865 (number of pieces).

Sources: 1837 from R.M. Martin, *Statistics of the Colonies of the British Empire in the West Indies, South America, North America, Asia, Australasia, Africa and Europe*, London, WM. H. Allen and Co., 1839, pp. 402–412; 1840–65 from *Tabular Statements of Singapore*, 1840–65.

Notes: Data for 1838, 1839, and 1858–61 are not available.

In addition, because the price of British textiles fell in Singapore after the 1830s, trade in textiles became more lucrative for both traders and native consumers.[35] British plain textiles were dyed by native craftsmen and printed with patterns that suited the local consumers' tastes.[36] Up to the late nineteenth century, British textiles reached the rural areas, such as mountainous villages in Northern Thailand and the hinterland in Central Sumatra.[37] Owing to the price competitiveness of British products and the decision by natives to incorporate new items into their clothing consumption, British-manufactured cotton goods gradually prevailed in Southeast Asia for use as ordinary cloth.

Conclusion

This final section summarises the pattern of regional trade development discussed earlier. During the eighteenth century, the expansion of Chinese overseas trade prompted the rise of exports of Southeast Asian tropical produce, including both luxury goods and staples. In maritime Southeast Asia, an entrepôt connecting regional trade with extra-regional trade developed. For instance, Riau prospered as a trade centre where various commodities and merchants gathered and engaged in trade relationships with Southeast Asia. Entering the nineteenth century, Singapore emerged as a trade hub and inherited the role of an entrepôt for regional trade. Its trade activities began growing by incorporating China-oriented exports. In addition to the development path of exports of native produce, this chapter stresses the significance of imported consumer goods for the early growth in Singapore's trade. In the period of transition from the early modern era to the modern era, along with the growing export of Southeast Asian produce, the imports of Indian textiles also steadily increased, with conventional fine cloth being the primary imported product. The growth of Indian textile imports facilitated the production and export of native produce in Southeast Asia. In Singapore, Indian cotton goods became the dominant commodity and led the trade growth of Singapore until the 1820s. British manufactured goods did not immediately succeed in the Southeast Asian market owing to their bad reputation, both in terms of quality and appearance. Indian textiles persisted in the Southeast Asian market and induced the temporary rise of domestic production of Malay cotton goods. These competing but complementary developments in cotton goods' trade sustained the trade growth of Singapore and transformed Southeast Asia's consumer goods market. Finally, British textiles became the ordinary cloth in the whole of Southeast Asia via the trade in Singapore, and the low-priced cloth motivated local populations to engage in the commercial production of native produce. As Webster's chapter in this volume shows, the declining importance of Indian textile exports to Southeast Asia from the 1820s underpinned the political reorientation of Straits Settlements' commercial interests away from its older India connections and reinforced a movement towards breaking with the EIC's Indian governing structures. Singapore assumed the role of entrepôt for the intra-Asian trade, and its trade growth prompted the region towards the division of labour with Western industrial countries.

Acknowledgements

This study was supported by JSPS KAKENHI Grant Number 17K13774.

Notes

1 R. Fernando and A. Reid, 'Shipping on Melaka and Singapore as an Index of Growth, 1760–1840,' *South Asia: Journal of South Asian Studies*, vol. 19, no. 1, 1996, pp. 82–84; A. Reid, 'Chinese Trade and Southeast Asian Economic Expansion in the Late Eighteenth and Early Nineteenth Centuries: An Overview,' in N. Cooke and L. Tana (eds.), *Water Frontier, Commerce and the Chinese in the Lower Mekong Region, 1750–1880*, Singapore: Rowman & Littlefield Publishers, Inc, 2004, pp. 22–24; A. Ota, 'Tropical Products Out, British Cotton In: Trade in the Dutch Outer-Islands Ports, 1846–1869,' *Southeast Asian Studies*, vol. 2, no. 3, 2013, pp. 503–506.
2 C.A. Trocki, *Prince of Pirates: The Temenggongs and the Development of Johor and Singapore 1784–1885*, Singapore: NUS Press, 1979, pp. 32–36; Fernando and Reid, 'Shipping on Melaka,' pp. 66–69; T.P. Barnard, *Multiple Centres of Authority: Society and Environment in Siak and Eastern Sumatra, 1674–1827*, Leiden: KITLV Press, 2003, pp. 23–25.
3 A. Reid, 'Southeast Asian Consumption of Indian and British Cotton Cloth, 1600–1850,' in G. Riello and T. Roy (eds.), *How India Clothed the World: The World of South Asian Textiles, 1500–1850*, Leiden: Brill, 2009, pp. 34–35.
4 E.H. Pritchard, *The Crucial Years of Early Anglo-Chinese Relations, 1750–1800*, London: Routledge, 1936, pp. 149–150; M. Greenberg, *British Trade and the Opening of China 1800–42*, London: Routledge, 1951, p. 64.

5   D. Lewis, 'The Growth of the Country Trade to the Straits of Malacca 1760–1777,' *JMBRAS*, vol. 43, no. 2, 1970, pp. 114–115; D.K. Bassett, 'British "Country" Trade and Local Trade Networks in the Thai and Malay States, c. 1680–1770,' *Modern Asian Studies*, vol. 23, no. 4, 1989, pp. 634–636; W.G. Miller, 'English Country Traders and Their Relations with Malay Rulers in the Late Eighteenth Century,' *Journal of the Malaysian Branch of the Royal Asiatic Society*, vol. 84, no. 1, 2011, pp. 24–25.

6   E. Tagliacozzo, 'A Necklace of Fins: Marine Goods Trading in Maritime Southeast Asia, 1780-1860,' International Journal of Asian Studies, vol. 1, no. 1, 2004, pp. 23–48; A. Ota, 'Tropical Products Out, British Cotton In: Trade in the Dutch Outer-Islands Ports, 1846-1869,' Southeast Asian Studies, vol. 2, no. 3, 2013, pp. 499–526.

7   A. Kobayashi, 'The Role of Singapore in the Growth of Intra-Southeast Asian Trade, c. 1820s-1852,' *Southeast Asian Studies*, vol. 2, no. 3, 2013, pp. 468–470.

8   L.K. Wong, 'The Trade of Singapore 1819–69,' *JMBRAS*, vol. 33, no. 4, 1960, p. 160; D.R. SarDesai, *British Trade and Expansion in Southeast Asia 1830–1914*, New Delhi: Private Publish, 1977, pp. 50–53; A. van der Kraan, *Contest for the Java Cotton Trade, 1811–40: An Episode in Anglo-Dutch Rivalry, Occasional Paper No. 32*, The University of Hull, Centre for South-East Asian Studies, 1998, pp. 12–14.

9   Reid, 'Southeast Asian Consumption,' pp. 46–47; A. Kobayashi, 'The Growth of Intra-Southeast Asian Trade in the First Half of the Nineteenth Century: The Role of Middlemen in Singapore,' in T. Shiroyama (ed.), *Modern Global Trade and the Asian Regional Economy*, Monograph Series of the Socio-Economic History Society Japan, 2018, p. 50.

10 J.G. Williamson, *Trade and Poverty: When the Third World Fell Behind*, Cambridge, MA: MIT Press, 2011, pp. 30–33.

11 A. Kobayashi, 'Price Fluctuations and Growth Patterns in Singapore's Trade, 1831–1913,' *Australian Economic History Review*, vol. 57, no. 1, 2017, pp. 122–123.

12 D. Bulbeck et al. (eds.), *Southeast Asian Exports since the 14th Century: Cloves, Pepper, Coffee, and Sugar*, Leiden: KITLV Press, 1998, pp. 12–13.

13 A. Reid, 'A New Phase of Commercial Expansion in Southeast Asia, 1760–1840,' in A. Reid (ed.), *The Last Stand of Asian Autonomies: Responses to Modernity in the Diverse States of Southeast Asia and Korea, 1750–1900*, New York: St Martin's Press, 1997, pp. 74–75.

14 N. Hussin, *Trade and Society in the Straits of Melaka: Dutch Melaka and English Penang, 1780–1830*, Singapore: NUS Press, 2007, pp. 72–74.

15 Reid, 'A New Phase of Commercial Expansion,' p. 74; Hussin, *Trade and Society*, p. 71.

16 *Madras Commercial Reports, 1802–30.*

17 C.A. Trocki, *Opium and Empire: Chinese Society in Colonial Singapore 1800–1910*, Ithaca, NY: Cornell University Press, 1990, pp. 50–52, 137–138.

18 Reid, 'Southeast Asian Consumption,' p. 35.

19 Ibid., pp. 41–42.

20 A.R. Sarada, *Economic Conditions in the Madras Presidency, 1800–1850*, Madras: Madras University Press, 1941, p. 205.

21 J.H. Drabble and P.J. Drake, 'The British Agency Houses in Malaysia: Survival in a Changing World,' *Journal of Southeast Asian Studies*, vol. 12, no. 2, 1981, pp. 304–305; Kobayashi, 'The Growth of Intra-Southeast,' p. 45.

22 P.P. Lee, *Chinese Society in Nineteenth Century Singapore*, Kuala Lumpur: Oxford University Press, 1978, pp. 14–16.

23 The noted and rich Chinese, some of them acquiring the status of British subject, were assigned to the Chinese Justices of the Peace that assisted the local courts concerned with Chinese inhabitants. They also had advisory roles in setting the regulation of Chinese society in Singapore. O.S. Song, *One Hundred Years' History of the Chinese in Singapore*, Singapore: Oxford University Press, 1902, pp. 21, 170, 174–176.

24 Kobayashi, 'The Growth of Intra-Southeast,' p. 53.

25 van der Kraan, *Contest for the Java*, pp. 19–25; Kobayashi, 'The Growth of Intra-Southeast,' pp. 42–44.
26 H.R.C. Wright, *East-Indian Economic Problems of the Age of Cornwallis & Raffles*, London: Luzac and Company, 1961, pp. 224, 226–229.
27 Wright, *East-Indian Economic Problems*, p. 224.
28 Ibid., p. 228.
29 Ibid., pp. 225–228.
30 T.J. Newbold, *Political and Statistical Account of the British Settlements in the Straits of Malacca, viz. Pinang, Malacca, and Singapore: With a History of the Malayan States on the Peninsula of Malacca*, London: John Murray, 1839, p. 353.
31 Reid, 'Southeast Asian Consumption,' p. 40.
32 M. Mohamad, *The Malay Handloom Weavers: A Study of the Rise and Decline of Traditional Manufacture*, Singapore: Institute of Southeast Asian Studies, 1996, pp. 79–83.
33 R. Maxwell, *Textiles of Southeast Asia: Tradition, Trade and Transformation*, revised edn., Singapore: Periplus Edition, 2003, pp. 366–370.
34 R. Mundy, *Narrative of Events in Borneo and Celebes, Down to the Occupation of Labuan: From the Journal of James Brooke, Esq.*, vols. 1 and 2, 2nd edn., London: John Murray, 1848, pp. 117–118.
35 Kobayashi, 'The Growth of Intra-Southeast,' p. 54.
36 J.H. Moor, *Notice of the Indian Archipelago, and Adjacent Countries*, Singapore: Singapore Free Press, 1837, p. 177.
37 A. Ooki, 'A Note on the History of the Textile Industry in West Sumatra,' in F. van Anrooij et al. (eds.), *Between People and Statistics: Essays on Modern Indonesian History*, The Hague: M. Nijhoff, 1979, pp. 147–148; K.A. Bowie, 'Unraveling the Myth of the Subsistence Economy: The Case of Textile Production in Nineteenth-Century Northern Thailand,' *Journal of Asian Studies*, vol. 51, no. 4, 1992, pp. 815–819.

Primary source references

Bengal Commercial Reports, 1795–1857/58. British Library India Office Records (hereafter BL IOR) (P/174).
Bengal Trade and Navigation Annual Statements, 1848/49–1875/76. BL IOR (V/17).
Bombay Commercial Reports, Internal and External Commerce, 1801–1857/58. BL IOR (P/174).
Bombay Trade and Navigation Annual Statements, 1848/49–1875/76. BL IOR (V/17).
Madras Commercial Reports on the External and Internal Commerce, 1802–1863/64. BL IOR (P/174).
Madras Trade and Navigation Annual Statements, 1841/42–1874/75. BL IOR (V/17).
Singapore Free Press (*SFP*), 15–22 October 1835, Showing the Annual Quantities and Values of the Principal Articles of Import from Places to the Eastward of the Cape of Good Hope, from 1 May 1823 to 30 April 1835.
Singapore Free Press (*SFP*), 3 December 1835–30 November 1837, Commercial Tables, Showing the Nature, Quantities and Values of the Articles Imported and Exported at Singapore, and the Places from and to, During the Year Ending 30 April 1834–1836.
Straits Settlements Factory Record (*SSFR*), G/34/160, 162, Trade Statistics in the Straits Settlements for the Year of 1828, London, British Library.
The Straits Times and Singapore Journal of Commerce (*ST*).
Sumatra Factory Records (*SFR*), G/35/51, Commodity Imports and Exports in Singapore for the Year, 1819–1822, London, British Library.
Tabular Statements of the Commerce and Shipping of Singapore, 1839–1865, Calcutta.

3 Made in Singapore

'Good Steady Scotsmen', the Lion City and London, 1820s–1870s

G. Roger Knight

I had my tiffin with Frazer of Maclaine, Frazer & Co, but immediately thereafter the mail brought intelligence to Mrs Frazer of the death of a brother, a fine young man who was doing uncommonly well in Rio [di Janeiro] . . . I therefore would not dine at the house, then a house of mourning, and re-joined my fellow passengers at the Hotel. I slept, however at Frazer's and breakfasted with him next day – a good, steady Scotsman.[1]

An entry in the travel diary of Reverend Angus Maclaine, en route from London to Batavia (Jakarta) and thence to his sheep property in South Australia, records his brief stay in Singapore in June 1846 while waiting for a steamer to take him on to Java. His hosts, both Scots-born and known to Maclaine through their connection to his late brother's mercantile business, were Lewis Fraser (1811–1868) and his wife Sophie Cumming (1827–1876). Her husband – the 'good steady Scotsman' – had arrived in Singapore in the mid-1830s to join his considerably older brother, James Fraser (1801–1872), in the import-export trade. Both brothers were evidently successful enough in the Lion City to return with their families to the UK while still in their early forties, where they continued to be active in financial and mercantile circles until their deaths in 1868 and 1872, respectively.[2]

Their story is one intimately linked to the emergence of modern Singapore as a centre of international commerce – and to the blend of diasporic identities that underpinned this development. For although the Fraser brothers themselves left no permanent mark on the city's history, the interregional and intercontinental trade which they, together with their collaborators, were responsible for promoting during the middle decades of the nineteenth century was and remained an essential part of the Singapore narrative. The overriding theme of Singapore's location in the trade between the various regions of Southeast Asia and the Lion City's role in long-distance commerce 150 years or more ago is something on which several Japanese scholars, in particular, have been at work in recent years, uncovering in the process a great deal of the vital trade data. This chapter aims to complement and add another dimension to the hard-won statistical picture of the development of Singapore commerce during that era by focusing on social actors and their associated money trails.

A certain amount of interest has been directed in the last couple of decades to the role of such actors in the expansion of global trade in Asia generally.[3] Nevertheless, the paucity of such studies, relative to those lavished on political, administrative and military figures, has been commented upon by a number of leading scholars in the field.[4] In respect to Singapore in particular, with some few exceptions, there is a notable absence of modern case studies of the entrepreneurial and mercantile actors who articulated its regional and worldwide connections during the colonial era.[5] Much the same might be said for the money trails which such actors both created and in which they were enmeshed. It is this relative neglect that this chapter sets out to address, by way of a discussion predicated on a (renewed) interest in people. It begins by outlining the known facts about James and Lewis Fraser's family background in their native Scotland and ends with their business activities in the London to which they both relocated after their lengthy sojourn in Southeast Asia. It is that sojourn, however, that forms the essential core of the chapter. As such, it focuses on the Fraser brothers' success in inserting the business that they headed into the commodity chains of which the mid-nineteenth century port was fast becoming a crucial nodal point.[6] The most celebrated of those commodity chains, those based on cotton goods and opium, had their origins outside the Southeast Asian region and were supported by trade between continents. No doubt the Fraser brothers and the business that they operated in the Lion City for three or more decades benefited greatly from their participation in them. The chapter also argues, however, that in order to fully understand the 'made in Singapore' label attached to the Frasers, we need also to consider their success in capitalising on those intra-regional commodity chains – especially those involving the commerce in rice – that were the key to Singapore's rapid rise to prominence.[7]

Scotland

What little we know about the Fraser brothers' background strongly suggests that they left their hometown with little or no capital at their disposal but with potentially useful connections that were of crucial significance in securing them an opening in international commerce. Their family had been long resident in Forres, a town in the northeast of Scotland with a long association with Freemasonry. In addition to its local connotations in Scotland itself, Freemasonry was also, as one perceptive commentator has noted, '*the* secret society of empire'[8] and may have been the conduit through which the elder of the two brothers made his way from Forres to London – and thence to Southeast Asia – when scarcely out of his teens. It was perhaps not irrelevant, therefore, that the Fraser family had been prominent members of the Lodge St. Lawrence in Forres since the time of its inception in the 1770s, and James Fraser himself appears to have been inducted into the 'brotherhood' as a very young man in 1820.[9]

Of course, to the casual observer, Forres, between Inverness and Aberdeen, may seem an unlikely place to have had links to 'the East'. In fact, this was far from being the case. As early as the 1680s, for example, James Brodie from Forres worked (as did other Scots) as a ship's surgeon for the (British) East India

Company – and as such must have journeyed several times to the South Asian ports. A century later, another family member, Alexander Brodie (1748–1818), long-serving Member of Parliament for the seat of Elgin Burghs in the same area of Scotland's north-east, was a 'nabob' who 'had amassed great wealth in India both working for the [British] East India Company and as a private merchant in Madras before his return to the UK c.1783.[10] Meanwhile, Alexander Falconer (1797–1856), brother of the town's most illustrious son, Hugh Falconer (inter alia, an internationally famous geologist and botanist who also spent more than two decades in India), made a substantial mercantile career for himself in Calcutta almost contemporaneously with that of James Fraser and his brother.[11] In 1833, moreover, in response to an appeal for funds to erect a new building for the St Lawrence Masonic Lodge in Forres, four of the subscriptions – in addition to that of James Fraser himself – came from locations in British India or Southeast Asia (while another nine came from the West Indies).[12] This cosmopolitan roll-call of expatriate citizens of Forres was a reminder that the town was far from untouched by the diaspora that had dispersed so many Scots – quite disproportionate to the relatively small population of 'North Britain' – first to continental Europe and subsequently to the Americas and, ultimately, to southern Africa and the Antipodes as well as to Asia where, in contrast to other global destinations, they were overwhelmingly sojourners rather than migrant settlers.[13]

Singapore

James Fraser first surfaced in Southeast Asia early in the 1820s as a clerk in the newly opened mercantile office in Batavia (Jakarta) of Gillian Maclaine (1798–1840), a fellow Scot who was only a very few years older than Fraser himself. As Maclaine informed his mother in September 1823, 'our establishment here musters strong. I have lately got out two fine young men as assistants, a Mr Frazer and a Mr Bain, both Scotchmen, to whom I have given a room each at my house, which makes our society *un peu mieux*.'[14] A diminutive man, whom Maclaine habitually referred to as the *Bodachan* (an elf-like figure in Gaelic mythology), Fraser had most probably been 'sent out' to the East by Maclaine's own erstwhile employers and patrons, the (then) fairly prominent East India House of D & P McLachlan or by their close associate Donald McIntyre, a man with considerable business interests in the Indian subcontinent.

From Batavia, possibly at MacIntyre's behest, Fraser was soon dispatched northward across the equator to Singapore to join Maclaine's business partner there, John Argyll Maxwell (1790–1857), a Scot from the same part of the Western Highlands as Maclaine himself. However, after the latter two had an acrimonious parting of the ways toward the end of the decade, Fraser took over as head of the (new) firm of Maclaine Fraser, a position he held until he left the business and relocated permanently to the UK in the mid-1840s. Prior to that, he had been joined in Singapore by his younger brother, Lewis Fraser – the same man with whose family Angus Maclaine was later to lodge – and had evidently done well enough in business there by the late 1830s to embark on a short return visit to his home town of Forres. It was there that he both found himself a wife – Ann Cumming (1811–1888) – and left with his parents two of the Eurasian children – both boys – whom he had fathered in Singapore during the previous decade.[15] The boys were still there – listed, somewhat tersely perhaps, as young scholars 'born overseas' in the first Scots Census of 1841 (their sister, born in Singapore and christened Ann Fraser, appears to have remained in the Lion City and subsequently to have married there and raised a family).[16]

James Fraser arrived back in Singapore with his newly acquired – and by this time pregnant – Scots bride toward the close of 1839, and his brother 'came out' to join him a few years later. There can be no doubt that the pair established a substantial profile in the Lion City. In 1835, for example, James featured as a trustee of the Raffles Institution, newly established to celebrate the memory of the modern port's founder, while in the following year he was listed in the *Singapore Free Press* among those protesting a proposal emanating from the India Office (under whose jurisdiction Singapore fell until 1867) to impose duties on goods passing through the port. Returning from Scotland in 1839, Fraser cemented his position in Singapore's colonial community by buying a house in Kampong Glam – aka Beach Road – from his fellow Scot Charles Carnie (1810–1873), thereby establishing his young (second) family among many of the city's other European worthies.[17] It was also around this time that he also became one of the original subscribers to 'the establishment of theatrical performances' in the city. Among other things, it helped provide an opportunity for his fellow merchant – and recent arrival – W.H.M. Read (1819–1909) to tread the boards in drag. 'The leading lady in most amateur theatricals', including a star turn in the persona of Charles Dickens's Miss Petowker, these performances were something for which Read was well qualified by virtue of having, as well as a petite figure, 'the smallest waist and smallest feet of any in Singapore.'[18] Read, a partner in the firm of A.L. Johnson, subsequently became a member of the Fraser-Cumming family circle through his marriage in 1846 to Marjory Cumming (1828–1849), sister-in-law of both James and Lewis Fraser.

The brothers, moreover, evidently paid their dues to the Scots diaspora that accounted, in one dimension at least, for their presence in the East. If we accept the argument that 'clubbing together along ethnic lines' was a key defining characteristic of that diaspora,[19] then it is significant that in the mid-1830s Lewis Fraser – the younger of the two brothers – was one of the stewards at a 'Scotch Dinner' held in Singapore at the end of November to celebrate St. Andrew's Day.[20] They were a precursor of similar celebrations that were to become famous throughout the British colonial settlements in the East. 'Well-attended, ritualised events', they had an important part to play both in confirming and constructing – and romanticising – identity, as well as opening possibilities of 'promoting oneself in potentially profitable ways by playing up one's affinity for things Scottish'.[21] In the particular case of Singapore, it was again Lewis Fraser who, in 1845, was among the stewards at the city's inaugural 'St Andrew's Day Ball and Supper'.[22] Nevertheless, the Frasers' participation in the social life of the colony was not limited to occasions on which the colony's Scots might be expected to 'stick together'. In February 1843, for instance, Lewis Fraser (perhaps the more outgoing of the two) was one of the stewards at a ball held after Singapore's first Race Meeting, while in the following year he was among the subscribers involved in the setting up of a Library in the Singapore Institution.[23] Underpinning all this civic activity, of course, was what had become, by mid-century, very much a family business, dominated by the Frasers themselves and the family relations that they had acquired through marriage.

Ann Cumming's father was a banker in Forres, and as such, much involved in the financing of local flax production. By the 1830s, however, the industry was in decline, something that may help explain why several more of his offspring followed James Fraser to Singapore after he had returned there with his bride late in 1839. Fraser's newly acquired sister-in-law, Sophie Cumming (1827–1876) 'went out' to Singapore to marry Lewis Fraser in 1845, and three of her brothers joined them there. In partnership with younger Fraser (his elder brother had repatriated c. 1844) and together with several more Scots, they continued to do business in Singapore during the mid-century decades.[24] In 1862, there appears to have been a major split in the Maclaine Fraser concerns, when the two surviving Cumming brothers (John Purse Cumming had died in 1858) – in conjunction with a third party (Hugh Rowland Beaver) – formed their own Singapore business of Cumming, Beaver & Co.[25] Beaver subsequently achieved a degree of notoriety on account of the assistance he gave to the renegade Confederate cruiser *Alabama* when it sailed into Singapore harbour in search of repairs and supplies in December 1863.[26] Around 1865, Maclaine Fraser was joined by Lewis James Fraser (1841–1906), the Singapore-born eldest son of James Fraser and Ann Cumming. We shall meet him again later in the story.

It was, in short, largely as a family company, run by a Scots kin group, that Maclaine Fraser operated in Singapore in the middle decades of the nineteenth century. It was one bolstered, moreover by the Freemasonry that linked it to other Scots, and even the occasional Sassenach, both there and elsewhere in the region. In the major Central Java port of Semarang, for example, John MacNeill, a key figure in the firm of Maclaine Watson that Gillian Maclaine had co-founded in 1827, was responsible for *re*-establishing the Freemason's Lodge, La Constante et Fidele, during his sojourn there in the late 1820s.[27] In Singapore itself, meanwhile, Lewis Fraser was instrumental in the 1840s in setting up the Zetland-in-the-East Masonic Lodge in the city, His newly acquired brother-in-law (and business partner), James Bannerman Cumming (1819–1889) became the Lodge's secretary and treasurer and subsequently 'Worshipful Master'.[28] It was no accident, therefore, that when Lewis and Sophie Fraser themselves departed permanently for Europe early in 1853, the festivities surrounding his departure were marked by the members of the Zetland Lodge giving:

> [a] ball and supper in the Assembly Rooms as a farewell token of their regard. The assembly was numerous, and the rooms were most tastefully decorated with various masonic emblems. The Military band was in attendance, and everything went off in excellent style. At supper, Mr. W.H. Read, the present

Master of the Lodge, proposed the toast of the evening in a short but appropriate speech, and after it had been drunk with masonic honours as well as the hearty cheers of the uninitiated, Mr. Fraser made a suitable reply. After the company left the supper table, the dancing was resumed and kept up with great spirit to an advanced hour.[29]

Underpinning the Fraser-Cumming family enterprise in Singapore were the profits accruing from trade that was both regional and global. In the latter category, at least initially, was their firm's location on a major international commodity chain – the nineteenth century's foremost – that began in the slave plantations of Louisiana and other parts of the American 'deep south', continued in the cotton spinning and weaving factories of the United Kingdom and other parts of north-western Europe and culminated in the sale of ubiquitous 'cotton goods' – meaning bales of dyed, patterned and plain cotton materials – in Asia, Africa and any other part of the world that they were able to penetrate.[30] Gillian Maclaine himself had literally 'gone out' to Southeast Asia in 1820 with a substantial cargo of such goods consigned to Batavia by his London employers,[31] and there is little doubt that James Fraser was on a similar mission when sailed from Batavia to Singapore to join Maclaine's agent there a very few years later. The sale of such goods to locally based Chinese and other so-called 'middlemen' would likely have remained a key staple of Maclaine Fraser's Singapore business throughout the middle decades of the nineteenth century.

It was not, however, the only one. Though there is no direct evidence, it is also a fair assumption that Maclaine Fraser also made its money through engagement in the intercontinental trade in opium in which Singapore played a major role. Opium, most of it originating in the Indian subcontinent, passed through Singapore on its way to China – a burgeoning market from the 1810s onward, in which were made the fortunes of a number of Scots firms, with the 'China Coast' smuggling business of Jardine Matheson very much to the fore.[32] Yet large quantities of opium were also sold in Southeast Asia itself, both in the string of Chinese mining and plantation settlements running southwards from Bangkok to Singapore and in the Netherlands Indies (present day Indonesia), where the Dutch government's purported monopoly on the sale of the commodity was perpetually and successfully subverted by an extensive and lucrative smuggling trade.[33] James's Fraser's one-time boss in Singapore, John Argyll Maxwell, as was revealed by his evidence to a British Parliamentary Committee after he returned home to the UK at end of the 1820s, was thoroughly conversant with the opium trade, and had himself travelled to Canton, the destination for the opium clippers sailing to China, at least once, while Gillian Maclaine himself was sufficiently familiar with the trade to petition the Dutch colonial authorities in the mid-1830s to contract his firm to supply the quantities needed for its opium 'farms' on Java.[34]

In such circumstances, it seems probable that Maclaine Fraser – the Singapore branch of his firm – would have sought to capitalise on the trade in the commodity that passed through the port. In terms of value, between the 1830s and 1850s – the period during which James and Lewis Fraser were active there – Singapore's exports to neighbouring, regional destinations were dominated by cotton goods (and cotton thread) of United Kingdom and Indian origin. Opium, however, most of it from India but also from the Levant, invariably occupied second place, and, in respect to exports to the east coast of the Malay Peninsula (where there were many settlements of Chinese labourers), consistently far exceeded cotton goods in value. Moreover, 'value' alone says nothing about the comparative profitability of the two commodities – and there is good reason to believe that the profits from opium were usually considerably higher than those earned by the (re-) sale of cottons.[35]

Even so, it seems possible that from the mid-century onward (or perhaps a little later) neither cotton goods nor opium formed Maclaine Fraser's sole core business, and that rice had either taken their place or stood consistently alongside them on the firm's balance sheet. In part this may have reflected the declining importance of the Indian trade with Southeast Asia outlined in Kobayashi's chapter in this volume. Rice was an important item in interregional trade in Southeast Asia, but it was also a commodity that found a ready sale in Europe, where it was used extensively for animal feed; for industrial use in, for example, the starch and paper industries; among the middle classes as a 'nutritional complement or supplement'; and, perhaps above all, 'in the absence or instead of other cereals' as 'a versatile and cheap dietary staple', especially useful for feeding the likes of orphans, soldiers, sailors, inmates and the poor generally.[36] Around the middle of the nineteenth century, the commodity chain(s) that produced it started among peasant farmers in Java, Siam, Cochin China and Lower Burma, whose notionally 'surplus' output was levied by extra-village elites, sold directly to merchants or otherwise made available to commerce. That commerce, in turn, increasingly centred on the Lion City, which became the linchpin of the Southeast Asian rice trade 'as entrepôt, distribution centre, and intermediary between Southeast Asian producers and consumers both inside and outside of the region'.[37] The Fraser brothers evidently became heavily involved in this trade. Once established in London (see later in this chapter) after their sojourn in the East, they ran a trading company, J. and L. Fraser & Co., from premises in Mincing Lane, along the hub of the City's 'East Indies' commercial quarter. Judging by the advertisements appearing in various London newspapers, the firm began operations sometime in the late 1850s and dealt, as brokers, in several 'colonial' commodities, above all in rice imported from a variety of Southeast Asian locations.[38]

In short, additional to playing a part in intercontinental commerce between Singapore and Europe, the Fraser brothers were substantial participants in intraregional trade in Southeast Asia. This, in turn, would hardly have been possible without the active collaboration of Chinese interests there and elsewhere in the region. They and other Asian merchants and shippers provided the sinews of trade in the rapidly emergent economy of mid-nineteenth century Singapore – and it was no accident, therefore, that when [Lewis] Fraser became, in 1837, one of the founding members of Singapore's first Chamber of Commerce, he did so in the company of Chinese as well as other European, Arab and Armenian merchants.[39] Given the context, It is a fair assumption that the Frasers and their business associates in Singapore would have had to work closely with Chinese mercantile interests in the Lion City More than that, however: fragmentary surviving evidence demonstrates that the firm's rice exporting business brought them into direct contact with the Lion City's leading Chinese trader in the commodity, Tan Kim Ching (1829–1892).

A very substantial figure in the port's mercantile community, in addition to being the owner of two steamers, Tan possessed rice mills in Saigon and in Bangkok, where his close connections with the Thai court presumably strengthened his hold over the latter port's rice trade.[40] Something of the extent – and character – of the Fraser brothers' dealings with him is evidenced by the fact that when one of their (ex-) partners, Simon Fraser Cumming (1823–1874), retired to the UK late in the 1860s, he left 10,000 Singapore dollars with Tan Kim Ching, secured by a mortgage 'on certain godowns or warehouses in Singapore' (the loan was subsequently repaid and the sum invested by Cumming in £2,500 (GBP) worth of stock in the London and South Western Railway Company).[41] To be sure, Tan Kim Ching's greatest days were still before him during the period in which the Frasers were operating in or trading with Singapore. Indeed, he only reached the apogee of his commercial career post-1870 (inter alia, his steam-driven rice mill in Bangkok dated from 1872), but his commercial importance in Singapore, and that of his father Tan Tock Seng (d. 1850), dated from some decades earlier. In short, given the Fraser brothers' dealings in rice and their association with an individual who was a commanding figure in the regional trade in that commodity, it is necessary to see their business not simply, or perhaps even primarily, in terms of its positioning in Singapore's commercial ties to the world outside Southeast Asia but also in terms of its deep involvement in intra-regional trade.

London

Despite the length of time they spent in Singapore and the fact that, in the case of Lewis and Sophie Fraser, most of their children were born there, the Lion City did not become home to the Fraser brothers, but neither, for that matter, did their native Scotland. Rather, when they left Singapore, they relocated to London and set themselves and their families up in fine style in London's West End, in the Marylebone-Paddington-Hyde Park-Bayswater area of the city much favoured by returnees from the East. Having left Singapore in the middle of the previous decade, James and Ann Fraser were living at the southern end of London's Regent's Park by the time of the 1851 Census (our sole guide in these matters), where they took up residence in a rather grand stuccoed terrace – Park Square East – built some quarter of a century earlier to the plans of the great Regency architect and entrepreneur John Nash. A few years later they shifted just over the road to similar accommodation on the east side of Park Crescent, which is where the family remained until after James' death in 1872. The locale is significant: it helps establish something of the social milieu of business and professional men and their families in which James Fraser moved in the metropolis after their mid-century return to the UK – as, indeed, did his brother Lewis, who occupied a large Victorian house in Paddington's Oxford Square before moving to the equally fashionable Montague Square a little to its east. By way of underscoring his new-found social status in London, he commissioned a *carte de visite* – showing himself standing next to his seated wife against a background of rich furnishings – from the studio of Camille Silvy, the most celebrated society photographer of the day.[42]

The 1851 Census data includes James Fraser's self-description as a 'retired East India merchant'. Retired in any more general sense, however, he most certainly was not: during the course of the 1850s and 1860s, both James and his brother associated with high-profile people in London's mercantile and financial circles. As business historian Charles Jones remarked, 'the availability among the growing group of returned merchants in London of men with local experience which they were willing to trade for a directorship' was a significant element in the City's growing mid-century position at the epicentre of global commerce and finance.[43] It was in this context that that (as far as can be ascertained) the Frasers withdrew much of their capital from the colony and re-invested it in a number of the newly incorporated merchant-banking and insurance companies that sprang up in London's financial district (aka 'the City') in the early 1860s in the wake of far-reaching government deregulation.[44] With positions on the boards of directors of a score or more of such companies, they participated in a period of unprecedented boom – and bust. Their story, in short, illuminates just how, in the case of the two men of substance, capital accumulated in the colonies was deployed in metropolitan investments after their return to the United Kingdom.

First and foremost – and hardly surprisingly – it clear that most of the boards on which they sat as directors were of companies that had an overseas, imperial focus rather than a domestic one. Indeed, in James Fraser's case, the most significant of the companies in which he was involved – at least in terms of its global reach and long-enduring character – was the Chartered Bank of India, Australia and China (eventually part of the Standard Chartered combine). Founded in 1853, it established offices throughout the East,[45] including one in Singapore in 1859 – presumably not coincidentally around the same time that Fraser joined its board. He was still one of its directors at the time of his death in 1872.[46] In this respect, the changing fortunes of the Fraser family provide strong evidence to support the strengthening connections between London and Southeast Asian interests cited in Webster's chapter in this volume, which fuelled the political pressure which secured Crown Colony status for the Straits Settlements by the end of the 1860s. But this was not the only City financial institution with which he became associated. Among the others were the English and Swedish Bank, the London Financial Association, and the London Chartered Bank of Australia.[47] His brother Lewis, meanwhile, held a similar string of City directorships, including those in the Bank of British Columbia, the Union Bank of Ireland, the Merchant Banking Company of London and – the most obviously empire-oriented – the Home and Colonial Insurance Co. of London.

What we know about their fellow directors in the companies concerned underlines the extent to which, after Singapore, the Fraser brothers had become part of the City establishment. On the board of the Home and Colonial, Lewis, for instance, sat alongside (among others) William Frederick Baring (1822–1903), scion of the well-known London family of merchant bankers and himself, inter alia, director of the Bank of Hindustan.[48] Most immediately, and again unsurprisingly, one of the obvious strengths of the brothers' connections was with business people with ties to the East. Among them were Peter Scott and William Nichol, both fellow directors of James Fraser's on the board of the Chartered Bank. Scott's firm of Scott, Bell & Co had traded with India and China since the late 1820s through the intermediary of Binney & Co of Madras, themselves correspondents of the rising 'China-Coast' firm of Jardine Matheson. In Calcutta they traded through Adam, Bell & Co and Mackinnon Mackenzie & Co., as well as having equally long-standing connections with cotton goods manufacturers and dealers in Manchester and Glasgow. At the time of its failure in 1865 (the victim, it was said, of a major downturn in Asian markets for cotton goods), Scott Bell was reported as 'occupying a high position in the commercial world': indeed, the fact that it closed its doors with debts estimated at around £800,000 (GBP) was indicative of the sheer scale of its operations.[49] William Nicol (1790–1879) likewise had deep mercantile roots in the East. Nicol likewise had a background in trade with the subcontinent, as founder (1820) of the long-enduring Bombay firm of Wm. Nichol & Co., from which he had officially retired in 1839, ten years after returning to the UK, where he subsequently became the Conservative Member of Parliament for Dover (1859–1865).[50] Like Scott Bell, Nicol's firm was at the upper end of mid-century business enterprises engaged in the massive trade in cotton goods from the UK to India and other parts of Asia: indeed, '[B]y the 1850s, it had grown into arguably the most important business group in [Bombay], with a large and diverse business portfolio . . . [and] as agents for Scottish manufacturers selling cotton textiles in western India, owned property and warehouses in the port of Bombay, and managed three of the coastal lines of the newly established British India Steam Navigation Company.'[51]

As this history of involvement in metropolitan business circles with a substantial stake in eastern Asia implies, 'the made in Singapore' designation of the Frasers and their commercial trajectory remained an apt one even after they had left the colony. Not only were the brothers able to capitalise (as we have just seen) on their lengthy experience in doing business there: they were also active members of a London-based lobby group that promoted the interests of the port-city in which they had made their money – and where they continued to run a business. Very shortly after his return from the colony in 1853, for example, Lewis Fraser had been among a 'deputation of gentlemen interested in Singapore' who had called on the president of the Board of Control (probably in relation to currency matters),[52] while two years later, in 1857, both Lewis and James Fraser were among the signatories – a veritable roll call of the Singapore-Penang mercantile interest in London – of a 'memorial to the president of the India Board, (again) opposing the imposition of tonnage dues in the Straits' ports'.[53] Consolidating the brothers' interests, moreover, early in 1868 James Fraser became an inaugural committee member of the newly established Straits Settlements Association, on which his fellow 'Singaporean' James Guthrie was deputy chair.[54]

The Association was founded, however, not in the boom conditions that had prevailed earlier in the decade but amid the detritus of the biggest financial crisis to hit the City during the entire nineteenth century. Predictably, the lure of London had its pitfalls, as we must assume the Frasers – as Good Steady Scotsmen – were well aware. Nonetheless, it seems unlikely they could have anticipated the depth of the financial turmoil – in present-day parlance the 'meltdown' – in which they were embroiled in the second half of the decade. The sudden collapse on 10 May 1866 of Overend Gurney, the London clearing house whose operations were central to the discounting of the bills of exchange which formed the lifeblood of international commerce in the middle decades of the nineteenth century, has been widely enough written about not to need rehearsing again here.[55] Suffice to say that one contemporary account spoke of 'great confusion all day, the streets were crowded and almost impassable . . . a day of the most intense excitement and panic in the City, in fact such a day as has never been experienced . . . in the memory of anyone.'[56]

For James and Lewis Fraser, both caught up in the expansive company growth of the preceding years, the results did not spell outright ruin, as it did for many others. Most – though not all – the companies on whose boards they sat survived the crisis. For some years, however, dividends were meagre or non-existent, and payments to Board Members dried up in consequence. The brothers and their families were still domiciled at the time of their deaths – Lewis in 1868 and his elder brother four years later – in the houses in which they had been living prior to the crisis. It must be assumed, however, that their financial circumstances were much reduced. Indeed, Lewis, dying while the repercussions of the crisis were still being experienced in the City, left only a modest estate of less than 20,000 GBP, while James apparently left some 60,000 GPB (we have no way of calculating what his or his brother's net worth might have been prior to the crisis). Shared between two widows, five sons and nine daughters, this was not the stuff of which dynastic fortunes were made. Other of the Fraser brothers' Singapore contemporaries managed to establish lasting businesses that endured long after their own demise. Indeed, in the case of the Guthries and Bousteads, they still do. The Fraser family's experience, however, was a very different one.

Postscript

In May 1882 a notice in the *St James Gazette* – that graveyard of unsuccessful businesses – notified the public that George John Fraser and Lewis James Fraser 'trading as J. & L. Fraser & Co, 6 Jeffrey's Square, Mary Axe in the City of London . . . and also as Maclaine Fraser & Co of Singapore' had filed for bankruptcy, with debts estimated around 85,000 GBP.[57] That was a relatively small sum which may suggest that the business which James Fraser's two sons were conducting was a fairly modest one. George John Fraser (1846–1887), the younger of the two, died five years later at the age of forty-two, having left no mark on the world. His elder brother, the Singapore-born Lewis James Fraser (1841–1906) fared rather better: indeed, he was the only one of the Fraser family to 'pass into history' and to become the stuff of legend. In the wake of the collapse of the family firm, sometime around 1890 he quite literally took to the hills, and, as the 'mysterious Scots prospector' or some such (depending on which modern-day tourist website is consulted) who 'disappeared' as obscurely as he had arrived, went on to discover tin deposits at what became known as Fraser's Hill or Bukit Fraser on the Malaysian mainland to the north of Singapore.[58] The settlement bearing his name became a hill-resort after the tin had run out (which it did fairly soon) and achieved notoriety at the end of the 1940s as the location near which the British High Commissioner, Sir Henry Gurney, was gunned down by communist guerrillas. Long before that, however, Lewis James Fraser himself had settled in the much less physically hazardous environs of the Kentish Spa-town of Tonbridge Wells in the southeast of England and – rather prosaically it might be thought – married a clergyman's daughter who was a widow of about his own age.

In fact, it was the women of the Fraser connection who generally managed things rather better than the men. In 1881, one of them – Lewis James Fraser's widowed older sister, Sophie Cumming Fraser (1840–1904) – wed the elderly James Guthrie (1814–1900), nephew of the eponymous firm's founder and himself a leading figure in the business over several decades. On his death, his estate, worth nearly 24,000 GPB passed to his widow.[59] It was her younger sister, Adelaide Fraser (1850–1929), however, who was the more socially successful. Already the widow of one British Army officer, in 1882 she married again, this time to Lieutenant-Colonel Herbert Locock (1837–1910), co-author of a famous *Drainage Manual* and son of a celebrated medical man who had at one time held a position as Queen Victoria's obstetrician.[60] After a society wedding in the fashionable Christ Church, Lancaster Gate (immediately to the north of Hyde Park), the couple took up residence in a rather grand house in London's affluent South Kensington, where Adelaide presided over a household of five children (two of them hers) and thirteen servants. When the Colonel's army days were over, the couple retired to a country house – Frensham Grove – just outside the Surrey town of Farnham, in England's leafy home counties.

This was not exactly the stuff, however, from which *business* dynasties were made, and well before the nineteenth century's end the Fraser family had faded into mercantile obscurity, a trajectory for which 'made in Singapore' but 'unmade in London' might well be the most apt description. Yet the importance of the story of James and Lewis Fraser and their long connection with Singapore should not be underestimated. Their family history back in their birthplace in Scotland suggests that they would have arrived in Southeast Asia with virtually no capital of their own but with potentially profitable connections in the business world that already tied the region into intercontinental commodity chains. Equal importantly, nonetheless, they were able to enrich themselves as a result of the Lion City's mid-century position in the intra-regional trade that linked the port to other key centres of commerce in Siam, Cochin China, Burma, 'the Indies' and the Malay Peninsula to its immediate north. They were able to exploit this situation, moreover, because of their ties not only with fellow ethnic Europeans but also with similarly ethnic Chinese whose own diasporic community overlapped in Singapore with the tiny but consequential Scots one to which the 'Good Steady' Lewis and James Fraser belonged.

Notes

1 Copy of on-voyage diary kept by Angus Maclaine between [Marseilles?] and Batavia, 26th July 1846, Osborn-Maclaine MSS, Gloucester Records, Gloucester, UK.

2 Except where otherwise stated, the biographical and suchlike information in what follows comes from UK Census Data, Probate Records, Marriage Banns etc. accessible via the *Ancestry.com* website, where it may be searched using the relevant name.

3 Inter alia, J. Forbes Munro, *Maritime Enterprise and Empire. Sir William Mackinnon and his Business Network, 1823–1893,* Woodbridge, UK: The Boydell Press, 2003; Christof Dejung, *Commodity Trading, Globalization and the Colonial World*, New York and London: Routledge, 2018; Richard J. Grace, *Opium and Empire: The Lives and Careers of William Jardine and James Matheson,* Montreal: McGill-Queens University Press, 2014; Anthony Webster, *The Richest East India Merchant,* Woodbridge: Boydell & Brewer, 2007; J.D. Wong, *Global Trade in the Nineteenth Century: The House of Houqua and the Canton System*, Cambridge: Cambridge University Press, 2016.

4 See, e.g., Christof Dejung and N.P. Petersson, 'Introduction: Power, Institutions and Global Markets – Actors, Mechanisms and Foundations of World-Wide Economic Integration, 1850–1930,' in C. Dejung and N.P. Petersson (eds.), *The Foundations of Worldwide Economic Integration,* Cambridge: Cambridge University Press, 2013, pp. 1–14.

5 Important work is reported in Ching-wang Yen, *Ethnic Chinese Business in Asia: History, Culture and Business Enterprise*, Singapore: World Scientific, 2014. For ethnic European business houses, Sjovald Cunyngham-Brown, *The Traders*, London: Newman Neame, 1971– dealing almost exclusively with the Guthrie family – has yet to be superseded.

6 The classic accounts remain C.M. Turnbull, *The Straits Settlements, 1826–1867*, London: Athlone Press, 1972; Wong Lin Ken, in C.H. Gibson Hill (ed.), *The Trade of Singapore, 1819–1869*, Singapore: Malayan Branch of the Royal Asiatic Society, 1961.

7 Inter alia, the present paper draws gratefully on the work of Kaoru Sugihara and Tomotaka Kawamura, 'Reconstructing Intra-Southeast Asian Trade, c. 1780–1870,' *Southeast Asian Studies,* vol. 2, no. 3, 2013 – and, in particular, on Atsushi Kobayashi's article in that issue (pp. 443–474) on 'The Role of Singapore in the Growth of Intra-Southeast Asian Trade, c.1820s – 1852.' See also: A.J.H. Latham and H. Kawakatsu (eds.), *Intra-Asian Trade and the World Market,* Abingdon, UK: Routledge, 2006.

8 T.N. Harper, 'Globalism and the Pursuit of Authenticity: The Making of a Diasporic Public Sphere in Singapore,' *Sojourn*, vol. 12, no. 2, 1997, pp. 273–275.

9 I owe a particular debt to Mrs. Ann Pickett of Brisbane, Australia (a descendent of the Fraser-Cumming families), for her generous help in detailing her ancestor's story, and to Mr. Brian Kerr, Secretary of the Lodge St Lawrence in Forres, for information relating to Masonic matters and to the Fraser family in nineteenth century Forres, kindly supplied to my assistant, Alexander Bouchet in December 2017.

10 Mackillop, 'Locality, Nation and Empire,' p. 61; 'Brodie, Alexander,' in J. M. MacKenzie and T. M. Devine. (eds), *Scotland and the British Empire*, Oxford: Oxford University Press, 2011, p. 61; 'Brodie, Alexander,' in L. Namier and J. Brooke (eds.), *The History of Parliament. The House of Commons, 1754–1790*, 1964, Woodbridge, Boydell & Brewer. Accessed online 27 December 2016 at https://eur02.safelinks. protection.outlook.com/?url=https%3A%2F%2Fwww.historyofparliamentonline.org

%2F&data=02%7C01%7C%7C8d391b3217a248cd10fd08d7468cdfc2%7C84df9e7
fe9f640afb435aaaaaaaaaaaa%7C1%7C0%7C637055443169098922&sdata=7QfGJ
CA0xBb%2BCh06qLlk4%2BEes%2FHLVx41khrWdzSo%2BTI%3D&reserved=0.

11 https://en.wikipedia.org/wiki/Hugh_Falconer, accessed 17 November 2018.
12 Transcript 'St Lawrence Lodge Forres . . . Forres March 1833,' kindly supplied by Mr. Brian Kerr (see above).
13 For a significant recent addition to the large body of literature, see Angela McCarthy and John M. Mackenzie (eds.), *Global Migrations. The Scottish Diaspora since 1600*, Edinburgh: Edinburgh University Press, 2016; T.M. Devine and Angela McCarthy (eds.), *The Scottish Experience in Asia. c. 1700 to the Present*, Basingstoke: Palgrave Macmillan, 2016.
14 Gillian Maclaine to Marjorie Maclaine, 10 September 1823, Osborn-Maclaine MSS.
15 Justin J. Corfield, *Singapore: Cathedral Church of St. Andrew: Baptisms 1823–1871, Marriages 1826–1871, Burials 1820–1875*, Singapore: Corfield & Co., 1999, pp. 4, 5, 7, 19.
16 Information kindly supplied by Mrs. Anne Pickett (see note 9 above).
17 C. Buckley, *An Anecdotal History of Old Times in Singapore*, Vol. 1, Singapore: Fraser & Neave, 1902, pp. 216, 377.
18 Turnbull, *Straits Settlements*, p. 24.
19 T. Bueltmann, *Clubbing Together: Ethnicity, Civility and Formal Sociability in the Scottish Diaspora to 1930*, Oxford: Oxford University Press, 2015, p. 12.
20 Buckley, *Anecdotal History*, Vol. 1, p. 320.
21 See E. Buettner, 'Haggis in the Raj: Private and Public Celebrations of Scottishness in Late Imperial India,' *Scottish Historical Review*, vol. 81, no. 2, 2002, pp. 215, 221.
22 Buckley, *Anecdotal History*, Vol. 2, p. 439.
23 Ibid., Vol. 1, p. 387, Vol. 2, pp. 419, 531.
24 The roll call of partners between the 1830s and 1860s included (along with the Fraser brothers themselves) Gilbert Angus Bain; Robert Bain, John Purse Cumming, Simon Fraser Cumming James Bannerman Cumming, R.O. Norris, N.B. Watson and Charles Dunlop. See Buckley, *Anecdotal History*, Vol. 1, p. 233.
25 Buckley, *Anecdotal History*, Vol. 2, p. 696.
26 The US Confederate cruiser *Alabama* (a major destroyer of Union shipping in the ongoing Civil War) had called into the port in December 1863 in search of repairs and supplies. Described by the *Alabama*'s captain as 'a clever English merchant [who] came on board and offered to facilitate us all in his power in the way of procuring supplies,' Beaver featured (with much gratitude expressed) in both captain Semmes own memoirs and in those of one his officers. See the provenance information re the *Alabama*'s flag in Sotheby's 2011 Catalogue, available at: www.sothebys.com/en/auctions/ecatalogue/2011/fine-books-and-manuscripts-n08755/lot.157.html, accessed 8 February 2017.
27 Information kindly supplied (August 2018) by dhr. Jac. Piepenbrock, of Het Cultureel Maconniek Centrum 'Prins Frederik,' Java Straat, The Hague.
28 Buckley, *Anecdotal History*, Vol. 2, pp. 437, 497.
29 Ibid., Vol. 1, p. 173, quoting *The Singapore Free Press*.
30 Sven Beckert, *Empire of Cotton. A Global History*, New York: Alfred A. Knopf, 2015, passim.
31 G. Roger Knight, *Trade and Empire in Early Nineteenth Century Southeast Asia: Gillian Maclaine and His Business Network*, Woodbridge: The Boydell Press, 2015, pp. 52–55.
32 Grace, *Opium and Empire*, passim.
33 Eric Tagliacozzo, *Secret Trades, Porous Borders. Smuggling and States Along a Southeast Asian Frontier, 1865–1915*, New Haven and London: Yale University Press, 2005, pp. 186–196. See also: Anthony Webster, 'The Development of British Commercial and Political Networks in the Straits Settlements 1800 to 1868: The Rise of a Colonial and Regional Economic Identity?' *Modern Asian Studies*, vol. 45, no. 4, 2011,

pp. 899–929; Carl A. Trocki, 'The Rise of Singapore's Great Opium Syndicate 1840–1886,' *Journal of Southeast Asian Studies*, vol. 18, no. 2, 1987, pp. 58–80.

34 Knight, *Trade and Empire*, pp. 146–147.

35 Kobayashi, 'The Role of Singapore,' pp. 443–474.

36 Peter A. Coclanis, 'Southeast Asia's Incorporation into the World Rice Market: A Revisionist View,' *Journal of Southeast Asian Studies*, vol. 24, no. 2, 1993, p. 254.

37 Ibid., p. 265.

38 In addition to rice, J and L Fraser & Co. ('Brokers, 1 Hammond Court/21 Mincing Lane/17 Mincing Lane) also traded in such commodities as Java Sugar, Coffee. 'Bengal Saltpetre' and Central American Coffee. See, for example, *Public Ledger and Daily Advertiser, 18 September 1862,* 12 February 1869, and 17 April 1871.

39 Buckley, *Anecdotal History*, Vol. 1, pp. 313–314.

40 T. Miyata, 'Tan Kim Ching and Siam "Garden Rice",' in Latham and Kawakatsu, *Intra Asian Trade*, pp. 115–132.

41 Court of Chancery Clerks of Records and Writs Office, Pleadings 1861–1875. *Cumming v Cumming*, [C 16/921/C117] National Archives, Kew, UK. Plaintiffs: Elizabeth Chambers Cumming, widow. Defendants: James Bannerman Cumming and William Anastasius Barff.

42 www.19thcenturyphotos.com/Lewis-and-Sophia-Fraser-125699.htm.

43 C.A. Jones, *International Business in the Nineteenth Century. The Rise and Fall of a Cosmopolitan Bourgeoisie,* Brighton: Wheatsheaf Books, 1987, p. 160.

44 S. Chapman, The *Rise of Merchant Banking*, London: Routledge, 1984, pp. 39–69; P. Cottrell, *Investment Banking in England 1856–1881*, Vol. 1, London: Routledge, 2012 *passim.*

45 See 'Chartered Bank of India, Australia and China,' *Wikipedia,* 2017, available at: https://en.wikipedia.org/wiki/Chartered_Bank_of_India,_Australia_and_China, accessed 30 June 2017; Jason Toh, *Singapore Through 19th Century Photographs*, Singapore: Editions Didier Millet, 2009, p. 35 (for an early 1900s photo of its impressive offices in the Lion City).

46 See, inter alia, Buckley, *Anecdotal History*, Vol. 2, p. 673; *London Evening Standard*, 1 May 1862; *Morning Advertiser*, 11 June 1866; *Money Market Review*, 19 April 1873, as cited in *Java Bode*, 19 June 1873.

47 E.g., *Morning Advertiser*, 3 November 1863; *London Daily News*, 8 January 1867; *London Evening Standard*, 3 October 1864.

48 E.g., *London Daily News,* 3 October 1863.

49 J. Forbes Munro, *Maritime Trade and Empire: Sir William Mackinnon and His Business Network*, Woodbridge, UK and Rochester: The Boydell Press, 2003, p. 30; *London Gazette,* 31 December 1830; A. Le Pichon, *China Trade and Empire: Jardine, Matheson & Co. and the Origins of British Rule in Hong Kong, 1827–1843*, Oxford and New York: Oxford University Press for the British Academy, 2006, pp. 230, 395; *London Evening Standard*, 26 August 1865; *Examiner*, 8 July 1865.

50 'William Nichol (surgeon),' available at: https://en.wikipedia.org/wiki/William_Nicol_(surgeon), accessed 2 July 2017.

51 S. Hazareesingh, 'Interconnected Synchronicities: The Production of Bombay and Glasgow as Modern Global Ports c.1850–1880,' *Journal of Global History*, vol. 4, no. 1, 2009, p. 18.

52 *Morning Post*, 26 May 1855.

53 Buckley, *Anecdotal History*, p. 647.

54 W. Makepeace et al., *One Hundred Years of Singapore*, Vol. 2, London: John Murray, 1921, pp. 297–298; Webster, 'British Commercial and Political Networks in the Straits Settlements,' *passim.*

55 E.g., www.bankofengland.co.uk/quarterly-bulletin/2016/q2/the-demise-of-overend-gurney, accessed 24 November 2018; D. Foucaud, 'The Impact of the *Companies Act* of 1862 Extending Limited Liability to the Banking and Financial Sector in the English Crisis of 1866,' *Revue Economique*, vol. 62, no. 5, 2011, pp. 867–897.

56 Quoted in D. Kynaston, *The City of London, Vol. 1. A World of its Own, 1815–1890*, London: Pimlico/Random House, 1995, pp. 238–240.

57 *St. James's Gazette,* 18 May 1882.

58 *The Sussex Agricultural Express*, 12 July 1901, for a report that on 4 July of that year, at St Mary Abbots, Kensington, West London, Lewis James Fraser, said to be of 'Tras Lahang [sic: Pahang],' married Marie Ellen, daughter of the late Rev. Frederic Cheere, Papworth Hall, Cambridge, and Mrs Cheere of Beverly, Tonbridge Wells. [*Tras is a village in the Highlands of Malaya, a few miles from Fraser's Hill*]. He died some five years later, presumably while on holiday, in Salzburg, Austria, in August 1906.

59 *Illustrated London News,* 17 November 1900.

60 https://en.wikipedia.org/wiki/Charles_Locock, accessed 28 October 2018.

4 Trade, finance, and the 'Anglo-Dutch' international order in Southeast Asia

The case of the British Eastern exchange banks, 1870–1890

Tomotaka Kawamura

Introduction

In December 2015, the Southeast Asian Common Alliance was established, with the aim of achieving greater economic integration across the region. It was the latest step in the process of securing an effective organisation to represent the countries of Southeast Asia, which began with the founding in 1967 of the Association of South East Asian Nations (ASEAN). What was particularly noteworthy about the Common Alliance was its aim to create a single regional economic zone that encompasses more people than the European Union. In respect of ASEAN trade in 2017, Singapore's importance as the hub of the region is evident from trade statistics. It commanded 26.8 per cent of ASEAN trade, compared to Thailand's 18.1 per cent and Indonesia's 12.8 per cent, respectively. Singapore thus continues to play a prominent role in international commerce and finance, having more strong connections with neighbouring countries.[1] However, Southeast Asia as an integrated region, and Singapore's predominance in it, have a much longer and more complicated history than has been assumed.

Japanese scholars argue that the roots of the dynamic growth of 'intra-Southeast Asian regional trade' lie in the period between the later eighteenth century and the mid-nineteenth century, during which Southeast Asia became integrated into both long-distance trade and the wider intra-Asian trade.[2] Crucial to this process was the transition from the dominance of the Dutch East India Company to the regime of colonial free trade under the Anglo-Dutch Treaty (1824), which shaped long-distance, regional and local trade in Southeast Asia. Their studies highlight the commercial role which Singapore played in the formation of intra-Southeast Asian trading networks in the first half of the nineteenth century. Sugihara also stresses that the region's economic integration between the 1880s and 1930s was connected in a certain extent to the establishment of the two nations' mutual benefit relationship, namely, the 'Anglo-Dutch international order'.[3] These works persuade us of the need to reconsider the international context in the Southeast Asian economic integration.

The subject has been shaped by the contrasting perspectives of British and Dutch historians, who have tended to remain so aloof from each other that the Southeast Asian archipelago might have been academically divided between north and south along the Straits of Malacca. There are some key texts that do seek to reach across the divide. For example, Knight explores how some British merchants developed new business in Java even after the Treaty of 1824 divided the region into separate British and Dutch spheres of influence. Kuitenbrouwer and Schijf also attempt comparative studies of capitalism and imperialism between Britain and the Netherlands with special reference to the Dutch colonial business elites in the last quarter of the nineteenth century.[4] In the same spirit, this chapter recognises the importance of transcending these imperial boundaries to build a clearer picture of developments across the region as a whole.

This chapter traces the formative processes of the 'Anglo-Dutch' international order in Southeast Asia, particularly through an examination of the British Eastern exchange banks during the 1870s and 1880s.[5] These banks profited from providing financial services linked with the growth of the international trade of Southeast Asia and other parts of Asia, through networks of offices and branches in key Asian port-cities. Central to the chapter will be an exploration of the ways in which those banks helped facilitate Southeast Asian economic integration. In so doing, it highlights the continuing pivotal role played by Singapore in the process of regional economic integration and wider globalization. It will argue that the image of Southeast Asia as a disjointed economic region similar to Africa at the end of the nineteenth century is misleading and in need of major revision.

The emergence of the Anglo-Dutch international order of 1824

Since the mid-eighteenth century the British East India Company had been expanding maritime trading activities from India to Southeast Asia and China, and consequently incorporated the Straits of Malacca into its sphere of influence in 1824. The Dutch government opposed the acquisition of Singapore in 1819 by Thomas Stamford Raffles from the Kingdom of Johor, which historically had been subject to Dutch influence. There followed several years of diplomatic negotiation between the British and Dutch which culminated in the establishment of separate spheres of influence in the Indonesian Archipelago. Under the Anglo-Dutch Treaty of 1824, trade between the British and Dutch would be conducted on the basis of 'the most favoured nation'. Britain took permanent possession of Singapore and Melaka, surrendering in return Bencoolen (today known as Bengkulu) and its other possessions on Sumatra, and all claims to the Karimun Islands and any other islands 'south of the straits of Singapore', which now comprised the Dutch sphere of influence. However, ambiguity in the precise position of the border between the two spheres would fuel future conflict in the region. In 1826, Penang, Melaka and Singapore were placed under the control of the Bengal government. The 'Straits Settlements', like British Burma, also recently acquired, was expected to serve the interests of British India in the maintenance of the old colonial system.[6]

The Netherlands had been developing its colonial policies from Java and the neighbouring islands. But the Java War (1825–30) further strained the Dutch financial status and political presence, together with the independence of Belgium

(1830), where most of the lucrative cotton industrial areas were concentrated. During the decades following the end of the Napoleonic wars, the Dutch King, William I, encouraged by leading private companies in Amsterdam and The Hague, sought national revival through strengthening both the domestic and colonial economies. Policies included the granting of Royal Charters to key enterprises and the creation of new, large corporations (137 by 1850) involved in transport, welfare, trade regulation and banking. An important new chartered company, founded in Amsterdam in 1824, was the Netherlands Trading Society (Nederlandsche Handel-Maatschappij), which was empowered to monopolize the East and West Indian colonial trades. The largest shareholder was William I, and in 1826 it opened its Batavia office. These new companies enriched the mercantile and banking elite from several aristocratic families, who concurrently served as directors and other executives.[7] The Bank of Java, owned by the Netherlands Trading Society and the Dutch Government, also commenced business in 1827.

In 1830, following the end of the Java War, Governor-General Johannes van den Bosch, in charge of the Dutch East Indies colonies, introduced the Cultuurstel (Cultivation System) in Java. After 1847 it was extended to coffee growing areas in West Sumatra. Under the system in Java, peasants were forced to allocate one-fifth of their land or one fifth of their labour for the cultivation of profitable export crops.[8] The role of the Netherlands Trading Society in the system was pivotal. In Amsterdam, it sold export crops on behalf of the Batavia office and paid the enormous profits to the home government. In return, it purchased and exported Dutch manufactured goods to Dutch possessions in Asia. The profits accounted for on average almost one-fifth of the total Dutch public revenues before 1850 and almost one-third during the period 1851–60.[9] These figures underline the importance of the contribution of the Netherlands East Indies to the Dutch state and economy. Significantly, the Cultivation System never excluded foreign private capital. British merchants and engineers in particular migrated to Java, bringing new technologies and capital acquired elsewhere, such as the tropical plantations in Latin America. Thus British private firms served the processing departments of sugar factories, which included Maclaine & Watson (Batavia), Fraser Eaton & Co. (Surabaya), and McNeal (Semarang). Thus British interests played an important role in the economic development of the Netherlands East Indies.[10]

But the East India Government Act of 1854 began the abolition of the Cultivation System. After that, Dutch private enterprises began to invest in Java and other parts of the Netherlands East Indies. The Netherlands Trading Society continued its central role in the trade between the Netherlands and Java, and greatly encouraged the development of shipbuilding industries in Amsterdam and Rotterdam. Colonial banks were also established to support of agriculture and industries in the Netherlands East Indies, including Netherlands-Indian Escompto Company, Netherlands-Indian Commercial Bank, and the Internationale Crediet- en Handelsvereeniging 'Rotterdam'. In developing an export-oriented economy, the Netherlands East Indies Government prioritised the construction of infrastructure such as railways, irrigation schemes and ports. Prior to 1870, these priorities were also reflected in the policies for Sumatra and the Outer Islands, notably in the promotion of tin mining on the Island of Billiton and tobacco production in Deli. The export values from Java/Madura doubled between 1840 and 1870, with over 80 per cent of all exports going to the Netherlands.

The British Asian colonial system centred on India also experienced major transformation in the 1850s and 1860s following the Great Indian Rebellion and the consequent dismantling of East India Company's rule. An important result in Southeast Asia was the transfer of jurisdiction of the Straits Settlements from the East India Company to the Colonial Office in 1867. As a 'Free Port', Singapore enjoyed the strongest connections with the Netherlands East Indies in Southeast Asia, though Penang's trade with Sumatra was also substantial.[11] Since the 1830s, the Straits mercantile communities had supported the principle of free trade, becoming increasingly dissatisfied with policies which threatened to undermine this made in British India. Singapore leaders in particular urged the Straits Settlements be released from Indian rule. Once this was secured in 1867, new opportunities arose to develop joint British/Dutch commercial initiatives across Southeast Asia.

New phases of British imperialism and Dutch imperialism

The Anglo-Dutch treaty of 1824 had provided a political basis for the integration of insular Southeast Asia into the wider international economy. The relationship between the two powers was refined further by the Sumatra Treaty in 1871, which sought to consolidate their respective colonial regimes in Southeast Asia. Notwithstanding Sumatra's position within the Dutch sphere after 1824, the British, especially from Penang, still maintained trade with the island, which formed an important source of prosperity. When in 1858 the Netherlands East Indies government annexed the Kingdom of Siak and taxed British merchants and trade there, tensions between the two powers intensified. The Sumatra Treaty sought to diminish these by allowing British merchants to enjoy the same rights and advantages of Dutch merchants on the island.

The treaty marked a major turning point in Dutch policy in the region. At the beginning of 1873, the Netherlands invaded the Kingdom of Aceh in northern Sumatra and introduced liberal economic policies to attract additional private investment. The government shifted to a policy of aggressive expansion, overturning the earlier principle of non-intervention in the Outer Islands.[12] Colonial expansion was expected to increase tax revenues, and indeed from 1876 to 1884 the Netherlands East Indies government reduced its accumulated budget deficit, notwithstanding the gradual abolition of the Cultivation System and the associated increase of public expenditure.[13] From its fiscal point of view, the Netherlands Indies government clearly had a strong motivation for encouraging economic development and private investment in the Outer Islands.

The Netherlands East Indies government needed to promote Dutch shipping interests to strengthen its position in relation to the British, but until the late 1880s it depended heavily upon British shipping to meet its needs. In 1852, the Netherlands East Indies government granted a Dutch shipowner, Cores de Vries, government postal business between Singapore and Batavia. De Vries came to monopolize the steamboat service connecting the major Dutch ports of the Indonesian Archipelago. But the government saw this monopoly as very inefficient, and signed a postal contract in 1865 with a London-registered Dutch flag company the Netherlands India Steamship Company (Netherlands Indische Stoomvaart Maatschappij).[14] This company had been established by a corporate group of British and Dutch politicians and merchants, including William Mackinnon and William Poolman. But it was actually owned by the British through the 'sister' firm British India Steamship Company that Mackinnon had formed in 1856 to carry mail between Calcutta and Rangoon. He made his friend Alexander Fraser the chief-agent in Batavia, who was one of the most prominent merchants within the British mercantile community in Singapore and Java. Fraser also had a friendship with Poolman, who had long been an active merchant in Java. The Netherlands India Steamship Company ran lines between Singapore, Batavia and the Outer Islands, through which Mackinnon and the British India Steamship Company could eventually connect the Netherlands East Indies with South Asia, Middle East, and East Africa. Only in 1888 was a fully Dutch-owned shipping concern, the Royal Packet Navigation Company (Koninklijke Paketvaart-Maatschappij), founded in Batavia for services within and beyond the Netherlands East Indies.

The Pangkor Treaty of 1874 marked growing British interference in the western states of the Malay Peninsula specifically aimed to protect essential commercial interests, especially in the tin industry. The Straits government placed the western Malay states under the influence of British Residents who developed a system of support and surveillance over the Sultans, effectively controlling them. Concerned by intensifying conflicts between Chinese interests over western Malay tin, the Chambers of Commerce in Singapore and Penang had long pressed for the Straits government to impose order in the increasingly conflict-ridden states of Perak, Selangor and Negeri Sembilan. Thus they warmly welcomed the Straits government's intervention there. These commercial interests ultimately led to the establishment of the Federated Malay States in 1897, placing the capital in Kuala Lumpur, Selangor. The 1870s and 1880s saw an increase of tin production in the Malay Peninsula in response to the rapid expansion of demand from tinplate industries (especially canned and drum-can manufacturing) in Europe and North America. But the Malay tin industry was dominated by Chinese enterprises that could mobilize cheap Chinese workers on a massive scale. Only after the 1880s did European capital entered this industry in earnest. The first was a French mining company awarded the right to dig tin in Perak in 1881. In 1887, the British-owned Pahang Corporation took control of a mining concession at Sungai Lembing. A Dutch company, the Netherlands Trading Society also took advantage of this trend in 1888 and set up an office in Penang. Among the European tin companies, the most prominent was the Straits Trading Company Limited in Singapore, incorporated in 1887. These European tin enterprises took advantage of advanced refining technology and large capital resources to establish a dominant position in Southeast Asia.[15] By 1913, the Straits Trading Company had become the largest tin-smelting company in the world.

As mentioned previously, the Sumatra Treaty guaranteed access for British merchants to that island. But from the early 1880s, complaints from Penang's inhabitants and the Chamber of Commerce indicated that great difficulties were being encountered by those carrying on trade between Penang and the several ports on the northeastern and western coasts of Sumatra.[16] In Penang, Chinese and Indian merchants imported peppers, rattans, gutta percha, tobacco and other items from Sumatra. They objected strongly to the actions of the Dutch Authorities in closing trade with a number of Acehnese ports as a result of the Aceh War, demanding Dutch compliance with the Sumatra treaty. Huttenbach Brothers & Co. of Penang complained bitterly of the disruption inflicted on their trade between Penang and the Indian Coromandel Coast via key ports in Sumatra.[17]

The Straits government contended to the Colonial Office that the restrictions on British trade threatened to severely undermine Anglo-Dutch relations in the region. The Colonial Office immediately transmitted confidential despatches to the Secretary of State for Foreign Affairs, then visiting The Hague. Raising the issue with the Dutch Netherlands Government, he was told that concerns about the import of arms from the Straits Settlements to the Netherlands East Indies meant that the Dutch restrictions in Sumatra could not soon be withdrawn.[18] Rather, the Dutch policy strengthened the continued restrictions on regional trade by the establishment of the so-called blockade in 1888: only the ports of Olehleh, Poela Rajaj and Teluk Semawe were open to general trade. All other ports were open only for coasting trade, that is, local trade between these ports themselves. The Netherlands East Indies government understood that the policy would have a serious impact upon Penang's trade.[19] The Penang Chamber of Commerce indeed complained that the trade of Penang was suffering incalculable harm, but little was done about the problem.[20] The existing Anglo-Dutch international order was preserved, notwithstanding these local disagreements between the two countries.

British Eastern exchange banks in Southeast Asia

From the 1840s, the British Eastern exchange banks became interested in establishing themselves in the Straits Settlements. The first was the Oriental Banking Corporation, which opened its Singapore office in 1842. Other banks followed into Singapore and Penang between the 1850s and the 1880s, establishing themselves as part of the European mercantile communities in the Straits Settlements, including Melaka, where the Chartered Mercantile Bank established its office. In the Netherlands East Indies, the Chartered Bank set up in Batavia in 1863, followed by the Chartered Mercantile Bank in 1872 and the Hong Kong & Shanghai Banking Corporation in 1884. The Chartered Bank also opened offices in Surabaya and Deli, and became the most influential British bank in the Netherlands East Indies. In June 1884 it was reported that a large quantity of notes issued by the Singapore offices of the Chartered Mercantile, Chartered, and Hongkong & Shanghai Banks were in circulation for which no authority had been given in the Protected States of the Malay Peninsula. In reality, it was the practice in each of those States for the Resident to make temporary advances, with or without security, to assist natives to open agricultural or mining lands.[21] In Selangor, the British Resident and the Straits Trading Company stressed that Selangor should own a State Bank or issue its government notes to the exclusion of all other notes.[22] However, the Colonial and Home governments declined such proposals, and instead arranged an institutional foundation that facilitated the new entry of private international banks.[23] Though both governments did not permit any note issuance in the Protected States, the Chartered Bank of India opened the offices at Kuala Lumpur and Taiping in 1884 and at Perak and Selangor in 1888.[24] The Hongkong & Shanghai Banking Corporation competed against the Chartered Bank in the Malay Peninsula and managed to open an agency in Perak.[25] The former expanded into Ipoh, Kuala Lumpur and Johor to finance rubber plantations and the export trade while the latter concentrated upon Taiping and Kuala Lumpur to engage in tin mining.[26]

In 1870, 49 per cent of the total business of the Chartered Mercantile Bank (CMB) was connected with India and Ceylon, and 34 per cent with China.[27] The Singapore and Penang offices shared only 12 per cent of the total. But this changed dramatically in the late 1870s. In 1875, the South Asian business (45 per cent) remained the most prominent while its activities in China (21 per cent) declined rapidly. But the CMB expanded its Southeast Asian business considerably (28 per cent). It lost no opportunity to make profits in the Netherlands East Indies under the liberal economic system, and opened new offices in Batavia and Surabaya during the years 1872–73. The Batavia office (11 per cent) enjoyed about the same share as the Singapore office (12 per cent) in 1875. The CMB also opened a Rangoon office in 1879. It won profits primarily by financing the export trade in rice. Burmese rice was exported to European markets for industrial and non-industrial uses. Demand for this crop in the world market had been expanding since the early nineteenth century, and exports increased sharply after the Second Anglo-Burmese War in 1852. The volume of export of rice from Burma became larger than that from Siam and Vietnam, and Burma developed from the mid-nineteenth century as the largest rice exporting country in Southeast Asia.[28] The CMB's finance of rice exports in Rangoon, added significantly to the rapid growth of Burma's export trade to the Straits Settlement as well as India and Ceylon in the 1880s.[29] This was reflected in the growth of the bank's exchange operation between Rangoon and Singapore.[30] Here was just one example of how colonial banking helped develop intra-regional trade in Southeast Asia. Southeast Asia continued to grow in importance for the bank during the 1880s. It's share of the CMB's business grew to 32 per cent, while China (14 per cent) had a smaller presence in the bank's Asian business, and South Asia commanded 51 per cent. This geographical pattern seems to reflect a shift in the bank's administrative strategy. George Garden Nicol, who gave the CMB long service as chairman after 1858, had previously worked in Hamilton, Gray & Co. of Singapore, long-established agency house, and had also been the president of the Singapore Chamber of Commerce (1850). In the 1880s, the CMB welcomed into its management two prominent merchants, Alexander Fraser (Maclaine Watson and Netherlands-Indian Escompto Company) and Thomas Scott (Guthrie & Co.). They belonged to a closed political circle of gentlemen capitalists, having a wealth of knowledge and experience of Southeast Asian commerce. By 1890, Southeast Asia accounted for about 35 per cent of the CMB's business, with South Asia enjoying 48 per cent and China just 16 per cent.

Developing the CMB's business: from Straits Settlements to Netherlands Indies

In order to evaluate the impact of the CMB's activities in developing commerce in Southeast Asia, it is helpful to examine the growth of the bank's role within both the wider region and in important key locations in which it had an office. This section will provide an overview of this development.[31]

Trans-Southeast Asian business

In Singapore, Penang, Rangoon, and Batavia, the most significant business of the CMB was foreign exchange business, comprising the purchases and sales of bills on London with merchants based in Southeast Asia. Those operations facilitated commodity exports and imports between Southeast Asia and other parts of the world. This business was central to all of the other British banks involved in the region. Exchange operations at the four main offices of the CMB in 1880 and 1890, respectively, were £791,230 and £488,491 in Singapore, £491,144 and £385,920 pounds in Penang, £1,013,699 and £1,353,923 in Batavia, £190,252 and £394,880 in Rangoon. The Southeast Asian offices collected current/fixed deposits in local currencies and employed much of them in foreign exchange operations. The amount of deposits of the CMB in 1880 and 1890, respectively, were £242,501 and £330,533 in Singapore, £167,527 and £216,971 in Penang, £70,132 and £63,389 in Batavia, £101,043 and £89,031 in Rangoon. The bank's deposits increased in its Singapore and Penang offices, especially in the former. Deposits were invested in local bill discounting or lending operations. The increase in these services dem-onstrates that the CMB financed agricultural production, mining, construction of infrastructure, and internal trades in the Southeast Asian domestic economy. Bill discounts respectively in 1880 and 1890 amounted to £89,626 and £22,929 in Singapore, £0 and £155,137 in Penang, £166 and £154,193 in Batavia, and £0 and £5,140 in Rangoon. Loans in 1880 and 1890 amounted respectively to £36,757 and £67,987 in Singapore, £41,561 and £15,090 in Penang, £166 and £154,193 in Batavia, and 0 pounds and £5,140 in Rangoon. All in all, these figures underline the growing importance to the bank of its Southeast Asian activities. In South-east Asia, the CMB issued its own bank notes in Singapore and Penang. Given the shortage of bullion and capital in the region, this helped stabilise the supply of local currencies and the collection of working funds. The bank's issuance in 1870, 1880, and 1890, respectively, was worth in sterling £53,372, £143,630 and £142,506 in Singapore, and £93,130, £42,614 and £121,957 in Penang. From the 1870s onward, the social and economic demand for bank notes increased in the Straits Settlements. In the 1860s, the issuance of the British banks had been con-sidered essential to help promote social stability and commerce in Singapore.[32]

The CMB's role was thus vital for the development of the economic and social structures of the Straits Settlements and other parts of the Malay Peninsula.

Penang

Since its foundation in 1786, Penang had steadily flourished and built intimate relations with ports on the western coast of the Malay Peninsula, the eastern coast of Sumatra, the Coromandel Coast of India, continental Southeast Asia, and mainland China.[33] This small island became a major gateway to the Malay Peninsula and Sumatra. From the late nineteenth century to the early twentieth century, the tin industry and rubber plantations developed as the core of the Malayan colonial economy. Penang grew as a collecting and exporting port for tin produced primarily on the West Coast of the Malay Peninsula, especially in Perak. Leading European merchant houses were important customers of the CMB in Penang, including Brown & Co., Gilfillan, Wood & Co., Behn Meyer & Co., Katz Brothers, and Frederick & Co.[34] These firms, also engaged in international trade with Europe, took advantage of the bank's services such as foreign exchange, overdraft, loans and advances on Bill of Lading and real estate securities. Main exports subject to exchange operations were tin, tobacco, sugar, and petroleum produced in the Malay Peninsula and Sumatra, which were transported in large quantities to Britain, Germany, and the Netherlands. These commodities were exported to Hong Kong and other Chinese ports as well.[35] In the Penang office, more significant were loans and advances to European companies involved in the tin industry and commercial agriculture. These branches of the CMB's business were so important and large that the London Court of Directors, fearful of large and unmanageable debts, instructed the office to refrain from overdrafts or advances on the guarantee of real estate and other securities.[36] Through this involvement in tin the Penang office also dealt with related firms and industries. It repeatedly advanced large sums to major tin companies such as Huttenback Brothers & Co., Frederick & Co., and Perak Mining Company.[37] As the tin industry became more important and expanded in the Malay Peninsula, the Chartered Bank and the Hong Kong & Shanghai Bank also became increasingly interested in Taiping and Kuala Lumpur. The CMB always watched closely the strategies of its two rivals in the Malay Peninsula.[38]

The important customers in commercial agriculture were Frederick & Co., the Sumatra Tobacco Plantation Company, the Amsterdam Deli Company, and the Allendburg Tobacco Company, which owned and operated tobacco plantations in Sumatra.[39] The Deli Company, in which the Netherlands Trading Society held half of the shares, was one of the leading companies with interests in the Netherlands East Indies, and was a leader of the tobacco industry in eastern Sumatra. Meanwhile, the CMB designated Brown & Co. as their agent in Medan, Sumatra, to develop the bank's commercial interests in tobacco in the Netherlands East Indies.[40] The Penang office was particularly interested in Aceh, with which it had long-standing commercial relations. Inevitably, it was deeply concerned at the effects of Dutch colonial violence in Aceh from 1873. It was therefore a major priority for the CMB to stabilise relations and maintain the Anglo-Dutch international order on Sumatra.

Singapore

As with Penang, on Singapore the CMB built intimate connections with major European agency houses.[41] For example, the Singapore office often mediated transfers of payments between the North Borneo Company and A.L. Johnstone & Co.[42] These two firms represented the leading companies in the Singapore mercantile community, and with them exerted a measure of political influence over the City of London and the Parliament. From its Singapore office, the CMB financed domestic production and distribution within the Malay Peninsula. In the tin industry, the Singapore office made large advances to the Huttenback Brothers and the Rawan Tin Mining Company. It also financed the Huttenbacks' oil and coal business in the Malay Peninsula.[43] Furthermore, the CMB financed the construction of the Sungei Ujong Railway from 1891, which connected Seremban and Port Dickson, especially backing Hill & Rathbone's activities in real estate and railway construction in the Malay Peninsula.[44] In this way, the Singapore office played a pivotal role in the development of Malayan export-oriented industry by the end of the nineteenth century. In addition, the Singapore office frequently made loans and advances to leading Chinese merchants who managed revenue-farms of opium, liquor, and gambling in the city and other Malayan towns.[45] These merchants controlled the supply of Chinese labour and dominated their daily lives on agricultural plantations and in tin mines, particularly through the Chinese secret societies in Singapore. Thus the CMB's balance sheet included a substantial element of finance for Chinese mercantile activities stretching from Singapore to the Malay Peninsula. Such loans and advances were also made available to Singapore-based Indian merchants as well, a practice also followed by the Chartered Bank and the Hong Kong & Shanghai Bank.[46] In this way, the British Eastern exchange banks were heavily involved in the development of intra-Asian mercantile networks under the 'Anglo-Dutch' international order.

The CMB's Singapore office extended its coverage across the region, including continental Southeast Asia. In the 1880s, Windsor Rose & Co. in Bangkok and the French Indochina Bank in Saigon acted as agents for the CMB. Through these channels, the Singapore office was able to alert the London Head Office on commercial conditions in Siam and the French Indochina office.[47] It also developed important links within the Netherlands East Indies. For example, the Sumatra Tobacco United Company in London imported Sumatra tobacco through the British agency house Guthrie & Co. in Singapore. Guthrie & Co. was heavily involved in the tobacco plantation industry in western Sumatra. This international trade in Sumatra tobacco was financed by the Singapore office.[48] The office also financed intra-regional trade by buying Guilder bills of exchange that Singapore Chinese merchants drew on Batavia Chinese merchants.[49] Thus, Singapore came to operate as a major hub of the CMB's activities across the region.

Batavia

During the 1870s and 1880s, the CMB's Batavia office commanded 10 per cent of the bank's activities in Asia, roughly the same share as the Penang office. But in Batavia, the CMB struggled to attract sufficient deposits and faced serious financial difficulties. Securing local capital became a priority for the British banks, not least because they met intense competition for customers from Dutch banks like the Java Bank, the Netherlands-Indian Escompto Company, and the Netherlands-Indian Commercial Bank. To compensate for the deposit shortage, the Batavia office attempted to acquire local currency (guilders) by selling bills of exchange on Europe. The major purchasers were in most cases the European trading companies that wanted to remit payments arising from the importation of commodities into the Netherlands East Indies. The selling of import bills enabled the Batavia office to purchase export bills and to discount inland bills in the Netherlands East Indies.[50] For example, the Batavia office bought the drafts on Amsterdam drawn by a Dutch company, the Internationale Crediet-en Handelsvereeniging 'Rotterdam'.[51] But the financial difficulties continued, and sometimes large sums had to be supplied by the Singapore office. The monies were used to purchase export bills on the Singapore office for goods transported from the Netherlands East Indies.[52] Bullion was also trans-shipped from the Singapore and Penang offices. In this way, both offices served to compensate for the shortage of working capital and cash in Batavia. The Batavia office borrowed additional monies from the Bank of Java as well.[53] In Batavia, the CMB offered services chiefly to European companies such as Maclaine Watson, Hope & Co. and John Peet & Co., which were heavily involved in exporting tea, coffee, sugar, spices, tin, and oil. Foreign exchange bills purchased by the Batavia office were mostly drawn by exporters on Britain and the Netherlands, similar to the bills drawn on import firms. This underlines the importance of European trade finance to the day-to-day operations of the Batavia office, and from time to time, such as in the bank's Batavia report of 1882, this raised anxieties about Java's external trade.[54] Nevertheless, the Batavia office financed intra-Asian and intra-Southeast Asian trades between the Netherlands East Indies and other parts of Asia. The office often purchased rupee drafts on Calcutta, Colombo, and Rangoon, and sold dollar drafts on Hong Kong and Shanghai. However, the largest line of business in the Batavia office was exchange transactions with Singapore and Penang. In the 1870s and 1880s, more than 90 per cent of both imports and exports of the Netherlands East Indies were with Singapore and the Malay Peninsula.[55] The export trade to China began to grow in the 1890s, but it was only from the early twentieth century that the Netherlands East Indies significantly expanded trade with China, India, and Japan. The Batavia office sold its drafts on Singapore and China not only in Batavia but also in Surabaya, Semarang, and Padang. The Batavia office had agency agreements with local companies that had operated in Java and other islands of the Netherlands East Indies. These included Frazer, Eaton & Co. in Surabaya, McNeill & Co. in Semarang, Leith & Co. in Makassar, and C.J. von Buren in Padang.[56] To make up for the shortage of working capital and to compete with the rival banks, the Batavia office intended to expand business through these agency networks across the

Netherlands East Indies. It attempted to expand the discount operations in local bills to offset the stagnation of foreign exchange transactions. The Bank of Java re-discounted them in the Netherlands East Indies, so the CMB could develop a growing business with Chinese merchants in Java and the Outer Islands.[57]

Conclusion

The Anglo-Dutch Treaty of 1824 demarcated territories and the spheres of influence in insular Southeast Asia. However, British private merchants and engineers continued to play an important role in Java's economic development under the cultivation system. In the Netherlands and Java, Dutch colonial private enterprises emerged from the 1850s onwards; notably the Netherlands Trading Society opened the Singapore office at the same time as the dissolution of British East India Company rule in India in the late 1850s. In this sense, it coincided with the liberation of the Straits Settlements from the Indian-based East India Company's system, creating new opportunities to expand British and Dutch private investment there and in the Malay Peninsula. The Sumatra Treaty of 1871 reorganized the 'Anglo-Dutch' international order on the principle of free trade, which promoted both countries' imperialist expansion into the Malay Peninsula, Sumatra, and other parts of the outer islands. That treaty stimulated further advancement of European private capital in insular Southeast Asia. This played a very important role in laying the foundation of Singapore as the leading commercial and financial centre in Southeast Asia. In turn, the island's commercial prosperity helped promote export-oriented production and economic structures across the region. It also underlines the importance of non-state actors in building Singapore as a commercial and financial centre which could serve the region and beyond. On the turbulent frontier between the British and Dutch empires, however, this sometimes led to tensions, such as those leading to the closure of the Sumatra coastal trade in the 1880s.

The CMB had three offices engaged chiefly in international trade finance in insular Southeast Asia. The Singapore office was undoubtedly the most vital. The bank also became involved in the Southeast Asian domestic economy through influential Asian merchants in Singapore and Batavia. It often transferred the funds from Singapore to Batavia, and some monies were employed by its agencies to meet the needs of Chinese entrepreneurs in Surabaya and Semarang. Thus, the British Eastern exchange banks became central to regional economic integration in the age of modern globalisation, and within this process, Singapore's role was paramount.

Notes

1 Asian and Oceanian Affairs Bureau, Ministry of Foreign Affairs of Japan, 'Me De Miru ASEAN: ASEAN Keizai Tokei Kiso Shiryo (Visual ASEAN: Basic Economic Statistics of ASEAN),' [Website], 2017, pp. 6–8, available at: www.mofa.go.jp/mofaj/files/000127169.pdf, accessed 28 October 2018.
2 K. Sugihara and T. Kawamura, 'Introduction: Reconstructing Intra Southeast Asian Trade, c.1780–1870: Evidence of Regional Integration Under the Regime of Colonial Free Trade,' *Southeast Asian Studies*, vol. 2, no. 3, 2013, pp. 437–441.

3 Sugihara also highlights the importance of Chinese overseas networks to the region's economic integration. Kaoru Sugihara, 'Kokusai Bungyo to Tounan Ajia Shokuminchi Keizai [International Division of Labour and Colonial Economy in Southeast Asia],' in Hiroyoshi Kano (ed.), *Tounan Azia Shi 6: Shokuminchi Keizai No Hanei To Choraku* [*History of Southeast Asia Vol. 6: Prosperity and Decline of Colonial Economy*], Tokyo: Iwanami Shoten, 2001.

4 G.R. Knight, 'Commodity Chains, Mercantile Networks and the Early Years of the Batavia Firm of Maclaine Watson (1820–1840),' *South East Asia Research*, vol. 22, no. 1, 2014, pp. 87–101; M. Kuitenbrouwer, 'Capitalism and Imperialism: Britain and the Netherlands,' *Itinerario*, vol. 18, no. 1, 1994, pp. 105–116; M. Kuitenbrouwer and H. Schijf, 'The Dutch Colonial Business Elite at the Turn of the Century,' *Itinerario*, vol. 22, no. 1, 1998, pp. 61–86.

5 T. Kawamura, 'British Exchange Banks in International Trade of Asia from 1850 to 1890,' in U. Bosma and A. Webster (eds.), *Commodities, Ports and Asian Maritime Trade since 1750*, London: Palgrave Macmillan, 2015, pp. 179–197.

6 A. Webster, *The Richest East India Merchant: The Life and Business of John Palmer of Calcutta 1767–1836*, Suffolk: Boydell Press, 2007.

7 A. Schrauwers, ' "Regenten' (Gentlemanly) Capitalism: Saint-Simonian Technocracy and the Emergence of the "Industrialist Great Club" in the Mid-nineteenth Century Netherlands,' *Enterprise and Society*, vol. 11, no. 4, 2010, pp. 753–783.

8 G.C. Allen and A.G. Donnithorne, *Western Enterprise in Indonesia and Malaya: A Study in Economic Development*, London: George Allen & Unwin, 1957.

9 C. Fasseur, *The Politics of Colonial Exploitation: Java, the Dutch, and the Cultivation System*, Ithaca, NY: Southeast Asia Program, 1992, p. 150.

10 G.R. Knight, 'Technology, Technicians and Bourgeoisie: Thomas Jeoffries Edwards and the Industrial Project in Sugar in Mid-Nineteenth Century Java,' in U. Bosma, J. Giusti-Cordero, and G.R. Knight (eds.), *Sugarlandia Revisited: Sugar and Colonialism in Asia and the Americas, 1800 to 1940*, New York and Oxford: Berghahn Books, 2007.

11 L.K. Wong, 'The Trade of Singapore 1819–69,' *Journal of the Malaysian Branch of the Royal Asiatic Society*, vol. 33, no. 4, 1960, p. 315.

12 J.T. Lindblad, 'The Outer Islands in the 19th Century: Contest for the Periphery,' in H. Dick, V.J.H. Houben, J.T. Lindblad, and T.K. Wie (eds.), *The Emergence of a National Economy: An Economic History of Indonesia, 1800–2000*, Honolulu, HI: University of Hawaii Press, 2002, pp. 82–110.

13 N.P. van den Berg, *Financial and Economic Condition of Netherlands India Since 1870 and the Effect of the Present Currency System*, 3rd edn., The Hague: Netherlands Economical and Statistical Society, 1886.

14 J.F. Munro, *Maritime Enterprise and Empire: Sir William Mackinnon and His Business Network, 1823–1893*, Suffolk: Boydell & Brewer, 2003, pp. 121–153.

15 P.P. Courtenay, *A Geography of Trade and Development in Malaya*, London: G. Bell & Sons, 1972.

16 Inhabitants of Penang to Frederic A. Weld, Governor of Straits Settlements, 2 December 1880, no. 2892, CO/273/107, The National Archives of the United Kingdom (hereafter TNA); A British Subject at Penang to F.A. McNair, Resident Councilor of Penang, 18 October 1883, no. 20619, CO/273/123, TNA; Merchants and Traders of Penang to Earl of Derby, Secretary of State for the Colonies, 27 February 1885, no. 7150, CO/273/133, TNA; Singapore Chamber of Commerce to Colonial Secretary, 14 September 1886, no. 5082, CO/273/139, TNA; Penang Chamber of Commerce to Resident Councilor of Penang, 18 August 1893, no. 16706, CO/273/189, TNA.

17 Huttenbach Brothers & Co. to Resident Councilor of Penang, 23 December 1885; Government House (Singapore) to Colonial Office, 13 May 1886, no. 10448, CO/273/140, TNA.

18 Foreign Office to Colonial Office, 21 November 1881, no. 20431, CO/273/112, TNA; Foreign Office to Colonial Office, 27 October 1886, no. 19341, CO/273/142, TNA.

19 Netherlands India to Straits Settlements, 6 January 1891, no. 2853, CO/273/172, TNA.

20 'Report of Penang Chamber of Commerce and Agriculture for the Year 1890,' Singapore: Straits Printing Office, 1891, Appendix H, pp. 24–26; A.G. Wright, Chairman, Chamber of Commerce at Penang, to A.M. Skinner, Resident Councilor at Penang, 18 August 1893; Skinner to Colonial Secretary at Singapore, 22 August 1893, no. 16706, CO/273/189, TNA.

21 Government House (Singapore) to Colonial Office, 18 June 1884, no. 12795, CO/273/128, TNA.

22 British Residency Selangor to Colonial Secretary, 20 February 1884, 17 February 1888 and 16 November 1888; Straits Trading Company to British Residency Selangor, 13 November 1888, all in no. 517, CO/273/156, TNA.

23 Colonial Office to Government House (Singapore), 26 August 1884, no. 12795, CO/273/128, TNA; Treasury Chamber to Colonial Office, 27 September 1884, no. 16643, CO/273/131, TNA; Government House (Singapore) to Colonial Office, no. 24378, CO/273/155, TNA; Government House (Singapore) to Colonial Office, 5 December 1888, no. 517, CO/273/156, TNA.

24 In 1888–89, Chartered Bank proposed to issue Bank Post Bills (a form of negotiable instrument to be payable at three days' sight in favour of person therein named) in its four agencies by way of compensation for the absence of a local note circulation, but was refused to sanction such issuance by the Government of Singapore. Chartered Bank (London) to Colonial Office, 5th November 1888, no. 21864, CO/273/157, TNA; Chartered Bank (London) to Colonial Office, 27 February 1889, no. 4290, CO/273/164, TNA; Chartered Bank (London) to Colonial Office, 9 April 1889, no. 7901, CO/273/164, TNA; Government House (Singapore) to Colonial Office, 20 May 1889, no. 12562, CO/273/160, TNA.

25 Hong Kong & Shanghai Bank (London) to Colonial Office, 25 January 1889, no. 2162, CO/273/164, TNA.

26 J.J. van Helten and G. Jones, 'British Business in Malaysia and Singapore Since the 1870s,' in R.P.T. Davenport-Hines and G. Jones (eds.), *British Business in Asia Since 1860*, Cambridge: Cambridge University Press, 1989, pp. 175–178.

27 On the share of the CMB's business, the figures are calculated by the following sources: Statements of General Balance, MBH 2368, Chartered Mercantile Bank of India, London and China Archives, HSBC Group Archives (hereafter HSBC GA).

28 T. Saito, 'Biruma Ni Okeru Kome Yushutu Keizai No Tenkai (Development of Rice Export Economy in Burma),' in H. Kano (ed.), *Tounan Azia Shi 6 [History of Southeast Asia Vol. 6]*, pp. 161–165.

29 Siok-Hwa, *The Rice Industry of Burma*, p. 201.

30 'Half Year Reports from Branches,' 29 January 1883, mbhist., no. 436, HSBC GA.

31 On the figures of the CMB's business in Southeast Asia, see Statements of General Balance, MBH 2368, Chartered Mercantile Bank of India, London and China Archives, HSBC GA.

32 Kawamura, 'British Exchange Banks,' pp. 184–185.

33 Loh Wei Leng, 'Penang's Trade and Shipping in the Imperial Age,' in Yeoh Seng Guan et al. (eds.), *Penang and its Region: The Story of an Asian Entrepôt*, Singapore: National University of Singapore, 2009, pp. 83–102; T. Kawamura, 'Maritime Asian Trade and Colonization of Penang, c. 1786–1830,' in T. Mizushima, G.B. Souza, and D.O. Flynn (eds.), *Hinterlands and Commodities: Place, Space, Time and the Political Economic Development of Asia Over the Long Eighteenth Century*, Leiden and Boston: Brill, 2015.

34 'Board Minute Book,' 17 November 1885, 6 November 1886, 29 November 1887, 12 June 1888 and many others, mbhist., no. 2308/1, HSBC GA.

35 'Half Year Reports,' 14 January 1883, mbhist., no. 436, HSBC GA.

36 'Board Minute Book,' 8 June 1886, mbhist., no. 2308/1, HSBC GA.

37 'Board Minute Book,' 24 November 1885, 8 November 1885, 23 November 1886 and many others, mbhist., no. 2308/1, HSBC GA.
38 'Board Minute Book,' 11 December 1888, 9 July 1889, mbhist., no. 2308/1, HSBC GA.
39 'Board Minute Book,' 26 April 1886, 20 November 1888, 16 September 1890 and many others, mbhist., no. 2308/1, HSBC GA.
40 'Board Minute Book,' 12 March 1889, 30 April 1889, 28 May 1889 and many others, mbhist., no. 2308/1, HSBC GA.
41 'Board Minute Book,' 18 May 1886, 29 March 1887, 28 June 1887, 11 November 1887, 6 March 1888, 26 June 1888 and many others, mbhist., no. 2308/1, HSBC GA.
42 'Board Minute Book,' 8 December 1885, mbhist., no. 2308/1, HSBC GA.
43 'Board Minute Book,' 16 June 1886, 29 September 1887, 26 June 1888, 4 September 1888, mbhist., no. 2308/1; 9 February 1892, mbhist., no. 2308/2, HSBC GA.
44 'Board Minute Book,' 2 April 1889, 9 July 1889, and many others, mbhist., no. 2308/1, HSBC GA.
45 'Board Minute Book,' 17 November 1885, mbhist., no. 2308/1, HSBC GA.
46 R. Mahadevan, 'Pattern of Enterprise of Immigrant Entrepreneurs: A Study of Chettiars in Malaya, 1880–1930,' *Economic and Political Weekly*, vol. 13, no. 4/5, 28 January–4 February, 1978; C.P. Lim, P.S. Nooi, and M. Boh, 'The History and Development of the Hongkong and Shanghai Banking Corporation in Peninsular Malaysia,' in F.H.H. King (ed.), *Eastern Banking: Essays in the History of The Hongkong and Shanghai Banking Corporation*, London: Athlone Press, 1983, pp. 350–391.
47 'Board Minute Book,' 2 November 1886, 25 January 1887, 13 November 1888, mbhist., no. 2308/1, HSBC GA.
48 'Board Minute Book,' 25 September 1888, 26 March 1889, mbhist., no. 2308/1, HSBC GA.
49 'Board Minute Book,' 2 February 1886, mbhist., no. 2308/1, HSBC GA.
50 'Half Year Reports,' 24 January 1883, mbhist., no. 436, HSBC GA.
51 'Board Minute Book,' 14 February and 26 June 1888, mbhist., no. 2308/1, HSBC GA.
52 'Half Year Reports,' 12 January 1883, mbhist., no. 436, HSBC GA.
53 'Statements of General Balance,' mbhist., no. 2368, HSBC GA.
54 'Half Year Reports,' 24 January 1883, mbhist., no. 436, HSBC GA.
55 W.L. Korthals Altes (ed.), *Changing Economy in Indonesia, Vol. 12a: General Trade Statistics, 1822–1940*, Amsterdam: Royal Tropical Institute, 1991.
56 S. Muirhead, *Crisis Banking in the East: The History of the Chartered Mercantile Bank of India, London and China, 1853–93*, Aldershot: Scolar Press, 1996.
57 'Half Year Reports,' 24 January 1883, mbhist., no. 436, HSBC GA.

5 Singapore, Global city *ante litteram* in early twentieth century Southeast Asia

Valeria Giacomin

Introduction: global cities in historical perspective

Two centuries after its foundation in 1819, Singapore is one of the world's major global cities. Due to its prominent role of commerce, finance and transport hub, it stands as a crucial node of the global economic architecture. In the 2010s, the Southeast Asian city-state surfaced as the third-largest foreign exchange market, fourth global financial centre, a major oil refining and trading centre, and the second-busiest container port in the world.[1] Indeed, Singapore is a preferred destination for foreign direct investment in services and for multinational enterprises' (MNEs') headquarters in the region. This position was cemented during the twentieth century, as Singapore established itself as the global leader in natural rubber and palm-oil trading, hosting the headquarters of the world's largest agribusiness corporations and of their major global MNEs clients.

The term 'global city' emerged in the 1990s to identify a group of highly interconnected centres, such as London, New York and Tokyo.[2] These centres differ from other cities in three ways: a high degree of connectivity in terms of transport and communication infrastructure; primary roles as prominent cultural centres; and significant service, especially financial, specialisation.[3] In respect of the last point, global cities can also be thought of as service clusters – including banking, insurance, consulting, marketing, legal services, etc. – and home of MNEs' headquarters, thus hosting highly educated (white collar) workers and a transnational capitalist class.[4] This in turn makes these locations catalysts of global migration, magnets for foreign direct investment and home for entertainment and cultural institutions.[5]

Global cities often emerge in connection with or as support for industrial clusters, defined as 'geographically concentrated agglomerations of specialized firms and associated institutions in a particular field.'[6] A cluster's dense networks and co-located institutions combine with MNEs' international linkages and generate positive externalities that reinforce the service specialisation and global connectivity of these cities.[7] Seminal studies on global cities identified them as a relatively recent phenomenon resulting from the expansion of global capitalism since the 1980s, or the period that Jones has defined as the second global economy.[8] This scholarship prioritised the analysis of the dynamics occurring within and between these cities over the role of agents and contingency in their development.

In the last several decades, new contributions in both history and geography studied how global cities impacted the development of global capitalism. This work documented how cities historically fostered global connectivity and how they participated in shaping the global economy. Urban historians acknowledged the value of a global perspective for researching cities,[9] while recent studies in global history investigated the role of cities in the spread of capitalism, showing that these centres emerged in support of global trade routes attached to colonial empires.[10] McCann and Acs analysed global connectivity in historical perspective and argued that hosting multinationals drove economic growth for cities in times of intense globalisation.[11] In his *Capitals of Capital*, Cassis mapped the historical development of global finance across a net of command centres (or global cities).[12] Bunnell offered an extremely thorough account of how Liverpool developed a global profile, contributing to the integration of Southeast Asia in the global economy.[13] Recent historical research also addressed the relationship between industrial clustering and export-led development in emerging economies. Evren and Ökten analysed the historical trajectory of the Istanbul jewellery cluster.[14] Cirer-Costa studied the roots and external influence of Majorca's tourism cluster.[15] Declercq's study of the Saxony fur district in the nineteenth century scrutinized the relationships between industrial concentration and global value chains by retracing the long-term trans-border interactions among Leipzig entrepreneurs.[16] Similarly, Henn's analyses of Antwerp's diamond cluster stressed the relevance of transnational entrepreneurs and their strategic action in shaping value chains between clusters in India and Belgium.[17]

While these contributions provided contextual depth to the topic of global cities and connected them to other frameworks such as global value chains, only fragmentary attention has been paid to the connection between global cities (or service clusters) and industrial clusters, as ways to organize entrepreneurial networks and corporate activity. In fact, the relationship between global cities and industrial clusters is particularly relevant to understanding the spread of global capitalism. In colonial territories, economic activity clustered around ports and capital cities due to the lack of widespread infrastructure in the interior and the need for proximity to supporting services. In a rare account of the relationship between global cities and clusters, Bathelt and Li analysed the flow of FDIs among these centres as long-standing cross-cluster patterns referred to as 'global cluster networks' and pointed out that 'little is known about the wider structure of global linkages between clusters and city-regions that is generated through FDIs.'[18]

Following these authors' work on the connectivity of clusters, this chapter uses the case of Singapore and the Southeast Asian plantation cluster to bridge this lacuna. Several historical analyses have extensively reconstructed the genesis of Singapore and its contribution to Southeast Asia development. Among them, W.G. Huff's seminal work on the city's economic growth illustrates that the roots of its current success lie in networks and institutions developed during the colonial era.[19] Few studies, however, explicitly conceptualise Singapore as a global city *ante litteram*. As an exception, Oswin and Yeoh cite the first public mention of Singapore as a global city in the early 1970s to legitimise its recently acquired status of nation-state.[20] This chapter, however, argues that Singapore qualified as a major global city in the early twentieth century and that this was strongly connected to the emergence of the rubber plantation cluster.

The analysis draws on empirical material on agency houses, shipping companies and the colonial plantation economy since the late nineteenth century sourced from seven different UK archives and from further research in Malaysia and Singapore National Archives.[21] The next section focuses on Singapore's entrepôt economy prior to the introduction of natural rubber. The third section covers the emergence of the rubber cluster and its institutional foundation on shared private-public objectives and cartelisation up to the 1920s. The fourth section focuses on Singapore's rise as regional cultural pole while the plantation cluster started diversifying towards palm oil during the interwar period. The fifth section draws key points together in conclusion.

The Western-Chinese nexus: the first steps
towards global Singapore (1870–1905)

Sir Stamford Raffles founded modern Singapore in 1819 on an extremely well-located island at the intersection of the Malay Peninsula, Borneo and Sumatra, between the Indian Ocean and the China Sea.[22] The island became a British colony in 1824, when Britain and the Netherlands signed the Anglo-Dutch treaty, defining their distinct spheres of influence across the Malay Archipelago. Two years later, in 1826, the city was grouped together with two other Malayan ports, Penang and Malacca, into a single administrative unit, the Straits Settlements, under the control of the East India Company.[23] Singapore continued to work as Britain's major transhipment port for Indian opium to China and as sorting centre for agricultural produce and raw materials from the Nanyang (Southeast Asia) for most of the nineteenth century,[24] but until the 1870s the city's trade remained largely regional in scope.[25] By then, the city hosted one of the world's most diverse and dynamic trading communities – European, Indian, Hadhrami-Arab and overseas Chinese traders, operating the local commerce, each with defined and complementary spheres of expertise. The long-standing interaction in the form of competition, cooperation and emulation among different ethnic groups was one of the crucial ingredients behind Singapore's emergence as a service cluster and global city at the turn of the twentieth century.[26]

While Arab and Indian traders managed trading routes with their own reference markets, such as South Asia or the Middle East, Chinese traders were a dominant force of Singapore's economy in control of the bulk of the cross-regional trade.[27] Chinese merchants mediated a barter-based system extending to the most remote areas of the Malay archipelago, where they could rely on family ties or trust-based networks to exchange local produce with regional foodstuff or manufactured imports.[28] In the city, they functioned as distributors of imported products and bulk buyers of produce for re-sale. Finally, they also controlled most of the 'coolie trade,' namely the inflow of unskilled – often indentured – labour from overpopulated regions of south China, and eventually Java, to employ in

mines and plantations of the surroundings.[29] The combined expansion of tin mining and plantations in the region boosted demand for cheap labourers so much
that between 1881 and 1932 more than 100,000 coolies per year reached Singapore from China to work primarily in the Malay peninsula and Sumatra.[30] As a
consequence, the number of Indian, Chinese and Western merchant houses more
than doubled.[31] The city also infamously became a major centre for human trafficking for sexual and labour exploitation.[32] After 1877, the British had indeed
established three colonial Protectorates of Chinese Immigrants in Singapore,
Penang and Malacca with the purpose of handling and regulating the increasing
flow of migrants. In 1890, the Chinese Advisory Board was formed, grouping the
representatives of the major Chinese *pangs*, to ensure constant consultation with
the Chinese community.[33] These institutions were particularly effective at pulling
resources and collecting charitable donations to fund hospitals and schools and to
support the life of Chinese migrants.[34]

During the nineteenth century, Chinese entrepreneurs had come to dominate the
planting of tropical produce (tapioca, pepper, gambier, tobacco and sugar) near
Singapore and the mining of tin ore in the Malay peninsula. Tin was smelted *in
loco* and either bartered regionally in exchange for produce or resold to Western
traders for further refining in the closest local ports.[35] In relation to these activities,
Chinese traders also controlled the bulk of intra-regional shipping lines through
the famous 'mosquito fleet,' more than 50 companies managing small-tonnage
vessels.[36]

In 1867, Britain made the Straits Settlements a Crown Colony. The opening
of the Suez Canal in 1869 and the launch of the 'open door' policy for foreign
investment in the Dutch East Indies (DEI) since the 1870s accelerated the pace of
commerce and economic growth and increasingly enveloped the city into intercontinental routes.[37] The increase of global demand for tin and tropical commodities at the end of the century scaled back the position of Chinese interests relative
to their Western counterparts and informed a reorganisation of the major regional
industries and trade routes.

Although the Singaporean Chinese business community certainly profited
from this increase in trade, Western interests were the ones to ultimately reap
the largest rewards. During the last decades of the nineteenth century, Singapore
underwent a sixfold increase in its value of commerce driven by growing Western
demand for Malayan tin and agricultural produce from the Dutch East Indies.[38]
Western merchants, initially organized in single or partnership outlets (merchant
houses, later agency houses), were fewer than their Asian counterparts but grew
fast, as they operated on bigger volumes.[39] They managed long-distance connections with the major European markets mostly via London as well as with other
colonial locations (i.e. Ceylon, Burma and Indochina), supervising inflows of
manufactured products and outflows of local primary goods. They also acted as
merchant charterers, agents for shipping lines and intermediaries for European
planters and entrepreneurs. In this context, Europeans realized the value of establishing sound relationships with the Chinese community and competed with each
other for exclusivity with Chinese, wholesalers, managers and clerks.[40] As for

the British colonial authorities, they strictly monitored Chinese political activity while adopting a relaxed *laissez-faire* policy in the business sphere.[41] Within the Straits' favourable business climate, several Chinese entrepreneurs accumulated vast fortunes from partaking in the entrepôt trade. At the turn of the century, the city's most influential tycoons were three Malacca-born men, Tan Chay Yang, Tat Chin Seng and Lee Keng Liat, and two entrepreneurs from China, Yap Ah Loy and Loke Yew. Most of them had large interests in planting and mining ventures as well as in shipping.[42]

As for banking, by 1877 three major international British banks (Chartered Bank of India, Australia and China; Mercantile Bank of India; and Hongkong and Shanghai Banking Corporation) held branches in the city for the financing of Western ventures and bulk export from the region.[43] Conversely, Chinese intermediaries continued to rely on barter and informal financing until the creation of the first Chinese banks in the mid-1910s. Rural areas started to use cash systematically only towards the 1930s.[44] The fact that Chinese entrepreneurs could not easily access London capital markets, lacked knowledge of overseas company law and did not master European contractual agreements allowed Western traders to easily sidestep the Chinese barter system.

On the wave of increasing Western demand for tin, in 1887 the German entrepreneur Herman Muhlinghaus and the British trader James Sword founded the Straits Trading Company (STC) for the smelting of tin in Singapore, starting a process of centralisation of the tin trade under the control of the city's European community.[45] In 1890, the company opened a state-of-the-art reverberatory furnace in the nearby island of Pulau Brani, offering large storage capacity and direct access to the Singapore port coaling stations.[46] Due to the scale and efficiency of these processing facilities, the STC could beat competitors' prices and quality while concentrating marketing functions in Singapore. Leveraging its network, the STC soon secured favourable regulations to operate the trade from the city.[47] Finally, the increases in cargo for tin, agricultural produce and related immigrant labour to employ in the territory drove the reorganisation of regional shipping, as traffic through Singapore quickly expanded and infrastructure was updated accordingly.

Again, Europeans conducted the process of centralisation and up-scaling of shipping services in Singapore. By 1880, three European players had joined the city's maritime community to serve the trade from Dutch East Indies and Malaya, the Dutch major liner KPM, the German Lloyd and Liverpool's Alfred Holt & Co.'s Ocean Steamship Company (also known as Blue Funnel).[48] The agency Mansfield & Co. managed Holt's interests in Southeast Asia under the direction of the Dutchman Theodore Cornelius Bogaardt, who expanded Ocean's reach by building a network of 'feeder lines.'[49]

Bogaardt valued highly Chinese backing to operate in the regional seas. In 1890, he joined three Malaccan Chinese tycoons, Tan Jiak Kim, Tan Keong Saik and Lee Cheng Yan and founded a new liner on behalf of the Holts, the Straits Steamship Company (SSC).[50] The venture began 'with four little [white funnelled] ships, a few hundred tons each. They traded with the west coast of the peninsula where no roads or railroads existed, and were occupied largely in carrying tin ore from Perak and Selangor to the newly established tin smelters on Pulau Brani.'[51] By 1914, the fleet counted 17 ships and had extended its operations to the rubber and coolie trade.[52] In 1891, Ocean also joined the Java trade opening a fully owned Dutch subsidiary (Netherlandische Stoomvaart Maatschappij Oceaan) after Bogaardt secured a tobacco concession from Sumatra.[53]

Meanwhile, European liners sealed the monopoly of the transoceanic routes from Singapore to Europe though cartel-like arrangements. In 1897, the Straits Homeward Conference was formed, setting freight rates between 23 shipping lines (among which Ocean, KLM and Lloyd) and four British merchant houses specialised in commodity procurement: Adamson & Gilfillian, Edward Boustead, Paterson and Simons and Borneo Co., and the German Otto Meyer. In 1905 the Straits-New York Conference joined the British Conference for the homeward service to the US coasts.[54] This occurred in connection to Holt's acquisition of the China Mutual Steam Navigation Company in 1902, which put an end to the intense competition on the Pacific route.[55]

In total, Singapore hosted extensive partnerships, often competing with each other, between Western and local, especially ethnic Chinese, merchants. These dynamics of cooperation and competition among different entrepreneurial communities are typical of clusters and drove the organisation of the city's service sector in response to the growth of tin and produce trades after the 1870s.[56] During most of nineteenth century, Singapore had been the linchpin of regional commerce for Chinese traders. From 1870s, the scope of Singapore's commercial activity became increasingly connected with the West (especially Europe) following changes in demand during the Second Industrial Revolution, which saw the introduction of machineries for mass production, and the acceleration of trade and communication thanks to new technologies such as the steamship and the telegraph. The much smaller community of Western traders in Singapore found itself at the centre of this transformation, acting as a link between the Asian producers, via their partnerships with Chinese traders, and the Western markets. Thanks to their privileged access to larger financial means and to colonial government protection, European entrepreneurs were able to centralise and scale up the tin processing industry, cartelise shipping and secure increasing stakes in these traditional Chinese traders' activities. Despite being increasingly multicultural and international, at this point Singapore still worked as a local branch of major London interests and did not yet achieve the status of a global city.

The institutionalization of the rubber cluster and Singapore as a global city (1905–1920)

The growth of the tin and produce trades at the end of the nineteenth century set the basis for a reinforcing pattern of growth between natural resource extraction in the region and an increasingly sophisticated service sector in Singapore. The existing infrastructure allowed the quick expansion of rubber and the emergence of a cluster organization around it in the first decade of the twentieth century.

On the other hand, rubber represented a game-changer in the globalisation of the Nanyang.

World demand for natural rubber had experienced a first 'boom' between 1890 and 1900, when production more than doubled from 20,000 to 52,500 tons. Driven by the expansion of the automotive industry in the US, demand continued to grow at a rate of 5.5 per cent per year up to 1908, followed by a second three-year boom with double-digit increases, averaging over 16 per cent per year until 1917. Following the frantic opening of plantations in the 1910s, Malayan production grew from 130 tons in 1905 to 5,000 tons in 1910 and reached 196,000 tons in 1915.[57] By the 1920s, Southeast Asia (FMS and Netherland Indies) had already outcompeted South America and West Africa as global rubber producer, with a total of about 3.5 million acres, accounting for 80 per cent of world supplies. By then, rubber represented a third of Singapore's total exports, doubling the share of tin and dwarfing other agricultural produce.[58]

Before the introduction of the natural rubber tree from South America, and its domestication as a plantation crop, the Southeast Asian economy was still dependent on a range of minor primary commodities such as tobacco, sugarcane and tapioca, which made it somewhat peripheral and vulnerable to the competition of other tropical locations. The emergence of the rubber plantation cluster and its formalisation through the creation of several specialized institutions marked the transformation of Singapore into a global city and its integration within the automotive value chain, one of the most advanced and globalised industries at that time.[59]

In 1876, the British adventurer Henry Wickham had smuggled what was allegedly the best rubber variety, *Hevea Brasiliensis*, from the Amazon region around Manaus, where the bulk of global rubber supply was sourced from wild trees. The *Hevea* seedlings were introduced to the Asian colonies via London, using the institutional net of the Imperial Botanic Gardens.[60] Since the 1880s, the director of Singapore Kew Gardens, Henry Ridley, had distributed *Hevea* seedlings to planters in British Malaya and Netherlands Indies and promoted research efforts among the local community of agronomists for domesticating the crop into plantations.[61] At the turn of the century, the first rubber estates in Southeast Asia completed the seven-year maturation period and became available to tap, making the fortune of early investors and luring several new ones from Ceylon and West Africa, to the superior climate and business environment of the Nanyang.[62]

Unlike the Chinese community, which could count on a plethora of informal associations, the European rubber traders and entrepreneurs coordinated via the Singapore International Chamber of Commerce (SICC) and received constant backing from the colonial government. The SICC had been founded in 1837 as a multiracial organization but came to comprise primarily Europeans in the period between 1870 and 1915.[63] While rubber spread through the Malay Peninsula and East Sumatra, several linked institutions emerged in both London and Singapore; among them were industrial associations representing different groups of producers, specialised supporting services, as well as public and private research organizations. In Malaya, European planters converged in the Planting Association

(PAM), while the AVROS grouped Sumatra Western planting experts. In 1906, the Chinese élite continued to formalize their interests through the Singapore Rubber Dealer Association, representing Chinese rubber brokers.

Revealing a major source of taxable income, rubber companies increasingly benefited from the very close relationships – mostly forged in white-people-only clubs – among the Western expats.[64] For instance, the British officials Sir Frank Swettenham, Sir William Taylor and Sir William Treacher, long remained involved with the rubber institutions after serving in different colonial posts across the region.[65] Alongside the institutionalisation of the rubber cluster, the colonial authorities used rubber fiscal revenues to upgrade the regional communication and service infrastructure. Singapore was the linchpin of this transformation. Firstly, the Public Works Department was instituted to absorb and reorganize several existing health and education institutions, until then relying primarily on private funding and donations from wealthy local magnates and entrepreneurs.[66] This led the region to boast a health and medical infrastructure unique in Asia and comparable to several European counterparts, albeit it long remained characterized by strict class and ethnic segregation.[67] Secondly, from the 1910s, the government launched new telephone and railway lines, connecting Singapore with the Federated Malay States.[68] This ensured continuous contact between the estates and their headquarters in the city, where price and market updates from brokers, graders and manufacturers could be accessed in real time. Finally, in 1913, the colonial government set up local port trusts called Harbour Boards in Singapore and Penang to support the construction of modern facilities in response to the expansion of ocean-going cargos.[69] In the Netherland Indies, the government provided bare wharves, sheds and other equipment in all major port locations.[70]

To respond to the increasing demand for rubber in early 1900s, the homeward (to Europe and the US) Conference had quickly extended its services to rubber, driving a quasi-cartelisation of the industry culminating in the mid-1910s.[71] The major merchant houses holding shipping agency, like Barlows and Bousteads, had capitalised their position by integrating upstream into rubber estates. Similarly, well-established agency houses lacking shipping agency, such as Guthrie and H & C, were eventually able to obtain agency with the Conference on the grounds of their large plantation holdings and supremacy in rubber trading and processing.[72] Therefore, in one way or another, concentration downstream transferred upstream, with the bulk of the rubber cluster converging into the hands of a small group of agency houses and plantation companies. The tendency towards cartelisation was further cemented with the creation of the Rubber Growers' Association (RGA), established in London in 1907 out of a preliminary meeting of 30 rubber estate agencies operating in Southeast Asia. Among those present were Herbert Brett for H & C, L.T. Boustead of Boustead Brothers and several other representatives of the most prominent rubber interests in the British Asian colonies.[73]

The RGA represented a major institutional catalyst behind the emergence of the cluster, as it ensured the cluster's global reach as well as internal cohesion, by strengthening the linkages among different rubber institutions, the colonial government and London interests. In 1913, H & C's director Arthur Lampard supported the creation of the International Association for Rubber Cultivation in the Netherlands Indies to integrate the RGA with the substantial rubber investment outside British Malaya, primarily in Sumatra.[74] The RGA also lobbied for publicly funded research and enhanced coordination among existing research projects across the Empire.[75] These efforts would materialise in the formation of the Rubber Research Institute (RRIM) in 1926. The RRIM complemented long-standing private and public research work by the Singapore Royal Botanic Gardens and the Malayan Agricultural Department. As a result, Singapore gradually became the main reference site for a thriving epistemic community of high-skilled expats employed by foreign multinationals and colonial institutions, comprising agronomists, botanists, chemists, engineers and estate managers operating in different plantation-related activities.[76]

The concentration of ownership in the cluster increased after 1912, once rubber prices stabilized, smaller estates and trading houses succumbing to the deep pockets of a few large players. Singapore-based firms directed this process and rose to dominance: above all the arch-enemies – H & C and Guthrie, followed by Barlow, Boustead, Sime Darby and Cumberbatch.[77] However, in the 1910s the Shipping Conference system started to encounter resistance from upcoming buyers in America, Japan, Russia and Australia, as it forced the commodity to transit through London on its way to its destination. This endangered the competitive position of Singapore, as new routes emerged serving these locations directly from other Southeast Asian ports.[78]

The result was increasing service specialisation and increasing homogenisation of the city's rubber institutions with London, at the time the undisputed global rubber market. As a first step, the Rubber Exchange was instituted in Singapore in 1911, transferring several auctioning and trading functions directly to Southeast Asia. As a result, in the mid-1910s, Japan's official trade mission[79] and several manufacturers such as Dunlop and the US giants Firestone and Goodyear opened in Singapore, signalling the increased centrality of the city for global trade.[80] In the same period, Singapore also introduced the standard qualities for rubber grading similar to the ones applied in London, while storage and processing facilities increasingly expanded in the city.[81] This move was initially not welcome in London, especially by the local dealers, who responded in 1913 by forming the Rubber Trade Association.[82] However, after the outbreak of the war, centralisation of grading and selling in Singapore was revealed to be crucial, as it allowed the Allies to secure strategic supplies.

In total, the introduction of rubber both amplified and revolutionised the institutional framework at the core of Singapore's economy. During the 1910s, a set of formal institutions emerged underpinning the Southeast Asia rubber cluster. While rubber production increasingly expanded to serve global markets, Singapore strengthened its role of gateway to world demand and upgraded its specialisation in rubber-related services. Rubber exports generated increasing income to reinvest in the transport, communication and public service infrastructure in both Singapore and Malaya. Finally, Singapore also benefited from the outbreak of

WWI, as London lost momentum and the city became established as global rubber trading, financing, processing and bulk shipping centre.

Diversification and cultural primacy in the interwar period

In the first two decades of the twentieth century, the emergence of the rubber cluster led to the transformation of Singapore into a global city. During the interwar period, rubber production further expanded to the extent that trading and purchasing started decentralising in the Malay Peninsula, while Singapore remained a major reference port for producers in the Netherland Indies.[83] Despite these developments and the weakening of global trade in the interwar period, the city maintained its role of global city by further upgrading its intermediary functions as rubber market and by supporting the diversification of production towards new crops, importantly, palm oil. Further, the city lived its own version of the Roaring Twenties, blossoming as a major cultural centre and as an entertainment pole in the region.[84]

During the 1910s, the concentration of estate ownership in the hands of agency houses had produced increasing decentralisation of estate management services. In order to monitor profitability, agency houses had managers touring several client estates on a regular basis, and hence needed detached offices to coordinate field operations. In the 1920s, Kuala Lumpur and Medan established themselves as the regional plantation capitals, and direct shipping was organized from regional ports, unburdening Singapore from cargo congestion.[85] Although rubber did not physically pass through the port, rubber auctions and major transactions continued to be handled in the city.

Despite the rise of agency houses, Singapore's Chinese (and to a lesser extent Indian) trading community had also profited enormously from rubber's unprecedented expansion. While Western agency houses were focusing on estates in Malaya and East Sumatra, Chinese traders in Singapore continued to work as wholesalers for regional produce. First, they included a whole new base of supply to the cluster by purchasing rubber from Asian producers. Since the early 1900s, Singapore Chinese had leveraged their intra-regional trading network to provide seeds, basic equipment and agency services to native farmers in Malaya and across the outer islands.[86] This sector grew further, especially in Sumatra and Borneo, as a result of former indentured labour occupying peripheral land and taking advantage of the infrastructure available to the estates.[87] By sourcing smallholders' rubber and channelling it through Singapore, the Chinese were providing them with a bundle of services that levelled the playing field with the European estates.

Alongside their intermediation activities, several Chinese traders followed the steps of the Western houses, resolving to implement vertical integration. They invested upstream into mid-sized rubber estates, mostly in the proximity of Singapore and in the Johor state, and financed the long maturation of the *Hevea* through inter-planting rubber trees with pineapples, then processed in their canning facilities.[88] Tan Kah-Kiee, the Lim brothers (founders of the Ho Hong group), and

Lim Nee Soon, also known as 'pineapple king,' emerged as Singapore's most legendary Chinese tycoons. Their financial interests were tightly knitted within the Chinese community and spread in a diversified range of activities, such as real estate, banking, shipping and rice trading. In the 1920s, Chinese capital flowed downstream into milling facilities to process the smallholders' rubber and transforming the city into the largest processing centre in the region. Tan Kah-Kiee also occupied a segment left open by the Western agency houses by moving into manufacturing of cheap rubber products for the regional market and then expanding into China and India.[89]

By the 1920s, smallholdings in the Netherlands Indies almost equalled estates in terms of acreage, posing a serious challenge to the profitability of European plantations in a time of high rubber price volatility.[90] In 1922, the British government supported a scheme for restricting production within the British territories, the Stevenson Plan.[91] Although the plan's intent was to curtail volume and maintain profitability, the opposite ensued. In response to the higher prices, producers in the Netherlands Indies, and particularly smallholders, expanded rubber cultivation not just in the outer islands, but also in Indochina, Siam and Burma, and prices collapsed following expectations of increased volumes.[92] In the long run, this situation was most detrimental for the Singapore Chinese. Lower rubber prices and dropping demand due to the Great Depression put the Chinese businesses under strain and their financial institutions with them. In 1932, Lee Kong Chian, Kah-Kiee's son-in-law and former employee, absorbed most of his father-in-law's assets in liquidation and reorganized the struggling Chinese banking sector, forming the Overseas Chinese Banking Corporation (OCBC).[93] As for shipping, Blue Funnel took advantage of the struggling Chinese ventures to replenish its fleet after the losses of WWI. In the 1930s, Ocean acquired several Chinese-owned regional liners such as the Ho Hong Line, the Sabah and Sarawak Steamship Companies and the Koe Guan Line. In 1935, it purchased the collapsing Glen and Shire Lines. Finally, it took over the Siam Steam Navigation Company from the Danish EAC while also expanding its Pacific routes.[94]

While the Singapore Chinese were hit by the developments in the rubber market in the interwar period, the biggest Western players were able to remain competitive thanks to their deeper pockets, which allowed for more radical diversification strategies. A small group of plantation firms, headed by Guthrie's, identified the palm oil crop as the most suitable diversification option.[95] The oil palm (*Elaeis guineensis*) was sufficiently similar to the rubber tree to leverage the synergies of the existing rubber cluster, but being more capital-intensive, the crop had the advantage of shielding large estates from local smallholders' competition.[96] The oil palm was introduced in Bogor and Singapore's Botanic Gardens from native regions of West Africa earlier than rubber but had not been domesticated for commercial plantations.[97] Adrien Hallet, a Belgian entrepreneur with experience in Belgian Congo and vast rubber holdings in Sumatra, was the first to launch oil palm estates in DEI in the 1910s.[98] In Malaya, he helped the Frenchmen Fauconnier and Posth with the floating of the very first local estate in 1917.[99] The Sumatran estate sector acted as frontrunner, leading a very fast expansion of the new commodity during the interwar period, which was immediately perceived as the 'Sumatran menace' among West African competitors.[100] In the 1920s, Hallet's company, by then renamed Société Financière des Caoutchoucs (Socfin), opened the first bulking facility for shipment to Europe in Belawan (Sumatra), introducing a tank system for palm oil storage.[101] Some Malaysian players followed suit despite their smaller acreage.[102] Due to the proximity of Malayan palm oil estates in Johor and Negeri Sembilan, Singapore quickly became the main port for the trade in Malayan palm oil, facilitating the diversification of the cluster towards this new commodity.[103] Singapore provided palm oil producers with economies of scope, as existing services supporting the rubber cluster, such as packing, storage and logistics, could be easily adapted to the requirements of the new product.[104] The city's shipping segment was revealed to be particularly important for the swift development of palm oil. For instance, despite its director Eric Miller's scepticism, H & C introduced the crop in its estates after realizing that the oil could be shipped in the same vessels used for liquid latex, which the company had expertise in.[105] In 1932, Guthrie founded the Malayan Palm Oil Bulking Company, cooperating with the Singapore Harbour Board to finance a joint facility in West Wharf, eventually upgraded with new tanks in 1939.[106] In the 1930s, SSC constructed three new 750-ton vessels to serve the Bulking Company.[107] Finally, palm oil helped balance out the volatility of rubber also in the processing sector. When Singapore lost milling volumes as a result of the introduction of a new restriction, the International Rubber Scheme in 1934, several millers in the city shifted to oil processing.[108] Although the palm oil share of the regional export portfolio remained negligible compared to rubber until the 1960s, this new crop helped to cushion the interwar volatility in rubber demand. In this period, rubber companies set the basis for their future leadership of Southeast Asia in palm oil production. In 1936, Sumatran output surpassed the global leader Nigeria and by 1939 Malayan and Sumatran volumes combined accounted for over 50 per cent of world exports.[109]

Alongside the diversification towards new crops, Singapore's transport infrastructure was further developed in the 1920 and 1930s. The city's civilian and military railway system was expanded, and a new airport was inaugurated in Kallang in 1937. Singapore thrived as major regional urban centre and developed into a cultural pole in this period. Its modern landscape resembled one of a major global metropolis, busy with motor cars, large buildings and a distinctively urban nightlife. The electrification of the city, started at the turn of the century, continued supporting the development of the city's entertainment industry. In 1923, the Chinese entrepreneurs Ong Boon Tat and Ong Peng Hock created Singapore's first entertainment park, 'New World.'[110] In the 1930s, the Hong Kong production house Shaw acquired the park and funded new ones, as part of its widespread investment in the city's burgeoning show business.[111] Since the early 1900s, Singapore had been at the forefront of cinema development in Asia. The first non-European venue to show films among other entertainment was the Parsi Theatre in Queen Street.[112] The Paris Cinema in Victoria Street was the first dedicated establishment, following closely the launch of first cinemas in the UK and the US.

In the interwar period, going to the movies became the most popular form of local entertainment. By the mid-1930s, after the introduction of the 'talkies', about 8,000 people per night visited the cluster of cinemas located between Beach and North Bridge Roads.[113] By then, the city offered a large range of shows in terms of genre, language, and price.[114] Hollywood films, representing the majority (70 per cent) of productions screened, had a major impact in shaping Singaporean culture and familiarising locals with Western values. Already in the 1930s, Singapore was among the tour destinations of international performing artists; for instance, Charlie Chaplin was greatly acclaimed during his two trips to the city in 1932 and 1936.[115] In terms of cultural institutions, the city hosted museums, art centres and educational outlets at the level of major European cities. Finally, Singapore boasted an extremely diverse cultural life, from the religious rituals practiced by locals, to typical colonial entertainment, including grand parties serving multicultural cuisines.[116]

Despite the slowdown in international trade, the mutual dependence between Singapore and the plantation cluster further strengthened during the interwar period. Singapore's Chinese business community specialised in rubber services and favoured the inclusion of the smallholding sector in the cluster by offering intermediation in Singapore. Western interests leveraged their greater financial resources to diversify their plantation activity towards more capital-intensive crops, using the rubber cluster infrastructure to set the basis for a regional palm oil industry.[117] Finally, in the 1920s, Singapore developed as a major cultural centre and further blossomed during the 1930s. Cultural dynamism was driven by a booming entertainment industry, and was supported by several institutions promoting education, arts and sciences.

Conclusions

Today Singapore scores among the highest in all global city rankings thanks to its Information and Communication Technology infrastructure and its specialised service sector. While the city's natural endowments – its position at the crossroads between two oceans, its extremely favourable port geography, and its proximity to resource-rich regions – may explain part of its early success, these conditions are not sufficient to account for Singapore's steady inflows of foreign investment and prominent role as global trading hub since the early twentieth century. Several locations in West Africa and Latin America showcased similar climatic and soil features for the cultivation of tropical commodities and the extraction of raw materials but did not experience the same development path, nor similar sustained growth during the colonial era.

W.G. Huff observed that the elements 'which made Singapore unique before WWII made it so afterwards.'[118] This chapter historicised the concept of global city and specified Huff's observation by showing that the (rubber) plantation cluster turned Singapore into a global city long before this term was introduced in local political circles and addressed by academic research. Specifically, the historical analysis of the first three decades of the twentieth century documented that following the introduction of rubber, Singapore displayed the three major dimensions that define a global city. First, service specialisation significantly expanded, and the introduction of rubber grading equalled Singapore to London as a global rubber trading centre. Since then, MNEs such as Goodyear and Firestone started flocking to the region. Second, the income resulting from rubber taxation supported the financing and the upgrading of transport and communication infrastructure that is unparalleled in the region. Third, the city also established itself as a prominent cultural centre in Asia, hosting a thriving cultural scene between the 1920s and 1930s for the entertainment of the city's highly international and wealthy business community.

Finally, the analysis contributed to clarification of the relationship between clusters and global cities by stressing their complementarity in shaping the global economy and in fostering sustained economic growth at the local level. By supporting the expansion of the plantation cluster, Singapore was instrumental in integrating the regional producers within the global automotive value chain and providing access to global markets. On the other hand, cluster expansion reinforced Singapore's prominence as a global service hub and pushed local firms to diversify away from their excessive dependence on rubber. Overall, the interaction between the plantation cluster and Singapore produced a globally competitive institutional setup which still endures today.

Notes

1 Chia Yan Min, 'Singapore Is Largest Forex Centre in Asia, Third Largest Globally,' *Straits Times*, 1 September 2016, available at: www.straitstimes.com/business/banking/singapore-is-largest-forex-centre-in-asia-third-largest-globally, accessed 9 December 2018; Top 50 World Container Ports, World Shipping Council, 2018, available at: www.worldshipping.org/about-the-industry/global-trade/top-50-world-container-ports, accessed 9 December 2018.
2 The notion of global city has emerged during the 1990s, when it was popularized by several pioneering contributions. See J. Friedmann, 'The World City Hypothesis,' *Development and Change*, vol. 17, no. 1, 1986, pp. 69–83; S. Sassen, *The Global City: New York, London, Tokyo*, 2nd edn., Princeton, NJ: Princeton University Press, 2001; A.D. King, *Global Cities: Post-Imperialism and the Internationalization of London*, London: Routledge, 1991.
3 A. Ren, *The Urban State of Mind: Meditations on the City*, available at: Amazon Digital Services, 2013, accessed September 2018.
4 J.V. Beaverstock, 'Transnational Elites in Global Cities: British Expatriates in Singapore's Financial District,' *Geoforum*, vol. 33, no. 4, 2002, pp. 525–538.
5 J. Friedmann, 'Where We Stand: A Decade of World City Research,' in P. Knox and P. Taylor (eds.), *World Cities in a World-System*, Cambridge: Cambridge University Press, 1995, pp. 26, 21–47.
6 M.E. Porter, 'Location, Competition, and Economic Development: Local Clusters in a Global Economy,' *Economic Development Quarterly*, vol. 14, no. 1, 2000, p. 16.
7 J.L. Trujllo and J. Parilla, 'Redefining Global Cities. The Seven Types of Global Metro Economies,' in *Global Cities Initiative*, Washington, DC: Brookings Institution Press, 2016.
8 G. Jones, *Multinationals and Global Capitalism: From the Nineteenth to the Twenty First Century*, Oxford: Oxford University Press, 2004.

9   A.K. Sandoval-Strausz and N. Kwak, *Making Cities Global: The Transnational Turn in Urban History*, Philadelphia, PA: University of Pennsylvania Press, 2018. Available at: Ebooks Pen Press, accessed 14 November 2018.

10 G. Clark, *Global Cities: A Short History*, Washington, DC: Brookings Institution Press, 2016; O. Gelderblom, *Cities of Commerce: The Institutional Foundations of International Trade in the Low Countries, 1250–1650*, Princeton, NJ: Priceton University Press, 2013; F. Gipouloux, *The Asian Mediterranean: Port Cities and Trading Networks in China, Japan and Southeast Asia, 13th-21st Century*, Cheltenham: Edward Elgar Publishing, 2011.

11 P. McCann and Z.J. Acs, 'Globalization: Countries, Cities and Multinationals,' *Regional Studies*, vol. 45, no. 1, 2011, p. 24; B. Aitken, G.H. Hanson, and A.E. Harrison, 'Spillovers, Foreign Investment, and Export Behavior,' *Journal of International Economics*, vol. 43, no. 1, 1997, pp. 103–132.

12 Y. Cassis, *Capitals of Capital: The Rise and Fall of International Financial Centres, 1780–2009*, 2nd edn., Cambridge, UK: Cambridge University Press, 2010.

13 T. Bunnell, *From World City to the World in One City: Liverpool Through Malay Lives*, New York: John Wiley & Sons, 2016, and see also Bunnell's chapter in this volume.

14 Y. Evren and A.N. Okten, 'Stickiness and Slipperiness in Istanbul's Old City Jewellery Cluster: A Survival Story,' *Journal of Economic Geography*, vol. 17, no. 4, 2017, pp. 893–911.

15 J.C. Cirer-Costa, 'Majorca's Tourism Cluster: The Creation of an Industrial District, 1919–36,' *Business History*, vol. 56, no. 8, 2014, pp. 1243–1261.

16 R. Declercq, *World Market Transformation: Inside the German Fur Capital Leipzig 1870 and 1939*, New York: Routledge, 2017; R. Declercq, 'Transnational Entrepreneurs? German Entrepreneurs in the Belgian Fur Industry (1880 to 1913),' *Zeitschrift für Unternehmensgeschichte*, vol. 60, no. 1, 2015, pp. 52–74.

17 S. Henn, 'Transnational Entrepreneurs and the Emergence of Clusters in Peripheral Regions. The Case of the Diamond Cutting Cluster in Gujarat (India),' *European Planning Studies*, vol. 21, no. 11, 2013, pp. 1779–1795; S. Henn, 'Transnational Entrepreneurs, Global Pipelines and Shifting Production Patterns. The Example of the Palanpuris in the Diamond Sector,' *Geoforum*, vol. 43, no. 3, 2012, pp. 497–506.

18 H. Bathelt and P.F. Li, 'Global Cluster Networks – Foreign Direct Investment Flows from Canada to China,' *Journal of Economic Geography*, vol. 14, no. 1, 2014, pp. 45–71.

19 W.G. Huff, *The Economic Growth of Singapore: Trade and Development in the Twentieth Century*, Cambridge: Cambridge University Press, 1994.

20 N. Oswin and B.S.A. Yeoh, 'Introduction: Mobile City Singapore,' *Mobilities*, vol. 5, no. 2, 2010, pp. 167–175.

21 The National Archives in Kew, London (henceforth TNA); the Harrison & Crosfield (henceforth H & C) collection at the London Metropolitan Archives (henceforth LMA); the Guthrie Collection at the SOAS Archives in London (henceforth GC); the Barlow Collection at Cambridge University Library (henceforth BC); the Unilever Archives in Port Sunlight (henceforth UA); the Maritime Archives Guildhall Library (henceforth GL) in London; the archives at Merseyside Maritime Museum (henceforth MMM) in Liverpool; and the National Archives of Singapore (henceforth SNA).

22 MMM 4/A/508, C.E. Wurtzburg, *Raffles of the Eastern Isles*, London: Glen Line, 1954.

23 R.J. Jarman (ed.), *Straits Settlements Annual Reports (Singapore, Penang, Malacca, Labuan) 1855–1941*, Cambridge: Cambridge Archive Editions, 1998.

24 A. Kobayashi, 'Price Fluctuations and Growth Patterns in Singapore's Trade, 1831–1913,' *Australian Economic History Review*, vol. 57, no. 1, 2017, pp. 108–129.

25 A. Kobayashi, 'The Role of Singapore in the Growth of Intra-Southeast Asian Trade, c.1820s – 1852,' *Southeast Asian Studies*, vol. 2, no. 3, 2013, pp. 443–474; K.W. Thee, 'Plantation Agriculture and Export Growth: An Economic History of East Sumatra, 1863–1942,' PhD Thesis, University of Wisconsin, 1969.

26 V. Giacomin, 'The Emergence of an Export Cluster: Traders and Palm Oil in Early Twentieth-Century Southeast Asia,' *Enterprise & Society*, vol. 19, no. 2, pp. 272–308.

27 U. Freitag and W.G. Clarence-Smith, *Hadhrami Traders, Scholars, and Statesmen in the Indian Ocean, 1750s-1960s*, Leiden: Brill, 1997; S. Dhoraisingam, *Peranakan Indians of Singapore and Melaka: Indian Babas and Nonyas–Chitty Melaka*, Singapore: ISEAS Publishing, 2006.

28 H.D. Chiang, 'Sino-British Mercantile Relations in Singapore's entrepôt trade 1870–1915,' in J. Ch'en and N. Tarling (eds.), *Studies in the Social History of China and South-East Asia: Essays in Memory of Victor Purcell (26 January 1896–2 January 1965)*, Cambridge, UK: Cambridge University Press, 1970, p. 255.

29 R.L. Irick, *Ch'ing Policy Toward the Coolie Trade, 1847–1878*, Taipei: Chinese Materials Center, 1982; A. Stoler, *Capitalism and Confrontation in Sumatra's Plantation Belt, 1870–1979*, 2nd edn., Ann Arbor, MI: University of Michigan Press, 1995; N.S. Yoong, 'The Chinese Protectorate in Singapore, 1877–1900,' *Journal of Southeast Asian History*, vol. 2, no. 1, 1961, pp. 76–99; A. McKeown, 'Chinese Emigration in Global Context, 1850–1940,' *Journal of Global History*, vol. 5, no. 1, 2010, pp. 95–124.

30 Statistics show that annual flows of Chinese coolies into the Federate Malay States fell below 100,000 only in 1918–1919 between 1880 and 1932. By the early 1900s, three quarters of Singapore's population was of Chinese origin. A. Reid, 'Early Chinese Migration into North Sumatra,' in J. Ch'en and N. Tarling (eds.), *Studies in the Social History of China and South-East Asia: Essays in Memory of Victor Purcell (26 January 1896–2 January 1965)*, Cambridge, UK: Cambridge University Press, 1970, p. 309; McKeown, 'Chinese Emigration in Global Context,' p. 113.

31 J.H. Drabble and P.J. Drake, 'The British Agency Houses in Malaysia: Survival in a Changing World,' *Journal of Southeast Asian Studies*, vol. 12, no. 2, 2011, pp. 297–328; W.G. Huff, 'The Development of the Rubber Market in Pre-World War II Singapore,' *Journal of Southeast Asian Studies*, vol. 24, no. 2, 1993, p. 290.

32 J. Warren, 'Prostitution and the Politics of Venereal Disease: Singapore, 1870–98,' *Journal of Southeast Asian Studies*, vol. 21, no. 2, 1990, pp. 360–383; B. Chapman-Schmidt, 'Sex in the Shadow of the Law: Regulating Sex Work and Human Trafficking in Singapore,' *Asian Journal of Comparative Law*, vol. 10, no. 1, 2015, pp. 1–21.

33 Yoong, 'The Chinese Protectorate in Singapore, 1877–1900,' pp. 79, 95.

34 S. Cunyngham-Brown, *The Traders: A Story of Britain's Southeast Asian Commercial Adventure*, London: Newman Neame, 1971, p. 176.

35 J.F. Hennart, 'Internalization in Practice: Early Foreign Direct Investments in Malaysian Tin Mining,' *Journal of International Business Studies*, vol. 17, no. 2, 1986, pp. 131–143.

36 MMM 1/A/164 Mosquito Fleet; M.B. Miller, *Europe and the Maritime World: A Twentieth Century History*, New York: Cambridge University Press, 2012, p. 63.

37 A. Booth, 'Varieties of Exploitation in Colonial Setting: Dutch and Belgian Policies in Indonesia and the Congo,' in E. Frankema and F. Buelens (eds.), *Colonial Exploitation and Economic Development: The Belgian Congo and the Netherlands Indies Compared*, Routledge Explorations in Economic History, Hoboken: Routledge, 2013, pp. 60–87.

38 Huff, *Economic Growth*, p. 11; L.K. Wong, *The Malayan tin Industry to 1914, with Special Reference to the States of Perak, Selangor, Negri Sembilan, and Pahang*, Tucson: Association for Asian Studies, 1965.

39 Drabble and Drake, 'The British Agency Houses,' pp. 298, 306–307.

40 H.D. Chiang, 'Sino-British mercantile relations,' p. 255.

41 C.F. Yong, J.A. Gonzalo, and M.M. Carreira, *Tan Kah-Kee: The Making of an Overseas Chinese Legend*, Revised edn., Singapore: Wold Scientific Publishing Co., 2014.

42 The Chinese community in Singapore was quite fragmented. A major distinction was between Strait born (often English educated) Chinese and China born Chinese (hua'

chiao), in turn divided into several ethnic groups (*pang*) depending on their dialect and region of origin. During the colonial period the British chose the first group as representatives of the whole Singaporean Chinese, while remaining wary of the latter because of their ties with political and business groups in China. See LMA CLC/B/112/ MS37390 Recollections from Employees; LMA CLC/B/112/MS37394/006 H & C Compradore Division, Henry Beng, 1987. D.J. Tate, *The RGA History of the Plantation Industry in the Malay Peninsula*, Kuala Lumpur, New York: Oxford University Press, 1996, pp. 102–103.

43 Huff, *Economic Growth*, pp. 18, 63–64.
44 MMM 1/C/2348 Java Gazette, 1933, 1(10), 487.
45 K.G. Tregonning, 'Straits Tin: A Brief Account of the First Seventy-Five Years of the Straits Trading Company,' *Journal of the Malayan Branch of the Royal Asiatic Society*, vol. 36, no. 1, 1963, pp. 79–152.
46 SNA WO/78/3044(1) Singapore New Harbor 1891; SNA WO 78/5365(4) Pulo (Pulau) Brani Survey Map, 1901.
47 Huff, *Economic Growth*, pp. 61–63.
48 M.E. Falkus, *The Blue Funnel Legend: A History of the Ocean Steam Ship Company, 1865–1973*, Basingstoke, UK: Palgrave Macmillan, 1990; H.D. Chiang, *A History of Straits Settlements Foreign Trade, 1870–1915*, Singapore: National Museum, 1978.
49 MMM OA/1/A/334 Short History of Ocean Steam Company, 6.
50 MMM OA/1/B/486 Historical Notes; *Straits Steamship Company Limited*, Singapore: J.M. Sassoon & Co., 1974, pp. 7–9.
51 MMM OA/1/A/879 Mosquito Fleet, p. 2.
52 MMM OA/1/A/334 Short History, p. 9.
53 MMM OA/1/A/164 The Blue Funnel Line, 1938.
54 Chiang, *A History of Straits*, p. 132; Huff, *Economic Growth*, p. 129.
55 MMM OA/1/A/334, Short History, p. 6; Falkus, *Blue Funnel*, p. 28.
56 Huff, 'The Development of the Rubber Market,' p. 286; J.H. Drabble, 'Investment in the Rubber Industry in Malaya c. 1900–1922,' *Journal of Southeast Asian Studies*, vol. 3, no. 2, 1972, pp. 247–261, Reid, 'Early Chinese Migration,' pp. 290–291.
57 J.H. Drabble, *Rubber in Malaya, 1876–1922*, Kuala Lumpur: Oxford University Press, 1973, Appendix VII, p. 220; Barlow, 'Agricultural Development,' p. 84.
58 Kobayashi, 'Price Fluctuations,' p. 119; Huff, *Economic Growth*, p. 87, Table 3.6.
59 Giacomin, 'The Emergence of an Export Cluster,' pp. 26–29.
60 L.H. Brockway, 'Science and Colonial Expansion: The Role of the British Royal Botanic Gardens,' *American Ethnologist*, vol. 6, no. 3, 1979, pp. 449–465; J. Jackson, *The Thief at the End of the World*, London: Gerald Duckworth and Company, 2009.
61 LMA CLC/B/112/37394/005 MacFadyen Notes on Planters, 1936; P.R. Wycherley, 'Introduction of the Hevea to the Orient,' *The Planter*, vol. 4, 1968, pp. 1–11; W. Dean, *Brazil and the Struggle for Rubber: A Study in Environmental History*, New York: Cambridge University Press, 2002. Plantations of rubber had proved impossible in Latin America, due to environmental factors such as the presence of the leaf blight disease, providing Southeast Asia with a major advantage for large-scale production of the commodity.
62 S. Martin, *The UP Saga*, NIAS Monograph, Vol. 94, Copenhagen: NIAS, 2003, pp. 27–28; Tate, *RGA History*, pp. 132–139.
63 Singapore International Chamber of Commerce, *From Early Days: SICC*, Singapore: The Chamber, 1979, p. 22.
64 LMA CLC/B/112/MS37390 Recollections from Employees.
65 Tate, *RGA History*, pp. 270–271, notes 17 and 23.
66 C. Cheong, *Framework and Foundation: A History of the Public Works Department*, Singapore: Times Editions for the Public Works Department.
67 S. Cunyngham-Brown, *The Traders: A Story of Britain's Southeast Asian Commercial Adventure*, London: Newman Neame, 1971, p. 191.

68 SNA NA/3347 SICC Annual Report, 1913–1916; SNA CAOG/10/46: Construction of Johore State Railway, 1904–1910; G.C. Boon, *Technology and Entrepôt Colonialism in Singapore, 1819–1940,* Singapore: ISEAS Press, 2013.
69 [Microfilm: NL 15150] The Singapore Harbour Board, Singapore: Tien Wah Press, 1959, pp. 4–5; 'The Ports Bill,' *The Straits Times*, 11 May 1912, p. 8, available at: http://eresources.nlb.gov.sg/newspapers/Digitised/Page/straitstimes19120511-1.1.8, accessed August 2017.
70 MMM OA/1/A/164 The Blue Funnel Line 1938, p. 17.
71 SNA FCO/141/15785–86 Migrated Archives, Shipping Conference 1899.
72 Chiang, *History of Straits*, pp. 47–49; Huff, *Economic Growth*, pp. 186–187.
73 LMA/RGA Council Meetings Minute Books, 1907–1922; Tate, *RGA History*, p. 258; Drabble and Drake, 'British Agency Houses,' pp. 53–54.
74 LMA CLC/B/112/MS37045 Dutch Rubber Growers Association, 1914.
75 TNA/DSIR/36/1495 Rubber Research in Malaya, Report on the state of research, 1918–1919.
76 Ibid.; Martin, *UP Saga*, pp. 40–52; V. Giacomin, 'The Transformation of the Global Palm Oil Cluster: Dynamics of Cluster Competition Between Africa and Southeast Asia (c. 1900–1970),' *Journal of Global History*, vol. 13, no. 3, 2018, pp. 374–398.
77 Tate, *RGA History,* pp. 251, 268.
78 Cunyngham-Brown, *Traders*, pp. 193–195.
79 H. Dick, 'Japan's Economic Expansion in the Netherlands Indies Between the First and Second World Wars,' *Journal of Southeast Asian Studies,* vol. 20, no. 2, 1989, pp. 244–272; Y.C. Leng, 'Japanese Rubber and Iron Investments in Malaya, 1900–1941,' *Journal of Southeast Asian Studies*, vol. 5, no. 1, 1974, pp. 18–36.
80 LMA CLC/B/112/MS37418 Plantation Management in Transition, 1970.
81 Huff, 'The Development of the Rubber Market,' p. 291.
82 LMA CLC/B/112/MS37418 Plantation Management in Transition, 1970.
83 Huff, 'The Development of the Rubber Market,' pp. 298–299.
84 A.L. Chua, 'Cultural Consumption and Cosmopolitan Connections: Chinese Cinema Entrepreneurs in 1920s and 1930s Singapore,' in C. Rea and N. Volland (eds.), *The Business of Culture: Cultural Entrepreneurs in China and Southeast Asia, 1900–1965*, Toronto: UBC Press, 2015, pp. 207–233.
85 MMM 1/C/2348 Java Gazette, 1933, 1(10), 483–485; LMA CLC/B/112/MS37170 Report on the general trade and commerce of the East coast of Sumatra, 1914.
86 K.T. Joseph, 'Agricultural History of Peninsular Malaysia: Contributions from Indonesia,' *Journal of the Malaysian Branch of the Royal Asiatic Society,* vol. 81, no. 1, 2008, pp. 7–18.
87 C. Barlow, 'Indonesian and Malayan Agricultural Development, 1870–1940,' *Bulletin of Indonesian Economic Studies*, vol. 21, no. 1, 1985, pp. 81–111.
88 J.A. Shriver, *Pineapple-Canning Industry of the World [Microform]*, 1915, Washington, DC: Govt. Print. Off.; R.A. Hawkins, 'The Pineapple Canning Industry During the World Depression of the 1930s,' *Business History*, vol. 31, no. 4, 1989, pp. 48–66.
89 W.G. Huff, 'Capital Markets, Sharecropping and Contestability: Singapore Chinese in the Interwar British Malayan Estate Rubber and Pineapple Industries,' in K. Sugihara and G. Austin (eds.), *Local Suppliers of Credit in the Third World, 1750–1960*, Basingstoke, UK: Palgrave Macmillan, 1993, pp. 226–227.
90 LMA CLC/B/MS37623 SSIC Annual General Meeting, 27 March 1924, p. 2; C. Barlow and S.K. Jayasurija, 'Stages of Development in Smallholder Tree Crop Agriculture,' *Development and Change,* vol. 17, no. 4, 1986, pp. 635–658.
91 P.T. Bauer, 'The Working of Rubber Regulation,' *The Economic Journal,* vol. 56, no. 223, 1946, pp. 391–414.
92 TNA/CO 54/882/3 Rubber Export Restriction Scheme, 1925–1928.
93 MMM OA/1/A/879 Mosquito Fleet, 4; 'Chinese Banks to Join Forces,' *The Straits Times,* 30 August 1932, p. 9, Newspaper SG, available at: http://eresources.nlb.gov.sg/newspapers/Digitised/Article/straitstimes19320830-1.2.40.1, accessed 25 August 2017.

94   MMM OA/1/A/164 The Blue Funnel Line, 1938, p. 15; MMM OA/2/B/2303 Agreement between SSC and EAC; Miller, *Europe and the Maritime World*, p. 127.

95   GC/01/03/11 Correspondence General Private Matters, no. 14, 8 May 1928; V. Giacomin, 'Negotiating Cluster Boundaries: Governance Shifts in the Palm Oil and Rubber Cluster in Malay(si)a (1945–1970 ca.),' *Management & Organizational History*, vol. 12, no. 1, 2017, pp. 1–23.

96   R.H.V. Corley and P.B.H. Tinker, *The Oil Palm*, 5th edn., London: John Wiley & Sons, 2015. The oil needs to be processed within 48 hours after harvesting, requiring milling facilities to be located near the trees. Moreover, as the crop needed domestication, the European estate sector could leverage its existing research facilities.

97   J.C. Jackson, 'Oil Palm: Malaysia's Post-Independence Boom Crop,' *Geography*, vol. 52, no. 3, 1967, pp. 319–321.

98   W.G. Clarence-Smith, 'The Rivaud Hallet Plantation Group in the Economic Crises of the Interwar Years,' in P. Lanthier and H. Watelet (eds.), *Private Enterprises During Economic Crises: Tactics and Strategies*, Ottawa: Legas, 1998, pp. 117–132.

99   P. Labrousse, 'Retour en Malaisie de Henri Fauconnier,' *Archipel*, vol. 54, no. 1, 1997, pp. 207–224; Henri Fauconnier, *Malaisie*, London: Macmillan, 1931.

100 TNA/CO/879/122 Palm Oil Industry in West Africa, 1924–1932, pp. 11–15; TNA/CO/85/61/12 Oil Palm Research in Nigeria, 1945–1947.

101 TNA CO/96/670/4, Auchinleck's Notes on Sumatra, 1928, p. 32; Martin, *UP Saga*, p. 68.

102 BC TBB/870, Correspondence with Grut, 1930s; GC/01/03/11 Correspondence General Private Matters No. 14, 8 May 1928.

103 W. Clarence Smith, 'Rubber Cultivation in Indonesia and the Congo from the 1910s to the 1950s: Divergent Paths,' in E. Frankema and F. Buelens (eds.), *Colonial Exploitation and Economic Development: The Belgian Congo and the Netherlands Indies Compared*, Routledge Explorations in Economic History, Hoboken: Routledge, 2013, pp. 193–210.

104 Giacomin, 'The Global Palm Oil Cluster,' pp. 12–15.

105 Tate, *RGA History*, pp. 466 note 23, 593 note 13; Miller, *Europe and the Maritime World*, p. 121.

106 'Shipment in Palm Oil in Bunk,' *The Planter*, vol. 1, no. 12, 1931, pp. 353–354.

107 GC 01/04/09 Memorandum to James Robertson, Esq., 1936; G.W.A. Trimmer, *The Port of Singapore*, Singapore: National Museum of Singapore, Rare Books Collection, 1933, p. 25.

108 J.H. Drabble, *Malayan Rubber: The Interwar Years*, London: Springer, 1991.

109 E.J. Usoro, *The Nigerian Oil Palm Industry: Government Policy and Export Production, 1906–1965*, Ibadan: Ibadan University Press, 1974, p. 48.

110 K.L. Tan, 'The "Worlds" Entertainment Parks of Singapore (1920s–1980s): New Urban Form and Social Space for Culture and Consumption,' MA thesis (unpublished), National University of Singapore, 2004.

111 X. Huang, *Shanghai Filmmaking: Crossing Borders, Connecting to the Globe, 1922–1938*, Leiden and Boston: Brill, 2014.

112 Lin, 'Cultural Consumption,' p. 208.

113 A.L. Chua, 'Singapore's "Cinema-Age" of the 1930s: Hollywood and the Shaping of Singapore Modernity,' *Inter-Asia Cultural Studies*, vol. 13, no. 4, 2012, pp. 592–604.

114 K.T. Lim, *Cathay: 55 Years of Cinema*, Singapore: Landmark Books for Meileen Choo, 1991.

115 Chua, 'Singapore's "Cinema-Age",' p. 601.

116 R. Braddell, *The Lights of Singapore*, Kuala Lumpur: Oxford University Press, 1982.

117 MMM 1/C/2348 Java Gazette, 1933, 1(10). Shipping companies had started diversifying into civilian airlines. From the early 1930s, Mansfields held the agency for Imperial Airways, and Ocean was among the shareholders of Malayan Airways, but these initial steps were halted by WWII and resumed slowly only in the late colonial period.

118 Huff, *Economic Growth*, p. 28.

6 Singapore during the World War II Japanese occupation

Gregg Huff and Gillian Huff

When Singapore fell on 15 February 1942, its Japanese conquerors had no more than a general idea of how to administer and control the city. Formal Japanese planning for Southeast Asia's occupation by the military and military-dominated governments came remarkably late and took the form of broad policy guidelines, not detailed prescriptions. In reality, little time existed for more than guidelines, because of the determination only in the summer of 1941 that Southeast Asia, not the Soviet Union, was Japan's preferable invasion target. On 20 November, with war a near certainty, the Liaison Conference, as part of the 'Essentials of policy regarding the administration of occupied areas in the southern regions' adopted the three *gunsei* (military organization) principles: the restoration of law and order in occupied areas, strategic materials acquisition in Southeast Asia and occupying army self-sufficiency.[1] The 20 November 1941 document was the first definitive policy statement for military administration in Southeast Asia.[2] Finally, on 12 December 1941, when war was already underway, the 'Outline of economic policies for the southern areas' became available.[3]

This chapter examines, in light of the three *gunsei* principles and hasty Japanese planning for war, how Japan controlled and managed Singapore and the effect of Japanese policies on the city's economy and people. From the outset, Singaporeans suffered serious deprivation and hardship. As occupation continued, and until Japan's 15 August 1945 surrender, unremitting deterioration in Japan's Pacific War military fortunes added greatly to the burdens occupation imposed.

The rapidity with which the Japanese military occupied Southeast Asia, a lack of detailed instructions and the size of the conquered region offered little choice other than what Japan did in Southeast Asia: to set up administrations based on pre-war structures and local personnel. Japan's wartime empire emerged as ad hoc and haphazard.[4] Although before the war the Japanese had studied Southeast Asian societies and cultures, most administrators sent to Southeast Asia lacked local expertise and language skills.[5] Few of those in Japan with knowledge of the Chinese in Southeast Asia were sent to the region. The Southeast Asian Command had just one person charged with Nanyang (Southeast Asian) Chinese affairs.[6]

That lack of expertise made social control in Singapore a problem for the Japanese because Chinese comprised over three quarters of the city's population. Moreover, even before the Japanese occupation a large proportion of Singaporean

Chinese had become implacable enemies of the Japanese. Singapore Chinese were acutely aware of Japan's ongoing war in China, where many Singaporeans had close ties, and of the history of Japanese war atrocities there.

Soon after occupation, Japanese administrators faced two further problems, both serious. One was how to feed Singapore, a city with a population of about 750,000 before the war but which by 1942 had swelled to around a million as refugees streamed down the peninsula. Although Malaya specialized in rubber and tin and grew little rice, pre-war Singapore had always had an abundant supply of food because of its situation in the middle of the world's great rice-producing region consisting of Burma, Thailand and Indochina. After occupation, that changed abruptly because the Japanese military established autarky within Southeast Asian countries to try to transform them into self-sufficient units, cutting off Singapore from its main sources of food. In the 1930s, Malaya produced less than a quarter of the rice it consumed; the rest of Malayan consumption of about 610,000 metric tons had come as imports. At first, the Japanese could draw on rice stockpiled by the British to feed Singapore's population, but this supply was soon exhausted, and over the course of the war food shortages became increasingly serious.

The other problem was that Singapore's economy collapsed, since it depended on exports of rubber and tin. Occupation closed export markets for both commodities, and Japan could use only a fraction of Malayan output of either. No more than partially industrialized before the war, Japan consumed just 5 per cent of world rubber and less than 4 per cent of world tin production. Malayan rubber consumption was at most about 1,000 tons annually. That compared with Malayan exports of well over 500,000 tons a year before the war. Large rubber stockpiles built up, even though output of the commodity plummeted. The size of Singapore's informal economy swelled as resident civilians, thrown out of work, scrambled to find some way of making a living.

Population, social control and labour supply

Terror served as the principal approach to achieve the *gunsei* principle of restoring law and order. Throughout occupation, it remained central as a strategy of social control. The organisation of Singapore's population into *tonari-gumi* or neighbourhood associations, the granting of rations and employment in the Japanese military and firms afforded further leverage over society. Together, Japanese control mechanisms proved successful. Although few Singaporeans supported the Japanese or aspired to emulate them, open social protest was conspicuously absent.

Once in Singapore, the immediate Japanese concern was how to counter Chinese hostility to Japan and anti-Japanese Chinese. 'Hard-line military officers had . . . a ready-made solution – punish them severely' and Japanese administrators opted for this policy as a military necessity.[7] Colonel Watanabe Wataru, characterised as the architect of military administration in Malaya, was a principal figure during the start and early phase of the occupation of Singapore. Watanabe's administrative approach was shaped by his previous tenure with the *Tokumu*

Kikan (Special Service Agency) in occupied China and the unquestioning acquiescence of a coterie of lieutenants, like Watanabe all from the Japanese prefecture of Okayama. Draconian social control methods were apparently formulated on high authority. They are believed to have been masterminded by Colonel Tsuji Masanobu and were ordered by Yamashita Tomoyuki who had led the invasion of Singapore and after the war was executed for his part in the Rape of Manila. Repressive measures applied upon occupying Singapore emphasized violence and the aim of 'spiritual cleansing'. The latter had its fullest expression in the slaughter of perhaps 23,000 (estimates vary from between 5,000 to upwards of 40,000) Singapore Chinese soon after occupation.[8]

By the time Watanabe left Singapore in March 1943, strong repression in Singapore, especially towards the Chinese, had become institutionalised. Torture was commonplace and extreme, often resulting in death and atrocities practiced if any dissent emerged. Japanese methods created a real fear of the Japanese and hardened and expanded deep Chinese resentment, often hatred, towards them. Understandably, most of those in Singapore opted for caution and discretion. Although underground resistance emerged, particularly in the Malay peninsula where the Chinese-dominated, mainly communist Malayan People's Anti-Japanese Army operated, in Singapore organized opposition to the Japanese did not develop. As Virginia Thompson has observed, the strictness of Japanese rule seems to have eliminated any possibility of strikes.[9] Most Singaporeans got on with life as best they could under increasingly difficult circumstances.

Through *tonari-gumi* the Japanese could closely monitor Singapore's population. The *tonari-gumi*, a system of used in Japan, was pyramid-like in structure with a base of neighborhood units of about 10 to 30 houses. Above these, the pyramid narrowed sharply towards its apex. Section heads were responsible for a number of neighborhood units and overseeing the section heads was a small number of headmen or supervisors. In Singapore, the *tonari-gumi*, founded in September 1943 and called the Peace Preservation Corps, comprised 5,500 neighborhood units of 30 households, 550 subsections, and 55 sections, each with a leader. The corps registered all families in a neighborhood and so, as well as monitoring local behaviour, served as a form of census and a basis for the distribution of rations.[10]

Working for the Japanese

After the collapse of Singapore's economy, as unemployment and underemployment grew and food became increasingly scarce, the Japanese ability to offer work, often partly remunerated in food, became an important means of achieving acquiescence to occupation, if generally not support. The only available employment might be work with the Japanese, and people who worked for them were almost certainly better able to protect their living standards than most others in the city. Japanese firms and the military employed about 70,000 persons, more than a fifth of the labour force. Some, although subject to accusations of being sympathizers, were happy to work for the Japanese.[11] Others were not.

Employment by the Japanese could not, however, possibly take up all the slack in the primarily commercial economy of Singapore once pre-war commerce had effectively ceased and the labour supply was swollen by inwards migration. Many Singaporeans turned to types of self-employment occupations with minimal entry barriers such as hawking and prostitution. While these were well-established occupations, queue standing was not. During the occupation, however, it became a recognised 'profession' for many unemployed and older and less agile civilians. For those who lacked other work, queuing and the sale of rationed goods at enhanced prices was 'always a possible source of livelihood'.[12] By 1944, people queued for rationed goods from 2 a.m. onwards.[13]

Japanese administrators attempted to use resettlement outside Singapore to counter the problems of food shortages and lack of work in the city but without much success. In August 1943, when the population of Singapore was estimated to be a million, the Japanese military set an evacuation target of 300,000 with transport to be provided by the Army. There was, however, never any major evacuation; the largest organized re-settlement programme was the Chinese settlement of Endau, 136 miles from Singapore in northeastern Johor which after its first year had about 12,000 settlers. A parallel attempt to resettle Singapore Eurasians and Catholics in Negeri Sembilan was a dismal failure. Even to sustain Endau, the Japanese had to send rice to support the population.[14] No significant resettlement of Singapore's population appears to have been possible, at least under Japanese direction.

Finance and resource acquisition

Financing occupation

The *gunsei* principle of resource acquisition found expression in Japanese financing of Singapore's occupation. Occupied areas are typically expected to be resource contributors, not a burden, and Japan adhered to this idea: occupied Singapore must pay the cost of its occupation. War can be financed by selling bonds to banks or to the public, through taxation and by printing money. This last, as well as printing in the literal sense of currency rolling off presses, includes indirect creation of money in the form of bank deposits, matched by holdings of bonds in the banks' balance sheets. Indirect money was, however, unimportant in Singapore and the rest of Malaya. All the main banks, including the three great British banks – the Hongkong and Shanghai, the Chartered Bank of India, Australia and China and the Mercantile Bank of India – were taken over by the Japanese and eventually liquidated. A number of local Chinese banks were allowed to reopen, but they were small in banking terms and offered at best a negligible market for bonds.

While the destruction of the pre-war European banking system effectively ruled out bonds as a way for the Japanese to finance occupation, taxation remained a possibility. That was difficult, however, because pre-war export specialisation in Malaya in rubber and tin was in response to a global, predominately American, market. Once the occupation cut off Singapore and the rest of Malaya from world markets and their economies collapsed, so too did their tax bases.

To try to mobilize finance, Japanese administrators initiated savings campaigns, including compulsory post office saving. Numerous new taxes were introduced in an attempt to retain pre-war tax arrangements and milk them as much as possible. Chinese businessmen were an easy target for new taxation and 'Donations from the overseas Chinese have, for them, been a considerable burden'.[15] Probably the most notorious of these donations was a 'voluntary' 50-million Malayan dollar gift from Chinese businessmen. No doubt in part it aimed to limit inflation by taking currency out of circulation, but the donation must also have been partly intended to cow influential Chinese opposition to occupation.[16]

Over the course of the war, the Japanese administration instituted lotteries such as the Southern Dream Lottery (Konan Lottery), using variations in timing and prizes to promote a sense of anticipation. Gambling became a way to tax and some 300 betting establishments, farmed out under licence, sprang up all over Singapore. The Shaw brothers, leading figures in post-war Singapore society, are said to have become prosperous by virtue of gaining a license to run gambling farms.[17] Japanese officials also levied taxes on amusement parks, including Great World and New World, and on cinemas, hawkers, dogs and fishing licenses. Prostitutes were taxed to try to generate revenue from the great wartime spread of prostitution, as were waitresses, taxi dancers, restaurants and coffee shops.[18] But taxes, like saving, raised only relatively small amounts of finance.

Despite energetic and sometimes inventive ways to tax devised by the Japanese and their use of other non-financial methods such as price controls and direct confiscation to obtain resources in Singapore, the occupation had, almost inevitably, to be paid for mainly by the taxation of printing money. Money, like any commodity, can be taxed, and governments can finance themselves, perhaps even chiefly, through monetary expansion and therefore seigniorage, defined as the revenue that governments realize from their right to issue money. Seigniorage is the difference between the cost of printing money and what it will buy. Such taxation continues and remains a viable source of government revenue so long as the public is willing, or can be forced, to hold a substantial proportion of its wealth as money. Willingness depends partly on the public judging inflation as not too high and on money's usefulness as a medium of exchange, if not as a store of value. At the same time, coercion was used to enforce compliance. The Japanese administration prohibited, and enforced with strong sanctions, the use of other monies, including the pre-war Malayan dollar. The population of Singapore continued to hold Japanese money because, apart from some clandestine use of pre-war currency, almost no other money was available, making scrip useful as a medium of exchange. Wages were paid in Japanese money, taxes collected in it and the currency was needed for everyday transactions such as buying goods, including rationed items, and paying for lottery tickets and amusement parks.

Money to finance the occupation was not difficult for the Japanese to create. Military scrip, unbacked paper money, could be printed at will and at minimal cost while the nominal spending power generated was the face value of the notes.

The Japanese therefore transferred resources to themselves simply by printing as scrip the required amount of currency. Scrip – printed expressly for Singapore and Malaya – was, as before the war, denominated in dollars. Now, however, currency carried new, 'appropriate' pictures. Banana plants featured on the Malayan ten-dollar note. However, as the war turned against Japan and the need for finance increased, scrip was issued in such large quantities that it continuously lost value, and the Japanese had to print even greater quantities of notes – which became known derisively as 'banana money' – in an attempt to achieve the same real (actual) transfer of resources to themselves as previously. Monetary promiscuity led to extremely high inflation in Singapore and finally, during the last stages of the war, hyperinflation. Inflation was further exacerbated by acute shortages of most essential goods, especially rice, the preferred staple of almost everyone in Singapore and basic to the standard of living.[19]

Prices in Singapore doubled between February and June 1942; doubled again in June 1943, and doubled a further time by January 1944. In March 1944, prices, were rising at some 25 per cent a month, consistent with a yearly increase of around 1,355 per cent. Unsurprisingly, most Singaporeans became continuously more unwilling to hold Japanese banana money, and as the speed at which it changed hands (its velocity of circulation) accelerated, so too did inflation. Between February 1942 and July 1945, while money supply rose 15-fold, prices increased by a factor of 150.

Resource acquisition of materials

In realizing the *gunsei* principle of strategic materials acquisition, Singapore offered the Japanese limited scope. A city's principal potentially extractable resources are industrial capacity and labour. Neither were of much immediate interest to Japan, which looked instead to Southeast Asia's oil and mineral wealth. Industrial capacity in pre-war Singapore was not well developed and although until around mid-1943 Singapore had large labour surpluses, the Japanese could think of little to do with these workers except to send some to labour on construction of the Siam-Burma railway.

Singapore afforded, however, a vital resource in its geography and infrastructure. Strategic location at the centre of Southeast Asia and on the Straits of Malacca, along with superb port facilities, made Singapore a Japanese military and supply centre. By serving as a collection and shipment point for oil from Sumatra and Borneo, Singapore's port was fundamental to the war effort.

Industrialization

Following *gunsei* occupying army self-sufficiency had become more difficult by mid-1943, as shortages in Southeast Asia and a struggling economy at home pressed on the Japanese military. The *gunsei* principle of resource acquisition now more urgently extended towards trying to source manufactured goods through production in Singapore. While it has been suggested that in some parts of wartime

Southeast Asia Japanese firms and the military initiated substantial new import substitution industrialization, they did not do so in Singapore. Its industrialisation beginning in the late 1960s is not explained by wartime occupation.

Pre-war industry in Singapore was relatively limited. For example, there was no chemical industry before the war and although a Ford factory had assembled automobiles in Singapore, all the parts for assembly and repair were imported from Britain and the United States.[20] Although many of Singapore's industrial facilities were taken over intact, the city's limited industrialisation continued to be a constraint during the war.[21] Despite Japanese claims of new industrialisation, factories in Singapore seem, from a Japanese perspective, to have done disappointingly little to meet either military requirements or the needs of Singapore consumers. It frequently proved difficult to keep even the pre-war industrial base operative owing to lack of raw material inputs and spare parts, and this added to the limits to potential industrialisation.

For the military, one of the most useful of Singapore's pre-war enterprises was United Engineers. Before the war it had extensive facilities and manufactured a variety of engineering goods for the rubber and tin industries.[22] Under Japanese control, United Engineers was converted to a munitions factory. The Singapore Gas Works were restarted and supplied gas lighting in the city. In March 1943, however, this public good component of the standard of living remained restricted, and just 840 of some 4,050 gas lights in Singapore were operative.[23] Electricity generation for the city was similarly curtailed.

A major new Japanese enterprise was the attempt to build wooden boats. Although ultimately this was a failure because the boats proved unusable, the industry employed about 1,000 people and absorbed substantial resources, including imported wood. Early in 1943, this was intended to be teak from Burma, but shipping difficulties soon forced a reliance on local wood. The Japanese appear to have started an enterprise to make steel drums as well as a carbolic acid gas factory and in 1943 planned to build a bottle-making plant. Resumption of production at the pre-war Malayan Breweries and Archipelago Brewery Co. was no doubt welcomed by Japanese military and civilian personnel. Mamoru Shinozaki recalled 'the reasonably-priced and very tasty Kirin beer . . . brewed by the Kirin Beer Kaisha on the premises of Tiger Brewery, off Alexandra Road.'[24]

In March 1943, pre-war stocks of raw material imports still kept a number of industrial concerns operating, but for others the wartime unavailability of imported inputs like caustic soda to manufacture soap forced adaptation and the use of substitutes. Some of these were effected only through highly labour-intensive processes, such as the use of rice paper for the manufacture of cigarettes, the recycling of paper, described as resembling a handicraft, and the separation by hand of pineapple fibres from plant leaves as a substitute for cotton.[25]

Little effort appears to have gone into the production of consumer goods, with the exception of soap. Shortages of basic goods were to some extent alleviated by substitutes devised by local entrepreneurs. Small firms, often Chinese, cropped up in the city to make replacement goods for items no longer available. Lee Kuan Yew describes how he, along with a friend and the families of both men, manufactured stationery gum in their homes. Branded as 'Stikfas', the gum was brewed from a mixture of tapioca, carbolic acid and palm oil.[26]

Consumer goods

In keeping with its *gunsei* principles, Japan had no intention of sending goods to Southeast Asia to support the military or local populations. The *gunsei* principle of occupying army self-sufficiency came at the expense of Singapore's population. Military needs would have to be met from what was on hand and what could be produced locally. In the distribution of available food and goods, the military would always have priority. A November 1941 outline of administration in Southeast Asia made Japanese policy clear: 'During the war, the great burdens which will fall on natives on account of the acquisition of natural resources and the process of making the army self-supporting must be borne with the utmost patience. Any requests regarding welfare, which are contrary to this object, will be refused'.[27]

After occupation, Singapore functioned as a 'stock economy': the city became reliant on whatever goods existed in the city at the time of invasion and whatever could be purchased or stolen and brought down from the Malay peninsula. Acute shortages quickly developed, since pre-war Singapore had relied on imports for almost all of its supply of textiles and basic consumer goods like thread, matches, light bulbs and essential medicines. It is unclear how a Japanese research report defined consumer goods, but its calculation that before the war Singapore imported 75 per cent of these is roughly accurate.[28] Even when a few goods like matches and soap had been produced locally, this depended on importing some raw or manufactured materials necessary for production.

Wartime living standards were badly impacted by Singapore's extreme dependence on imported consumer goods and its lack of local manufacturing. Even in 1943 cloth and clothing were apparently largely unavailable. Rations in 1944 of one yard of cloth per person per year were too little to be of much use.[29] A Japanese research report found that no one surveyed had been able to buy new clothes since the start of the occupation. A 'desperate' state of affairs with regard to clothing was 'becoming the norm'.[30] Soap to wash clothes and, more important, underwear, was in scarce supply. Washing had often to be only in water or with ash as a soap substitute.

Among Chinese, the lowest standard of living existed among those crammed into the two densely packed Chinatowns (the old town) on either side of the Singapore River. Here the large majority of Singapore's low-paid factory workers, coolies, hawkers and rickshaw-pullers were housed. All of these occupational groups were badly affected by inflation. Malays, however, located on the fringes of the city, were found to be in a 'far more desperate' condition than the 'overseas Chinese' who dominated Singapore's Chinatowns. Tamils were the poorest Indians, and because they accounted for the great bulk of Singapore Indians, probably placed that community last in terms of wartime living standards. In Johor, rubber coolies, whose wages apparently remained largely static between

1941 and 1943, were especially adversely affected. They 'live desperate lives at bare subsistence levels'.[31]

Food supply

The Japanese had no interest in starving Singaporeans but, as the *gunsei* principles suggest, the approach was to supply food only at a bare minimum except to those whose work for the Japanese directly contributed to the war effort. Even this modest goal was not easily achieved. This section considers how Singapore's population obtained food in sufficient quantities to avoid famine, if not widespread malnutrition. Early in the occupation, rice stockpiled by the British could be distributed as rations and used to feed the population.[32] Throughout occupation rations provided one source of food, but by the later stages of the war fell far below subsistence levels. Increasingly, Singaporeans had to grow their own food and rely on smuggled black market supplies.

Rationing

Initially the Japanese authorities used registers kept by retailers to control amounts given as rations, as had the British colonial government after the outbreak of war. But from August 1942 rationing was through cards issued to individuals.[33] Possession of a card entitled the bearer to purchase a specified amount of rationed goods at controlled prices.

While the aim remained to guarantee at least a subsistence level of essential foods, rationed amounts increasingly fell short of this target. Food available for rations decreased because pre-occupation stocks were soon depleted; because of a continuously widening gap between controlled and black market prices; and because of a shortage of transport both to bring food to Singapore and to distribute it within the island. In March 1942, immediately after occupation, rice rations were 12,066 grams per person per month (397 grams per day equivalent to about 1,421 calories). That was not excessively adrift of an estimate, reproduced in an official British report, of daily pre-war rice consumption in Malaya of 499 grams (1,786 calories) per capita.[34] By February 1944, however, monthly rice rations had fallen to 158 grams (566 calories) per day for men and 119 grams (426 calories) for women, although small amounts of tapioca noodles and tapioca bread flour were also available through official channels.[35] Since the basal metabolic rate (the level at which no surplus for physical activity exists) is around 1,080 calories for women aged 18 to 30 and 1,450 for men aged 18 to 60, Singaporeans had clearly to find energy sources alternative to rice. Even if food were available, it could not always reach consumers. In late 1944, when 30 lorries should have been available to bring food from collection points in Malaya, the actual fleet was only 11 and three of these had broken down. Some perishable foods were left to rot for lack of transport.[36]

Although in early 1944 the ration target was 1,400 calories per day, only 905 calories were being provided, less than required for survival. A Japanese research report found that consumption of staple foods was 32 per cent of pre-war levels, while for vegetables and fruit the percentage was 29 per cent and for fish and meat 59 per cent. On the basis of the estimated figure for pre-war rice consumption of 499 grams per person per day, this Japanese research finding for staple foods suggests that by the latter stages of the war Singapore residents may on average have been able to consume something like 160 grams (573 calories) of rice daily, and that for people to survive rice must have been supplemented by a substantial amount of other foods like tapioca and sweet potatoes and extensive recourse to the black market, discussed later.

While Singapore's middle class might be able to sell gold, jewellery, other valuables and furniture to improve food intake, many others did not have such assets. There was considerable inequality in the distribution of food. By October 1943, many people, although preferring rice, no longer ate it. Since in late 1943 rations apparently still provided 280 grams of rice a day (so long as the distributing system functioned as intended), many people must have sold their rations on the black market to be able to buy adequate quantities of cheaper foods and non-food necessities.[37]

Growing food

The Japanese vigorously promoted campaigns to grow your own food with instructions on how this might be done and the dissemination of information on the preparation of unfamiliar foods. Main suggestions of substitutes for rice as the staple food were root crops like cassava (tapioca) and sweet potatoes. Although easily grown and calorific, shortages of almost all other foods meant that the diets of Singaporeans were badly lacking the essential nutritional components of oils, fats and protein. Singaporeans universally loathed tapioca.

Available spaces in central Singapore were soon covered with food crops, but the city was exceptionally densely populated and offered limited scope for cultivation: in 1947, an area of 2,285 acres which made up the inner city wards amounted to 11 per cent of the land area of the municipality but just under half its population. Where land was available some municipal residents kept chickens and ducks which they fed on the city's two-inch cockroaches trapped in the sewers at night. Additionally, the area of Singapore island under market gardens expanded from 1,500 acres to 7,000 acres. That was, however, just 0.021 of an acre for each of the 263,600 additions to the city's population between 1938 and 1944. Cats and dogs afforded an obvious source of high protein. These animals disappeared in sufficiently great numbers to qualify as endangered species.[38]

'The failure of the Japanese Government to provide and to maintain adequately the supply of rice for the Malayan population was', according to Chin Kee Onn, the 'fundamental cause of all the economic ills of the country'.[39] In 1944, however, the Japanese attempted to redress the critical shortage of rice reaching Singapore. Policies were introduced to reorganize the import of rice and to provide greater incentives for Chinese rice traders.

On 20 March 1944, Japanese administrators responded to the difficulties of Mitsubishi (the official government supplier) in obtaining rice in competition with private purchasers in Thailand and the depreciation of the Japanese version of the Malayan dollar. In an attempt to exercise control over rice supplies, they banned private imports. The measure was, however, short-lived. Within a month, on 13 April 1944, Japanese authorities turned to Singapore Chinese enterprise to arrange for the supply of rice, and just over a month later set up the Singapore Rice Import Association, which involved a large body of Singapore Chinese traders and liberalized the rice trade. Along with levy (or taxed) rice required to be delivered to the military administration at set prices, these traders were entitled to sell unregulated (non-taxed) rice on the open market.[40] As a Japanese research report emphasized in regard to the new association: 'A successful operation requires the support of the overseas Chinese, which would be difficult to gain without the prospect of adequate economic profits'.[41]

Once the Japanese liberalised trade in rice and an officially sanctioned trade route between Singapore and Songkhla in Thailand opened, Singapore Chinese began furiously to build boats to carry back rice from Thailand. According to Ng Seng Yong, speaking much later but calling on what were apparently vivid memories, 'Most of us were doing boat construction and everyone was rushing to get this rice'.[42] The traders organized themselves into cooperative groups. An essential component of any group was a 'leg man', almost certainly with Japanese connections, to secure various official permits. Another person or persons financed the venture. Finance included funds to build a ship of about 35 tons and pay for an engine as well as petrol to run it. Permits were also required to get engines and petrol. These may not have been easy to acquire without some official connections.

Black markets

A stock economy, unsuccessful Japanese attempts at price control and high inflation together ensured an extensive black market. As official rations dwindled and even stated entitlements became more difficult to obtain in practice, Singapore's black market grew proportionately, and the gap between prices in it and official selling prices for rations increasingly widened. By mid-1943, most Singaporeans probably had to rely for food on both constituents of a parallel structure of controlled and black markets.

During the war, the black market became a way of life. People in Singapore began to think of it as normal and 'when the stage arrived at which the public was compelled to pay black-market prices for such things as bus-tickets, railway-tickets, cinema-tickets, cloth-coupons and even newspapers, the situation was beyond redemption'.[43] Encumbered by the wartime legacies of a pervasive black economy, social breakdown and severe shortages of food and consumer goods, the post-war British Military Administration became popularly known as the Black Market Administration.

The black market gave rise to new classes of brokers who, often as part of complex networks, facilitated the discovery of scarce goods. Chin Kee Onn describes those in the upper echelons of an informal economy that grew up as part of a wartime distributive system: '[T]he highest class of brokers were the "arm-chair" brokers [who each] had a corps of co-operatives. Chief among these were "lieutenant brokers"' who specialized in one type of goods or another. Lieutenants alone had the right to approach the chief and directed 'field brokers'. These latter went about the city nosing for contacts and relied on a yet larger group of brokers, the so-called 'nondescripts'. Such men were the first point of contact between buyer and seller. Like packs of reporters, they haunted the coffee shops, hotels, restaurants and lodging houses and roved the country in search of goods.[44]

At the bottom of Singapore's new wartime informal economy, hawkers had an important distributive role. Uniquely, they had informational advantages which derived from an area-specific knowledge and a known clientele. In Singapore, retail black market distribution of basic goods like food was generally through coffee shops, eating shops and hawkers. One reason for this was that most 'wholesale' distributors assessed contact with the public as too risky.[45] For a great number of people, however, hawking appears to have been a residual occupation. It was explained that: 'groups such as street vendors have no choice about their work. If they are able to find a better job, they will willingly change their occupation. But 'in present conditions they cannot find satisfactory work and are compelled to do what they can to buy food.'[46]

Social and welfare indicators

Urban health and nutrition

Wartime statistics on death rates and infant mortality for Singapore confirm a sharp drop in living standards and show the differing impact of occupation on the city's three main races. By the end of the war, almost no one in Singapore had escaped significant nutritional deprivation and associated impairments to health. The returning British found 'a very large percentage of the population was suffering from serious under-nourishment'.[47] Between about two-fifths and two-thirds of Singapore school children were malnourished by pre-war standards.[48] Most children showed stunted growth and very poor musculature.[49]

During the Japanese occupation in Singapore, as elsewhere in Malaya, health services and anti-malarial work were progressively abandoned. Death rates surged due to declining health services, reduced availability of clean water and inadequate diets, this last evidenced, for example, by a much higher incidence of beri-beri (dietary deficiencies associated with an overload of carbohydrates) and infantile convulsions. The latter, indicative of malnutrition among infants under one year old, was high because poorly fed women were unable to suckle their infants and could not obtain milk.[50] Between 1941 and 1944, Singapore's crude death rate more than doubled. Birth rates fell more slowly than deaths rates rose, but by 1945 the crude birth rate of 27.5 per thousand was not much above half its 1940/1941 average and far below crude deaths of 39.8.[51]

Infant mortality is a good indicator of health trends and, in particular, a usual measure of access to clean water. In Singapore, the infant death rate rose markedly during the Japanese occupation. An 86 per cent rise in Singapore's' infant death rate between 1940 and 1942 compares with a 40 per cent increase in occupied Europe over a similar period and indicates how quickly and how greatly conditions deteriorated in Singapore.[52] Between 1942 and 1945, infant deaths accounted for a quarter of total deaths but for a much higher share of the increase in deaths. In comparison to 1940, between 1942 and 1945, while average annual deaths excluding infants increased by 56 per cent, infant deaths rose by 256 per cent.

In 1940, much higher Malay than either Chinese or Indian infant death rates points to pre-war deprivation compared to the other races. During the war, however, Indians were more adversely affected than Malays. A wartime explosion of Indian infant mortality provides clear evidence for the collapse in Indian living standards. Substantially because of the high 1940 pre-war Malay starting point, between then and 1944 the percentage increase in Malay infant deaths (61.4 per cent) was considerably less than for Chinese infants (100 per cent). However, both races were far outdistanced by an increase of 166.7 per cent for Indian infants. Between 1940 and 1944, while infant death rates for Singapore as whole doubled, they were 2.7 times higher among Indians.

Post-war Singapore

Japan never came close to converting Singaporeans to a Japanese way of life. An attempt to teach the Japanese language in schools and to persuade people to learn it failed miserably. Unlike in much of Southeast Asia, where income per capita languished below pre-war levels for two or three decades, Singapore's per capita GDP recovered quickly. By 1950, it easily exceeded its 1938 level. However, Singapore emerged from the war a changed place.

Occupation and wartime deprivation left a legacy of social problems and cruelly exposed others. After becoming a 'million city' during the war, rapid population growth continued in Singapore. To accommodate more people and in response to a brisk wartime demand for food from local market gardens, during the war large squatter settlements on the fringes of the city developed for the first time.[53] In Singapore, the social consequences of Japanese conscription of women as 'comfort girls' for the troops, the closing of schools, a breakdown in social services and the spectre of near-starvation lasted well beyond the end of the war. The convergence of all these aspects of Japanese occupation in Singapore 'made easier the revival of the practice of selling female children to brothel keepers and others who trained them for prostitution'. In 1946, Singapore's medical authorities drew attention to the large numbers of girls aged 10 to 14 appearing for the treatment of venereal disease.[54]

After 1945, Singapore existed in a political environment radically different than before the war. Post-war Singapore soon became a political battleground. Wartime inflation, combined with attempts after the war to re-establish pre-1940 nominal wage levels, gave rise to widespread labour unrest and promoted trade union organization. Singapore political parties could make use of social and labour discontent and, moreover, now had a clear agenda of political independence and examples of it elsewhere in Southeast Asia. The Japanese occupation was not an economic turning point in Singapore's history. However, the war and occupation provided the context in which British planning fundamentally changed Singapore's political relationship with Malaya. The Malayan Union, and after its failure the February 1948 Federation of Malaya, divorced Singapore politically from the Malay states, Penang and Malacca. And yet that ultimately left Singapore even more outward looking and globally oriented than before the war – themes which will be picked up on further in the chapters by Kah Seng Loh and Nicholas J. White which follow. In comparison with most of the rest of Southeast Asia, Singapore's independence, as part of Malaysia in 1963 and then after the 1965 separation from Malaysia, came late. When it did, the new city-state of Singapore was left to chart its own future, something it has done with marked economic success.

Notes

1 Liaison Conferences, which took place from late 1937 to 1944, were meetings between the Government and military to discuss various issues and formulate policy. Major policy decisions agreed at the conferences were ratified by Imperial Conferences.
2 Gotō, Ken'ichi, *Tensions of Empire: Japan and Southeast Asia in the Colonial and Postcolonial World*, Athens, OH: Ohio University Press, 2003, pp. 52–53, 78.
3 Nobutaka Ike (ed. and trans.), *Japan's Decision for War: Records of the 1941 Policy Conferences*, Stanford: Stanford University Press, 1967, pp. 249–253; Harry J. Benda, James K. Irikura, and Koichi Kishi (eds.), *Japanese Military Administration in Indonesia: Selected Documents*, New Haven: Yale University Southeast Asia Studies, 1965, pp. 1–3, 17–24; Yoshimura Mako, 'Japan's Economic Policy for Occupied Malaya,' in Akashi Yoji and Yoshimura Mako (eds.), *New Perspectives on the Japanese Occupation in Malaya and Singapore, 1941–1945*, Singapore: NUS Press, 2008, pp. 113–114, 113–138.
4 Gotō, *Tensions*, p. 77.
5 Paul H. Kratoska and Ken'ichi Gotō, 'Japanese Occupation of Southeast Asia,' in R.J.B. Bosworth and Joseph Maiolo (eds.), *The Cambridge History of the Second World War: Vol. 2: Politics and Ideology*, Cambridge: Cambridge University Press, 2015, p. 539.
6 Akashi Yoji, 'Japanese Policy Towards the Malayan Chinese 1941–1945,' *Journal of Southeast Asian Studies*, vol. 1, no. 2, 1970, p. 62.
7 Akashi, 'Japanese Policy,' p. 62.
8 Akashi Yoji, 'Colonel Watanabe Wataru: The Architect of the Malayan Military Administration, December 1941-March 1943,' in Akashi Yoji and Yoshimura Mako (eds.), *New Perspectives on the Japanese Occupation in Malaya and Singapore, 1941–1945*, Singapore: NUS Press, 2008, pp. 33–64; Akashi Yoji, 'Japanese Policy,' pp. 61–89; Yuma Totani, *The Tokyo War Crimes Trial: The Pursuit of Justice in the Wake of World War II*, Cambridge: Harvard University Asia Center, 2008, pp. 163–164.
9 Virginia Thompson, *Labor Problems in Southeast Asia*, New Haven: Yale University Press, 1947, p. 12.
10 Office of Strategic Services [hereafter OSS], R&A 2072 *Japanese Administration in Malaya*, Washington, DC: Research and Analysis Branch, Office of Strategic Services, 8 June 1944, pp. 20–21; OSS, R&A 2137 *Industrial Facilities in Malaya*, Washington, DC: Research and Analysis Branch, Office of Strategic Services, 15 May 1944; OSS, R&A 2423 *Singapore Under Japanese Domination*, Washington, DC: Research and Analysis Branch, Office of Strategic Services, 8 September 1944, pp. 2–3.
11 National Archives of Singapore [hereafter NAS], Oral History interviews 000021 Chan Chee Seng and 000007 Wong Lau Eng.

12 M.V. Del Tufo, *Malaya: A Report on the 1947 Census of Population*, London: Crown Agents, 1949, p. 34.
13 Yamada Isamu, 'Methods of Increasing Food Production on Syonan Island (October 1944),' in Gregg Huff and Shinobu Majima (eds.), *World War II Singapore: The Chōsabu Reports on Syonan-to*, Singapore: National University of Singapore Press, 2018, p. 420.
14 Mamoru Shinozaki, *Syonan – My Story: The Japanese Occupation of Singapore*, Singapore: Times Books International, 1975, pp. 79–92.
15 Commiittiee for the Problem of Prices, 'Counter-Measures for Prices in Syonan Municipality (March 1944),' in Huff and Majima, *World War II Singapore*, p. 349.
16 Tan Yeok Seong, *The Extortion by the Japanese Military Administration of $50,000,000 from the Chinese in Malaya*, Singapore: Nanyang Book Co., 1947.
17 Lee Kuan Yew, *The Singapore Story*, Singapore: Times Editions, 1998, p. 76.
18 Chin Kee Onn, *Malaya Upside Down*, Singapore: Jitts & Co., 1946, pp. 54, 192.
19 Gregg Huff and Shinobu Majima, 'Financing Japan's World War II Occupation of Southeast Asia,' *Journal of Economic History*, vol. 73, no. 4, 2013, pp. 938–978.
20 OSS, *Industrial Facilities*, p. 3.
21 Ibid., p. 1.
22 Gregg Huff, *The Economic Growth of Singapore: Trade and Development in the Twentieth Century*, Cambridge: Cambridge University Press, 1994, pp. 216–217.
23 Military Administration, Department of General Affairs, Research Office, 'An Overview of Important Industrial Factories in Syonan Municipality (March 1943),' in Huff and Majima, *World War II Singapore*, p. 305.
24 Shinozaki, *Syonan – My Story*, p. 57.
25 'An Overview of Important Industrial Factories in Syonan Municipality (March 1943),' p. 317.
26 Lee, *Singapore Story*, p. 67.
27 The National Archives of the United Kingdom, Kew [hereafter TNA], WO203/6310, 'SEATIC Special Intelligence Bulletin,' p. 2.
28 Commiittiee for the Problem of Prices, 'Counter-Measures for Prices for Syonan Municipality (March 1944),' in Huff and Majima, *World War II Singapore*, p. 327.
29 Ibid., p. 347.
30 Yamada Isamu and Kawai Mikio, 'A Study of the Lowest Levels of Living by Ethnic Group in Syonan Municipality (October 1943),' in Huff and Majima, *World War II Singapore*, p. 505.
31 Ibid., p. 490.
32 TNA, CO852/327/9, 'Food Supplies: Malaya,' in *Details the Pre-War Build up of Stocks of Rice and Other Foodstuffs*.
33 TNA, WO 852/327/9, 'Food Supplies Malaya,' p. 2.
34 Arkib Negara Malaysia (National Archives of Malaysia) [hereafter ANM] 1957/0575131 Intelligence 506/30, 'Appreciation of the Economic Position of Malaya Under the Japanese,' p. 3.
35 TNA, WO 203/4499, 'Rice – S.E.A.C. Territories,' pp. 54–55; WO 203/2647, 'Summary of Economic Intelligence No. 130, 15 October 1945,' p. 5.
36 Yamada, 'Methods of Increasing Food Production on Syonan Island (October 1944),' p. 414.
37 'Conditions of Economic Security in Syonan Municipality and Johore (March 1943),' in Huff and Majima, *World War II Singapore*, p. 381.
38 He Wen-Lit, *Syonan Interlude*, Singapore: Mandarin Paperbacks, 1991, p. 156.
39 Chin, *Malaya Upside Down*, p. 55.

40 According to TNA, Kew, WO203/44, 'Rice – S.E.A.C. Territories,' p. 60 all private imports of rice by civilians using their own junks were utilized by the Food Control Department but other evidence indicates that this was not the case.

41 Matsu'ura Shigeharu, 'Rice Imports to Malaya with Special Reference to Syonan Municipality (September 1944)' in Huff and Majima, *World War II Singapore*, p. 457.

42 NAS, Oral History Department 000283, Interview Ng Seng Yong.

43 Chin, *Malaya Upside Down*, p. 37.

44 Ibid., pp. 42–43.

45 Paul H. Kratoska, *The Japanese Occupation of Malaya and Singapore: A Social and Economic History*, Singapore: NUS Press, 2018, p. 175.

46 Odabashi Sadatoshi and Ōmura Junzaburō, 'Population by Occupation in Syonan Municipality (December 1943),' in Huff and Majima, *World War II Singapore*, p. 153.

47 Singapore, *Annual Report of the Medical Department 1946*, Singapore: Government Printing Office, 1947, p. 13 and see Singapore Department of Social Welfare, *First Report of the Singapore Department of Social Welfare, June to December 1946*, Singapore: G.H. Kiatt, 1947, p. 15; Commiittiee for the Problem of Prices, 'Countermeasures for Prices for Syonan Municipality,' in Huff and Majima, *World War II Singapore*, p. 334. According to the Countermeasures report in March 1944 food consumption of staple foods was around 32 per cent of pre-war levels.

48 Geoffrey H. Bourne, 'Nutrition Work in Malaya Under the British Military Administration,' *International Review of Vitamin Research*, vol. 21, 1949, p. 286.

49 ANM, BMA Dept/1/3 pt. II, British Military Administration, 'Final Report Nutrition Unit' (April 1946), Appx. A(i); and see Bourne, 'Nutrition Work,' pp. 286–287.

50 Singapore, *Report of Medical Department 1946*, p. 2.

51 For this and the following data on measures of health, see Gregg Huff, *World War II and Southeast Asia: The Economic and Social Consequences of Japanese Occupation*, Cambridge: Cambridge University Press, 2020.

52 League of Nations, *World Economic Survey, 1941/42*, Geneva: League of Nations, 1942, p. 18.

53 Gregg Huff and Gillian Huff, 'Urban Growth and Change in 1940s Southeast Asia,' *Economic History Review*, vol. 68, no. 2, 2015, pp. 522–547.

54 Singapore Department of Social Welfare, *First Report*, pp. 37–38.

7 The economics of Singapore's exit from Malaysia[1]

Nicholas J. White

Introduction: a moment of relief?

After a surprise return to power in May 2018, Malaysia's prime minister, Mahathir Mohamad, announced his government's intention to cancel a high-speed rail link between Singapore and Kuala Lumpur because it would 'make no money at all' for Malaysia. Most of the track would (necessarily) be in Malaysia, and the implication, therefore, was that Singapore was the principal beneficiary. As with simultaneous disputes over port limits, airspace and water supplies, this was a revisiting of the economic squabbles which had punctuated relations between Malaysia and Singapore since their political separation over five decades previously.[2] Indeed, as a novice backbencher in October 1966, Mahathir dismissed the calls of Singapore-based businesses for the preservation of the currency union between island and mainland since 'money made in Malaysia will be spent in Singapore to give jobs, build houses and generally develop the Republic'.[3]

As this chapter demonstrates, economic tensions also bedevilled the period of merger between September 1963 and August 1965 and were central to Singapore's exit from the Malaysian federation. The standard explanation in the existing historiography is that ethnic tensions lay at the heart of Singapore's expulsion. Sino-Malay rivalry apparently proved insurmountable, epitomised by the Singapore communal riots of July 1964. The 'Malaysian Malaysia' espoused by Singapore's People's Action Party (PAP) clashed irreconcilably with the Malay special rights rhetoric of the dominant party in the central government in Kuala Lumpur, the United Malays National Organisation (UMNO), in which Mahathir was a leading anti-PAP activist. The racial issue was intensified by ideological divides (the PAP's Fabian socialism versus the ruling Alliance's laissez-faire economic philosophy) and personal animosities between the leading politicians on either side of the Causeway.[4]

The forewarnings and post-split assessments of British business leaders, at the head of enterprises long associated with Malaysia and Singapore, appear to confirm the ethno-political view. The Mercantile Bank of India, a subsidiary of the Hongkong and Shanghai Banking Corporation (HSBC) after 1959, was part of the cluster of British exchange banks which Kawamura shows in this volume was crucial to Singapore's colonial phase of globalization. Mercantile's chief manager in London, Charles Pow, visited Kuala Lumpur in November 1963 and discovered 'much anxiety about how Lee Kuan Yew will behave in the Federal Parliament'. Lee 'may campaign [Malaysia-wide] for his PAP . . . and will try to supplant the MCA [Malaysian Chinese Association, a key component of the Malay-dominated Alliance coalition in Kuala Lumpur]'. Pow foresaw a 'quite explosive situation' developing 'overnight'.[5] The Liverpool-based Ocean Steam Ship Company (OSSCo; alternatively known as the Blue Funnel Line or Alfred Holt & Co.) was Britain's leading shipping group in Southeast Asia. Controlling the shipping agents Mansfield & Co and the regional feeder services of the Straits Steamship Company, Blue Funnel was one of Singapore's premiere companies.[6] OSSCo's chairman, Sir John Nicholson, visited Singapore in September 1965, and from discussions with expat 'commercials, commanders, [and] commissioners', he found 'almost unanimous evidence' that secession confirmed his personal 'disbelief in the compatibility of Malays and Chinese'.[7] As a Bank of England staffer commented back in January 1959, the 'main obstacle' to Singapore's desired merger with the Federation of Malaya, even if the latter shifted leftwards politically, 'remain[ed] the Malays' fears of Chinese domination'.[8]

But British business archives, and those of the UK government, interrogated in this chapter (to compensate for a deficit in local material given official restrictions in Malaysia and Singapore) point to economic tensions as uppermost in the 'Greater Malaysia' debacle. This archival Anglo-centricity is additionally justified because Britain's business, military and diplomatic nexus continued to dominate Commonwealth Southeast Asia's economic and geo-political externalities in the end-of-empire era. Singapore remained Britain's largest overseas military base in the 1960s. Moreover, 70 per cent of Malaysia's foreign investment (often administered and financed on a day-to-day basis by British agency houses and banks with regional headquarters in Singapore) was UK-owned as late as 1972 when parity between sterling and the Singapore and Malaysian currencies finally ended. Top US policy-makers certainly viewed the region as a British sphere of influence. Secretary of State Dean Rusk informed President John F. Kennedy in February 1963 that it was a 'British responsibility' to provide both military and economic assistance to the prospective new state of Malaysia, as well as 'to protect the country against any internal subversion if outside assistance [was] needed'.[9] Indeed, Nicholson of Blue Funnel feared in the demise of 'Mighty Malaysia' that bilateral frustrations would be taken out 'on the excessively ubiquitous British'.[10]

Rather than a racial struggle, the British records reveal that two of the principal protagonists were ethnic Chinese and cousins: Goh Keng Swee, Singapore's finance minister, and Tan Siew Sin, the federal finance minister in Kuala Lumpur. On 9 August 1965 Lee Kuan Yew, the prime minister of Singapore, famously shed tears on national television when announcing that his micro-state had left Malaysia to become a separate republic. But Lee's 'moment of anguish' might well have been a 'moment of relief' given that the economic constraints of the Malaysia years were ended. Singapore was free to pursue its own economic policy in its own interest.

This rethinking of the Malaysia-Singapore split relates to wider recent debates about the failure of decolonisation through federalisation (in Africa and the Caribbean especially).[11] Vaughan focuses on the high politics of unachieved federation in postcolonial East Africa but does acknowledge that centrifugal political tendencies were magnified by national-level concerns about common trade, financial and immigration proposals in Kenya, Tanganyika/Tanzania and Uganda.[12] Cohen notes that the 'economic advantage' of the Central African Federation (CAF), inaugurated in 1953, was 'assumed rather than proved', Colonial Office (CO) mandarins doubted the supposed developmental benefits for Nyasaland from the outset, and a perceived bias towards Southern Rhodesia in finance and economic decision-making strained relations with Northern Rhodesia.[13] Indeed, reflecting in 1962 that 'it would be fatal to go ahead' with 'Greater Malaysia' on the 'off chance' that financial and economic matters would 'right themselves afterwards', a CO bureaucrat drew comparisons with the CAF and also the West Indies Federation which had 'come unstuck'. The 'lack of any development policy by the Federal Government in Nyasaland' was, he believed, 'a substantial contributory factor'. One of 'the principal reasons for the collapse of the West Indian Federation', meanwhile, 'had been in the fiscal field'.[14] Bank of England officials likewise appreciated in 1963 that the desire of the central government to be financially independent rather than go 'cap in hand to the component territories' proved 'very largely' why Caribbean integration 'foundered'. Concurrently, the stymying of 'Greater Malaysia' from the outset through Brunei refusing to sign up in July 1963 partially reflected political considerations (the Sultan being 'clearly worried about . . . his position . . . in the Conference of Rulers'). But, a 'further disincentive', proved Royal Dutch Shell's offshore oil discoveries in Brunei (and, hence, the prospect of having to surrender the sultanate's royalties from this bounty to Kuala Lumpur).[15]

Even so, separatism throughout decolonising Southeast Asia has been explained by ethnic and religious polarities.[16] On top of Straits Chinese objections to Malay domination, however, the (ultimately unsuccessful) Penang Secession Movement of the late 1940s and early 1950s was fired by a desire for the settlement 'to resume its former position as the free trade port of the Northern part of the Straits of Malacca'.[17] Singapore might have matched Penang's economic stagnation in the 1960s and 1970s, through the further erosion of its free-port status and neglect of industrialisation had it lingered longer inside Malaysia.[18] As Huff argues, Singapore's long-term incorporation into Malaysia could have been economically disastrous for the island.[19]

The common market

In a post-separation diagnosis of September 1965, Laurence Hope, the UK's commercial attaché in Singapore, appreciated that a suspicion on the island had developed during the Malaysia years that the federal government in Kuala Lumpur had no intention of recognising Singapore as the business capital of 'Greater Malaysia'. Rather, the thinking north of the Causeway appeared inclined to reduce Singapore's economic status. The chief irritant was the failure to establish a common market.[20] Lee Kuan Yew regarded Malaysia primarily as a customs union central to the island's economic survival (especially since the British military presence, a key employer and source of revenue for Singapore, could not be counted on indefinitely).[21] In March 1960, the assessment of the CO's Sir John Martin was that the socialist but 'ardently anti-communist' prime minister believed that the solution to Singapore's principal and interlinked problems – the radical left-wing threat and the 'feeding' of its rapidly expanding population – lay in closer relations with mainland Malaya. The quasi-colonial regime, as far as Lee was concerned, could not inspire loyalty in its people. Full independence, on the other hand, was only viable through merger with the Federation of Malaya since Singapore was too small to stand alone (both economically and politically).[22] The PAP had won the elections of November 1959 which presaged Singapore's incarnation as a semi-independent, self-governing state. Lee's government oversaw domestic affairs (including economic matters), as British responsibility was reduced to foreign policy and security. In introducing his first budget, Goh Keng Swee proposed a common market and an integrated industrialisation strategy with Malaya (which had achieved full independence in August 1957).[23] Goh's scheme followed on from a 1959 report commissioned by Singapore's colonial administration which 'endorsed the prevailing sentiment for the island to establish a common market with . . . Malaya'.[24]

Lee came to regard agreement with the Federation on some form of common market as an 'essential prerequisite to merger'.[25] Key to Singapore's development was the expansion of secondary industry; to compensate for the declining entrepôt trade and the absence of natural resources. But the Singapore market in itself was tiny and could not sustain the level of industrialisation required to meet full-employment. 'By creating a common market with . . . Malaya, Singapore would be able to sell its goods to the larger population up north'.[26] For PAP leaders, the 'whole question of Singapore's future prosperity within the [Malaysian] Federation' hinged on a customs union.[27] This view was shared by business opinion in Singapore, especially as the radical left of the PAP split with the party's moderate leadership, fronted by Lee and Goh, in August 1961 to form the Barisan Sosialis (Socialist Front). The break-away leftists campaigned for immediate Singaporean independence but *outside* the Malaysia bloc (which they regarded as a neo-colonial smokescreen for genuine autonomy).[28] In dismissing the Barisan's obstructionism, the pro-business *Straits Times* argued in February 1962 that the 'interdependence' of 'the Five' (Singapore, Malaya, North Borneo, Sarawak and Brunei) was not properly appreciated. The latter four were essentially primary producers with Singapore linking them to overseas markets. Moreover, 'the much larger trading unit which Malaysia will make possible' offered 'considerable advantages' because currently 'the smallness of the domestic market is a major handicap to all industrial enterprise'.[29]

The federal government in Kuala Lumpur, and particularly Finance Minister Tan Siew Sin, disagreed. Alliance leaders feared that coordination of industrial policy would result in new factories in 'Greater Malaysia' settling in Singapore,

given the port city's existing status as a developed industrial and commercial centre with a central geographical position between Malaya and the Borneo states,
good communications and an abundant supply of cheap labour. The new manufacturing zones on the mainland, at Petaling Jaya on the outskirts of Kuala Lumpur, especially, would be bypassed. This view was not without justification given
the massive Jurong project in western Singapore, the centrepiece of an industrial
expansion policy for job creation which pre-dated merger in the PAP government's State Development Plan for 1961–64.[30] Though state-led via Goh's Economic Development Board, Jurong was designed to attract private investment
from overseas multinationals through tax concessions and an integrated, tailor-
made infrastructure (including a coastal location facilitating the construction of
deep-water berths to import raw materials and heavy machinery). Lee's government dedicated 13 per cent of its industry and commerce budget to Jurong
alone.[31] In visiting the project in November 1963, a Blue Funnel manager was
highly impressed, believing that 'we shall have to take [Jurong] seriously into
our calculations'. Already, 9,000 out of the 25,000 projected acres were cleared,
resembling images of 'the surface of the moon'. Hills were being levelled and
swamps filled, and 'thousands and thousands of tons of earth-moving equipment
and trucks were on the area'. Dual carriageways were 'going hither and yon', and
'a few off the peg factories [were] already up'. Federal ministers in Kuala Lumpur
would not have been pleased by the assessment of the British shipping executive
that Petaling Jaya, by comparison, was 'a junior concept': 'The toothpaste may go
into tubes in Petaling Jaya, but it will be made in Jurong'.[32]

Even more irksome for Kuala Lumpur in Singapore's plans for merger was
the PAP's desire to have its 'cake (of protected infant industries) and eat it (by
retaining the entrepôt business)', as an Australian diplomat put it in March 1963.
Singapore would 'benefit from a protected Malaysian market' while, concurrently, retaining 'most of [its] advantages of a free port'.[33] The long-established
British agency houses supported the PAP's position. The chairman of the Singapore Chamber of Commerce (SCC) declared in March 1963 that 'it is essential
that maximum free port status is maintained for Singapore whilst industrialisation
grows in Malaysia'.[34] Tan Siew Sin was not enamoured with the reasoning of the
PAP top brass or the self-styled 'heirs of Raffles' in the SCC. He expressed his
concerns to Bank of England staff on a visit to London in May 1963: 'Singapore's
demand for a complete Customs Union at the same time as the continued maintenance of the Free Port was something which Malaya could not tolerate'. Tan
would be 'quite content' if Singapore introduced a 'bonded area for the Free Port'.
However, Tan accepted the reasoning of a Bank official that a 'high level of protection in Malaysia, quite apart from the undesirable effect on domestic costs . . .
with a Free Port nearby' would encourage 'a well organised smuggling system'.[35]
The prevailing dilemma remained, therefore. Not only would Singapore enjoy
advantages through cheap and plentiful labour but also from the import of raw
materials tariff-free followed by duty-free access to Malaysia for its manufactures
vis-à-vis mainland industries which consumed raw materials subject to Malayan
tariffs. The potential sucking of industrial investment southwards in Singapore's

'best of both worlds' scenario was appreciated not only by Federal Finance Minister Tan but also by the minister of commerce and industry in Kuala Lumpur, Lim Swee Aun, and his permanent secretary, Raja Mohar.[36] As early as August 1961 (three months after Malaya's prime minister, Tunku Abdul Rahman, made his first public announcement in favour of 'a political and economic cooperation'), Mohar told the UK's economic adviser in Kuala Lumpur that his ministers remained to be convinced that a common market with Singapore 'or indeed any other form of closer association offers them any economic advantage'. Rather, the MCI head stressed the economic risks for the Federation in any such association, including loss of new industrial investment to Singapore and potential reduction of revenue through the difficulty of securing an equitable distribution of duties collected at Singapore on imports for ultimate use or sale on the mainland.[37] Moreover, the Federation didn't have a particular need for the Singapore market in the way that Singapore coveted mainland Malaya's. The island's population was just 1.5 million compared to the Federation's seven million plus; Malaya already had duty-free access for its products into Singapore; and, the unstable and politicised labour scene in Singapore could act as a deterrent to pan-Malaysian industrialisation (particularly in the attraction of foreign investment).[38]

Indeed, Kuala Lumpur's ministers and mandarins were reluctant aggrandisers, viewing merger primarily in political and strategic terms. No longer able to rely on the British to do their dirty work for them, Alliance leaders latched on to 'Greater Malaysia' as a means of suppressing the so-called 'communist undertow' in Singapore, especially as Lee's moderate regime was threatened by the formation of the Barisan Sosialis. The Borneo Territories, meanwhile, would act as a safeguard against demographic domination of Malaysia by ethnic Chinese. Once the radical leftists had been imprisoned through Operation Coldstore in February 1963, Kuala Lumpur's focus turned to Singapore's economic and financial containment.[39] Far from integrating economic development with Singapore, the Alliance regime continued into the 1960s with strategies – such as developing a central bank, an international airport and stock and rubber exchanges in Kuala Lumpur and upgrading Port Swettenham (Klang) – which were aimed at making Malaya as economically autonomous as possible from the old colonial business capital.[40]

By November 1962, Lee received intelligence from an Australian businessman that Malaya had plans to keep Singapore out of the Malaysian common market altogether (but to include the Borneo Territories). The Alliance government agreed in the summer of 1961 to a visit from World Bank experts (known as the Rueff Mission) with specific terms of reference to advise on a customs union. Yet Singapore's finance minister experienced 'difficulties . . . with Tan Siew Sin in getting it agreed that the common market arrangements should be examined by the Rueff Mission', as Goh recited to a British official. The Federation 'was looking for ways to do down Singapore', Goh claimed, and Kuala Lumpur was 'not thinking in terms of the contribution that Singapore could make to the economy of Malaysia as a whole'.[41] The UK commissioner-general for Southeast Asia reported in January 1963: 'There is little evidence at present of co-operative economic planning between the Federation and the Singapore governments'. The trend was rather 'towards a jealous rivalry'. Fearing exclusion from the common market, the PAP government was 'embarking on a programme designed significantly to increase protection of their industries'. To aggravate matters, a minor economic war had broken out with the Federation placing a virtual ban on imports from Singapore of hatch-able eggs and day-old chicks. In retaliation, Singapore was not issuing licences for the import of foodstuff from Malaya.[42]

Shortly before the merger, the Rueff Mission recommended that priority be given to the establishment of a common market in Malaysia, permitting the free movement of goods internally with external tariffs set at the existing Malayan levels. The long-established entrepôt trades of Singapore and Penang could be preserved in special free-trade zones, and a policy of differential incentives might be implemented if excessive industrial concentrations developed.[43] Yet Lee's government had to engage in some hard bargaining to gain economic concessions in the merger terms. 'On a number of occasions [during 1963], the disagreements over financial arrangements threatened the progress towards Malaysia'.[44] In return for the Federation's assent to the 'progressive establishment' of a common market, Singapore agreed to surrender 40 per cent of its revenue to the central government in Kuala Lumpur; to allow the federal Ministry of Finance control over the approval of Singapore's pioneer industries; and, to provide a loan of M$150 million for the development of the Borneo states. Moreover, the Malaysia Agreement of July 1963 did not give Singapore unfettered access to the federal market and was vague on the longer-term preservation of Singapore's entrepôt trade.[45] Tan highlights that: 'Singapore's position as a possible site for the manufacture of materials imported at a cheaper rate by being free of duty was curtailed' in a key clause 'which provided that the common market provisions "shall not be construed to prevent the imposition . . . of any special tax on producers in a low-tariff state which would offset the cost inequalities arising from differential import duties" '.[46] Tan Siew Sin boasted to Charles Pow that he had achieved 'a favourable bargain with the Singapore government' and 'did not think they knew how much power they had given up to him'.[47]

Furthermore, once Singapore achieved decolonisation through becoming a state in the Malaysian federation in September 1963, the progressive establishment of the common market proved extremely progressive. A Tariff Advisory Board (TAB) was immediately established to advise the federal government on the establishment of a common market.[48] Chambers of commerce throughout the new Malaysia met several times and had 'fruitful discussions', 'delineating the problems' which would arise if free-port status was withdrawn (from Penang as well as Singapore). But, seven months into the creation of Malaysia, the chairman of the Penang chamber reported the 'unfortunate' situation whereby the services of a 'suitably qualified impartial Chairman' for the TAB had still not been secured. Only in August 1964 did Penang merchants finally meet with the TAB chairman. But he was vague: the common market would 'definitely' include Penang but 'the timing was not yet known'. Moreover, in a scenario which would not please Singapore, assurances were given that protective duties would be imposed 'gradually' but 'there were no such assurances in respect of revenue duties'.[49] Meanwhile, rather than thinking on a pan-Malaysian basis, there was a suspicion in PAP circles that Kuala Lumpur was poaching prospective industrialists from Singapore.[50] US intelligence gatherers wryly observed in December 1965 that there had been very little disruption to either Malaysian or Singapore economies post-separation precisely because 'only loose economic ties had been created in the federation'. Some harmonisation of taxes had been achieved but generally 'no effective steps had been taken to coordinate industrial policy or planning'. Rather, 'additional barriers' to intra-Malaysian trade in manufactures had been erected during 1964 and 1965 to protect local industries.[51]

Konfrontasi

Another source of economic tension between Singapore and Kuala Lumpur, as Hope noted in September 1965, was that *Konfrontasi* (Confrontation) with Indonesia hit Singapore's trade far more than the mainland's. Singaporean leaders believed that the loss was not taken fully into account in the policies of the federal government.[52] Political incorporation with Malaysia had immediate economic consequences out-of-kilter with the historical trajectory of Singapore's intra-Southeast Asian commercial linkages, especially with Indonesia (which had burgeoned in the Anglo-Dutch colonial era).[53] Indonesia-Singapore exchanges intensified after World War II and became even more significant following Indonesian independence in 1949: 'Most of Singapore's rubber came from outside Malaya' during the 1950s and 'the bulk of it from Indonesia'. Non-Malayan imports, four-fifths from Indonesia, were sufficient on their own 'to make Singapore easily the world's biggest primary rubber market'. Meantime, 'mainly reflecting Indonesian production, [Singapore's] traders dealt in half the world's pepper'.[54] A director of Maclaine Watson & Co., the long-established British merchant firm which had branches in both Jakarta and Singapore, stressed to Blue Funnel executives in December 1963 that 'the level of Singapore's trade with Indonesia since the war has been far larger than before the war'. That was down to three main factors: Indonesian foreign exchange regulations which encouraged smuggling and the barter trade (with Sumatra particularly); the decline in intra-archipelago shipping given the dislocations of the Japanese Occupation, anti-colonial insurgency and decolonisation; and, likewise, Indonesia's failure to recover its pre-war position in grading and re-milling rubber (which meant that the archipelago's producers, smallholders especially, had to rely upon processing in Singapore).[55] By 1963, the emporium handled about half of Indonesian rubber production, and the archipelago's coffee and spices were major features of Singapore's produce markets. Return exports to Indonesia of rice and manufactured goods (notably textiles and spare parts for automobiles and machinery) made another significant contribution to Singapore business life.[56]

Claiming that the creation of Malaysia was a 'neo-colonialist plot' designed to secure rubber, tin and oil supplies for 'the imperialists', President Sukarno announced a policy of severing all economic relations with Malaysia on 21

September 1963. As British diplomats appreciated, this was likely to hit Singapore much more than the rest of Malaysia, and the smaller-scale ethnic Chinese traders and processors in the port particularly.[57] In Malaya, Confrontation would affect import-export firms in Penang and Port Swettenham and would reduce the operations of the two tin smelters at Penang.[58] However, the general effect on the mainland economy was likely to be 'small' and could well be outweighed by a likely increase in commodity prices if Indonesian production faced obstacles reaching world markets. Indeed, principally a primary producer, Malaya benefited by filling the gap left by Indonesia's economic implosion in the aftermath of the sequestration of Netherlands assets and the expulsion of Dutch personnel from the end of 1957, which was only made worse by the Malaysia Confrontation.[59] At the height of the Indonesia-Malaysia estrangement in April 1965, the States of Malaya Chamber of Commerce reported that, overall, the Malayan mainland economy experienced a good year. The volume of trade increased by one per cent, rubber production reached a new record output approximating 818,000 tons and the number of tin mines in operation increased from 709 to 800.[60]

However, because Singapore remained principally an import-export and processing centre, British High Commission (BHC) staff predicted 'much more serious' consequences on the island than the mainland. Working on estimates given in the Rueff Report, BHC analysts calculated that the loss of Indonesian trade would mean a reduction in Singapore income of some £12–15 million per annum (or 5–6 per cent of GNP), resulting in a substantial loss of employment in rubber processing especially.[61] By November 1963, British business leaders reported to the BHC that Singapore's pre-boycott imports from Indonesia amounted to 30,000 tons per month of which 10,000 tons consisted of wet slab and dirty rubber which needed further processing in the port city. Present imports of (contraband) rubber were down to just 500 tons per month. The number of likely unemployed was put at 10,000. Coastal shipping between Singapore and Indonesia was 'dead' and there was 'no banking business with Indonesia'.[62]

The Singapore government's estimate of loss of income through *Konfrontasi* was considerably higher than the BHC's, suggesting that the total effect (including the cessation of exports to Indonesia) might be as much as £22–23 million per annum or 8–9 per cent of GNP.[63] A deeper impact was confirmed by British shipping representatives on the spot, predicting in December 1963 a drop of about 12 per cent (or 540,000 tons) annually in the total general cargo handled by the Singapore Harbour Board (SHB). The official estimate of Singapore's trade with Indonesia amounting to 8 per cent of state income was considered to be 'pitched quite low'. After vising Jakarta, an American shipping manager reported pessimistically that 'very little' of the Singapore-Indonesia trade would be revived. The Indonesian regime organised at least 20 small coastal companies to carry inter-island produce for export from the major ports of Java and Sumatra to substitute for Singapore. These firms were effectively government-subsidised through favourable freight rates given the importance attached to earning foreign exchange.[64] That negative view was confirmed by Maclaine Watson's visitors to Liverpool in December 1963. *Konfrontasi* was expected to be a 'long drawn out affair' in which Indonesia could permanently dispense with Singapore by 'putting [its] produce house in order' or by 'accept[ing] a discount on the prices [it] could formerly obtain via Singapore'. There was 'no reason', for example, 'why re-milling machinery, which is already available in Indonesia – although often in the wrong place – should not be satisfactorily brought into use'.[65] Indeed, the BHC in Kuala Lumpur had reported in November 1964 on a general belief in Malaysian business circles that Confrontation made Sukarno's regime 'determined to eliminate Singapore from [its] export pattern'. Indonesia had 'lost heavily in foreign exchange through using Singapore' and *Konfrontasi* now provided 'the opportunity for making a clean break'.[66] In March 1964 the UK's ambassador in Jakarta reported to the British taipans in Singapore that the slumping of Indonesia's economy 'to an unbelievably low level' had been largely 'due to the lacka-daisical handling of money matters' which had enabled Singapore merchants 'to take considerable advantage'. Jakarta could hardly be blamed for 'trying to pull [its] economy together and in so doing cut out the Singapore financial loophole'.[67] Albert Winsemius, the highly influential Dutch economic adviser to the PAP government (who features heavily in Loh's essay in this volume), noted in February 1966 that the 16,000 jobs created on the island in 1964 and 1965 through the growth of manufacturing were cancelled out by the loss of employment in rubber processing and the entrepôt trade due to Indonesia's embargo.[68]

In the short term, the state government took a more conciliatory line towards Indonesia than the federal regime in Kuala Lumpur. Disagreement revealed itself in the issue of exporting petroleum products from the Pladju refinery on Sumatra to Shell's installations on Pulau Bukom in Singapore harbour. By 1960, when oil refining commenced in Singapore, the island could claim to be one of the world's (and certainly Southeast Asia's) 'biggest oil storage, blending, packing and bunkering base'.[69] Of the £100 million worth of Indonesian exports to Malaysia as a whole in 1962, petroleum, virtually all handled in Singapore, was the fourth largest (after rubber, spices and tin ore).[70] When a Shell manager discussed his company's problems with Toh Chin Chye, Singapore's deputy prime minister (DPM), in October 1963, the latter 'indicated that the Singapore Government would like to seek ways and means by which trade might be opened up with Indonesia and to avoid any action which would help cut off Indonesia's dependence on Singapore as an entrepôt centre'. But Toh counselled that 'this would not necessarily be the Federal Government's view'. He was right. Lim Swee Aun 'made it quite clear [to Shell] that the Federal Government's policy [and Tunku's strategy especially] was to squeeze the economy of Indonesia as much as possible'. Continued use of Bukom 'would provide foreign exchange openings for Indonesia and would ensure that the Indonesian population continued to get their kerosene [in the return voyages by Shell's tankers]'. Kuala Lumpur persisted with this hard-line despite it being relatively straightforward for Pladju to switch to kerosene production, while making up foreign-exchange losses by shipping refined products direct to world markets, thus leading to Singapore permanently losing the Indonesian petroleum trade. Concurrently, Persian Gulf oils would need to be imported into Singapore in order to maintain the Bukom supply lines; an operation which was more costly than importing Sumatra's production.[71] Indeed, by the end of October, to keep Pladju operating at full tilt to satisfy its Indonesian host, Shell was shipping white oils to alternative ports in Southeast Asia (notably Bangkok) to the detriment of Singapore.[72]

By the end of 1963, however, Singapore's political leaders were pitching for full-scale economic warfare. That included the possibility of action against third countries, such as The Netherlands, which were deemed to be aiding and abetting Indonesia. But, as BHC staff appreciated, retaliation was likely to produce further discord between the central and Singapore Governments because of the 'serious effect' economic sanctions could have 'on the Malaysian economy as a whole' (and especially the primary-producing Malay peninsula). For example, the EEC might react to discrimination in Singapore against Dutch shipping by imposing a substantial import duty on natural rubber (still Malaya's major export), thus accelerating the movement towards the substitution of synthetic for natural rubber in Western Europe.[73] By April 1964, George Palmer Holt, a Blue Funnel director, found 'a strong inclination' in Singapore to 'Ganjang Indonesia' (Crush Indonesia) and 'conduct some sort of economic offensive against Indonesia' to match Sukarno's 'Ganjang Malaysia' campaign which had 'hit Singapore's trade' and was now 'manifesting itself in sporadic bomb explosions in which people [were] being killed'.[74] In March 1965, combining economic and military sabotage, an incendiary device was set off by two undercover Indonesian marines at HSBC's MacDonald House, causing massive damage to the first four floors of the 10-storey building and killing three people (including two bank staff).[75] This was the worst of the terror attacks on Singapore during *Konfrontasi*. Yet even before the HSBC incident Blue Funnel found the Singapore authorities scrutinising businesses known to be trading with Indonesia. Sight of vessel manifests of cargo destined for or loaded in Indonesia, for example, was demanded. DPM Toh, whose ministerial remit encompassed shipping, interrogated Holt in September 1964 about the Indonesian trade. Toh refrained from directly criticising Blue Funnel's continuing Indonesian activities, but the DPM expressed displeasure at the Dutch KPM (Koninklijke Paketvaart-Maatschappij), the former inter-island shipping provider whose ships were sequestered at the end of 1957, selling and chartering ships to Indonesia. A remark by President Charles de Gaulle about expanding French activity in the archipelago was also referred to 'disapprovingly'. Holt learned that Finance Minister Goh was even more gung-ho, having set up a special section, 'a kind of economic warfare department', to study Indonesia. It was feared that the PAP government might contemplate refusing admission to ships carrying cargo to or from the archipelago. But, as the BHC informed Holt, 'economic warfare was not at present a feature of K[uala] L[umpur] policy'.[76] Tunku remained opposed to a general embargo beyond restricting military stores and/or explosives.[77]

Aside from these differences on how to react to Confrontation, the loss of the Indonesian trade pushed Singapore's government into stepping up economic strategies liable to further inflame relations with Kuala Lumpur. In particular, that meant the attraction of new manufacturing industry 'to try and fill the employment gap', as Britain's trade commissioner in Kuala Lumpur reported in November 1963.[78]

Pow hit the nail on the head in noting that while pan-Malaysian finances were 'in good order' and the economy 'if not exactly booming can tick on very well', Singapore had 'a special finance problem arising from the trade embargo with Indonesia'. Looked at from Kuala Lumpur, however, that did 'not appear to be so serious'.[79] But Singapore's difficulties arising from the Indonesian downturn only served to focus PAP minds on the apparent inequities of the 60:40 division of revenues which, as Commercial Attaché Hope realised, became a growing concern in the merger years.[80] After all, Singapore's budget shortfall impaired its ability to pursue the PAP's $100 million industrialisation plan plus ambitious social initiatives, in housing especially, which reflected a more interventionist ideology on top of the more pressing unemployment problem compared to the rest of Malaysia.[81] Once the island was out of Malaysia, both British shipping agents and US intelligence analysts found Singaporean merchants eagerly anticipating the reignition of Indonesian trade.[82]

The future of the Singapore hub

The divergence between Malaysia and Singapore was manifest also in the role of Singapore as the de facto financial and commercial centre of the Malaysia region. On a Malayan tour in autumn 1962, Jake Saunders, chief manager of HSBC, found 'no doubt that the Federation Government intends to govern Malaysia strongly from Kuala Lumpur'. Tun Abdul Razak, Malaya's DPM, had said that 'Kuala Lumpur will be to Singapore as Washington to New York', and told Saunders that he foresaw 'a partnership between the two administrations'. But this was not the view held by 'many leading foreigners, who consider that the Government will control Singapore'. That didn't merely mean political and security matters; it extended to economic measures. '[U]ltra-left wing politicians would be removed for security reasons'. Concurrently, however, Bank Negara (Malaysia's central bank) would 'control its branches from Kuala Lumpur'.[83] As such, Singapore's fluidity and flexibility within the international financial system, and the sterling area particularly, were also threatened by the Malaysia merger. In August 1963, HSBC managers fretted over liquidity problems in Singapore with the imminent merger and the extension of Bank Negara powers to the island. The central bank would 'inevitably take an ever-increasing control over Government funds', and its assertive governor, Ismail Mohd Ali, had 'already referred to the needs for banks to reduce their balances abroad and invest more in Malaya and it may be difficult in the future to justify holding more than adequate working balances abroad'.[84] During November 1963, Saunders told Ismail that HSBC had 'lost ground' in budgeting for the anticipated liquidity squeeze, through adopting a very cautious approach to advances. Saunders had advised his Singapore manager that he 'could not see how the liquidity arrangements currently in force in the Federation could be imposed on Singapore unless a breathing space were allowed'.[85] In the same month, Pow expressed similar thoughts in an interview with Ismail, pointing out that 'after the Central Bank took over Singapore it would create a monetary stranglehold if we went on being required to provide 100 per cent cover for other banks' money'. Ismail was apparently 'interested but non-committal'.[86] By the end of 1964, Bank Negara was asking the exchange banks to meet the liquidity requirements of the mainland in Singapore, and this, as Hope in the BHC noted, created a shortage of bank money on the island.[87]

Concurrently, additional evidence of Kuala Lumpur's disregard for Singapore's wider financial and commercial interests was provided by Tan Siew Sin's unilateral decision to shut down the Bank of China on the island. An incensed S. Rajaratnam, the PAP minister of culture, believed that China's central bank was providing a 'useful' function in facilitating trade with mainland China. Yap Pheng Geck, vice-president of the Singapore Chinese Chamber of Commerce, was equally perplexed because, in the negotiations on the formation of Malaysia, 'there was an understanding between the Singapore and Malayan Governments that the bank [of China] could continue to function as long as it behaves'. Underlining intra-Malaysian tensions irrespective of race and political affiliation, Yap, a leader of the Singapore Alliance opposition to the PAP, found 'no justification' for a potentially provocative move that appeared to be politically rather than commercially driven: 'just because Indonesia is flirting with Communist China'. Revisiting the island's free-trade heritage which was now constrained by political union with the mainland, the president of the Singapore Manufacturers' Association, T.L. Whang, believed the closure 'unwise' because 'practically the whole world is advocating more trade among all nations' and Malaysia's security depended 'on our sound economic condition'. The island's trade with the People's Republic was 'purely commercial' and the Bank of China 'helped to stimulate economic activities in Singapore'.[88] Significantly, one of the first acts of Lee Kuan Yew's government after divorce from Malaysia in August 1965 was the reopening of the Beijing-controlled bank, and Blue Funnel personnel anticipated burgeoning trade between Singapore and mainland China.[89]

Suspicions surrounding Singapore's influence also abounded in service provision, especially in pan-Malaysian port development and coordination. In 1964, Malaysia's expat transport adviser, Sir Eric Millbourn, believed that SHB continued to oversee the efficient working of the emporium's port. Shipping companies and agents agreed. Provided there was 'no drastic political change', there was 'a very good chance' that the Port of Singapore Authority (PSA; due to supersede SHB during 1964) would maintain 'a high standard of efficiency'. Toh Chin Chye was regarded by Sir Eric as a 'practical, tough person who knows what is needed for Singapore'. Millbourn was less impressed with the situation at Port Swettenham, however, let alone Malaysia's Minister of Transport Sardon Jubir. If there was no improvement in congestion and delays at Port Swettenham, Sir Eric pointed out that the international lines would impose a surcharge on cargo. Meanwhile, from his vantage point in Singapore, Toh was taking an interest in Port Swettenham's affairs. SHB personnel were asked for comments on the North Klang Straits (NKS) expansion project (completed in May 1963 but the wharves only transferred from contractors to the Port Swettenham Authority in January 1964). '[L]ittle notice' seemed to have been taken of the Singaporean advice, however. It appeared to be 'the old story of Kuala Lumpur not liking Singapore'.

SHB members expressed the view that with the creation of Malaysia 'this non-sense should stop'; Singapore as Southeast Asia's premiere port 'should see that its efficiency and methods . . . spread to other ports in Malaysia'. '[P]etty jealous-ies' continued to exist at interdepartmental level, and SHB 'suggested that some effort should be made at an intergovernmental level to make better use of Singa-pore's efficiency and experience'.[90] Underlining how economic frustrations could spill over into personal sniping, the UK Ministry of Transport's representative in the Far East reported that when Millbourn put the 'whole blame' for inefficiencies at Port Swettenham on the general manager of the port authority, a nominee of Sardon's, Toh 'could not have been more pleased'.[91]

Rivalries between Singapore and Kuala Lumpur were similarly centre stage in the question of a national shipping line for Malaysia. Preceding the merger with Singapore, the original proposal, code-named 'Primrose', involved the Malayan government and a combination of the leading British shipowners in the UK-dominated Far East Freight Conference. The PAP government was kept informed of developments from October 1962.[92] By February 1964, however, there were serious doubts on the Singapore side about the desirability and viability of the project, especially as the island's business interests were excluded. Abu Bakar, permanent secretary to the Singapore Treasury, told Peter Gardner, the UK Min-istry of Transport representative, that a Malaysian ocean-going shipping line was 'too big a step forward . . . at the present time'; it was 'a wrongful employment of capital'.[93] By the end of 1964, the PAP government was supporting the views of a group of Singapore shipowners, facing the squeeze through exclusion from Indonesia and allegedly backed by the leading local and interconnected trading and banking syndicates on the island (Lee Rubber and the Oversea-Chinese Banking Corporation). 'Primrose' was dismissed by these Singapore Chinese interests as a 'second-class scheme' with a fleet of 'three old tubs'. Newer and faster vessels, more cheaply built in Japan and with better credit terms, would operate more efficiently and competitively, permitting profits from the outset rather 'some years hence'. Moreover, a line with 'more of a National character was required'.[94]

Here was a potential clash of Singapore and Federation Chinese interests since MCA senator and rubber grower-cum-trader, Gan Teck Yeow, was favoured by federal minister Sardon as a director of 'Primrose'. So enthused by the project, Gan offered to invest some of his own capital.[95] In October 1963, the British High Commissioner stressed that the MCA, with Tan Siew Sin and Lim Swee Aun as its ministers in the federal cabinet, feared 'encroachment by Singapore and Borneo on Malaya's wealth' especially if the interests of its core support amongst the Malayan Chinese towkay were threatened.[96] The Singapore separa-tion can be seen as product of a political struggle between the MCA and PAP for the pan-Malaysian Chinese vote, exacerbated by personality clashes between Tan Siew Sin and Lee Kuan Yew, in which Lee's decision to fight the 1964 elections (on a Malaysia-wide basis and not just in Singapore) was the 'straw that broke the camel's back'.[97] But the struggle between Malayan and Singapore Chinese for business opportunities also needs to be considered. As Gardner alerted Nicholson in February 1964, there were 'signs of increasing pressure by the Chinese interests on Sardon' and 'stories that the Chinese Ministers have got their eye on this particular portfolio'.[98]

What was certain by the end of 1964, however, was that the national line issue had 'been added to the list of subjects on which the Central Government and the Government of Singapore are voicing opposing views'. In this, Mansfields anticipated a scenario whereby, if the central government decided to proceed with 'Primrose', the conference could be faced with an application for membership from the Singapore shipowners 'with the very strong backing of the [PAP] Government'. It was rumoured that Abu Bakar would call a meeting of Singapore local shipping interests on how a national line 'could and should be organised'. If true, 'the atmosphere existing between Kuala Lumpur and Singapore on this subject is in a most explosive state'.[99] During February 1965, Mansfields was passed 'two most Secret papers' by Raja Mohar. These were counter-proposals to the 'Primrose' scheme from the Singapore Shipping Association and Guan Shipping for Goh's ministry. Mansfields subsequently passed on the confidential documents to Glen Line, the London-wing of Blue Funnel, to produce a paper for Mohar 'exploding' the Singaporean calculations and conclusions. Mohar insisted that 'any such paper produced for him should have no evidence of authorship'.[100] Such was the distrust inspired by the economic tensions of merger. By April 1965, the British shipping barons had intelligence that a Hong Kong-based group, said to be behind the Singaporean objections to 'Primrose', had put up a rival scheme. There was 'a danger' that the alternative plan would get the 'tacit agreement of the Singapore Government', provoking a 'head on clash' between Kuala Lumpur and Singapore.[101]

As conflict over the national line escalated in December 1964, Mansfields reported that Tan Siew Sin's recent budget proposals for payroll and turnover taxes were 'being fiercely criticised' by the Singapore government.[102] Nevertheless, these controversial levies were introduced by the federal government in January 1965, and, as Laurence Hope noted, they were liable to bear down more heavily on the balance sheets of Singapore-based businesses.[103] So much so that Washington's spooks reported post-split that the Singapore Chinese business community was 'gratified by the prospect' not only of 'reopening profitable commercial relations with Indonesia' but also by 'an end to federal taxes'.[104] Added to the list of disagreements on the commercial-cum-service side was Malaysia's international airport and the intra-Commonwealth telecommunications link (both of which Kuala Lumpur insisted should be sited on the mainland). In conversation with Blue Funnel's chief executive in September 1965, PSA's chairman 'spoke contemptuously, from personal experience' about the Malayan attitude on both issues.[105]

Conclusion: 'A Heart without a Body'?

'We inherited the island without a hinterland, a heart without a body', recalled Lee Kuan Yew of the situation facing his PAP government in August 1965.[106] There lay the rub, however. During the merger years, Kuala Lumpur had not accepted Singapore as the heart of Malaysia and regarded the island more as an extraneous limb. Moreover, as the discussion of *Konfrontasi* emphasises, Singapore served not only Malaysia but Indonesia as well, and indeed was economically connected to the wider Southeast Asian region. Singapore's time in Malaysia was contrary to the island's prevailing regional and global trajectory (as was the Japanese Occupation of 1942–1945 which Gregg and Gillian Huff highlight in a previous chapter in this volume).

According to British observers after Singapore's exit, Lee's judgement was 'clouded by excitement and exhaustion' and the prime minister was believed to be suffering from 'nervous insomnia'.[107] Yet Lee's mental state may have reflected elation rather than depression in his enlightenment about the new possibilities in Singapore's return to globalism. This was inherent in the export-oriented industrialisation (EOI) strategy announced by Goh at the end of 1965. As Loh points out, EOI had been anticipated as early as 1960–1961 in the UN mission led by Winsemius. The Dutch planner recommended that Singapore should manufacture 'for the world rather than the home market', and that Malaysia be just 'one of several regional export markets Singapore should cultivate'. In reiterating the importance of export-led growth after August 1965, Winsemius regarded separation as an opportunity, not a threat: 'the best day in Singapore we ever had', as he recalled in 1982.[108] PSA's chairman was down in the dumps in September 1965 (believing that Kuala Lumpur's plans to expedite the building of deep-water wharves at Butterworth [Penang] and to add at least three berths to Klang would 'probably destroy the case for four extra berths in Singapore').[109] But Singapore's new docks could be just as easily utilised for shipping manufactured goods out as raw materials and machinery in. Consequently, after 1966, 'no government anywhere was more aggressive in preparing for the container age than Singapore's' through embracing the cost advantages of the new shipping technology. The Republic's combination of containerisation and EOI shifted up a gear after 1968 with the UK's announcement of accelerated military withdrawal 'East of Suez'.[110] By 1973, a year after the first container vessels docked, British shipping interests noted that Singapore's aim was to become a 'World City'; a 'financial and communications centre, with a broad manufacturing base oriented towards exports to world markets [of] goods of high technological content'. Maintaining the openness of the Raffles inheritance, the 'offshore operations of multinational groups' would be 'strongly encouraged'.[111]

Continuities with the merger era persisted. Malaysia remained Singapore's largest trading partner in the early 1970s 'thanks to the large volume of exports there'. Even so, traditionally close economic ties were being eroded, evidenced in the end of parity between the two currencies in 1973.[112] Earlier, in 1971, OSSCo's chairman noted that the imminent break-up of Malaysia-Singapore Airlines reflected divergent interests: 'Singapore in its long haul trades on a purely commercial basis, Kuala Lumpur in Malaysian communications, partly on a social necessity basis'.[113] A 'somewhat prickly' relationship continued between Kuala Lumpur and Singapore. 'Neither wishes to be helpful to the other', reported Blue Funnel's strategists in 1973. Malaysia remained 'resentful of Singapore's ambition to be the economic and financial centre for South East Asia'.[114]

Notes

1 As well as at the 'Singapore 200' workshop, Liverpool John Moores University (LJMU), September 2018, earlier versions of this chapter were aired at the 'Regionalism, Federation and Supranational Community in the Era of Decolonisation' conference at the University of York in June 2017, and the History Department 'Brown Bag' Seminar, LJMU, March 2019. I am grateful to participants at these forums for their insights.
2 'Singapore and Malaysia Clash Over Water and High-Speed Rail Link,' *Asianews.it*, 10 July 2018, available at: www.asianews.it/news-en/Singapore-and-Malaysia-clash-over-water-and-high-speed-rail-link-44394.html, accessed 3 January 2019; Jason Koutsoukis and Anisah Shukry, 'Why Singapore and Malaysia are Locking Horns Again,' *Bloomberg.com*, 6 December 2018, available at: www.bloomberg.com/news/articles/2018-12-06/why-singapore-and-malaysia-are-locking-horns-again-quicktake, accessed 3 January 2019.
3 Harrisons & Crosfield (H&C) Archive, London Metropolitan Archives, 37612/8, speech to the Malaysian lower house reported in J.W.B. Annesley, Director, H&C (Malaysia) to London, 13 October 1966.
4 Mohd Noordin Sopiee, *From Malayan Union to Singapore Separation: Political Unification in the Malaysia Region, 1945–65*, Kuala Lumpur: Penerbit Universiti Malaya, 1976, pp. 187–232; R.S. Milne and D.K. Mauzy, *Politics and Government in Malaysia*, Vancouver: University of British Columbia Press, 1978, pp. 71–73; Albert Lau, *A Moment of Anguish: Singapore in Malaysia and the Politics of Disengagement*, Singapore: Times Academic Press, 1998; Matthew Jones, *Conflict and Confrontation in South East Asia, 1961–1965: Britain, the United States, Indonesia and the Creation of Malaysia*, Cambridge: Cambridge University Press, 2002, pp. 273–275; Tan Tai Yong, *Creating "Greater Malaysia": Decolonization and the Politics of Merger*, Singapore: Institute of Southeast Asian Studies, 2008, pp. 133–134, 194–197.
5 HSBC Group Archive, London (hereafter HSBC), MB Hist 1045, transcript of tape received from Mr. Pow in Kuala Lumpur, 25 November 1963.
6 Tim Bunnell, *From World City to World in One City: Liverpool Through Malay Lives*, Chichester: Wiley, 2016, pp. 33–35 and Bunnell's and Giacomin's chapters in this volume.
7 Ocean Archive, Merseyside Maritime Museum (hereafter OA), OA/JLA/20/1, Note by Nicholson, 4 October 1965.
8 Bank of England Archive, London (hereafter BoE), OV 65/23, note by Mays-Smith, 14 January 1959.
9 *Foreign Relations of the United States* (hereafter *FRUS*), *1961–1963*, XIII, 329, Memorandum, 17 February 1963, online version available at: https://history.state.gov/historicaldocuments/frus1961-63v23/d329.
10 OA/JLA/20/1, Note by Nicholson, 4 October 1965.
11 Michael Collins, 'Decolonisation and the "Federal Moment",' *Diplomacy & Statecraft*, vol. 24, 2013, pp. 21–40; Frederick Cooper, *Citizenship Between Empire and Nation: Remaking France and French Africa, 1945–1960*, Princeton, NJ: Princeton University Press, 2014; Spencer Mawby, *Ordering Independence: The End of Empire in the Anglophone Caribbean, 1947–69*, Basingstoke: Palgrave Macmillan, 2012; Chris Vaughan, 'The Politics of Regionalism and Federation in East Africa, 1958–1964,' *Historical Journal*, online version, 31 October 2018.
12 Vaughan, 'Politics,' pp. 16–17, 18.
13 Cohen, *Politics and Economics*, pp. 40–41, 48, 50–51.
14 The National Archives of the United Kingdom (hereafter TNA), CO 1030/993, Minute by Selwyn for Roberts, 6 July 1962.
15 BoE, OV 65/7, note by Parsons for Haslam and Hogg, 20 May 1963; note by Shilson, 16 July 1963.

16 Clive Christie, *A Modern History of Southeast Asia: Decolonization, Nationalism and Separatism*, London: Tauris, 1996.

17 TNA, FCO 141/7391/1, D.A. Mackay, Eastern Smelting Company to Malcolm Mac-Donald, Commissioner-General for the UK in Southeast Asia, 10 December 1948. Penang Chinese merchants concluded in May 1950 that: 'Economically Penang has lost a good deal of her mainland trade since she was linked to the Federation [of Malaya]' after February 1948. Additionally, Penang was given a budget which the merchants found 'inadequate for the development of this Settlement.' TNA, CO 717/204, memorandum submitted to the Secretary of State for the Colonies, 30 May 1950 reproduced in Christie, *Southeast Asia*, pp. 211–213. See also Mohd Noordin Sopiee, 'The Penang Secession Movement, 1948–51,' *Journal of Southeast Asian Studies*, vol. 4, no. 1, March 1973, pp. 54–55, 59, 60–61.

18 Nicholas J. White, *British Business in Post-Colonial Malaysia: 'Neo-Colonialism' or 'Disengagement'?* London: Routledge, 2004, pp. 85–86.

19 W.G. Huff, *The Economic Growth of Singapore: Trade and Development in the Twentieth Century*, Cambridge: Cambridge University Press, 1994, pp. 27–30, 309–310.

20 TNA, DO 189/553, Hope to Twist, Commonwealth Relations Office (CRO), 29 September 1965.

21 Lau, *Anguish*, pp. 10–13. In 1965, it was reckoned that the British military establishment accounted for 20–25 per cent of Singapore's GNP with the entrepôt trade and related activities making up 20–30 per cent and industrial production 14 per cent. *FRUS, 1964–1968*, XXVI, 270, Prospects for Malaysia and Singapore. National Intelligence Estimate, 16 December 1965, online version available at: https://history.state.gov/historicaldocuments/frus1964-68v26/d270.

22 TNA, DO 35/9864, note of meeting of 21 March 1960. On Singapore's interconnected demographic and employment issues, Loh explains: 'Between 1947 and 1957, as families settled down with multiple children instead of returning to their home countries, Singapore's population grew at a rapid rate of 4.5% per annum. These settled families and locally-born children could no longer be repatriated in an economic downturn, and the entrepôt trade would not likely supply the jobs they needed, especially as newly-independent states in the region began to develop their own ports and industries, bypassing Singapore.' Loh Kah Seng, 'Imaginaries of Jurong Industrial Estate, Singapore,' *International Institute of Asian Studies Newsletter*, vol. 81, Autumn 2018, p. 6.

23 TNA, DO 35/9864, Woodruff to Reynolds, 2 July 1959; Tory to Hunt, 6 January 1960.

24 Loh, 'Imaginaries,' p. 6.

25 TNA, DO 189/219, telegram to Secretary of State for the Colonies from Selkirk, Singapore, 18 January 1963.

26 Tan, *Greater Malaysia*, p. 135.

27 Ibid., p. 124.

28 The Barisan was not opposed to Malaysia per se but rejected the existing 'unequal' merger terms as they affected Singapore (in relation to internal security, citizenship and parliamentary representation). See Gareth Curless, '"The People Need Civil Liberties": Trade Unions and Contested Decolonisation in Singapore,' *Labor History*, vol. 51, no. 1, 2016, pp. 62–63.

29 'Economics of Merger,' *Straits Times*, 8 February.

30 Loh, 'Imaginaries,' p. 6.

31 Ibid., p. 7.

32 OA/JLA/BOX 30/3, Eric Price to Lindsay Alexander, 13 November 1963.

33 Lance Joseph to Secretary, Department of External Affairs, 26 March 1963 cited in Tan, *Greater Malaysia*, p. 135.

34 Singapore International Chamber of Commerce, Singapore (hereafter SICC), *SCC Annual Report 1962*, Chairman's Address, 29 March 1963, p. 40.

35 BoE, OV 65/7, note by Parsons, 20 May 1963.

36 Tan, *Greater Malaysia*, p. 136.
37 BoE, OV 65/7, telegram from Kuala Lumpur to CRO, 5 August 1961.
38 Tan, *Greater Malaysia*, p. 51.
39 Ibid., p. 124; Andrea Benvenuti, *Cold War and Decolonisation: Australia's Policy Towards Britain's End of Empire in Southeast Asia*, Singapore: NUS Press, 2017, pp. 189–190.
40 HSBC, Chief Manager's Private File: Singapore (Personal & S/O OUT), January 1957–December 1960, Knightly to Turner, 19 July 1960; Tan, *Greater Malaysia*, p. 51.
41 TNA, DO 189/219, Roberts, CO to Drysdale, CRO, 6 December 1962 enclosing note by Radford, UK Commission in Southeast Asia, 26 November 1962.
42 TNA, PRO, DO 189/219, telegram to Colonial Secretary, 18 January 1963.
43 See Drabble, *Economic History*, pp. 176–177.
44 Tan, *Greater Malaysia*, p. 123.
45 Ibid., pp. 142–144.
46 Ibid., p. 142.
47 HSBC, MB Hist 1045, Pow tape, 25 November 1963. Tan would later oppose Tunku's plans from December 1964 for a looser federation which would have involved much greater economic and fiscal autonomy for Singapore. Lau, *Anguish*, pp. 225, 291.
48 TNA, DO 189/220, *Federation of Malaya Government Gazette*, 12 September 1963.
49 Arkib Negara Malaysia (hereafter ANM), AE/99/M, Penang Chamber of Commerce Minute Book (hereafter PCCMB), 1964–1972, Chairman's Speech at AGM, 10 April 1964, p. 3; minutes of a meeting of the committee of the PCC, 15 September 1964. Six months before the creation of Malaysia, the chairman of the Singapore Chamber of Commerce had stated that it was 'essential that maximum free port status is maintained for Singapore whilst industrialisation grows in Malaysia.' SICC, *SCC Annual Report*, Chairman's Address, 29 March 1963, p. 40.
50 TNA, DO 189/553, Hope to Twist, 29 September 1965.
51 National Intelligence Estimate, 16 December 1965.
52 TNA, DO 189/553, Hope to Twist, 29 September 1965.
53 Huff, *Singapore*, pp. 27–28, 51, 54–56, 84–86, 118 and the chapters by Giacomin and Kawamura in this volume.
54 Huff, *Singapore*, pp. 279–281.
55 OA/JLA/14/2, Alexander to Smyth, Mansfields, 10 December 1963. On Maclaine Watson see G. Roger Knight, *Trade and Empire in Early Nineteenth Century Southeast Asia: Gillian Maclaine and His Business Network*, Woodbridge: Boydell, 2013 and Knight's chapter in this collection.
56 TNA, DO 169/82, telegram to CRO, 23 September 1963.
57 TNA, DO 189/220, savingram from Deputy High Commissioner, Singapore to High Commissioner, Kuala Lumpur, 27 September 1963. Singapore Summary, 17–25 September 1963, p. 5.
58 TNA, DO 169/82, telegram to CRO, 23 September 1963. The chairman of the Penang Chamber of Commerce reported in April 1964 that Indonesian Confrontation had a 'distressing effect on the economy of Malayan entrepôt centres and Penang has not escaped scot-free,' particularly regarding the barter trade. ANM, AE/99/M, PCCMB, 1964–72, Chairman's Speech, 10 April 1964, p. 4.
59 Nicholas J. White, 'The Settlement of Decolonization and Post-Colonial Economic Development: Indonesia, Malaysia, and Singapore Compared,' *Bijdragen tot de taal-, Land- en Volkenkunde*, vol. 173, 2017, pp. 208–241, citation at 229–231.
60 ANM, AE/97/A, *States of Malaya Chamber of Commerce Yearbook 1964*, President's Address, 28 April 1965, pp. 9–10.
61 TNA, DO 169/82, telegram to CRO, 23 September 1963.
62 TNA, DO 169/82, note of a meeting with the economic panel of representatives of the British business community, 7 November 1963.
63 TNA, DO 169/82, telegram to CRO, 28 September 1963.
64 OA/JLA/14/2, Smyth to Alexander, 6 December 1963.

65 OA/JLA/14/2, Alexander to Smyth, 10 December 1963.
66 TNA, DO 169/82, telegram to CRO, 23 November 1963.
67 OA/JLA/14/2, Smyth to Alexander, 12 March 1964.
68 Loh Kah Seng, 'Albert Winsemius and the Transnational Origins of High Modernist Governance in Singapore,' in Lily Zubaidah Rahim and Michael D. Barr (eds.), *The Limits of Authoritarian Governance in Singapore's Developmental State*, Basingstoke: Palgrave Macmillan, 2019, p. 82.
69 Huff, *Singapore*, p. 279.
70 DO 169/82, telegram to CRO, 23 September 1963.
71 TNA, DO 169/82, Newns, British Trade Commission, Singapore to Cross, Senior British Trade Commissioner, Malaysia, 17 October 1963.
72 TNA, DO 169/82, telegram to CRO, 29 October 1963.
73 TNA, DO 169/82, Bottomley to Moore, 17 December 1963. With the settling of the Irian Jaya dispute between The Hague and Jakarta, the smelting of Indonesian tin was resumed in the Netherlands as per the position pre-1957. That resulted in a reduction by one quarter in pan-Malaysian ore throughput, including at Singapore's Pulau Brani plant. DO 169/82, telegram to CRO, 28 September 1963. In February 1965, copra, tea and timber shipments from Indonesia to the Netherlands recommenced. White, 'Settlement,' p. 230.
74 OA/JLA/14/2, note by Holt, 23 April 1964.
75 'Terror Bomb Kills 2 Girls at Bank,' Straits Times, 11 March 1965, p. 1; 'MacDonald House Bombing Occurs,' *HistorySG online*, 10 March 1965, available at: http://eresources.nlb.gov.sg/history/events/73fb133a-828a-4240-9801-421d7077369f, accessed 18 January 2019.
76 OA/JLA/14/2, note by Holt, 23 April 1964.
77 OA/JLA/14/2, note by Nicholson on Malaya-Ceylon visit, 2–6 November 1964; OA/JLA/BOX 20/1, note by Nicholson for Alexander, 12 November 1964.
78 DO 169/82, Sutton, British Trade Commissioner, Kuala Lumpur to Drysdale, 26 November 1963.
79 HSBC, MB Hist 1045, Pow tape, 25 November 1963.
80 TNA, DO 189/553, Hope to Twist, 29 September 1965.
81 Tan, *Greater Malaysia*, p. 127. Public housing, receiving 43 per cent of the $350 million social services budget in Goh's development plan, was central to the industrialisation push; socialising squatters and slum-dwellers as homeowners to 'become the incentivised [factory] workforce.' The Housing and Development Board blocks were also 'a visible sign of progress, proof to multinationals that Singapore was not "going down the drain".' Loh, 'Winsemius,' pp. 80–81.
82 OA/2116, Smyth to McNeill, Glen Line, 10 August 1965; National Intelligence Estimate, 16 December 1965.
83 HSBC, J.A.H. Saunders. Singapore Private, 1962–6, 'Malayan Tour, 24 October–8 November 1962,' note of 13 November 1962.
84 HSBC, J.A.H. Saunders. Singapore Private, 1962–6, Oliphant to Stubbs, Singapore, 16 August 1963 and attached note.
85 HSBC, J.A.H. Saunders. Singapore Private, 1962–6, draft note by Saunders, November 1963.
86 HSBC, MB Hist 2045, Pow tape, 22 November 1963.
87 TNA, DO 189/553, Hope to Twist, 29 September 1965.
88 'S'pore Govt Opposes Closure of Bank,' *Straits Times*, 31 December 1964, p. 16; Lau, *Anguish*, p. 217.
89 'Malaysia and Singapore: Hunt the Scoundrel,' *Economist*, 21 August 1965, pp. 684–685; OA/2116, Smyth to McNeill, 11 August 1965.
90 OA/JLA/14/2, Smyth to Alexander, 8 February 1964; *Port Klang: Malaysia's Maritime Marvel*, Port Klang Authority, 2011, pp. 50, 52, 55, available at: https://issuu.com/wildage/docs/coffee_book_20110303_, accessed 22 January 2019.

91   OA/2116, Gardner to Nicholson, 28 February 1964. Even before merger, in the course of 1961–2, the PAP regime oversaw the introduction of a more efficient, centralised system of personnel management in the Singapore docks, taking power away from the labour gangs and instituting the recommendations of a 1957 commission of inquiry which had been headed by Millbourn. Gareth Curless, 'The Triumph of the State: Singapore's Dockworkers and the Limits of Global History, c. 1920–1965,' *Historical Journal*, vol. 60, no. 4, December 2017, pp. 1121–1122. In contrast, still under the control of the Malayan Railways to July 1963, Port Swettenham was adversely affected by a strike of railway workers in December 1962 (because the port labourers remained members of the railway union). Into the mid-1970s, Port Klang 'continued to be the target of constant criticism due to frequent delays in loading and unloading cargo.' *Port Klang*, pp. 50, 54, 69.

92   OA/2116 'Summary' in Smyth to Nicholson, 22 April 1964.

93   OA/2116, Gardner to Nicholson, 28 February 1964.

94   OA/2116, Smyth, Mansfields to McNeill, 2 December 1964.

95   OA/2116, 'Summary'; note by McNeill, December 1963.

96   Tory to Commonwealth Secretary, 31 October 1963 cited in Tan, *Greater Malaysia*, p. 128.

97   Tan, *Greater Malaysia*, pp. 133–134, 195.

98   OA/2116, Gardner to Nicholson, 28 February 1964.

99   OA/2116, Smyth to McNeill, 4 December 1964.

100 OA/2116, Gardner, Kuala Lumpur to McNeill, 1 February 1965.

101 OA/2116, McNeill to Nicholson, 1 March 1965; Memorandum enclosed in Sir Douglas Thomson, WM. Thomson & Co (Ben Line), Edinburgh to McNeill, 6 April 1965.

102 OA/2116, Smyth to McNeill, 4 December 1964.

103 TNA, DO 189/553, Hope to Twist, 29 September 1965.

104 National Intelligence Estimate, 16 December 1965.

105 OA/JLA/20/1, note by Nicholson, 4 October 1965.

106 Lee Kuan Yew, *From Third World to First: The Singapore Story: 1965–2000*, Singapore: Marshall Cavendish, 2000, p. 19.

107 OA/JLA/20/1, note by Nicholson, 4 October 1965.

108 Loh, 'Imaginaries,' p. 7; Loh 'Winsemius,' pp. 79–80, 82–83; see also Loh's essay in this collection.

109 OA/JLA/20/1, note by Nicholson, 4 October 1965.

110 Marc Levinson, *The Box: How the Shipping Container Made the World Smaller and the World Economy Bigger*, Princeton, NJ: Princeton University Press, 2006, pp. 209–211.

111 OA/862, board memorandum, 20 August 1973, Appendix 5 enclosed in note by Alexander, 24 August 1973. The international spread of investment, however, would be much wider than under colonial rule given the PAP's desire to avoid dependency upon one source (combined with the poor performance of the UK economy).

112 OA/862, Appendix 5 and 6.

113 OA/JLA/22/3, note by Alexander for directors, 12 February 1971.

114 OA/862, Appendix 5.

Part II

Singapore – politics, culture & identity

8 Singapore, the Straits Settlements & the politics of imperial commerce, 1819–1867

Anthony Webster

The success of Singapore as a trading centre is a central theme in this volume. The rapid growth of the port's trade after 1819 is well known, as is the material base of its success in the first half of the nineteenth century: as an entrepôt collecting Malay produce for the China market, and as an outlet for Indian and British manufactures such as opium and cotton piece goods. The role of European merchants and Chinese merchants and labour in the success of the port has also been identified by historians, facilitating in due course an expansion from trade into tin production on the Malay peninsula, and ensuring the long-term development of Singapore as a major centre of commerce in Asia by the beginning of the twentieth century.[1]

This chapter is concerned with the political dimension of Singapore's success; namely, the emergence within the Straits Settlements of a political system and culture which enabled effective collaboration between the various ethnicities within them. This provided the settlements with a strong voice in political affairs for the interests of commerce which afforded protection to all those crucial to their economic success – especially Singapore. The argument presented here reinforces those offered by Neal and Kawamura, that Singapore and the Straits Settlements offered a unique commercial, sociological and political template for the governance of empire. Neal outlines the way in which Singapore became an exemplar for the management of a large migrant Chinese population which other colonial administrations in India, Australia and the West Indies would seek to follow.[2] Kawamura shows how Singapore and the Straits Settlements were pivotal in attracting the British Eastern Exchange Banks, whose activities helped forge a distinctive Anglo-Dutch dominated commercial regional order in the late nineteenth century.[3] It is further argued that the longer-term success of Singapore into the twentieth century, and the prominence of British Malaya as one of the most commercially successful colonies, based on tin and rubber, to a large degree was based upon the development in the early and mid-nineteenth century of a highly effective commercial lobby and a political system which protected its interests. Neal's work especially underpins how Singapore and the Straits Settlements came to be seen not only as a unique system of imperial governance but also one from which certain aspects could be transferred to other imperial contexts. It will be seen that an important factor in this was the effectiveness of commercial interests in Singapore and the Straits in proselytising about their system through some formidable links in the UK. A recent PhD thesis demonstrates, for example, that the China Association, a British- and Chinese-based cultural, political and commercial pressure group set up in the late nineteenth century, was consciously founded to imitate the Straits Association, a British-based pressure group established at the end of the 1860s to represent interests in the Straits Settlements in the UK.[4]

The next section will outline the development of imperial governance in the Straits Settlements during the period, describing how a unified system of government and political culture was fashioned from the very different British and Dutch colonial administrations of Penang and Malacca, and the new experiment in imperial administration unfolding on Singapore. It will be seen that this was a process interrupted and shaped by wider imperial developments, including the financial crises of 1830–34 and 1847–48, the termination of the East India Company's commercial role and monopoly of the China trade in 1833, British victory in the two wars in China of 1839–42 and 1858–60, the opening of Siam to British commerce in the 1850s, as well as the historic shift of colonial administration from the India Office to the Colonial Office in the wake of the India Rebellion of 1857 and the winding up of Company rule in the decade that followed. The third section of the chapter will then identify and explore the various factors which meant that commercial interests came to dominate the political system and were able to dictate key British colonial policies in the region. The final section will then evaluate the implications of this emergent system of governance for both wider British imperial policy, and for the subsequent trajectory of British rule and influence in Southeast Asia – especially in respect of the growing importance of Singapore.

The evolution of government in the Straits Settlements

To understand the evolution of governance in what became the Straits Settlements, it is essential to grasp that the three settlements of Penang, Melaka and Singapore were created at different times, by different national organisations and for subtly different purposes. Melaka, the oldest, had a very long history as a major commercial centre which reached back into the Middle Ages, after which it was conquered, first by the Portuguese in 1511 and then the Dutch in 1641.[5] It had accommodated Malays, Europeans and Chinese settlers for centuries, and as a result saw a high degree of intermarriage and cross-ethnic collaborations in commerce. It was a settled and stable community, dominated by its predominantly Dutch European settlers and administrators, which even boasted its own banking system based on the charitable organisation, the Orphan Chamber (Weeskammer).[6] Melaka town had experienced substantial population growth, rising from 7,216 in 1766 to 19,647 in 1817, though then falling to 11,180 in 1824 as the rapid growth of Singapore attracted people south.[7] It had a small but long-standing Chinese population of between 1,000 and 2,000, and the European population was always very small.

Penang was a far more recent creation, founded on the authority of the East India Company by the British private merchant Francis Light in 1786. It developed very quickly, and its population grew rapidly as Chinese, Malays and Europeans flooded onto the island. In 1788, Penang town's (Georgetown's) total population was 1,283, with the Chinese and the Malays constituting about 41 per cent each of the population and Europeans making up just 1.48 per cent. By 1810, the town's population had risen to 13,855, with the Chinese constituting about 37 per cent of the population, the Malays just 15 per cent, and Bengalis and Chuliahs forming 40 per cent of the population. Twelve years later, the population had fallen slightly to 13,781, and the Chinese portion had fallen to just 24 per cent, with the Bengalis and Chuliahs roughly staying the same.[8] The loss of population – especially of the Chinese – again probably reflected the attractiveness of Singapore as a more profitable location. Unlike Melaka, Penang was a far more turbulent and less orderly place. Rapid inward migration resulted in a much more ethnically segregated town and island, leading to conflict and tensions, even within specific communities such as the Chinese.[9] In addition, from the earliest days, successive administrations on the island enjoyed little support from the East India Company.[10] It was not until 1805 that the importance of the trade between India and China for the Company, involving exports of opium and Malay produce to China to finance lucrative exports of tea from China to Britain, led to Penang being granted Presidency status, and the establishment of a Court of Judicature there two years later.[11]

The material, political and social differences between the two settlements, as well as the imperial rivalry stemming from the respective dominance of the British and Dutch at Penang and Melaka, meant that between the establishment of Penang and the seizure of Melaka in 1795, there was a relationship of commercial rivalry bordering on hostility between the two settlements. The common perception was that the two settlements were competing to attract the Malay traders needed for commercial prosperity. The outbreak of the Napoleonic Wars in Europe in 1793 dramatically changed the relations between the British and the Dutch in Southeast Asia, with fateful consequences for the relationship between, and the standing of, Penang and Melaka. Fearful that Dutch Southeast Asian possessions might fall into French hands, in 1795 the British seized Melaka and the Maluku islands, a step followed in 1811 by the seizure of Java and its occupation under the leadership of Thomas Stamford Raffles until the end of the war in 1815. Strenuous efforts with only limited success were made by the Penang administration in the years that followed to divert Melaka's trade to Penang, and when Robert Townsend Farquhar was appointed governor of Penang he strongly advocated the destruction of Melaka, with a view to establishing a more central British outpost at Balambangan.[12] The authorities in both Calcutta and London agreed to the reduction of Melaka, but a memorandum in 1808 from Thomas Stamford Raffles, then seconded to Melaka, showed not only that the port had become valuable to British commerce but that Penang actually depended upon the transhipment at Melaka of commodities such as tin from the island of Bangka bound for the British port. As a result, Melaka was allowed to continue, albeit with the imposition of tariffs on trade there to try to persuade as much trade as possible to be redirected to Penang.[13]

However, it was the ending of the Napoleonic Wars in 1815 which precipitated a major upheaval in European geopolitical relations in Southeast Asia, and with it effectively creating the Straits Settlements. The initial British policy at the end of the war was to return all Dutch possessions that had been occupied in order to re-establish an economically strong Dutch state able to act as a buffer against any future French expansionism in Northern Europe. As a result, Melaka, the Maluku islands and Java were all restored to the Netherlands by 1818. But among merchants and East India Company administrators in Asia there were deep concerns about the prospect of the return of a protectionist Dutch regime in Southeast Asia which was likely to try to roll back the advances British commerce had made in the region during the period of British occupation. The opening of the Indian market to free trade from Britain by the Charter Act of 1813 had intensified competition for British private trade interests in Asia, as a new breed of trader came out from Britain to take advantage of the new trading opportunities in Asia. By 1818/1819, there was a glut of shipping and both British and Indian produce in the ports of India, and there was a real possibility of a major economic downturn. The prospect of the closure of parts of the Southeast Asian market by the Dutch and potential new impediments to trade between India and China threatened to intensify the impending economic crisis in India. Francis Rawdon, the Marquis of Hastings and governor general of India, was sufficiently alarmed by this danger that in November 1818 he despatched Raffles to establish a new, central port in the Malay Archipelago which could preserve access to the region for British trade. The result, of course, was the establishment of Singapore in 1819, and the beginning of a major dispute between the British and Dutch over the legality of the settlement, during which the port grew rapidly in terms of volume of trade and population. The outcome was negotiations leading to the Treaty of London of 1824, which divided the region into respective British and Dutch spheres of influence. Territory north of the Straits of Melaka, including the Malay Peninsula, was deemed to be the British sphere, and all south and west (including the island of Sumatra) formed part of the Dutch sphere. There was also an exchange of possessions, with the British abandoning to the Dutch the port of Bengkulu on Sumatra and its subsidiary outposts, and acquiring Melaka as a permanent possession. Crucially, Singapore was recognised as a British port, and in 1826, Penang, Melaka and Singapore were designated as the Straits Settlements. Notwithstanding the rapid growth of Singapore, Penang was still named as the seat of government for the Straits Settlements, with full presidential and legal authority over the other two settlements.[14] Turnbull shows that in the late 1820s, there were efforts by the Penang administration to use taxation and tariffs to curb the growth of Singapore, which it saw as a threat to Penang's leadership. But these were refused by the authorities in Calcutta and London, who wanted to keep trade duties as low as possible. This not only frustrated the Penang's administration's determination to assert its authority over the other settlements but also limited its ability to meet the growing costs of government, which were especially onerous for Penang itself.[15]

Moreover, Penang did not retain this status for long. By the end of the 1820s, a deepening financial crisis in India, caused partly by the ruinously expensive war with Burma between 1824 and 1826, was forcing the Company to implement dramatic spending cuts. The upshot has been described as a 'double humiliation' for the Penang administration: the ending of its Presidency status and its demotion, along with the other Straits Settlements, to Residency status subject to the direct authority of Calcutta, and the removal of the Straits Settlements administration to Singapore, with the Resident and Assistant Resident being located there.[16]

The next major development which was to affect the governance of the Straits Settlements occurred in India and London rather than in Southeast Asia. The looming financial crisis erupted in 1830, with the failure of John Palmer & Co., the leading agency house in Calcutta, which was merely a foretaste of the chain reaction of financial insolvencies which wiped out the rest of the Bengal agency houses by 1834.[17] The political fallout was even more dramatic. Under the Charter Act of 1833, The East India Company not only lost its monopoly of trade to China but also ceased to be a trading organisation, with its new role essentially being confined to administering on behalf of the British state the possessions it had accumulated.[18] As will be seen, the changes had important consequences for perceptions in the Straits Settlements. By the mid-1830s, there was a move among merchants in the Straits, as there was across many of the British colonial cities of Asia (Calcutta, Madras, Bombay, Rangoon) to form Chambers of Commerce to ensure that their interests would be adequately defended during a period of radical political change in the governance of British possessions in Asia.[19] This was in response to a range of concerns, including piracy and its impact upon the Asian trade upon which the Straits Settlements depended, plans by the Calcutta administration to impose duties on Singapore, and Dutch efforts to restrict British trade with their Southeast Asian possessions.[20] Moreover, as will be seen, the Straits merchants worked closely with trade organisations in Britain in pursuit of their objectives. In the following decades the Straits chambers would become pivotal in the assertion of commercial interests and opinion in the formation of policy in the Straits. Other mouthpieces for commerce also emerged. Before the creation of the Chambers, the Grand Jury operated as an important mouthpiece for mercantile opinion. Local newspapers were established such as the *Singapore Free Press* (1835) and the *Straits Times* (1845).[21]

The Chinese were also becoming vocal politically. As the population of the Chinese grew first in the Straits, and from the 1840s on the Malay peninsula with the development of tin production, they also began to organise. There were Chinese representatives on the first executive committee of the Chamber.[22] In addition, as the numbers of Chinese migrants into the Straits increased, the influence of internal Chinese organisations became more important in securing order within and cooperation with the European authorities. Ethnically based clans known as *kongsis* became more important for organising Chinese society throughout the Straits.[23] Neal's chapter in this volume provides evidence of how prominent Chinese merchants, such as Seah Eu Chin, were able to exert real political influence. British and European attitudes to the Chinese, as Neal's chapter shows, were racially stereotyped, complex and contradictory. On the one hand, the Chinese were regarded as treacherous, comically superstitious and volatile, the last being regarded as a cause of alarm given the sporadic problems of rioting and disorder in the Straits.[24] From this perspective, the Chinese were figures of contempt, though also ones to be feared. But, on the other hand, while recognised for their industry and entrepreneurial flair, the Chinese were also essential to both private commercial interests and the funding of the government of the Straits. Chinese *towkays* acted as intermediaries through whom trade with local merchants was conducted, while Chinese entrepreneurs ran sugar, gambier and pepper plantations, especially on Penang and Province Wellesley.[25] In due course, with the growing importance of tin mining, both Chinese merchants and labour became indispensable.[26] Even more important was the role that the Chinese played in the financing of government. A huge proportion of government income was raised through 'revenue farming' under the Straits government, which sold exclusive rights to syndicates of Chinese merchants to sell certain commodities to the public. The most lucrative of these were the opium farms, which conferred the exclusive right to retail the drug in the various Straits Settlements.[27] The upshot was that, notwithstanding endemic racial prejudice amongst the British ruling minority and the European population, the commercial interests of the Chinese were too important not to be defended. Hollen Lees shows how a peculiar and wider notion of 'Britishness' developed which incorporated the need to defend Chinese as imperial subjects, notwithstanding the sharp divisions which tended to characterise social relations between the Europeans and Chinese. This in part contributed to the adoption of a kind of 'dual identity' by the Chinese mercantile elite, who in their relations with their European rulers were careful to adopt behaviours which rendered them more palatable to Western sensibilities.[28] Herein lies an important point about one of the key factors in Singapore's success. Recent work in the field of regional studies indicates that an important element in many thriving business and entrepreneurial regions and locations is ethnic diversity with certain crucial characteristics. These include the transplantation of migrant community organisations, structures and institutions into the host location, creating 'Communities on the Move' (CoM).[29] CoM facilitate numerous advantages for their migrant populations, including transnational or even global links with the 'home' culture and business communities, enabling trade links as well as transmission of capital, expertise and specialist labour plus institutions able to mediate with the host governing and business structures in ways that enable the migrant population to succeed economically and achieve acceptance on the basis of their contribution to the wider economic and social success of the host. CoM also frequently are able to act as mediators between the host's elite and other migrant groups. The mass relocation of the Chinese to Singapore in the 1820s from ports such as Melaka were striking examples of CoM, and were essential not only in facilitating the later mass migration of the Chinese into Singapore, the Straits Settlements and Malaya but also in developing through an intermediary role commercial relations between the British merchants and the Malays. The Kongsis, as well as Chinese representation on the Grand Jury and Chambers of Commerce, were all key to ensuring a stable relationship with the 'host' British imperial elite and enabling key revenue structures such as the opium and other commodity farms. They facilitated political alliances between

European and Chinese commercial merchants, effectively trumping racism (at least in the field of commercial politics).

For the next 30 years, the development of governance and political culture in the Straits Settlements reflected this striving by the commercial elite to assert themselves and dictate policy. As will be seen, it was fuelled in part by frustration at what were perceived as policies imposed by the East India Company administration in Calcutta which were inappropriate for, and even harmful to, the long-term interests of the Straits Settlements and their commercial interests. It also, as has been argued elsewhere, helped forge a collective identity for Straits interests, together with a sense of the uniqueness of Southeast Asia as a region, overcoming the differences and squabbles between the Straits Settlements communities which had characterised the early decades of the nineteenth century.[30] Further political changes in the 1850s served to reinforce this sense of neglect by the British authorities in India, notably, the passing of control over the Straits Settlements from the Bengal presidency to the governor general of India in 1851, which seemed to suggest even greater remoteness from the needs of the Straits. As Kobayashi's chapter in this volume demonstrates, this sense of disengagement with India was reinforced by the declining importance of Indian cotton good exports to Southeast Asia from the 1840s onwards. By the mid-1850s, growing disenchantment with Company rule led to a campaign by the Singapore merchants and the *Singapore Free Press* for the Straits Settlements to be given Crown Colony status.[31] This was eventually successful in 1867, and shortly after the establishment of a new government and the appointment of Sir Harry Ord as the first governor of the Crown Colony, the Straits Settlements Association was formed in London by retired Straits merchants and by long-standing allies such as John Crawfurd, in direct response to, and rejection of, a tentative suggestion by Ord that customs duties might have to be introduced to pay for the costs of administration. The idea was quickly disowned.[32]

What emerged by the end of the 1860s was not merely a new position for the Straits Settlements within the British Empire but a political culture within which commercial interests had achieved a position of political dominance. This would prove to be pivotal in the long-term economic success of the British in Malaya, as the hegemony of commercial interests would be critical in the success of a range of policies and activities later in the century, including the development of the tin and rubber industries, and the pursuit of infrastructure projects which assisted that process, such as investment in roads, railways and docks. As Neal's forthcoming book and Kawamura's chapter show, in many respects Singapore and the Straits Settlements more generally came to be seen as an exemplar of imperial management of key economic issues, such as the provision of labour supplies and the facilitation of effective banking and financial services.[33] In addition, they were also an example of how commercial interests, by organising effectively in Britain as well as at the periphery of empire, could shape the political culture and systems of governance in ways which were distinctly favourable for economic growth and profitable business activity, especially through the development of regional and international networks which enabled business to flourish. This was certainly an important factor in the longer-term success of Singapore, the central focus of this book, but the networks and commercial infrastructure created enabled the Southeast Asian region to establish innovative and successful global leadership in new commercial fields. For example, in the early twentieth century the region eclipsed West Africa in the production of palm oil.[34] How and why did this commercial political dominance arise in what, in the first three decades of the nineteenth century, had been three settlements regarded as peripheral to the needs of the British Empire and the East India Company, and which were frequently at odds with each other?

The growth of commercial hegemony in the Straits Settlements

A striking feature of the rise of the commercial lobbies in the Straits Settlements, and the consolidation of their relative unity, was the growth of a common conviction that the East India Company not only was uninterested in the fortunes of the Straits' interests but was also actively at loggerheads with them on a range of policies. This section will identify those policies, but it is important first to consider the changing role of the East India Company during this period and its implications for policy towards the Straits and Southeast Asia generally. Recent research has offered new perspectives on the evolving role of British India in respect of wider British imperial policy in the nineteenth century. Washbrook contends that during the middle and later nineteenth century British governments in India increasingly became a vehicle for administering a wider imperial policy rather than merely governing India. They furnished the soldiers needed to fight imperial wars, labour supplies for such imperial assets as the rubber industry in Malaya from the 1890s, commodities such as opium which was crucial to trade in China and Southeast Asia and cotton as an alternative supply for British industry to the USA. It was this wider role which dictated British policy in India rather than the specific interests of India or indeed any other specific territory under British-Indian rule.[35] Markovits shows that this prioritisation of wider imperial policy over considerations or directly concerned with Company possessions was applied even during the earlier period of East India Company rule. This subservience to the British state was a direct consequence of the financial rescue of the Company by the former in 1773 and 1784, which resulted in the subordination of the Company to the British government, with a new government department, the Board of Control, exercising control over the Court of Directors of the Company.[36] Markovits shows that this was instrumental in prompting several military expeditions undertaken by the Company, at great cost to it, from which it gained relatively little; these included the expedition to seize Manila from Spain in 1762; Ceylon from the Dutch in 1795–96; Mauritius in 1810 and Java in 1811.[37] But the policy the Company had to accept towards the Netherlands in respect of that country's Southeast Asian possessions would bring it into direct and continuous conflict with British merchants and interests in that region. The Anglo-Dutch Convention of 1814 compelled the Company to return Java and the Maluku islands to Dutch control as part of the wider British strategy to strengthen the Netherlands against any future French expansionism, even though the Company and allied private interests mitigated the loss by the acquisition of Singapore and Melaka through the Treaty of London of 1824. This at least protected access for British merchants to the Malaya Peninsula, and theoretically to most of the Malay archipelago. Nonetheless, those British merchants who had developed commercial interests on Java now faced an uncertain future.

The Company's apparent reluctance to defend the interests of British merchants in Southeast Asia was not lost on the mercantile community of Penang, which, as seen, was not appeased by the acquisition of Melaka and Singapore, which threatened to be rivals. The Company appeared all too ready to sacrifice both its own and private interests in Asia at the behest of its political masters in London. Moreover, the Company's priorities, in part dictated by wider imperial interests, continued to frustrate the aspirations of the Straits merchants. The willingness of the Company authorities, clearly following state policy, to overlook Dutch efforts to hinder British trade between the Straits Settlements and the islands of the Malay archipelago controlled by them was a constant source of anger throughout the Straits. This began within a year of the Treaty of London being signed. In June 1825, John Crawfurd, then Resident at Singapore, complained bitterly to the Calcutta authorities that the Dutch had dramatically increased duties on British textiles imported into their East Indian possessions, as well as hiking duties on exports from there of coffee.[38] Nothing was done about it, and as will be seen, Straits' grievances against the Dutch would fester throughout the next 40 years, and serve to weld not only the disparate Straits interests together but also enable them to build powerful alliances in Britain.

The sense that the Company was no real ally, and a growing feeling of isolation amongst the Straits mercantile interests of all ethnicities, was intensified by events in India and Britain in the early 1830s. The Bengal financial crash had important consequences for British merchants in the Straits. Up till then, many merchants in the Straits Settlements had built their trade through connections with the major agency houses based in Calcutta, and as a result tended to regard their interests as being closely connected with the fortunes of their Calcutta partners, which in turn nurtured very close relations with the Company through handling the personal finances of many of its servants as well as from time to time providing a variety of financial services for the Company itself. Fairlie, Fergusson & Co. traded and collaborated closely with the firm of James Carnegy on Penang, and Clark & Hare in Melaka.[39] Palmer & Co. developed close relations with David Brown, the Penang pepper planter, and Syf Allam, a wealthy Arab Muslim merchant.[40] As well as becoming involved in successions rivalries in the Sultanate of Aceh on Sumatra, Palmer and the other agency houses also established links with Singapore merchants after 1819. But the failure of all the leading agency houses between 1830 and 1834 effectively severed this link with Calcutta. In fact, with the growth of the export of British textiles and other commodities to the Southeast Asian market, and the opening of trade with Southeast Asia by the 1813 Charter Act, the development of direct links with Britain became more attractive. Nonetheless, the sense of being cut off from the mercantile community in India was real and was exacerbated by the impact of the 1833 Charter Act which finally ended the East India Company's commercial career and opened trade to China. Prior to this, the Straits interests could take comfort that the strategic location of the Straits of Melaka as the main trade route between India and China, as well as the supplies of Malay produce in demand in the Chinese market (which could be gathered by Company and private merchants from the Straits Settlements), ensured that the Company could not simply disregard their needs. Now the Company itself had little vested interest in the Straits trade; there was deep suspicion among the Straits merchants that they were now very low indeed on the list of Company priorities.[41] This was not an unreasonable view.

East India Company priorities for the governance of the Straits Settlements also did not sit well with the Straits merchants' perception of their own needs. A reluctance to champion Straits interests against the Dutch has already been mentioned. Parsimony and a commitment to minimum government were central to the Company's strategy for administering the Straits. Keeping the numbers of local officials to a minimum, and as far as possible making the Straits pay for their own administration were the main priorities. One commentator even condemns the prevailing philosophy of Company governance of the Straits Settlements as 'spartan, casual and neglectful'.[42] The corollary of keeping costs down was a strict policy of non-interference in local politics, especially in the Malay states, for fear of this leading to friction and conflict which would prove expensive. While there was a nominal commitment to maintaining law and order, and respecting local governing traditions and ethnic sensibilities, this was largely a product of indifference and a desire not to 'rock the boat' rather than any real sensitivity to local complexities.[43] Inevitably these strictures chafed the Straits merchants, as their ambitions for commercial expansion depended upon a more generous and supportive regime in Calcutta which would be responsive to their needs. Nor were they represented in Calcutta, and this also propelled them towards self-organisation and the pursuit of a wider network of allies.

The Company's unwillingness to engage adequately with the complexities faced by the Straits mercantile communities, and its preoccupation with reducing costs, led to direct conflict with Straits interests on several pressing issues. Piracy in the Malay archipelago proved to be a recurring problem for maritime commerce. John Crawfurd had complained of it when he was Resident Councillor at Singapore, and in 1828 Edward Presgrave, registrar of imports and exports at Singapore, investigated the problem. His report stressed the organised and embedded nature of the practice among the 'Orang Rayat', an ethnic group that populated the islands to the south of Johor. He estimated that nearly 175 perahus (Malay vessels) were involved, each with a crew of 40 to 80 men, and that they served a variety of local Malay rulers, including the Raja of Terengganu.[44] In August 1833, Chinese and Malay merchants petitioned the Straits government about the problem, claiming that their losses were between 15,000 to 20,000 Spanish dollars per annum. They were so desperate that they indicated that they would even tolerate the introduction of customs duties to pay for protection, though the Straits government suspected they exaggerated the problem.[45] No serious action was taken as a result. But the disruption of trade became so bad in the mid-1830s that the British and European merchants in Singapore took up the fight. A general meeting was held at the Exchange Rooms in Singapore on 25 May 1835, and a petition signed by 36 European merchants was sent to the governor general of India, calling for the Straits government to be empowered to act on piracy.[46] But the merchants were dismayed by the response of the Bengal authorities, which indicated that they wanted to pay for dealing with piracy by introducing customs duties at Singapore.[47] The Singapore merchants began petitioning against this in January 1836 and followed this up with a series of meetings to oppose the measure later in the year.[48] The result was the establishment of the Singapore Chamber of Commerce in February 1837.[49] As will be seen, other issues would emerge as Straits' interests clashed with Company administrative priorities.

A key factor in the rise of Straits mercantile political influence was the growth of close contacts with business in the UK, both through commercial relationships and through links with British-based business pressure groups. Some Singapore trading firms enjoyed links in Britain from their inception. In 1827, the firm of Maclaine, Fraser & Co. was established. It was managed in Singapore by Lewis Fraser and Gilbert Angus Bain but maintained a continuous contact with a London-based partner, James Fraser.[50] Knight's chapter in this volume shows how the Fraser family proceeded from commercial success in Singapore and Southeast Asia to establish themselves as London merchants who represented Southeast Asian interests. Ker, Rawson & Co., set up in Singapore in 1828, corresponded with Thomas Sam Rawson in London and Christopher Empsan in China. By the end of the 1850s, the firm traded under the name of Paterson, Simons & Co. after several changes of partners, and William Paterson, its senior partner, became chairman in London of the Chartered Bank of India, Australia and China.[51] His earlier firm of William Paterson & Co. had links with a firm in Glasgow.[52] Syme & Co., established in Singapore in 1823, by 1846 had partners in Glasgow, Liverpool and Manila.[53] The firm of Hamilton, Gray & Co., set up in Singapore in 1832, by 1846 dealt with Walter and William Hamilton in London.[54] By the 1860s, Hamilton, Gray & Co. also traded with the Glasgow firm of Buchanan, Hamilton & Co.[55] George Garden Nicol, who had earlier been a leading light in Hamilton, Gray & Co., became chairman of the Chartered Mercantile Bank of India, London and China.[56] Boustead, Schwabe & Co. of Singapore enjoyed a close trading relationship with Sykes, Schwabe & Co. of Liverpool in the early 1840s.[57] The Singapore firm of William Macdonald & Co., established in 1852, had partners in Glasgow, and were commission agents for a Glasgow gunpowder manufacturer.[58] Some firms in the UK built their own links with Singapore. The Liverpool firm of Middleton, Blundell & Co. worked through a partner in Singapore in the early 1840s, William Blundell.[59] Penang also had its direct links with the UK. Brown & Co. supplied sugar to the Liverpool firm of Hossack & Co.[60]

These individual contacts provided a strong base for the promotion of Straits' interests in the UK, and for challenging the stultifying East India Company hierarchy, which seemed so indifferent to Straits' needs. But there emerged even stronger connections with British-based pressure groups with a strong interest in trade with Asia. Opposition to the East India Company and its privileges had emerged early in the nineteenth century, especially among manufacturers and merchants in the main provincial cities of Liverpool, Glasgow, Birmingham and elsewhere. All became vocal in the campaign which overturned the Company's monopoly of trade with India under the Charter Act of 1813. The East India Association of Liverpool (LEIA) and the East India Association of Glasgow (GEIA) played an especially important role.[61] Unlike other, similar provincial organisations, LEIA was not dissolved in the wake of the Act and continued to lobby on a range of issues throughout the 1810s and 1820s.[62] It was instrumental in the revival of provincial lobbying (and pressure groups) from 1829 that finally stripped the Company of its remaining monopoly of trade with China.[63] This time, however, there was no dissolution of either LEIA or GEIA, which continued to actively lobby the Company and the British government on issues related to the Asian trade in which they had an interest. Moreover, in 1836, so successful a model had Glasgow and Liverpool created that London merchants and East India agency houses formed their own East India and China Association (The London East India and China Association: LEICA).[64] As the 1830s progressed, they built contacts with the Chambers of Commerce which sprang up across the cities of the British Empire in Asia. Interestingly, merchants in Southeast Asia were among the first whose interests in Asia were to be defended by GEIA. John Crawfurd, a key adviser to GEIA and an ex-Resident of Singapore still interested in Southeast Asian affairs, persuaded it to lobby the British government on a number issues affecting the commerce and Singapore, including memorials protesting against Dutch protectionism and the reluctance of the East India Company authorities to permit American ships to trade at Singapore.[65] The Straits merchants pursued developing links with the East India and China Associations, and on Dutch protectionism, it managed to persuade GEIA, LEICA and the Manchester Chamber of Commerce to actively campaign against Dutch protectionism throughout the 1830s and 1840s.[66] Their relative lack of success only reaffirmed the Straits merchants' belief that the Company was irreconcilably set against their interests.

The British East India and China Associations were mobilised by entreaties from the Straits merchants on a range of other issues. The move by the Bengal government to introduce trade duties at the Straits Settlements in 1835 in order to finance anti-piracy measures was brought to the attention of LEICA, and through them, GEIA in August 1836.[67] They lobbied the India Board which promptly denied the plans and agreed to stop the move, information which was swiftly passed on to the merchants of Singapore by LEICA.[68] In 1838, Crawfurd and LEICA also successfully interceded on behalf of the Straits merchants in opposing Bengal's policy of limiting the duration of land tenure leases in the Straits to 20 years; Crawfurd's expertise was particularly important for the outcome.[69] Merchants in Penang also had their battles, particularly to reduce duties charged on sugar and rum exported to Britain from Penang, which had been excluded from the favourable terms of the Sugar Act of 1836 because foreign sugar required to pay a higher duty could be imported into the Straits and would therefore be indistinguishable from Straits sugar. Ultimately, the Penang merchants lost the battle by the mid-1840s, heightening still further Straits resentment at Company rule.[70] Conflict with the Company authorities continued into the 1850s: over an abortive attempt to introduce a Stamp Act on official and business transactions in 1851; for greater judicial devolution to the Straits Settlements in 1852; against the transportation of Indian convicts to Singapore in 1854; and an attempt to impose in 1855 a copper currency on the Straits in place of the well-established Spanish dollar. The full weight of LEICA, John Crawfurd and the Singapore merchants ultimately defeated the policy and reversed the convict transportation policy.[71] But the process dramatically radicalised Straits opinion, and by the late 1850s a movement for the granting of Crown Colony status for the Straits Settlements was gathering momentum both in Southeast Asia and London.

In fact, the first suggestions for such a move can be traced back to the 1840s, and in due course the powerful commercial interests of the Straits, especially Singapore, would rally behind it. As early as 1840, John Anderson, a former Straits government official, advocated the transfer of the Straits Settlements to the Colonial Office, partly because of Company disinterest in them and the need for a more robust, fully British state-backed political presence in Southeast Asia to deter Dutch protectionism and facilitate better relations with Siam, Burma and other polities in the region.[72] In the same year, William Clark of the Colonial Society urged GEIA to lobby for such a move and published articles pressing for transfer in the *London Journal of Commerce*.[73] While immediate steps did not follow, the evolving regional economic and political context in the 1840s and 1850s further strengthened Straits commercial opinion of the need to shape policy to defend their interests. The Opium War of 1839–42 concluded with the opening of the Chinese market and the establishment of a new island port to rival Singapore – Hong Kong. This new port began to capture a substantial share of the trade of the Malay archipelago, and together with Dutch protectionism, this drove an increasing share of Singapore trade to the Malay peninsula, which rose from 15 per cent in 1825 to 34 per cent in 1845.[74] This served to heighten Straits anxieties about the lack of protection of their interests in Calcutta, and this reinforced their efforts to build alliances in Britain. Later, the opening of commerce with Siam under the Bowring Treaty of 1855, and the growing interest in the tin trade in the Malay peninsula among Straits merchants, served to build confidence that the Straits Settlements were a distinctive economic and colonial entity, capable of self-government provided that commerce was able to lead the way in policy formation.

However, the financial crisis of 1847–48 threatened the strength of the Straits interests' links in Britain, destroying as it did many of the London-based East India agency houses and some provincial firms which did business with firms all over Asia, including the Straits. One consequence of this was the merger of GEIA into the Glasgow Chamber of Commerce, though both LEICA and LEIA survived for a time (LEIA was eventually subsumed into the Liverpool Chamber of Commerce).[75] However, by the late 1840s, so strong were Straits connections in the UK that they were able to survive the impact of the 1847/48 crisis. The leading Singapore merchant W.H. Read spent several years in the UK between 1848 and

1851, during which he built a very close working relationship with John Craw-furd, who was still a potent voice in British policy in Asia. This was to be very important during the campaign in the late 1850s to transfer the Straits to Crown Colony status.[76] In addition, throughout the 1830s and 1840s, Singapore and the Straits Settlements attracted the interest of merchants and officials in Asia and London, especially in its system for exploiting Chinese labour migration to the Straits. Neal shows that Singapore in particular was copied – not always success-fully – as a model for exporting Chinese labour to Assam, Ceylon and Australia from the 1830s to the 1850s.[77] This both enhanced support within Britain and across the empire for Straits mercantile interests. The colonial bank movement of the 1850s, given new impetus following the demise of many of its opponents during the crash of 1847–48, also nurtured some powerful allies of the Straits interests.[78] For example, James Fraser, the prominent Southeast Asian and Singa-pore Scots merchant, joined the Board of the Chartered Bank of India, Australia and China.[79] Significantly, the Chartered – and the Oriental Bank – had branches established in Penang and Singapore by the early 1860s.[80] Indeed, Kawamura cites the efforts of the Straits Settlements to develop their own Exchange Bank-ing connections, and Bengal's resistance to this, as another factor which made the Straits' interests even more intent on Crown Colony status.[81]

The upshot was that when the Singapore and Straits merchants began to cam-paign for Crown Colony status in the late 1850s, they were able to secure pow-erful and long-standing allies in the UK, including eminent opinion formers on Southeast Asian affairs such as John Crawfurd. The downfall of East India Com-pany rule in India in the wake of the Indian Rebellion of 1857 opened the way for the Straits to be granted Crown Colony status under the authority of the Colonial Office, though the resolution of financial questions for the Straits and the general reordering of British rule in India, meant that it was 1867 before the transition was complete. But without doubt it represented a major victory for commercial inter-ests, and it presaged continuing commercial dominance of policy in Straits affairs.

Conclusion: the long-term implications of commercial dominance

What then are the main implications of the dominance of commercial interests for an examination of the development of Singapore and British interests in Southeast Asia? Firstly, this was undoubtedly a factor in the continued rise and success of Singapore under British rule. It meant that the interests of commerce, of all ethnic-ities, occupied an important position of influence in policy formation in the Straits settlements, and later in the Malay States as British influence and power expanded there after 1874. Secondly, and deriving from this factor, it was an important rea-son why the Malay states came to occupy such a prominent position within the British Empire, especially within the fields of first tin and later rubber production. Thirdly, it also allowed the growth of cross-regional networks and infrastructures which connected commercial interests in the Dutch and British spheres in South-east Asia, as demonstrated in Kawamura's chapter in this volume. This provided the basis for future success in such commodities as palm oil, extending even into the postcolonial period. Fourthly, the strong links between British and Straits and Southeast Asian interests continued under British rule and indeed after – again helping underpin the longer-term success of Singapore.

From the point of view of the history of the British Empire, the hegemony of commercial interests in the Straits points to the potential value of comparison with imperial arrangements at other British ports in Asia (such as Hong Kong), India (Bombay and Calcutta) and elsewhere in the empire. How unique was Singapore and the Straits, and to what extent were efforts made to replicate aspects of the 'Straits system' elsewhere? Neal's work on Singapore as a template for managing labour migration, and Jones' identification of the Straits Settlements as a model followed by the China Association, certainly suggests anecdotally that this was the case. More systematic comparisons might reveal other examples of efforts to apply lessons learned in the Straits to other imperial contexts. Perhaps, in respect of the position of Singapore and the Straits Settlements, the British Empire proved itself a 'learning empire' which adapted successful initiatives to other contexts. Such a development would suggest that the British Empire was, in some instances at least, more than just the pragmatic and ad hoc creation by 'reluctant imperialists' of exclusively localised customised and unique systems of rule. It might help give the lie to that old notion of the 'absent-minded' imperialist.[82]

Notes

1 Y. Chung-Huang, *Community and Politics: The Chinese in Colonial Singapore and Malaysia*, Singapore: Times Academic, 1995; C.A. Trocki, *Opium and Empire: Chinese Society in Colonial Singapore, 1800–1910*, London: Cornell University Press, 1990; C.A. Trocki, *Singapore: Wealth, Power and the Culture of Control*, London: Routledge, 2006.
2 S. Neal, *Singapore, Chinese Migration and the Making of the British Empire, 1819–1867*, Woodbridge: Boydell, forthcoming, and see Neal's chapter in this collection.
3 Kawamura's essay in the present volume.
4 R. Jones, 'The China Association: Fostering Trade, Networks & Sociability, 1889 to c. 1955,' PhD Thesis, Northumbria University, 2018.
5 A. Reid, *Southeast Asia in the Age of Commerce 1450–1680 Volume Two: Expansion and Crisis*, London: Yale University Press, 1993, pp. 2, 27–30; N. Hussin, *Trade and Society in the Straits of Melaka: Dutch Melaka and English Penang, 1780–1830*, Copenhagen: NIAS Press, 2007, p. 13.
6 Hussin, *Trade and Society*, pp. 206–210, 271–290.
7 Ibid., pp. 166–168.
8 Ibid., pp. 185, 187, 190.
9 Ibid., pp. 310–311.
10 V. Sinha, *Religion-State Encounters in Hindu Domains: From the Straits Settlements to Singapore*, Singapore: Springer, 2011, pp. 32–33.
11 Ibid., p. 35.
12 A. Webster, 'British Expansion in South East Asia and the Role of Robert Farquhar, Lt Governor of Penang 1804–5,' *Journal of Imperial & Commonwealth History*, vol. 23, no. 1, 1995, pp. 18–19.
13 A. Webster, *Gentlemen Capitalists: British Imperialism in South East Asia 1770–1890*, London: Tauris, 1998, pp. 62–64.

14 C.M. Turnbull, 'Penang's Changing Role in the Straits Settlements, 1826–1946,' Conference paper, 'The Penang Story,' April 2002, Penang, Organised by the Penang Heritage Trust and Star Publications, pp. 2–4.

15 Ibid., pp. 2–4.

16 Ibid., pp. 4–5.

17 A. Webster, *The Richest East India Merchant: The Life and Business of John Palmer of Calcutta 1767 to 1836*, Woodbridge: Boydell, 2007.

18 A. Webster, *The Twilight of the East India Company: The Evolution of Anglo-Asian Commerce and Politics 1790–1860*, Woodbridge: Boydell, 2009, pp. 101–102.

19 I. Nish, 'British Mercantile Co-operation in the Indo-China Trade from the End of the East India Company's Trading Monopoly,' *Journal of Southeast Asia Studies*, vol. 3, no. 2, 1962, pp. 74–91.

20 C. Buckley, *An Anecdotal History of Old Times in Singapore*, Vol. 1, Singapore: Fraser & Neave, 1902, pp. 303–305, 313–314.

21 C.M. Turnbull, *The Straits Settlements 1826–67 Indian Presidency to Crown Colony*, London: Athlone, 1972, pp. 131–135.

22 Buckley, *Anecdotal History*, p. 314.

23 C.A. Trocki, *Opium and Empire: Chinese Society in Colonial Singapore, 1800–1910*, Ithaca: Cornell University Press, 1990, pp. 82–116.

24 For example, on concern about Chinese rioting, see *Singapore Free Press*, 9 June 1842.

25 Tan Kim Heng, 'Chinese Sugar Planting and Social Mobility in Nineteenth Century Province Wellesley,' *Malaysia in History*, vol. 24, 1981, pp. 24–38.

26 A. Webster, 'The Development of British Commercial and Political Networks in the Straits Settlements 1800 to 1868: The Rise of a Colonial and Regional Economic Identity?' *Modern Asian Studies*, vol. 45, no. 4, 2011, pp. 899–929, 911–912.

27 Trocki, *Singapore*, pp. 86–92; C. Trocki, 'The Rise of Singapore's Great Opium Syndicate 1840–1886,' *Journal of Southeast Asian Studies*, vo. 18, no. 1, 1987, pp. 58–80.

28 L. Hollen Lees, 'Being British in Malaya, 1890–1940,' *Journal of British Studies*, vol. 8, no. 1, 2009, pp. 76–101.

29 M.D. Parrili, S. Montresor, and M. Trippi, 'A New Approach to Migrations: Communities-on-the-Move as Assets,' *Regional Studies*, vol. 53, no. 1, 2019, pp. 1–5.

30 Webster, 'Development of British Commercial and Political Networks.'

31 Ibid., p. 924.

32 J. Legge, 'The Colonial Office and Governor Ord,' *Journal of Southeast Asian Studies*, vol. 29, no. 1, 1998, p. 4.

33 Neal, *Singapore, Chinese Migration and the Making of the British Empire*; Kawamura's chapter in the present collection.

34 V. Giacomin, 'The Emergence of an Export Cluster: Traders & Palm Oil in Early Twentieth Century Southeast Asia,' *Enterprise & Society*, vol. 19, no. 2, 2017, pp. 272–308.

35 D.A. Washbrook, 'The Indian Economy and the British Empire,' in D. Peers and N. Gooptu (eds.), *India and the British Empire*, Oxford: Oxford University Press, 2010, pp. 44–74.

36 C. Markovits, 'The Indian Economy and the British Empire in the Company Period: Some Additional Reflections Around an Essay by David Washbrook,' *Modern Asian Studies*, vol. 51, no. 2, 2017, p. 377.

37 Ibid., pp. 378–383.

38 Buckley, *Anecdotal History*, p. 181.

39 Undated memorandum of Governor Bannerman of Penang, Dutch Records, 1/2/29, OIOC BL (Oriental and India Office Collections, British Library).

40 Webster, *The Richest East India Merchant*, p. 62.

41 Webster, 'Development of British Commercial and Political Networks,' pp. 908–910.

42 Sinha, *Religion-State Encounters*, p. 40.

43 Ibid., pp. 34–38.

44 Presgrave to K. Murchison, Resident Councillor, 5 December 1828, Boards Collections (BC) F/4/1724 (69433), pp. 59–71, OIOC BL.

45 Letter from Straits government to Bengal government 19 August 1833 BC F/4/1724 (69433), pp. 29–30, OIOC BL.
46 C.R. Read, J. Hamilton and T. Fox to Governor General of India 25 May 1835 BC F/4/1724 (69433), pp. 83–86, OIOC BL.
47 Wong Lin Ken, 'The Trade of Singapore 1819–69,' *Journal of the Malaysian Branch of the Royal Asiatic Society*, vol. 33, no. 4, 1960, p. 182.
48 Buckley, *Anecdotal History*, pp. 301–306.
49 Ibid., p. 313.
50 Ibid., p. 233.
51 Ibid., p. 398.
52 Ibid., p. 380.
53 Ibid., p. 233.
54 Ibid., p. 234.
55 Case of Ashton & Others vs Bauer & Others, 25 October 1866 in J.W.N. Kyshe, *Cases Heard and Determined in Her Majesty's Supreme Court of the Straits Settlements 1808–1884*, Singapore: Singapore & Straits Printing Office, 1885, pp. 164–165.
56 Kyshe, *Cases Heard*, p. 566.
57 Buckley, *Anecdotal History*, p. 398.
58 Ibid., p. 567; Buchanan vs Kirby, 8 April 1870, Kyshe, *Cases Heard*, pp. 230–231.
59 Buckley, *Anecdotal History*, p. 401.
60 Scott, Sinclair & Co. v Brown & Co., Penang 26 October 1852 in Kyshe, *Cases Heard*, pp. 84–85.
61 For the most complete account of this, see Y. Kumagai, *Breaking into the Monopoly: Provincial Merchants and Manufacturers' Campaigns for Access to the Asian Market 1790–1833*, Leiden: Brill, 2013, especially chapter 2 in relation to the 1813 Act.
62 Webster, *Twilight of the East India Company*, pp. 75–76.
63 Kumagai, *Breaking into the Monopoly*, chs. 3–5.
64 Webster, *Twilight of the East India Company*, p. 109.
65 Kumagai, *Breaking into the Monopoly*, pp. 108–109.
66 Webster, 'Development of British Commercial and Political Networks,' pp. 914–915.
67 LEICA to GEIA 25 August 1836, MS891001/7 Glasgow East India & China Association papers, p. 73, Mitchell Library, Glasgow.
68 India Board to GEIA 26 August 1836; LEICA to GEIA 6 September 1836, MS891001/7 Glasgow East India & China Association papers, pp. 74–75; Buckley, *Anecdotal History*, p. 305.
69 Webster, 'Development of British Commercial and Political Networks,' pp. 916–917.
70 Ibid., pp. 918–919.
71 Ibid., pp. 922–925.
72 Sinha, *Religion-State Encounters*, p. 39.
73 Clark to GEIA 26 September 1840, MS891001/8, p. 60.
74 Wong, 'Trade of Singapore,' p. 54.
75 Webster, *Twilight of the East India Company*, pp. 131–134.
76 Webster, 'Development of British Commercial and Political Networks,' p. 919.
77 Neal, *Singapore, Chinese Migration and the Making of the British Empire*.
78 Webster, *Twilight of the East India Company*, pp. 138–142.
79 Knight's chapter in this volume.
80 T. Kawamura, 'British Business and Empire in Asia: The Eastern Exchange Banks, 1851–63,' in D. Bates and K. Kondo (eds.), *Migration and Identity in British History: Proceedings of the Fifth Anglo-Japanese Conference of Historians in London*, Tokyo September 2006, pp. 193–212.
81 T. Kawamura, 'British Exchange Banks in the International Trade of Asia from 1850 to 1890,' in U. Bosma and A. Webster (eds.), *Commodities, Ports and Asian Maritime Trade Since 1750*, Basingstoke: Palgrave Macmillan, 2015, pp. 184–185.
82 The eminent historian Sir John Seeley first cited the seeming 'fit of absence of mind' which accompanied the building of the British Empire in 1883. J.R. Seeley,

The Expansion of England: Two Courses of Lectures, New York: Cosimo, 2005, p. 8. A variation of the term was used to symbolise the allegedly marginal role played by the Empire in British domestic politics and culture in B. Porter, *The Absent-Minded Imperialists: What the British Really Thought About Empire*, Oxford: Oxford University Press, 2004. The concept of imperial conquest as a last resort when informal efforts at influence had failed – reluctant imperialism was a central tenet of Gallagher & Robinson's view of British imperialism: J. Gallagher and R. Robinson, 'The Imperialism of Free Trade,' *Economic History Review*, vol. 6, 1953, pp. 1–13.

9 Mediators, migrants and memories of colonial Singapore

The life and legacy of Seah Eu Chin

Stan Neal

Introduction

When a British trading post was established in 1819 Singapore was seen as a quiet island. By 1867 the Straits Settlements, with Singapore as capital, became a Crown Colony and Singapore, a flourishing trading port, was home to over 80,000 people.[1] At this point, the majority of the colony's population were designated as 'Chinese'. As Singapore underwent rapid transformation in the early colonial period, British rule was dependent on collaboration with Chinese mediators. One such example is the Chinese businessman and community leader Seah Eu Chin (1805–1883).[2] Seah was significant as part of Singapore's Chinese community and as a mediator cultivated a strong relationship with British colonial authorities. For the historian, Seah also provides an insight into Singapore's wider significance as a migrant colony. He is one of the few Chinese voices recorded as an English-language source on the Chinese migrant community in the nineteenth century.

As one of the most famous Chinese figures of the early colonial period, Seah's legacy is visible in various charitable organisations and place names. In recent years, Seah's celebrity has also led several descendants to write biographies, set up websites and create YouTube videos about their famous ancestor. The internet and popularisation of family history has facilitated this recent interest, but these accounts of Seah Eu Chin's life are also shaped by contemporary discussions about ethnicity and economic prosperity in modern Singapore. Discussions of Seah's life raise questions about the intersection between collective memory, family history and narratives of national progress.

In terms of sources, there is very little primary source material on Seah Eu Chin. Given the wealth and significance of Seah, this indicates a difficulty faced by scholars with an interest in Chinese migrant lives in the early colonial period. Certain details are substantiated by archival records. For example, the 1853 letter granting Seah Eu Chin a Certificate of Naturalization has been digitized as part of the Singapore Citizen Archivist Project.[3] Most discussions of Seah's life draw on the biographical details outlined in Song Ong Siang's *One Hundred Years' History of the Chinese in Singapore*.[4] Most of the basic elements of his story outlined here are repeated in the work of scholars who have examined the Chinese community in early colonial Singapore, such as Carl Trocki and Yen Ching-Hwang.[5] There have also been recent biographies from Seah Eu Chin's descendants. There is a biography published online by Brandon Seah and a book titled *Seah Eu Chin: His Life and Times* by Shawn Seah.[6] Notably, these family histories are not created or designed to be received in a vacuum. They are inherently political and blur the lines between personal interest, family history and broader discussions of the significance of the early colonial period in Singapore's history.

This chapter will examine Seah Eu Chin's story in three sections. First, it will examine Seah Eu Chin's background with an emphasis on his role as a mediator between British colonial authorities and the Chinese population, specifically as a Teochew community leader. Second, it will examine an article that discussed Chinese immigration to Singapore that was attributed to Seah Eu Chin. This is a rare and important source on migration history from this period, which is placed here in the broader context of perceptions of Chinese migrants in the British Empire. Third, this chapter will focus on the meanings attached to Seah Eu Chin in terms of heritage and family history. Drawing on conversations with two of his descendant-biographers, Brandon Seah and Shawn Seah, as well as considering the multifarious ways modern Singaporeans engage with this history beyond written biography, this chapter will critically assess the way that family histories intersect with Singapore's story and question the commonly held perceptions of the early colonial period 200 years from 1819.

Seah Eu Chin background

Seah Eu Chin was born on 30 August 1805 in the county of Chaozhou (Teochew) in Guangdong province. His father, Seah Keng Liat, was secretary to the yamen of P'o Leng subprefecture.[7] Most accounts of Seah's life suggest that he received a classical Chinese education and would have been expected to try to become an official through the civil service examination system.[8] However, we know that instead he followed a common path of emigration from southern China to Southeast Asia.

In the early colonial period, most Chinese migrants to Singapore were credit-ticket migrants: manual labourers who signed contracts to get their 'tickets' from China to Singapore paid. These systems of Chinese migration to Southeast Asia pre-dated British colonial control.[9] The credit-ticket system largely worked to the benefit of employers seeking cheap labour. Workers signed contracts for a set period with a broker in China before they were taken to their destination (in this case Singapore) where the Chinese brokers would sell the contract to a Chinese or European employer. The sale of the contract acted as payment to the broker for passage and the labourers repaid their new employers for the purchase of the contract from their wages.[10] Alternatively, some credit-ticket passengers were brought to Southeast Asia on the account of specific vessels, where on arrival the passengers would be detained until an employer secured their services by paying their expenses and a margin of profit to the ship.[11] This 'junk trade' was conducted entirely by Chinese brokers and operated in some form across most of Southeast Asia.[12] These trading vessels often carried labourers as supplementary cargo, meaning that the movement of people followed existing trade routes. In this context, given his family background, Seah Eu Chin was an unusual migrant when he travelled to Singapore in 1823. We can assume that Seah arrived in Singapore with some capital and no passage debt, as he started out working as a bookkeeper and investing in the 'entrepôt trade' selling local products as provisions to and from the junk crews arriving from China.[13]

Seah Eu Chin was able to rapidly grow his business and traded in cotton and tea. Crucially, he was able to invest in land in the 1830s when it was still cheap. In particular, it was Seah's timely investment in pepper and gambier plantations that gave him his fortune and earned him the nickname the 'gambier king'.[14] In 1835 Seah acquired rights from the East India Company to cultivate gambier and pepper over a ten-mile stretch of land.[15] Luckily for Seah, this investment was matched with increased demand for gambier, a 'miracle plant', to be used as a dye in Europe.[16] Seah was able to build his fortune further by providing finance to other plantation owners to buy land. In Trocki's words, this placed him at the top of the colony's 'debt pyramid'.[17] As the credit-ticket labourers were often indebted – from passage money, opium addiction, gambling debts – to their employers, those same employers were then indebted to finance providers like Seah Eu Chin. Sitting atop the 'debt pyramid' helped Seah Eu Chin to amass a wealth of $1.35 million at his death in 1883.[18]

Beyond his economic power, Seah Eu Chin was also able to establish himself as a community leader.[19] Most discussions of his importance to early colonial Singapore emphasize his role as the co-founder and head of the Teochew organisation the Ngee Ann Kongsi (founded as Ngee Ann Kun in 1830 and renamed in 1845).[20] The main function of the Kongsi was to pool resources in order to provide charitable services, such as paying for funerals.[21] Of course, the continued prominence of the Teochew Building (Tank Road) and the Ngee Ann Kongsi, with the Ngee Ann educational institutions, Ngee Ann Cultural Centre and the Yueh Hai Ching Temple, has served to build Seah Eu Chin's legacy and legend. Crucially, the Seah family maintained multi-generational control of the Ngee Ann Kongsi. Seah Eu Chin's two eldest sons, Cheo Seah and Liang Seah, both led the organisation and passed control to Seah Eu Chin's grandson, Eng Tong Seah.[22] Interestingly, whilst Seah Eu Chin's role as an important Teochew community leader is emphasised by his biographers, the coordinated attempts to wrestle control of the Ngee Ann Kongsi away from the Seah dynasty suggest that there is an element of revisionism in the centrality of the Seah family in the Teochew community. After an anti-Seah group of Teochew merchants failed to take control in 1906, Eng Tong Seah was deposed by another group led by Lim Nee Soon, after an expensive legal challenge, in 1930.[23]

One of the charges against the Seah dynasty in the twentieth century was that they were pro-British, in contrast to their more China-oriented rivals. This can be traced back to Seah Eu Chin himself. Seah had cemented his status as a community leader through marriage to the eldest daughter of Tan Ah Hun, the Chinese Kapitan of Perak, Tan Meng Guet and, following her death from smallpox, marriage to her sister Tan Meng Choo.[24] Marriage gave Seah an important brother-in-law, Tan Seng Poh, who controlled a profitable opium revenue farm in Johor.[25]

Seah Eu Chin and Tan Meng Choo had four sons – Seah Cheo Seah, Liang Seah, Song Seah and Peck Seah – and three daughters – two died at a young age, leaving Sin Seah as the surviving daughter.[26] Seah's sons were given an 'English' education at St. Joseph's mission school, whilst being schooled in Chinese at home. This combined education was designed to help them in business, which it evidently did. The Seah sons assumed control of the opium farm from Tan Seng Poh on his death in 1879, Liang Seah became known as the 'pineapple king' with his ownership of a pineapple processing factory and Peck Seah invested in shipping.[27] Beyond economics, the Seahs maintained important social roles as 'Straits Chinese'. For example, Liang Seah was a founding member of the Straits Chinese British Association.[28] The way that the Seahs were able to negotiate their position between colonial authorities and community leaders is a hallmark of the way Seah Eu Chin is characterised in the early colonial period.

Beyond his role as a wealthy business man and Teochew community leader, the main focus of historical discussions of Seah Eu Chin has been on his role as a mediator between the British colonial authorities and the Chinese community at large. During both the Anti-Catholic Riots in 1851 and the Hokkien-Teochew riots in 1854, the colonial authorities called on Seah to act as a mediator. He represented the Teochew community during negotiations in 1854.[29] Seah also had more formalised links with European merchant elites and the British colonial state. He joined the Singapore Chamber of Commerce in 1840, sat on several Grand Juries between 1851 and 1867, and served as a Justice of the Peace from 1872.[30] The colonial authorities clearly trusted him, not just as a last resort at points of crisis or as an influential financier but as a community leader with formalised roles in colonial legal processes. Seah further consolidated his position with the colonial authorities by naturalizing as a British subject in 1853 and organising a deputation of Chinese merchants that greeted the governor-general of India, Lord Dalhousie, on his visit to Singapore in 1850.[31] Again, this connection with the British authorities was maintained by Seah's descendants. Liang Seah was appointed to the legislative council of the Straits Settlements in 1883 and read the address of congratulation from the Chinese community in English during the Straits Chinese Recreation Club's celebrations of Queen Victoria's Golden Jubilee celebrations in 1887.[32] Seah Eu Chin's reputation as a mediator, who sat between communities or within multiple communities is a common feature of both historical discussions of him and a legacy passed to his family who continued to negotiate colonial power structures.

Chinese migrants in Singapore

With the lack of available primary sources from the early colonial period, many scholars have focused on a journal article attributed to Seah Eu Chin on the 'Chinese in Singapore'.[33] As a researcher working generally on Chinese migration in the British Empire, this is where I first encountered Seah Eu Chin. It is very rare to have an English-language discussion of Chinese migration in the nineteenth century that is attributed to a Chinese migrant. British colonial discussions of Chinese migration frequently provide vague attributions for their sources of information.

The dearth of first-hand literature from Chinese sources is partly a result of the colonial hierarchies at play in the construction of archives – there are plenty of English-language discussions of Chinese migrants in Southeast Asia from Western officials, merchants, missionaries, explorers – and partly a consequence of the fact that emigration from China was technically prohibited by the Qing state until 1860.[34] The 'Chinese in Singapore' article was translated by Dr Thomas Oxley, an East India Company surgeon from Dublin who served as senior surgeon for the Straits Settlements from 1844, and was based on answers to questions written in Chinese by Seah Eu Chin.[35] It appeared in the *Journal of the Indian Archipelago and Eastern Asia*, which was published by James Richardson Logan, the Scottish lawyer and orientalist who is credited with coining the term 'Indonesia' at Singapore's Mission Press and intended to disseminate 'scientific information' about the languages and cultures of Southeast Asia.[36]

In this article, Seah gives the total population of Singapore's Chinese community in 1848 as 40,000, with 10,000 arrivals annually aboard the junks from China, with 3,000 returns.[37] Beyond the numbers, Seah discussed average pay for Chinese labourers, typical food, medical problems and the gender imbalance in the colony.[38] Unsurprisingly, given Seah Eu Chin's strong identification with the Teochew community, he was keen to emphasize the different regional/dialect groupings of the Chinese in Singapore: 'Chinese from Hokien; Malacca born Chinese; Chinese from Tio Chiu; Chinese from Canton; The Khe Chinese; Chinese from Hai-nam'.[39] Notably, this emphasis stands in contrast to some of the most famous Western characterisations of the Chinese in the nineteenth century. For example, the missionary, linguist and China expert, Charles Gutzlaff described China as the 'largest and most homogenous nation' in the world.[40]

Seah also breaks down the Chinese community by occupation, giving a comprehensive list. He breaks down these occupations into a traditional fourfold hierarchy of 'literati, farmers, craftsmen, and merchants'.[41] The full list of occupations he provides is as follows:

> The different trades and professions of the Chinese in Singapore, are Schoolmasters, Writers, Cashiers, Shop-keepers, Apothecaries, Coffin-makers, Grocers, Gold-smiths, Silver-smiths, Tin-smiths, Blacksmiths, Dyers, Tailors, Barbers, Shoemakers, Basket-makers, Fishermen, Sawyers, Boat-builders, Cabinet-makers, Architects, Masons, Manufacturers of lime and bricks. Sailors, Ferrymen, Sago manufacturers, Distillers of Spirits, Cultivators of plantations of Gambier, Sugar, Siri, Pepper, and Nutmegs, Play actors, Sellers of cake and fruit, Carriers of burdens, Fortune tellers, idle vagabonds who have no work and of whom there are not a few, beggars, and, nightly, there are those villains the thieves.[42]

Significantly, we can detect in this quotation an indication of the social hierarchy within the Chinese community, especially from its conclusion with 'thieves'. Again, there is more nuance here than in many contemporary colonial sources. Many colonial observers generally essentialise the 'Chinese' into two homogenous blocks: the merchant elite and the impoverished labourers. For example, when John Crawfurd – the second British Resident of Singapore, ethnographer and Malay linguist – provided information on Chinese migration to Singapore to the Colonial Office in support of a projected Chinese migration scheme to the West Indies, he emphasized the contribution of the educated 'artizans' and 'merchants'.[43] Giving the example of 'one very enterprising merchant who had been for years a common porter. Having lived handsomely, he died the richest man in Singapore'.[44] By contrast, when discussing the majority of credit-ticket migrants, he lamented that 'No man brings capital any more than Irish labourers coming to England'.[45] This colonial dichotomy of the wealthy elite and poor labourers is reproduced time and again, presumably because these two groups were the economically important ones to colonial authorities. The rest of the Chinese community was only seen as important in the service of those groups.

Seah's discussion of the Chinese in Singapore also dealt with some of the challenges facing the Chinese workers who acted as the labour force for the plantations owned and financed by him. Notably, here Seah discusses the problem of opium addiction, which not only served the colonial debt hierarchy but featured heavily in British representations of Chinese migrants in an era of Anglo-Chinese relations defined by the Opium Wars. As described by Trocki, 'one of the most enduring European images of the Chinese was that of the opium wreck'.[46] Seah describes the process as follows:

> They become addicted to the prevailing vice of Opium smoking. After a continued residence here they learn the habit, which afterwards becomes fixed. Many of the Chinese labourers after having earned a little money, waste it upon opium or expend it in gambling . . . when these opium smokers are reduced to straits from want of money they resort to schemes of plunder and robbery.[47]

This is an interesting description from the top of the 'debt pyramid', as Seah personally benefited from cheap labour. As Markovits has demonstrated, there was a clear relationship between opium addiction and the opium supply.[48] Also, Seah goes on to be very critical of the opium trade generally, which again is of interest given that his sons took control of the colonial opium revenue farm after his death. Notably, placed in the broader context of British representations of Chinese migrants, the way that this account refers to Chinese opium and gambling addiction could be taken from a contemporary exclusionary critique of Chinese migrants in a white-settler colony. For example, note the frequency of opium and gambling in pictorial representations of the 'yellow peril' in nineteenth-century white settler newspapers.[49] Again, the extent to which Seah's account is mediated by Oxley here may be why this fits so closely with broader colonial discussions of Chinese opium addiction.

With these considerations in mind, Seah still offers us a rare English-language assessment of the Chinese community from the perspective of a Chinese migrant. As a mediator between the British authorities and the Chinese community at large, Seah Eu Chin was respected by colonial observers. Moreover, the political status and economic power Seah harnessed in his lifetime has left a legacy.

Legacy, family, memory

As one of the early pioneers in Singapore's agriculture and economy, Seah Eu Chin has become a feature of various elements of public history in modern-day Singapore. The most obvious physical legacy is in terms of street names. The various streets named after the Seah family, 'Seah Street/ Eu Chin Street/ Liang Seah Street/ Peck Seah Street', were the focus of Episode 7 of the television series 'My Grandfather's Road', first aired on Take 5 in 2015.[50] This television show features discussions with various descendants who largely emphasise Seah's charitable work through the Ngee Ann Kongsi and his role as a mediator during riots and colonial unrest. This take is unsurprising given the stated aim of the 'My Grandfather's Road' series to 'learn more about the country's past as well as the people who helped make Singapore the success that it is today'.[51]

Beyond these commercially produced videos, a quick Google search reveals various YouTube videos, Facebook pages and websites created by descendants. For example, a 2014 YouTube video created by Sean Seah, titled 'Search', depicts a journey from Singapore to Seah Eu Chin's home village in China.[52] Sean Seah's voiceover recounts being told about Seah Eu Chin by his father and learning more in history lessons. He ponders the question of why Seah Eu Chin took the risk of leaving for Singapore when he was educated and had opportunities at home, representing his ancestor as a 'fighter'.[53] The video focuses on a visit to a villa that Seah funded in the village in which he was born, further reinforcing his charitable image, and culminates with Sean Seah and the locals, having found his 'roots'. The interest of descendants in their famous ancestor is not new. According to an article in the *Singapore Free Press* in 1953, there was a now defunct Seah Eu Chin Descendant's Union.[54] The two major contributions to these commemorative acts of family history are a website biography, roughly 30,000 words, by Brandon Seah and a 172-page book titled *Seah Eu Chin: His Life and Times* by Shawn Seah. A discussion of both of these biographies outlines the intersection between family history, memory of the colonial past and narratives of nation-building in modern Singapore.

Brandon Seah is a postdoctoral microbiologist at the Max Planck Institute for Marine Microbiology in Bremen and five generations removed from his ancestor Seah Eu Chin. I was able to speak to Brandon via Skype to discuss his website.[55] His biography is very thorough, and he modestly suggests that he put it together to kill time after his national service, having been aware of Seah Eu Chin through his family and the obvious connections through street names. Brandon Seah's biography of Seah Eu Chin is in some ways critical and sceptical of his ancestor. For example, he is critical of too much being made of Seah as a mediator, positioning himself between different ethnic communities as a conscious and benevolent interlocutor:

> It might be a situation where we are reading our present day categories and ways of thinking and experience to the past. Because in Singapore today people are very aware of ethnicity, it's on your identity card and related to

language policy, so we have this idea that your identity is connected to your ethnicity. But, I think what he was doing back then was just trying to survive and trying to do business.[56]

Here Brandon Seah expresses a healthy scepticism – first, of Seah Eu Chin's motivations as a financier, and second, of the way that his historical role and actions have been understood in relation to modern categories and ethnic divisions.

More broadly, my conversation with Brandon Seah highlights the inherent tensions between family history and national narratives. He is also critical of what he sees as the education system's simplistic focus on Raffles's foundation of a British trading post, the Japanese occupation in the Second World War and independence in 1965. Again, Brandon Seah combines his criticism of the national story with scepticism of the emphasis on Seah Eu Chin as a primarily charitable character:

> The story of Singapore is told, from a nation-building perspective, that Singapore started from nothing and grew because these pioneers came and contributed. And it's sort of a moralistic tale because they came with very little, a rags to riches story, and created prosperity, which all sounds nice and benign but when you look into the details what these people did and you realise that they are not just contributing to prosperity they are out to make money for themselves. If along the way you have to do something charitable to improve your public image then so be it.[57]

Brandon Seah's criticism of the 'rags to riches' story stems from the characterisation of Singapore as a place where Chinese migrants arrived with nothing and were able to become wealthy. As we know from Seah Eu Chin's family background and his rapid ascent as an entrepreneur, he did not begin in 'rags' but started off with a good education and capital at his disposal. Brandon Seah appears to be cautious of Seah Eu Chin's story being co-opted into a broader narrative of Singapore as a site of economic miracles. Additionally, Brandon Seah clearly sees similar potential problems of an overly positive or simplistic narrative in both family and national histories where he expresses doubt of Seah Eu Chin's charitable motives.

In addition to Brandon Seah's online biography, Shawn Seah's *Seah Eu Chin: His Life and Times* gives a comprehensive account of Seah's life and the broader activities of his sons and ancestors. Shawn Seah is a descendant of Seah Peck Seah, Seah Eu Chin's youngest son, and felt compelled to write about his famous ancestor in order to 'help Singaporeans learn more about an important individual who played a significant part in Singapore's history'.[58] As a civil servant, he also sees Seah Eu Chin's story as important in 'helping build a larger Singapore national identity'.[59] His book is supported by the Singapore National Heritage Board. I was able to email questions to Shawn, which made for a more structured but useful conversation. His biography is highly detailed and effectively traces Seah Eu Chin's legacy through his children's lives too, which is a necessary approach given the lack of primary sources from the man himself.[60]

Whilst Shawn Seah credits Brandon Seah's work as a useful guide in navigating the topic, there is a clear difference in tone as he introduces Seah Eu Chin as follows on his website: 'In 1823, a gutsy and astute eighteen-year old from Swatow, China, arrived in Singapore to seek his fortune. He succeeded in his adopted country, and when he died 60 years later, he left a legacy that remains to this day'.[61] Shawn Seah also feeds the characterisation of Seah Eu Chin as a mediator into a narrative of Singaporean history: 'Most importantly, Seah Eu Chin brought peace and stability during Singapore's tumultuous early days. He played the role of mediator, negotiator, and peacemaker during the 1851 Anti-Catholic riots and the 1854 Hokkien-Teochew riots'.[62] Evidently, for Shawn, Seah Eu Chin's story can clearly be grounded in a broader 'Singapore story', which he describes as follows:

> To me, the early colonial period is very important in understanding the longer arc of history. Singapore did not start in 1819, or in 1965. It had a history before Sir Stamford Raffles landed in Singapore, and it certainly had a history between 1819 and 1965. I would argue that it was the particular path-dependent way in which we arrived here today – with a Westminster-style government, English as an official language, British common law, just to name a few examples – that made Singapore the way it is. And Seah Eu Chin and his descendants, and their families, who settled in Singapore and helped make it the way it is, and in their own ways, is an important embodiment of a more nuanced Singapore Story. Essentially, my Singapore Story or Stories is about the pioneering people who made Singapore the way it is today.[63]

Notably then, Shawn sees his biography as being as much about saying something about modern Singapore – and his own take on it as a remarkable success story – as it is about his family history.

Whilst Seah Eu Chin's charitable contributions cannot be dismissed, we can see scepticism from Brandon Seah that these were not ultimately beneficial to his business, either as a form of nineteenth-century public relations or more directly financially beneficial in terms of cementing his status as a community leader, which in turn gave him great access and control of the colonial labour force. By contrast, Shawn Seah is unequivocal in his view of Seah Eu Chin as a charitable community leader:

> The historical record is clear – he was indubitably a charitable entrepreneur who helped his community. Many examples stand out, including his leadership and establishment of the Ngee Ann Kun, which later became the Ngee Ann Kongsi, a charitable organisation for Teochews. He was also deeply involved in education; preservation of the peace; humanitarian aid through donations; being a member of Tan Tock Seng Hospital, which was for paupers; and writing on his observations of the conditions of the migrant worker in Singapore. One of the epithets he gained was "Emperor Seah", an informal title that suggested that he was seen as the government or a major leader.[64]

By highlighting the esteem in which Seah Eu Chin was held and his significance as a community leader, Shawn Seah is giving a conventional defence of his ancestor, rather than challenging the conventional 'Singapore story'. Across all of the biographies, websites and videos created by Seah descendants, the conflict between commemorating Singapore's past and shaping Singapore's future casts a clear shadow.

With the recent interest in Seah Eu Chin's story, his grave has taken on particular significance as a focal point for commemoration amongst descendants. Of course, this issue has political ramifications with the ongoing debate over the exhumation of the Bukit Brown cemetery in order to create space for urban development.[65] Many in Singapore have expressed concern at the destruction of heritage sites such as Bukit Brown in the name of economic progress and future development. In 2012 Charles and Raymond Goh discovered Seah Eu Chin's grave on Grave Hill in Toa Payoh West, adjacent to the Bukit Brown cemetery.[66] Whilst Seah Eu Chin's grave is not currently explicitly threatened by redevelopment, the proximity to Bukit Brown and his historical status as a community leader who was crucial to the success of early colonial Singapore means that he has been co-opted into the larger heritage debate.[67] For example, the website of the *All Things Bukit Brown* heritage group features a blog post titled 'Remembering Seah Eu Chin' that details a visit to Seah Eu Chin's grave by 27 descendants and the Goh brothers.[68] Alongside the photographs and description of the visit we can see family members connecting in the comments section and related posts titled 'Seah Eu Chin – Found!' and 'Found but Under Threat'.[69] In addition to this website there are also YouTube videos of family visits to the gravesite, with a continuing theme of the importance of cataloguing these heritage sites and 'rich heritage for our children' before they are lost to development.[70] In my conversation with Brandon Seah, he noted that there have been fundraising efforts between descendants to restore Seah Eu Chin's gravesite.[71]

The tensions between heritage and economic development are most clearly expressed in conversation with Shawn Seah. His biography features a section on the Bukit Brown debate and he references an unsuccessful attempt by Sean Seah, who visited southern China for the 'Search' video, to petition the National Heritage Board to protect Seah Eu Chin's grave.[72] Ultimately, despite his personal family interest in preserving heritage, he is cognisant of the pressures and economic realities that make redevelopment necessary:

> However, you have raised an important point, namely the conflict between development and heritage preservation. On the one hand, economic development – land for housing, business, industry, security, and amenities – means that the Bukit Brown cemetery, and in fact the surrounding area, will have to be redeveloped. It is a matter of time, as Singapore is a land-scarce country and there are real and pressing trade-offs. No amount of wishing or dreaming is going to change our constraints, and therefore we have to make hard-nosed decisions of weighing the benefits and costs of development.[73]

That said, Shawn Seah does identify possible solutions and compromises involving technology and cataloguing rather than preservation. In line with the broader discussions taking place online, he suggests that there is a duty to pass these stories on to future generations:

> On the other hand, heritage and history are intangible, and Bukit Brown is an important place where we can remember and honour our pioneers and ancestors. This is something that money cannot buy, and an invaluable part of our heritage. So, the question really is: how can policy-makers balance between what we need, and what we should have? One possibility is to leverage on technology, but that may take the soul out of Bukit Brown. Another possibility is to document the graves, similar to what I have done. Seah Eu Chin's grave at Grave Hill is near to Bukit Brown, and while it is one of the largest and grandest tombs in Singapore, at some stage, it may have to give way to redevelopment. While this is hopefully a long way off, I have taken the initiative to document and reflect upon Seah Eu Chin's story, and promote and advocate for it. In this way, I hope that everyone can develop a sense of where we came from as a people, who we are, and maybe what we must do to move forward can emerge.

Note here that Shawn Seah uses the threat of destruction, and the need to record and pass on these stories, as justification or possibly motivation for his family histories. This same process of connecting this story to a sense of loss is taking place on a broader scale when we consider the decline of the Teochew dialect.

The repeated emphasis on Seah Eu Chin as a 'Teochew pioneer', which is a key feature of the recent biographies, websites and articles, more so than some of the colonial sources which characterise him more broadly as 'Chinese', points to a broader sense of loss and change that overlays these new histories. In recent years there have been concerns about the decline of dialects, such as Teochew, amongst the younger generations of ethnic Chinese in Singapore:[74]

> In my view, the relative decline of *all* dialects, not just Teochew, compared to Mandarin in contemporary Singapore is due to policy direction from the government. It may come as a surprise to Western observers that Teochew is very much alive among the older generation. But regardless, knowledge of a dialect or not, having four streets named after you and your family is not a mean feat. Today, Seah Eu Chin is also regaining prominence on the Internet and in my book – a first in Singapore.[75]

Whilst Shawn Seah appears to be sanguine about the decline of the Teochew dialect, instead keen to emphasise the physical legacies of street names and the passing on of his story, there are broader concerns expressed by the Teochew community groups about the ethnic identities being lost. These family histories are not operating in a vacuum but are inherently political, highlighting tensions between the conventional presentation of Seah Eu Chin as a migrant mediator who held the colony together the colony during tumultuous early days and Singapore's national story.

Conclusion

In summary, Seah Eu Chin does provide a good example of the informal connections and mediators that facilitated colonial control in the early colonial period, particularly as Singapore developed as a multi-ethnic society. Rather than relying on formalised structures and official leaders, Seah Eu Chin's role demonstrates the intentionally limited role of the colonial state in colonial Singapore's early days. By providing a rare insight into the systems of Chinese migration and the Chinese community that has been characterised as the economic engine of the colony, Seah Eu Chin also left a legacy for English-language historians. His account adds regional and class nuances to a Chinese community often stereotyped and essentialised by colonial observers. However, there are problems with the article attributed to Seah Eu Chin in the *Journal of the Indian Archipelago*. Specifically, it repeats colonial tropes and assumptions, particularly around opium addiction. More problematic are the tensions exposed by the recent family histories and connected public debates about heritage and development in modern Singapore. In the context of the 2019 bicentenary, Seah Eu Chin's story raises questions about the intersection between collective memory, family history and nationalist narratives.

At first glance, Seah Eu Chin's life is a simple and straightforward story. Like many others, he left southern China for Singapore in the mid-nineteenth century to make his fortune, and he was successful. He repaid the opportunities offered by Singapore by leading his community, making charitable donations and offering peace and stability. He was a migrant and a mediator who offers an insight into the realities of life for Chinese migrants in early colonial Singapore and the workings of the colonial state. However, when we assess what his story means to his descendants in 2019, 200 years after a British trading post was founded, we can detect tensions both between competing narratives of Singapore's past as well as tensions between economic development and heritage. The irony here is that the narrative view of Singapore's past is as a rapidly developing and expanding economic base. The stories that celebrate Seah Eu Chin repeat a standard narrative of early colonial Singapore as indicative of the march of progress, civilisation and modernity, facilitated by British liberal economics. It is almost poetic, then, that Seah Eu Chin's grave is threatened by redevelopment necessitated by the insatiable need for land and economic growth in modern-day Singapore. Would an economic pioneer, such as Seah Eu Chin, save Bukit Brown?

Notes

1 Straits Settlements Blue Book, 1867. [CO 277/1] UK National Archives.
2 Note here that most discussions of Seah Eu Chin present his name in the traditional Chinese order with the family name first but name his descendants, such as Liang Seah, in the Western style with the family name second. This chapter follows this convention.

3 Secretary to the Governor, 28 December 1853. [Z27: Singapore: Letters from Governor] National Archives of Singapore.

4 S.O. Siang, *One Hundred Years' History of the Chinese in Singapore: The Annotated Edition*, Singapore: National Library Board, 2016, originally published 1923, pp. 24–31.

5 C.A. Trocki, *Singapore: Wealth, Power and the Culture of Control*, London: Routledge, 2006, pp. 21–49; Y. Ching-Hwang, *Ethnic Chinese Business in Asia: History, Culture and Business Enterprise*, Singapore: World Scientific, 2014, pp. 288–293. See also L. Pan (ed.), *The Encyclopedia of the Chinese Overseas*, Richmond: Curzon, 1998, p. 202.

6 B. Seah, *Seah Eu Chin*, [website], 2007–2016, available at: http://seaheuchin.info/index.html, accessed 30 November 2018; S. Seah, *Seah Eu Chin: His Life and Times*, Singapore: National Heritage Board, 2017.

7 Seah, *Seah Eu Chin: His Life and Times*, p. 12.

8 Seah Eu Chin's education is also evidenced by the characterisation of him as Singapore's first 'man of letters', see M.R. Frost, 'Emporium in Imperio: Nanyang Networks and the Straits Chinese in Singapore, 1819–1914,' *Journal of Southeast Asian Studies*, vol. 36, no. 1, 2005, p. 36.

9 D. Northrup, *Indentured Labour in the Age of Imperialism, 1834–1922*, Cambridge: Cambridge University Press, 1995, p. 54; P.C. Campbell, *Chinese Coolie Emigration within the British Empire*, London: P.S. King & Son, 1923, p. xii. There are references to migrants 'pawning' themselves in this fashion as early as 1805.

10 A.J. Meagher, *The Coolie Trade: The Traffic in Chinese Laborers to Latin America, 1847–1874*, Philadelphia: Xlibris, 2008, p. 189.

11 C. Chang, 'Chinese Coolie Trade in the Straits Settlements in the Late Nineteenth Century,' *Bulletin of the Institute of Ethnology Academia Sinica*, vol. 65, 1988, p. 2.

12 E.C. Arensmeyer, 'The Chinese Coolie Labour Trade and the Philippines: An Inquiry,' *Philippine Studies*, vol. 28, 1980, p. 189.

13 Seah, *Seah Eu Chin: His Life and Times*, p. 32; Ching-Hwang, *Ethnic Chinese Business in Asia*, p. 289.

14 J. Corfield, *Historical Dictionary of Singapore*, Toronto: Scarecrow Press, 2011, p. 74.

15 Seah, *Seah Eu Chin*. Land acquired by Seah in the early colonial period later became the subject of legal disputes between his descendants and other claimants. For example, details of a legal case in 1877, which was won by the Seah family, are given in Seah, *Seah Eu Chin: His Life and Times*, p. 115.

16 Seah, *Seah Eu Chin: His Life and Times*, p. 37.

17 C.A. Trocki, *Opium and Empire: Chinese Society in Colonial Singapore, 1800–1910*, London: Cornell University Press, 1990, p. 65.

18 Brandon Seah calculates this as comparable to an estate of $9 billion in the present day: Seah, *Seah Eu Chin*.

19 British modes of governance that relied on community leadership were more informal in Singapore than in other Southeast Asian colonies. See C. Liew, 'Ordo ab Chao at the Far End of India: Chinese Settlers and Their Colonial Masters,' *Journal of Asian History*, vol. 50, no. 1, 2016, pp. 147–152.

20 A good overview of the role of Kongsi in the broader political economy of colonial Singapore is given in Trocki, *Opium and Empire*.

21 Seah Eu Chin also donated to charitable causes not confined to the Teochew community, such as the Tan Tock Seng Hospital.

22 Y. Ching-Hwang, *Ethnicities, Personalities and Politics in the Ethnic Chinese Worlds*, Singapore: World Scientific, 2017, p. 65.

23 Ibid., p. 81. The importance of marriage ties between the Chinese and the Straits Chinese communities is discussed in H. Kuo, *Networks Beyond Empires: Chinese Business and Nationalism in the Hong Kong-Singapore Corridor, 1914–1941*, Leiden: Brill, 2014, p. 48.

24 Note that the Singapore administration quickly abandoned the 'kapitan' system of community leadership, which was used in the rest of colonial Southeast Asia, in favour of more informal relationship with the Chinese elite.

25 Note that the opium 'farm' was not a literal farm but the right to collect tax revenues on opium sales on behalf of the colonial state. See C. Trocki, 'Opium and the Beginnings of Chinese Capitalism in Southeast Asia,' *Journal of Southeast Asian Studies*, vol. 33, no. 2, 2002, p. 297.

26 Seah, *Seah Eu Chin: His Life and Times*, pp. 87–113.

27 Ibid., p. 97.

28 Seah, *Seah Eu Chin*.

29 Seah, *Seah Eu Chin: His Life and Times*, p. 67–83.

30 Siang, *One Hundred Years' History of the Chinese in Singapore*.

31 Ching-Hwang, *Ethnicities, Personalities and Politics in the Ethnic Chinese Worlds*, p. 65.

32 Siang, *One Hundred Years' History of the Chinese in Singapore*, p. 319.

33 U. Siah, 'The Chinese in Singapore,' *Journal of the Indian Archipelago*, vol. 2, 1848, pp. 283–290.

34 As evidenced by the long-standing Chinese communities across Southeast Asia.

35 Y. Tham, 'Oxley Road Home Was Where History Was Made,' *Straits Times*, 18 June 2017.

36 J.C.Y. Jia and B. Tan, 'James Richardson Logan,' *Singapore Infopedia*, [website], 2009, available at: http://eresources.nlb.gov.sg/infopedia/articles/SIP_1146_2009-10-27.html, accessed 30 November 2018.

37 Siah, 'The Chinese in Singapore,' p. 286.

38 Due to Qing restrictions on emigration and the tough manual labour on plantations and mines the majority of migrants were young, single men.

39 Siah, 'The Chinese in Singapore,' p. 283.

40 C. Gutzlaff, *China Opened, Vol. I*, London: Smith, Elder and Co., 1838, p. 286.

41 Siah, 'The Chinese in Singapore,' p. 284.

42 Ibid., p. 284.

43 J. Crawfurd, 'Chinese Emigration to the West Indies,' in Colonial Land and Emigration Commissioners, *Colonization Circular*, 30 October 1843, National Library of Australia, pp. 34–37.

44 Ibid.

45 Ibid.

46 Trocki, *Opium and Empire*, p. 1.

47 Siah, 'The Chinese in Singapore,' p. 285.

48 C. Markovits, 'The Political Economy of Opium Smuggling in Early Nineteenth Century India: Leakage or Resistance?' *Modern Asian Studies*, vol. 43, no. 1, 2009, p. 89.

49 On opium in 'yellow peril' settler discourse see R. Muirhead, *China: A Yellow Peril? Western Relationships with China*, Bideford: CFZ Press, 2009; M. Lake and H. Reynolds, *Drawing the Global Colour Line: White Men's Countries and the International Challenge of Racial Equality*, Cambridge: Cambridge University Press, 2008; D.C. Atkinson, *The Burden of White Supremacy: Containing Asian Migration in the British Empire and the United States*, Chapel Hill: University of North Carolina Press, 2017.

50 *My Grandfather's Road: Episode 7*, Take 5, 20 January 2015, available at: https://video.toggle.sg/en/series/my-grandfather-s-road/ep7/319548, accessed 30 November 2018. The naming of streets is also discussed in V.R. Savage and B. Yeoh, *Singapore Street Names: A Study of Toponymics*, Singapore: Eastern Universities Press, 2003, p. 118.

51 *My Grandfather's Road*.

52 *Search*, S. Seah, [online video], 6 June 2014, available at: www.youtube.com/watch?v=JGrP7x5-j78, accessed 30 November 2018.

53 *Search*.

54 Seah, *Seah Eu Chin: His Life and Times*, p. 145.

55 The conversation lasted roughly an hour in a free form interview, with a couple of pre-agreed topics, of which he was notified when signing a consent form, rather than set questions.
56 Brandon Seah, interviewed by Stan Neal, 2 September 2018.
57 Ibid.
58 Shawn Seah, interviewed by Stan Neal, 9 October 2018.
59 Ibid.
60 Shawn is currently working on a biography of Seah Eu Chin's second son, Liang Seah.
61 S. Seah, *Seah Eu Chin: His Life and Times*, [website], 2017, available at: https://seaheuchin.com/life/, accessed 30 November 2018.
62 Ibid.
63 Shawn Seah, interview, 2018.
64 Ibid.
65 A good summary of the broader conflicts around Singapore's urban development and heritage is provided here: K.K. Liew and N. Pang, 'Neoliberal Visions, Post-Capitalist Memories: Heritage Politics and the Counter-Mapping of Singapore's Cityscape,' *Ethnography*, vol. 16, no. 3, 2015, pp. 331–351.
66 Rachael Boon, 'Teochew Pioneer's Grave Found in Toa Payoh,' *Straits Times*, 28 November 2012.
67 There are concerns that the project to build the North-South Highway may affect the Seah Eu Chin burial site.
68 'Remembering Seah Eu Chin,' *All Things Bukit Brown* [website], 2012, available at: http://bukitbrown.com/main/?p=5605, accessed 30 November 2018.
69 Ibid.
70 *Seah Eu Chin Visit 2013*, Firewerkz Films, [online video], 13 July 2013, available at: www.youtube.com/watch?v=0koOJkZY_BA, accessed 30 November 2018.
71 Brandon Seah, interview, 2018.
72 Seah, *Seah Eu Chin: His Life and Times*, p. 149.
73 Shawn Seah, interview, 2018.
74 On the decline of Teochew and other Chinese dialects relative to Mandarin in Singapore, see L. Lim, 'Beyond Fear and Loathing in SG: The Real Mother Tongues and Language Policies in Multilingual Singapore,' *AILA Review*, vol. 22, no. 1, 2009, pp. 52–71.
75 Shawn Seah, interview, 2018.

10 Liverpool in the relational remaking of Singapore

Global city routes and Malay seafaring mobilities

Tim Bunnell

Since long before its official founding in 1819, Singapore's economic fortunes have been bound up with distant places and people.[1] Never simply a story about relations with neighbouring islands or a regional hinterland, modern Singapore even came to be dubbed a 'global city' before that term rose to prominence among urban scholars in the social sciences.[2] A danger with the term 'global' more widely is that its all-encompassing connotations can serve to obscure specific geographies of connection. While British imperial connections are of course widely appreciated in popular as well as academic imaginings of Singapore's spatially extended historical geography, in this chapter I attend to a smaller scale of analysis than metropolitan Britain as a whole. More specifically, my focus is on historical interrelations between Singapore and the city of Liverpool. Although not featuring prominently among Singapore's long-distance economic relations today, at independence and for a century before 1965, Liverpool was a maritime commercial centre of worldwide renown and influence. I consider the role that Liverpool played in the extended historical making of Singapore as a global city.

Part of the wider scholarly significance of examining the Liverpool-Singapore nexus arises from the fact that this is an intercity connection. Both historians and urban geographers increasingly recognize the dangers of 'methodological nationalism' (the tendency to treat the nation-state as the default unit of analysis, territorial framing device or actor in studies of social and political change).[3] Historical perspective compels appreciation of what political scientists and international relations scholars often seem to overlook – namely, that the nation-state as a 'container' for political, economic and social processes is a relatively recent phenomenon in most of the world. In urban studies, meanwhile, it is recognized not only that cities act beyond national systems but also that the economic 'command and control' functions of global cities or world cities preceded the era of neoliberal globalisation that began from the final decades of the twentieth century.[4] I adopt a 'relational comparative' historical approach to the Liverpool-Singapore nexus.[5] That entails treating Liverpool and Singapore not as wholly discrete entities for comparison but as cities that have been constitutively related during much of the past 200 years. Relational comparison allows examination of how Liverpool-Singapore relations – the geographies of power and vectors of influence between them – have changed over time.

The relational comparative analysis that follows draws upon and extends my previous work on the 'life geographies' of Malay seafarers in Liverpool.[6] Some of the men concerned were born in Singapore and almost all had obtained seafaring work from there before eventually settling in Liverpool in the 1950s and 1960s. The men whose mobilities I traced through interviews and archival research followed in the wake of several prior generations of Malay seafarers whose journeys to Liverpool were made in rather different historical structural contexts. I use Malay maritime linkages to sketch changing Liverpool-Singapore relations across three broadly chronological periods. The first concerns the role of Liverpool in the commercial (re)making of Singapore as a trans-shipment centre after 1819. In the second and main section of the chapter, I consider Singapore's growing role in colonial governance and economy from the middle of the nineteenth century in relation to the commercial networks of 'world city' Liverpool. The third and final section contrasts Liverpool's economic demise as an imperial maritime centre from the 1960s with Singapore's rise and consolidation as a global city-state.

Liverpool and the commercial (re)making of Singapore

While Stamford Raffles is often cast as having acquired Singapore for Britain, he was acting more specifically in the interests of the English East India Company (EIC) and 'motivated primarily by the commercial needs of British India'.[7] As Tony Webster has detailed, the impact of the end of the EIC's India monopoly on the India trade added greater urgency to the search for markets for the produce of British India; and this was what motivated Raffles to seek a new commercial base in southeastern Asia *despite* rather than in line with official British policy. One way in which 'Liverpool' figured in such developments was in name only. Lord Liverpool (Robert Banks Jenkinson) was British prime minister from 1812, and it was the 'Liverpool government' that ended the EIC's India trade monopoly in 1813 in response to demands from manufacturing interests seeking to gain access to foreign markets. However, lobbying by commercial groups from the city of Liverpool also contributed to those demands, and thereby to the political economic conditions under which Raffles was driven to expand into the Malay world. Commercial interests in Liverpool subsequently supported the establishment and retention of Singapore, with the Liverpool East India Association often acting alongside similar groups from Glasgow and Birmingham.[8] The China trade remained an EIC monopoly for 20 years after India (i.e. until 1833), but ships from Liverpool and other British 'provincial outports' subsequently participated fully in the trade with China and Southeast Asia.

It is in this mid-nineteenth century period that Malay seafarers, among other so-called 'lascars', begin to appear in writing about Liverpool.[9] While technically connoting Indian sailors, 'the term lascars was applied to all indigenous sailors of the Indian Ocean region'.[10] Figure 10.1, taken from Joseph Salter's (1873) account of work at the Strangers' Home for Asiatics in London, illustrates that diversity. As 'Missionary to the Asiatics in England', Salter visited port cities across the country. 'In Liverpool', he wrote, 'the natives of the distant East have been visited

LASCARS.

BURMESE   BENGALI   MALAY   SIAMESE   SURATI
CHINESE

Figure 10.1 A Malay seaman and other lascars.

frequently, and found in larger numbers than in any other provincial town'.[11] During one visit, '[a]bout one hundred strangers heard the Gospel – Arabs, Malays, East Indians, and Chinese'; and an unidentified lodging house was said to have been 'filled with Manillas and Malays'.[12] Malays were also among the lascar crew described by Herman Melville on board a ship called the *Irrawaddy* in Liverpool in around 1840.[13]

While Malay seafarers, among other lascars, were a transient population in Liverpool, and confined largely to specific dockside parts of the city, their presence was a sign of the growing role of the 'East' in Liverpool's economy, as both a source of commodities and of the labour that shipped them. As Webster has summarized, '[B]y the middle of the nineteenth century, Liverpool had become the principal exit point for British manufactures bound for the crucial specific markets of India and Pacific Asia, as well as a major warehousing and transit port for important produce from "the East" generally'.[14] Although the Atlantic trade remained central to Liverpool's commercial geography, 'eastern commerce' came to play a very significant part in the economic growth of the city. Liverpool, in turn, played a role in the development of Singapore as the main port through which commodities for industrial production in Britain were exported from the Malay world region.

World city networks

> [Liverpool] is the New York of Europe, a world city rather than merely British provincial.[15]

> [Singapore] is an international Liverpool with a Chinese Manchester and Birmingham tacked on to it.[16]

This second and main section of the chapter considers three roles played by Liverpool in the economic development of Singapore from the mid-nineteenth century: (1) in expanding Singapore's steamship connections with the metropole and a wider Atlantic-centred world economy; (2) through financing regional steamship operations that facilitated the flow of commodities to Singapore from its Malay world hinterland; and (3) in contributing to Singapore's emergence as a regional centre for commercial 'command and control' functions.

Steamship development: Alfred Holt and the Liverpool of the East

In 1879 a British traveller on his way to Borneo described Singapore as 'the Liverpool of the East'.[17] Given that F.W. Burbidge was a naturalist rather than an urbanist, his likening of Singapore to Liverpool was probably based on nothing more than casual observation. Nonetheless, at a time when Liverpool ranked among the port city 'capitals' of a British-dominated, Atlantic-centred cycle of global accumulation – a 'world city' rather than merely British provincial – Burbidge's comparison was a sign that Singapore had begun to thrive commercially.[18] What is more, in relational comparative terms, the notion of Singapore as the Liverpool of the East is a spur for thinking about ways in which Singapore's development may also have been attributable to Liverpool, or at least to key firms and individuals associated with the city.

Several studies suggest that Liverpool did indeed play a significant role in Singapore's development as a trans-shipment centre, although most are either corporate-sponsored accounts or works that celebrate Liverpool's historical maritime influence. One British historian has contended that in terms of direct metropolitan routes, 'the credit for the first regular steamship service to the Far East is due to one Liverpool man alone – Alfred Holt'.[19] From 1866 Holt's three pioneer vessels in the China trade, *Agamemnon*, *Ajax* and *Achilles*, travelled from Liverpool round the Cape of Good Hope to Mauritius (8,500 miles or 13,680 km), then to Penang, Singapore, Hong Kong and Shanghai. Holt was the first shipowner to install high-pressure, surface-condensing engines on transoceanic steamers, reducing fuel consumption and bunker space, and thereby making steam transport to the Far East via the Cape commercially viable. That innovation, combined with the subsequent opening of the Suez Canal (in 1869), meant that the number of vessels reaching Singapore with cargoes from Britain rose steeply.[20] By the mid-1870s, 14 of Holt's Blue Funnel Line vessels carried goods right through to Singapore.[21] Burbidge would no doubt have seen several on his trip to (and back from) 'the swamps and forests of Borneo'. By 1914 more Blue Funnel Line ships passed through the Suez Canal than that of any other company and the harbour in Singapore would have been 'forested with familiar blue funnels'.[22]

In terms of seafaring labour, the routes operated by the Blue Funnel Line vessels and other British steamships, like sailing ships before them, were sustained by lascars.[23] From the early twentieth century some Malay men from among this wider seafaring workforce began to settle in Atlantic port cities such as New York and Cardiff.[24] The foundation myth of Malay Liverpool is that seafarers who ended up staying in the city came over from New York after the First World War.[25] This has been impossible to verify, but the founder of the first club for Malay seafarers in Liverpool certainly came from across the 'Malay Atlantic' after the Second World War. The Malay club on St James Road was frequented not only by seafarers coming to and through Liverpool in the 1950s, some of whom worked on Blue Funnel Line vessels, but also by Malays already living the city who had first arrived in the interwar period. An indication of the scale concerned may be derived from a Home Office report of January 1932 that recorded the presence of 73 Malays among the 'coloured alien seamen' in Liverpool.[26] Malay seamen therefore contributed to the 'precocious multicultural-demographic profile'[27] of the city or, more precisely, of the south docks area that one sociologist termed 'the other Liverpool'.[28] More significantly for this chapter, Malays (some Singapore-born) contributed to the seafaring labour that sustained Liverpool and Singapore's connections to each other and to wider maritime worlds, in and (far) beyond the North Atlantic.

In Singapore, the influence of world city Liverpool in maritime commercial networks became more visibly manifest in successive iterations of the Ocean Building. In 1870, the agents for Holt's steamers moved into that building, the sea-facing back of which became known as 'Blue Funnel corner'. The agency house concerned, W. Mansfield and Co., was incorporated as a private company in Liverpool in 1903, with Alfred Holt and other members of the Board of the Ocean Steamship Company as directors, and W. Mansfield and Co. Ltd (hereafter 'Mansfields' for short) went on to acquire the Ocean Building.[29] The city of Liverpool was perhaps at its commercial zenith in 1914 and as K.G. Tregonning put it, '[T]he success of Singapore was of material benefit to Liverpool'.[30] Equally, however, Liverpool, and especially the Ocean Steamship Company founded by

Alfred Holt, had contributed to turning Singapore into 'the greatest tranship-ment port of the Orient'.[31] By this time, Singapore was the seventh-busiest port in the world in terms of shipping tonnage.[32] The Ocean Steamship Company (of Liverpool) played a significant role in making Singapore into 'the Liverpool of the East'.

Regional expansion: gathering commodities and governing territory

Singapore's expansion as a port from the 1860s involved a rather different rela-tionship to its surrounding region than had been imagined at the point of its incep-tion as an EIC outpost. Robert Elson has referred to this in terms of a shift from mercantile 'free trade imperialism' (when Britain had little interest in the regional 'interior') to one of colonial 'high capitalism' (when interior territories were grad-ually brought under colonial control).[33] The shift was about securing and profiting from the supply of commodities to Singapore that Blue Funnel and other steam-ships then took to feed industrial production in Britain and other industrializing parts of the world (notably for tin cans from the middle of the nineteenth century and rubber pneumatic tyres from its final decade). The increasingly territorial-ized political economy of the hinterland of British Malaya meant that Singapore assumed regional administrative 'capital' functions. In Elson's terms: 'Commerce and territorial administration had been welded together; capitals [such as Singa-pore] now stood at the termini of infrastructural grids through which produce was moved out of the interior, and administrative control of the hinterland established, maintained and enhanced'.[34]

Liverpool figured in this system not merely in terms of the mainline steamships that took tin and rubber from British Malaya to industrial Britain but also in the routes through which such commodities reached 'the great gathering ground' of Singapore in the first place.[35] The rapid expansion of shipping tonnage from the peninsula in the 1860s and 1870s – especially tin – was mostly accounted for by various forms of 'native' craft.[36] However, in 1890, the year when the Straits Trading Company's new smelter on Pulau Brani began operations, T.C. Bogaardt established the Straits Steamship Company (SSC), with involvement from Alfred Holt and Company, to handle regional commodity traffic. The Liverpool/Holts connection was not surprising given that Bogaardt had managed Mansfields from the first Ocean Building for much of the previous two decades. The tin ore trade from the 'west coast Malay ports', as K.G. Tregonning put it, became 'one of the bread and butter jobs of the Straits Steamships'.[37] During the First World War, German firms were liquidated and Alfred Holt and Company played a key role in replacing the services of the German shipping line, Norddeutscher Lloyd, through an agreement by which 'the Liverpool firm provided new ships for the SSC to expand its operations and in exchange acquired the ownership of just under a third of that company'.[38] Alfred Holt and Company thus effectively acquired the SSC as a 'local fleet to serve their main line steamers in South-east Asia'.[39]

It is with the SSC that the seafaring life geographies of most of the men in my study began. Almost all were from small coastal towns that formed part of the

Singapore-centred SSC network, and especially from villages around Malacca. More than three-quarters of the Malay men in the company's service came from 'kampongs behind Malacca'.[40] K.G. Tregonning, in his official history of the SSC, *Home Port Singapore*, specifically mentioned Serkam as a kampung where a 'family tradition of Straits service was maintained'. When I first started my research in Liverpool in 2003, the oldest surviving Malay ex-seafarer, Mr Majid, was from Serkam, and had worked for SSC in the 1930s before securing ocean-going work from Singapore.[41] In the working lives and seafaring mobilities of men such as Majid, as in the movement of commodities that their labour enabled, Singapore was the interface between regional and 'global' routes. More specifically, it was the (second) Ocean Building that housed regional coordination functions for world city Liverpool's commercial reach into the hinterland of Singapore (in and beyond British controlled territories).

After the First World War, the original Ocean Building had been demolished and replaced with a new one, modelled on New York's Flatiron Building.[42] The second structure was completed in 1923. Reportedly the 'handsomest' as well as the tallest building in Singapore at that time,[43] its design and iconography can be read in contrasting ways. I have suggested elsewhere that the second Ocean Building brought some of Liverpool's Atlantic world city, 'New York of Europe', commercial showiness to Singapore.[44] In contrast, others have read the second Ocean Building's 'stone-like claddings' as 'giving its façade a solid and enduring impression that captured the confidence of the Empire' in the 1920s.[45] Perhaps both readings are valid and the second Ocean Building encapsulates how Liverpool's Atlantic world city horizons were bound up with British colonial control and even wider imperial commercial reach. Certainly, while New York was a source of architectural inspiration and building innovation in Liverpool, the same is true of Liverpool's waterfront for port cities in Asia. The Bund waterfront in Shanghai is perhaps the best-known example of how Liverpool's Pier Head was considered 'worthy of emulation into the 1920s'.[46] In Singapore, Liverpool architects, Briggs and Thornley were initially engaged to design the second Ocean Building, and it is no coincidence that this and other grand buildings lining Collyer Quay have been recalled as 'Bund-like'.[47]

The second Ocean Building came to house: the Straits Trading Company (which owned the tin smelter at Pulau Brani) on the fourth floor; the SSC (whose regional fleet fed the smelter) on the first floor; and the Blue Funnel Line (which operated the mainline routes) on the second floor. Mansfields directly oversaw two Blue Funnel Line ships – the *MV Charon* and *MV Gorgon* – that ran on a Western Australia route, and which gave many of the men in my study their first seafaring experience beyond Southeast Asia (see Figure 10.2). However, it is also important to remember that the second Ocean Building formed a *regional* node in a global commercial network controlled from India Buildings, in Liverpool. As such, although they almost certainly did not realize it at the time, many of the men in my study – originating from across and beyond British Malaya – had been working on networks ultimately accountable to Liverpool for many years before they ever set foot in the city.

Figure 10.2 Crew of the MV Charon in Singapore (circa. 1946).

Command and control

In the language of the transdisciplinary field of urban studies today, colonial Singapore's historically subordinate regional relation to Liverpool may be cast in terms of world city networks of 'command and control'. As was noted in the epigram to this section of the chapter, Liverpool was labelled a 'world city' in one news magazine in the 1880s. It was some three decades later before that term was used in English language academic writing (by Patrick Geddes), and a further half-century before it rose to prominence.[48] An important turning point was publication (in 1966) of Peter Hall's book, *The World Cities*; this was the first to establish the understanding that a subset of the most powerful cities around the world forms the apex of an urban hierarchy.[49] Subsequent work by John Friedmann, Saskia Sassen and Peter Taylor among many others, consolidated conceptualization of world/global cities as command and control centres in the global economy. While use of the term in the *Illustrated London News* in 1886 thus bears no direct connection to today's scholarly usage – with scholars such as Friedmann casting world cities as historically products of the New International Division of Labour[50] – thinking about political economy in terms of hierarchically ordered urban networks with world city command and control nodes at the 'top' works very well for the Liverpool-Singapore nexus in much of the first half of the twentieth century.

Tony King was among the first scholars to historicize the urban studies literature in this way. In his 1990 book on London as a 'global city', King makes mention of the 'specialized industrial-commercial' roles of several British cities (including Liverpool) in the colonial mode of production.[51] Importantly, in that context, however, connections between London, Glasgow or Liverpool and Singapore were as part of 'a single political and economic unit' – the British Empire.[52] Singapore's function as what King termed a 'zonal' or 'regional' centre within that extended imperial territorial unit was broken down by the Japanese Occupation of British Malaya. The second Ocean Building changed from regional commercial node to headquarters of the Japanese Southern Air Transport Command (*Nanpo Koku Yosubo*).[53] After the war, Singapore and Liverpool rebounded economically, and so did commercial relations between them. The year 1951 was a record trading one for Singapore in both rubber and tin, and the Blue Funnel Line (run from India Buildings in Liverpool) was prominent among the companies shipping those commodities. Indeed, the return of Blue Funnel Line ships was seen as a barometer for the post-war recovery of Singapore's economic climate. The chairman of Mansfield and Company, A. McLellan, recalled how at the end of 1947,

> a senior Government official, after one of his visits to the Singapore Harbour Board wharves, remarked to one of his friends: 'It is a most cheering sight to see so many Blue Funnel vessels alongside the wharves – it is just like pre-war days and extremely encouraging to realise how rapidly the Blue Funnel Line and British shipping generally is again getting into its stride'.[54]

For the generation of Malay men in my study, post-war economic recovery meant that there were expanded opportunities to work at sea with British shipping companies, including in some cases with Blue Funnel Line on routes directly connecting Singapore and Liverpool. Other men took more circuitous routes before ending up on Merseyside. During the 1950s Liverpool was not only a maritime commercial command and control centre but was also an attractive base for men who wanted to continue to work at sea, and even as a migrant destination, given an abundance of 'shore jobs'. It was therefore no coincidence that in 1963 a group of Liverpool-based Malay men collectively purchased a terraced house in the Liverpool 8 postal code area as the city's second Malay club. However, the mini economic 'golden age'[55] soon came to an abrupt end; the opening of the Malay club took place at a point when the post-war 'high watermark' for British shipping had already passed.[56] Liverpool also subsequently lost out in the process of shipping containerisation, and in both international and national divisions of labour (with industrial activity in the north and midlands of England that had previously been fed through Liverpool moving to other parts of the world, including Southeast Asia, and growth in the increasingly service sector-oriented British economy concentrated in the southeast of England). The factor in Liverpool's economic decline most directly relevant to the Liverpool-Singapore nexus, however, was the dismantling of the colonial economic system upon which world city Liverpool had been dependent.

The making of the third iteration of the Ocean Building reveals much about the changing place in the world of both Liverpool and Singapore, and about the two cities' changing relations with each other. K.K. Seet's corporate account of the site's transformation casts the directors of SSC and Mansfields – especially Eric Wingate, who was chairman of both – as the 'driving force' behind rebuilding plans from the late 1960s. Yet these Singapore-based players required approval from India Buildings in Liverpool before they could proceed with their plans. As such, on the one hand, Liverpool retained ultimate control. On the other hand, the 'parent concern' there is depicted as having been reluctant to embark upon 'a grandiose scheme' of urban redevelopment, preferring to 'stick to things nautical and steer clear of bricks and mortar'.[57] When they 'finally relented', Ocean of Liverpool (along with Mansfields and a London-based property developer) formed Ocean Properties Pte Ltd. to build a state-of-the-art 28-storey commercial office tower with air-conditioning, computer-controlled lifts and the biggest underground car park in Singapore.[58] In hindsight, this may be regarded as a significant symbolic moment in shifting world city networks in that Ocean's apparently reluctant move towards land-oriented, 'bricks and mortar' business marked the end of Liverpool as a site of maritime imperial world city functions (or, as Malcolm Falkus put it: 'As sea gave way to land, Liverpool gave way to London').[59] Meanwhile, the third Ocean Building, as a signature component of the emergent 'golden shoe' financial district in Singapore[60] contributed to the independent city-state's own global city aspirations.

Rise, demise and relational decoupling

The economic fortunes of Singapore and Liverpool over the past half-century may be generalized in terms of 'rise' and 'demise' respectively. In the context of the relational comparative framing of this chapter, however, it is important to acknowledge that there has not been a straightforward inversion of the two cities in the global economic scheme of things. The global city – or, more precisely, what has become the 'global city-state'[61] – of Singapore is not a locus of 'command and control' functions for post-world city Liverpool in the way that Ocean Steamship once controlled significant aspects of colonial economic networks in (and through) Singapore. Singapore and Liverpool have instead largely been decoupled commercially, with the result that this final section of the chapter is more straightforwardly comparative rather than relational comparative; it considers their contrasting fortunes in wider worlds rather than how they have (re)shaped each other. I consider three short points of comparison in turn.

The first point entails a continuation of the world/global cities theme from the previous section, and has to do with the very different ways in which Liverpool and Singapore feature in the various city rankings that have proliferated in urban studies over the past two decades. The best known of these is the 'roster' of world cities compiled by the Globalization and World Cities (GaWC) research group since 1999. GaWC devised a hierarchical ranking of cities based on their importance to so-called 'advanced producer services' firms (in the fields of accountancy, advertising, banking and legal services).[62] In the initial GaWC analysis, Singapore appeared as an 'Alpha' world city, while Liverpool did not appear at all. Indeed, the one-time New York of Europe did not even feature on a list of 'next best' cities showing 'evidence of world city formation'. In the couple of decades since that original ranking, GaWC scholars have refined their methods and sought to become more encompassing – extending beyond the original top of the global urban hierarchy. In the 'World According to GaWC 2016', Singapore was a so-called 'Alpha+' city (ranked below only London and New York); Liverpool does now appear, but below the 'Gamma-' category, alongside Johor Bahru.[63] Inspired by GaWC methods and measurements, other scholars have devised rankings specifically for 'World Maritime Cities', seeking to calculate a hierarchy of influence in terms of where shipping companies make decisions from.[64] Again, Singapore is ranked near the top, as an 'Alpha world maritime city', while Liverpool does not appear (the 'Alpha' ranking European cities are Hamburg and London).

I have contributed to urban studies research on the problems and limitations of these kinds of ranking exercises and associated visualizations.[65] Nonetheless, whether we approve of them or not, they remain very influential in and beyond the academy, particularly in legitimising certain places and policies as 'successful' (and thereby worthy of emulation). In Singapore, the continued competitiveness of the container port and graduating to becoming a maritime world city decision-making hub (as well as having consolidated its position as a 'global city' financial services centre) form part of an even wider narrative of successful economic transformation: 'from third world to first'. This leads to my second point of comparison concerning how narratives of Liverpool's economic transition include conceptions of a shift in the opposite direction to Singapore. 'From Third World to First', of course, forms part of the title of one volume of Lee Kuan Yew's memoirs on the developmental rise of Singapore under his premiership and mentorship.[66] The phrase has already been subjected to critical scholarly scrutiny, while the fact that Singapore was likened to Liverpool, Birmingham and Manchester long before independence adds a further wrinkle to the story of transition from 'third world' in 1965.[67] Whatever 'myths' are bound up in 'From Third World to First', however, a valid central component of the transition narrative has to do with rising affluence and material wealth, which saw Singapore surpass the UK's per capita GDP in the mid-1990s. By that time, the economic troubles of Liverpool (and the wider Merseyside region) were well recognized and had fomented policy responses at various scales. In 1993 Merseyside was accorded 'Objective 1' status as a 'lagging' region of the European Union (EU) – one in which per capita income was less than 75 per cent of the EU average – meaning that it was eligible for regional developmental assistance (or 'aid'). It is in an essay by Alan Sekula on the Liverpool dock workers' dispute in the 1990s that we find explicit articulation of what sounds like *The Singapore Story* in reverse. Sekula's essay includes an image of sacked dock workers listening to a radio call-in show about a film that they co-wrote concerning their 28-month struggle. The accompanying text reads:

> Caller #1: 'Don't dockers know any other word but the F-word?'
> Caller #2: 'We're becoming a third world country'.[68]

Among the bewildering range of policy responses to economic de-development that have been attempted on Merseyside – and the one that relates most directly both to my work on Malay Liverpool, and to Singapore – is Liverpool's rebranding as 'The World in One City'. In connection with that, my third point of comparison has to do with how authorities in both Singapore and Liverpool have sought to capitalize on demographic diversity inherited from British colonial economy and labour mobilities. In the case of Singapore – and it is worth reiterating that since 1965, this has been a nation-state as well as a city, or even a 'city-state-nation'[69] – in addition to managing the population through colonially inherited racial categories (Chinese, Malay, Indian), demographic diversity has long been mobilized in tourist marketing. One example from 'Singapore Travel News' in the mid-1970s read:

> Singapore is a world within a world. Where so many groups have come together to make it one of the world's great melting pots of different races. It's a place where one can see a Malay wedding, a Chinese opera and an Indian dance all in a day.[70]

Britain and its cities, woke up to such marketing opportunities much later. In Liverpool, from the early 2000s, that included celebrating the cosmopolitan histories and demographic legacy of seafaring labour. According to one of the chief proponents of Liverpool's bid to become European Capital of Culture for 2008:

> Liverpool is a unique city. . . . The cultural wealth and diversity generated by 800 years of maritime history together with our long established Black, Chinese and Irish communities produces a unique identity which is both national and international. . . . We are truly The World in One City.[71]

I examined such civic discourse and how it was bound up with the city's successful European Capital of Culture bid in my book on Malay Liverpool. On the one hand, 'The World in One City' was a reflection of genuine concern to excavate historical diversity. On the other hand, attention tended to focus on specific communities with (real or imaginative) diasporic connections to economically booming parts of the world – especially to coastal cities of the PRC such as Shanghai.

But if there is one part of Liverpool that remains demographically marked by its maritime world city past, it is not so much Chinatown as the Liverpool 8 area – where the city's second Malay Club opened in 1963, and where (from 2003) I conducted much of my fieldwork, including speaking with elderly ex-seafarers about their return journeys to 'modern' Singapore. The clubhouse closed down in 2007, the year before Liverpool assumed the mantle of European Capital of Culture as 'The World in One City'. Nonetheless, more widely in the one-time New York of Europe, heritage marketing continues to capitalize upon the roots and routes of Liverpool's maritime world city past. In contrast, in Singapore (the one-time Liverpool of the East) recent urban development, most prominently at Marina Bay, inter-references London and New York as part of efforts to remain in the league of 'Alpha' global/world cities.[72]

Conclusion

There are few visible signs in Singapore today of constitutive relations with Liverpool. Not only did the making of the third Ocean Building from the late 1960s involve some of the last acts of command and control from Liverpool but that building was in turn demolished in 2007.[73] The primary aim of this chapter has been to excavate aspects of the historical commercial influence of formerly 'world city' Liverpool on the development of Singapore. As I noted in introducing the chapter, part of the wider significance of such an approach is in resisting the default tendency to frame histories and geographies at the national scale. To the extent that Singapore's imperial British connections have been framed in inter-urban terms, the focus has overwhelmingly been on London – the metropolitan centre of the British Empire – rather than other British cities. Relatedly, academic urban studies research remains stubbornly 'metrocentric' in foregrounding the experiences of an often deeply unrepresentative set of large and/or powerful contemporary cities and urban regions.[74] My hope is therefore that this chapter might be a spur for further work that diversifies examination of Singapore's relational historical geographies beyond recognized historical and contemporary world cities such as London and New York. That could mean other British imperial ports or manufacturing centres that I have mentioned in passing in this chapter – Cardiff, Glasgow, Birmingham or Manchester, among others – and other prominent ports in the colonial commercial networks of shipping companies such as the Blue Funnel Line (e.g. Colombo, Cape Town, or Hong Kong). However, the making of Singapore as a regional commercial centre and global city over the past two hundred years has clearly also been about much more than British roots or routes, as evidenced by Julia Lossau's recent work on firms from Bremen.[75] Finally, while examination of the relational remaking of Singapore demands that attention be given to firms as important actors and objects of analysis, historical geographies of connection may also be mapped by tracing flows of commodities and products, and the mobilities of the seafarers who shipped them between nodes in regional and global networks.

Acknowledgement

The research that is drawn upon in this chapter was originally funded by NUS research grant R-109–000–058–112. I am grateful to Julius Chang for collecting further documentary and archival material. Feedback from fellow presenters and participants at the conference on 'Singapore 200: Two Centuries of the Lion City', organized by Nick White and Tony Webster, helped me to develop an initial draft of the chapter. Andrew Tan kindly provided me with important insights into the Singapore 'Bund' waterfront.

Notes

1 J.N. Miksic, *Singapore and the Silk Road of the Sea, 1300–1800*, Singapore: NUS Press, 2013.
2 S. Rajaratnam, 'Singapore: Global city.' Text of address to the Singapore Press Club, 6 February 1972. See also: N. Oswin and B.S.A. Yeoh, 'Introduction: Mobile City Singapore,' *Mobilities*, vol. 5, no. 2, 2010, pp. 167–175; Valeria Giacomin's contribution to this volume on Singapore as a 'global city ante litteram' on account of its centrality to the world's most important 'rubber plantation cluster' from the early decades of the twentieth century.
3 J. Agnew, 'The Territorial Trap: The Geographical Assumptions of International Relations Theory,' *Review of International Political Economy*, vol. 1, no. 1, 1994, pp. 53–80.
4 See, for example, A.D. King, *Global Cities: Post-Imperialism and the Internationalization of London*, London: Routledge, 1990; P.J. Taylor, 'Historical World City Networks,' in B. Derudder, M. Hoyler, P.J. Taylor, and F. Witlox (eds.), *International Handbook of Globalization and World Cities*, Cheltenham: Edward Elgar, 2012, pp. 9–21. In definitional terms, 'world city' has long been used to connote cities deemed to be of worldwide importance or significance. 'Global city' entered the lexicon of urban studies much more recently through the work of Saskia Sassen, who used the term to denote more specifically a city with capacity for 'command and control' functions in a global(ised) economy (S. Sassen, *The Global City*, Princeton: Princeton University Press, 1991). In practice, world and global city are often used interchangeably in academic urban studies. S. Rajaratnam's description of Singapore as a global city, noted above, is one of several antecedents to Sassen's popularisation of that term).
5 K. Ward, 'Towards a Relational Comparative Approach to the Study of Cities,' *Progress in Human Geography*, vol. 34, no. 4, 2010, pp. 471–487.
6 T. Bunnell, *From World City to the World in One City: Liverpool Through Malay Lives*, Chichester: Wiley, 2016. As I note in the book, the men concerned were of geographically diverse origins – most from what are today the nation-states of Malaysia and Singapore, but some from dispersed coastal parts of the Indonesian archipelago – and had varied relations with the identity category 'Melayu' or 'Malay.' On Malay-ness as a historically 'contested and wandering identity', see: T.P. Barnard and H.M.J. Maier, 'Melayu, Malay, Maleis,' in T.P. Barnard (ed.), *Contesting Malayness: Malay Identity Across Boundaries*, Singapore: Singapore University Press, 2004, p. ix.
7 A. Webster, *Gentlemen Capitalists: British Imperialism in South East Asia 1770–1890*, London and New York: Tauris Academic Studies, 1998, p. 71.
8 A. Webster, 'Liverpool and the Asian Trade, 1800–50: Some Insights into a Provincial British Commercial Network,' in S. Haggerty, A. Webster, and N. White (eds.), *The Empire in One City: Liverpool's Inconvenient Imperial Past*, Manchester: Manchester University Press, 2008, pp. 35–54.

9   As trade expanded in the first half of the nineteenth century, and India became increasingly central to Britain's global trade and economy, so-called *lascars* 'became the mainstay of the labour force in British-registered ships bound for Europe.' R. Visram, *Asians in Britain: 400 Years of History*, London: Pluto Press, 2002, p. 16.

10 A. Ghosh, 'Of Fanas and Forecastles: The Indian Ocean and Some Lost Languages of the Age of Sail,' *Economic and Political Weekly*, 21 June 2008, pp. 56–62, 57.

11 J. Salter, *The Asiatic in England: Sketches of Sixteen Years' Work Among Orientals*, London: Jackson and Halliday, 1873, p. 230.

12 Ibid., pp. 158–159.

13 This is recorded in Melville's autobiographical novel, *Redburn*, which was published in 1849 but based on a journey he had made to Liverpool a decade earlier. Melville described the lascar crew of the *Irrawaddy* as comprising 'Malays, Mahrattas, Burmese, Siamese, and Cingalese.' H. Melville, *Redburn: His First Voyage*, New York: The Library of America, 1983 [1849], p. 187.

14 Webster, 'Liverpool and the Asian Trade,' p. 44.

15 *Illustrated London News*, 15 May 1886.

16 R.H.B. Lockhart, *Return to Malaya*, London: Putnam, 1936, p. 140.

17 F.W. Burbidge, *The Gardens of the Sun: Or, a Naturalist's Journal on the Mountains and in the Forests and Swamps of Borneo and the Sulu Archipelago*, London: John Murray, 1880, p. 14.

18 Ian Baucom casts Liverpool as one of the 'capitals' of a 'long nineteenth century' I. Baucom, *Specters of the Atlantic: Finance Capital, Slavery, and the Philosophy of History*, Durham, NC: Duke University Press, 2005.

19 G. Chandler, *Liverpool Shipping: A Short History*, London: Phoenix House, 1960, p. 212.

20 The opening of the Suez Canal in 1869 made the eastern trade more attractive to steamships and reduced the sea journey between England and Malaya from 116 days to 42. Federation of Malaya, *Annual Report of the Federation of Malaya*, Kuala Lumpur: Government Press, 1956. According to George Bogaars' historical analysis of the effects of opening of the Suez Canal on the trade and development of Singapore, the rise in shipping tonnage reaching Singapore from Britain by steamship would have occurred even without the canal (and the wider eclipse of sail tonnage by steamship) although the process would have been much more gradual. G. Bogaars, 'The Effect of the Opening of the Suez Canal on the Trade and Development of Singapore,' *Journal of the Malayan Branch of the Royal Asiatic Society*, vol. 28, no. 1, 1955, pp. 99–143.

21 M. Falkus, *The Blue Funnel Legend*, Basingstoke: MacMillan, 1990, p. 28.

22 Ibid., p. 4.

23 Although in the twentieth century, Malays were also often included among seafarers labelled 'Asiatic.'

24 M. Puteh, 'Menjengah ke teratak Melayu di Pulau Manhattan,' *Dewan Budaya*, February 1983, pp. 38–39.

25 Bunnell, *From World City to the World in One City*, p. 45.

26 India Office Records [IOR L/E/9/954]. The equivalent figure in Cardiff was 132, and it was only after the Second World War that Liverpool eclipsed Cardiff as the pre-eminent home for (ex)seafaring Malays in Britain.

27 J. Belchem, *Merseypride: Essays in Liverpool Exceptionalism*, Liverpool: Liverpool University Press, 2000, p. xiii.

28 T. Lane, *Liverpool: City of the Sea*, Liverpool: Liverpool University Press, 1997, p. 131.

29 K.K. Seet, *Prime: Pride of Passage*, Singapore: Straits Times Press, 2011, p. 59.

30 Ocean Archives, Merseyside Maritime Museum [OA 879]: K.G. Tregonning, 'The Mosquito Fleet', circa 1960. Richard Lawton identified the year 1914 as Liverpool's 'commercial zenith.' R. Lawton, 'Liverpool and the Tropics,' in R.W. Steel and R. Mansell Prothero (eds.), *Geographers and the Tropics: Liverpool Essays*, London: Longmans, 1964, pp. 349–375, 358.

31 OA 7.A.2.154, 'British Malaya and Adjoining Territories: Notes for Exporters,' 1936.
32 W.G. Huff, *The Economic Growth of Singapore: Trade and Development in the Twentieth Century*, Cambridge: Cambridge University Press, 1994.
33 R.E. Elson, 'International Commerce, the State and Society: Economic and Social Change,' in N. Tarling (ed.), *The Cambridge History of Southeast Asia, Volume 3*, 2001, pp. 127–192.
34 Ibid., p. 165.
35 Falkus, *Blue Funnel*, p. 31.
36 Bogaars, 'Suez Canal,' pp. 120–121.
37 K.G. Tregonning, 'Straits Tin: A Brief Account of the First Seventy-Five Years of the Straits Trading Company Limited,' *Journal of the Malayan Branch of the Royal Asiatic Society*, vol. 36, no. 1, 1963, pp. 79–152, 94.
38 Huff, *Economic Development*, p. 146.
39 Falkus, *Blue Funnel*, p. 51.
40 K.G. Tregonning, *Home Port Singapore: A History of Straits Steamship Company Limited, 1890–1965*, Singapore: Oxford University Press, 1967, p. 88.
41 Bunnell, *From World City to the World in One City*, p. 28.
42 E. Jennings, *Mansfields: Transport and Distribution in South-East Asia*, Singapore: Meridian Communications, 1973.
43 *Straits Times*, 24 March 1923, p. 9.
44 Bunnell, *From World City to the World in One City*, p. 36.
45 Seet, *Prime*, p. 60.
46 O. Sykes, J. Brown, M. Cocks, D. Shaw, and C. Couch, 'A City Profile of Liverpool,' *Cities*, vol. 35, 2013, pp. 299–318.
47 S.R. Nathan and T. Auger, *An Unexpected Journey: Path to the Presidency*, Singapore: Editions Didier Millet, 2011, p. 181. In addition, an exhibition at the National Museum of Singapore for the 50th anniversary of independence recreated 'Singapore's lost historic waterfront' under the title 'The Singapore Bund,' available at: www.nationalmuseum.sg/our-exhibitions/exhibition-list/the-singapore-bund, accessed 29 November 2018. On the initial engagement of Briggs and Thornley architects for the design of the second Ocean Building, see Falkus, *Blue Funnel*, p. 163.
48 P. Geddes, *Cities in Evolution*, London: Williams and Norgate, 1915.
49 P. Hall, *The World Cities*, London: Weidenfeld and Nicolson, 1966.
50 J. Friedmann, 'The World City Hypothesis,' *Development and Change*, vol. 17, no. 1, pp. 69–83.
51 King, *Global Cities*, p. 36. See also: S. Wilks-Heeg, 'From World City to Pariah City? Liverpool and the Global Economy, 1850–2000,' in R. Munck (ed.), *Reinventing the City? Liverpool in Comparative Perspective*, Liverpool: Liverpool University Press, 2003, pp. 36–52.
52 King, *Global Cities*, p. 34.
53 Seet, *Prime*, p. 67.
54 A. McLellan, *The History of Mansfield and Company: Part 2, 1920–1953*, Singapore: Mansfield, 1953.
55 J. Murden, '"City of Change and Challenge": Liverpool Since 1945,' in J. Belchem (ed.), *Liverpool 800: Culture, Character and History*, Liverpool: Liverpool University Press, 2006, pp. 393–485, 402.
56 Falkus, *Blue Funnel*, p. 302. Although Jon Murden notes that 1964 saw what was then an all-time record tonnage of cargo passing through Liverpool. Murden, '"City of Change",' p. 404.
57 Seet, *Prime*, p. 75.
58 *Straits Times*, 25 September 1970, p. 5.
59 Falkus, *Blue Funnel*, p. 376.
60 B.H. Chua, *The Golden Shoe: Building Singapore's Financial District*, Singapore: Urban Redevelopment Authority, 1989.

61 K. Olds and H. Yeung, 'Pathways to Global City Formation: A View from the Developmental City-State of Singapore,' *Review of International Political Economy*, vol. 11, no. 3, 2004, pp. 489–521.

62 J.V. Beaverstock, R.G. Smith, and P.J. Taylor, 'World-City Network: A New Meta-Geography,' *Annals of the Association of American Geographers*, vol. 90, no. 1, 2000, pp. 123–134.

63 'The World According to GaWC 2016,' www.lboro.ac.uk/gawc/world2016t.html, accessed 28 November 2018.

64 A. Verhetsel and S. Sel, 'World Maritime Cities: From Which Cities Do Maritime Decision-Makers Operate?' *Transport Policy*, vol. 16, no. 5, 2009, pp. 240–250.

65 T. Bunnell, 'Antecedent Cities and Inter-Referencing Effects: Learning from and Extending Beyond Critiques of Neoliberalisation,' *Urban Studies*, vol. 52, no. 11, 2015, pp. 1983–2000.

66 K.Y. Lee, *From Third World to First: The Singapore Story: 1965–2000*, Singapore: Marshall Cavendish, 2000.

67 P. Holden, 'Questioning "From Third World to First",' in K.S. Loh, P.J. Thum, and J.M-T. Chia (eds.), *Living with Myths in Singapore*, Singapore: Ethos Books, 2017, pp. 75–83.

68 A. Sekula, 'Freeway to China (Version 2, for Liverpool),' *Public Culture*, vol. 12, no. 2, 2000, pp. 411–22, 421.

69 B.H. Chua, 'Singapore as Model: Planning Innovations, Knowledge Experts,' in A. Roy and A. Ong (eds.), *Worlding Cities: Asian Experiments and the Art of Being Global*, Chichester: Wiley, 2011, pp. 29–55, 29.

70 Singapore Travel News, March 1976, cited in T.C. Chang, 'From "Instant Asia" to "Multifaceted Jewel": Urban Imaging Strategies and Tourism Development in Singapore,' *Urban Geography*, vol. 18, no. 6, 1997, pp. 542–562.

71 Mike Storey (leader of Liverpool City Council), cited in: Liverpool City Council, *Liverpool 2008: European Capital of Culture Bid*, Liverpool: Liverpool Culture Company, 2002.

72 E.X.Y. Yap, 'The Transnational Assembling of Marina Bay, Singapore,' *Singapore Journal of Tropical Geography*, vol. 34, no. 3, 2013, pp. 390–406.

73 The Ocean Financial Centre that replaced the third Ocean Building was opened in 2010.

74 T. Bunnell and A. Maringanti, 'Practising Urban and Regional Research Beyond Metrocentricity,' *International Journal of Urban and Regional Research*, vol. 34, no. 2, 2010, pp. 415–420.

75 J. Lossau, 'Hanseatic Imprints: Bremen's Contribution to the Making of Singapore,' Seminar presented at the Asia Research Institute, National University of Singapore, 13 March 2018.

11 Experts in the making of Singapore

Kah Seng Loh

In 1963, the People's Action Party (PAP) government declared 'war on the all too familiar ogres and giants in a subservient society – poverty, disease, ignorance, squalor, and idleness'.[1] This was a fitting slogan for the policy of 'democratic socialism in action' – the PAP's plan to take the lead in transforming the economy and the state of health, education, housing, and employment. But with Singapore poised to become independent by joining the Federation of Malaysia, the slogan of national self-determination belied the plagiarism of the 1942 Beveridge Report in Britain, which had decried the same five 'giant evils', laying the basis of the British welfare state.

To say that British colonialism shaped postcolonial Singapore is a truism. The salient issues are the forms and agents of influence, and the processes and outcomes. This chapter focuses on less visible and heralded actors: the international experts. Rather than bilateral, colonial influence worked through a tripartite relationship between the metropolitan/colonial establishment, the Singapore government and these advisers. The chapter considers four cases of expert influence, which though somewhat arbitrarily assembled, provide useful insights into the socio-economic war on 'ogres' and 'giants'. They throw light on the transition from the colonial to the postcolonial after 1959, when Singapore became a self-governing state and acquired control over economic and social policy.

The experts were third-party foreign advisers, appointed by the British government or international non-governmental organisations (INGOs) like the United Nations (UN). Their ties with Singapore were a corollary of its long-standing role as a port city, connected to global trade routes. Singapore actively cultivated external expertise in the way it welcomed goods, capital and migrants from outside. Despite its left-wing socialist ideology, the PAP expressed in 1958 its willingness to consult experts who were not doctrinaire socialists.[2]

Experts of the twentieth century

The early technical expertise which Singapore received at the dawn of the twentieth century stemmed from the aegis of development and welfare, tied to notions of new relationships between the colonial power and ruled population, namely, dual mandate and trusteeship. Expertise was a product of shifting imperial interests, rather than a direct response to local conditions. It was more notable for its rhetoric than any effect on policy.[3] In pre-war Singapore, British officials and doctors debated over the terrible state of housing and disease for over three decades without significantly improving either. The 1938 Weisberg Committee warned that the shophouses in the Municipality had 'become warrens of cubicles and form slums of the worst description, and are a proved menace to the health of the people'.[4]

At the end of the Second World War, expertise shed its rhetorical nature to shape emerging development policies and the socio-economic world, signalling, as Joseph Morgan Hodge terms it, the 'triumph of the expert'.[5] In Singapore as elsewhere, part of the reason was political: expertise facilitated British decolonisation and the Anglo-American Cold War, bridging the uncertain transition between the colonial and postcolonial order. It was key to the enhanced version of the Colonial Development and Welfare Act introduced for the British colonies in 1945. It sought to forestall revolutionary forces by proposing scientific solutions to poverty and underdevelopment, integral to what various historians have called 'welfare colonialism', 'developmental colonialism' and 'reformist colonialism'.[6] Its goal was not merely to tackle socio-economic 'ogres' but also to create a postcolonial order. Albert Winsemius, the Dutch adviser to the People's Action Party government, was strongly anti-communist, but he was not unique.

The post-war welfare state in Britain provided the institutional template for most experts, although others like Winsemius looked to their home countries. More importantly, they offered a consensus of interlocking ideas: there was a great crisis in the colony in which local actors were ignorant and hapless, and the state had to lead a massive response, utilising science and technology. Expertise was frequently authoritarian-high modernist, to use James Scott's term, being advised by experts and pushed through by state power.[7] Matters of housing, health, education and development, historically left to individuals, communities and the private sector, now came under the purview of the state-expert coalition. The post-war education programmes in southeast Asia, Tim Harper notes, were tools of transition to shape new states in the colonial image, replacing community- and vernacular-based school systems.[8] To congested cities, experts preached the ideals of Ebenezer Howard's 'Garden City', but with the proviso for the state to lead the way. The colonial third world, having grown with little regulation, now sent their best students to learn from the West in order to do so.[9]

Expertise appealed to many postcolonial regimes. Based on science or the social sciences, it appeared apolitical and universally applicable. In reality, it was drawn narrowly from victorious Western experiences and was being adapted, sometimes haphazardly, to difficult colonial and postcolonial contexts. Most experts were white, Western-educated and male, and nominated by colonial officials who admired their work. As Timothy Mitchell observes, the idea of expertise was inherently political: the solution came from outsiders, sidelining locals, while elevating the state above civil society and the private sector.[10] Development issues which stemmed from the imperial and extractive nature of colonial rule were reduced to technical matters requiring the application of science and technology.[11] Still, there was an earnestness in the assistance offered to client states, as manifest in the expert missions supported by INGOs. Akira Iriye sees in these organisations a semblance of a global community and international society, pursuing collaboration instead of competition between nation-states.[12] While this view is too idealistic, as INGOs were affected by Cold War and national politics, they did herald an attempt to redefine the basis of international relations. Without ignoring their failings, we can take INGOs seriously in the context of what they tried to accomplish. Experts were a third party, linked to politics in their home countries or the Cold War, but they were not merely agents of Western influence.

Singapore is interesting because the government-expert connection was more equal, dialogic and effective than in many cases. Studies are typically critical of expertise, likening it to a form of rule or tyranny imposed on the clients.[13] In Singapore, however, experts often submitted useful and relevant ideas, which guided the city-state's robust development. Some were willing to learn from Singaporeans, while the government was able to adapt the advice. On a personal level, experts and Singaporeans often got along well, or shared similar thinking on policy issues. Where most literature on socio-economic developments have tended to highlight the role of the state, the experts offer a more sophisticated view of transnational Singapore, acting in concert with the government and local factors.[14]

W.J.R. Simpson: tuberculosis to public housing

The unpredictable long-term impact of expertise is exemplified by W.J.R. Simpson, a sanitation expert who undertook studies of plague, cholera and tuberculosis in British colonies in Asia and Africa. Between 1895 and 1914, Simpson worked with the Colonial Office to conduct research on tropical diseases.[15] In 1906, he arrived in Singapore to advise the Straits Settlements government on the state of sanitation. The colonial administration was not clueless about the problem. Governor John Anderson's medical officers had advised him that Singapore's high death rate of over 40 persons per thousand was due to overcrowding in the town's shophouses.[16] But Anderson understood remedies such as cleansing or rebuilding the shophouses to be both difficult and expensive. An expert's recommendations would justify his administration's response and outlay. Simpson's report linked the overcrowding to environmental and social factors. He was interested in the physical state of dwellings, their proximity to one another and their access to air and sunlight.[17] He deemed locals to be deficient in sanitary matters, and the state had to take a leading role to form a sanitary service, establish building by-laws and demolish unclean dwellings.[18] In Singapore for only three months, he relied heavily on local statistics. The death rate had jumped 40 per cent between 1892 and 1905. Tuberculosis was a principal factor, killing 8,516 people in the last five years. But Simpson failed to acknowledge problems in his sources. Hospital records did not capture the working class people who avoided hospitals until they were seriously ill. The figures on deaths outside of hospitals were usually not certified by medical practitioners.[19]

To his credit, Simpson sent municipal inspectors to survey, map and photograph shophouses along eight streets in the town area. His findings concurred with those of Anderson and local doctors: the shophouses were built back to back without open spaces and backlanes. Inside, 'horrific conditions' prevailed as residents crowded into tiny cubicles, particularly at the back where there were no windows, air or light, and it was 'dark and cheerless'.[20] Simpson added a racial interpretation to the environmental observations, commonplace in his profession in the early twentieth century. Official statistics showed the death rate for tuberculosis to be highest among the Chinese. Simpson assessed that 'The Chinese prefer, where possible, to build horizontally rather than vertically', in creating the shophouse housing form.[21] Simpson drew a map titled 'Deaths from Tuberculosis', highlighting recurring deaths in two shophouses and concluding that tuberculosis was becoming an epidemic.[22] He urged administrative and environmental solutions. The government should make tuberculosis a notifiable infectious disease, making it mandatory for cases to the reported to the authorities. But mainly he linked the disease to 'haphazard and unhealthy development'.[23] The municipal administration should institute proper controls against insanitary housing and prevent overcrowding in shophouses. Expertise was crucial: Simpson recommended the creation of a sanitary board similar to the Improvement Trust in Bombay, chaired by the Principal Civil Medical Officer and filled with medical representatives.

Simpson's study was generally well received, but a reporter queried its relevance, remembering the call in 1905 by 'our active and energetic Health Officer, [W.R.C.] Middleton' for sanitary reform, ignored by the Municipal Commission. 'Why, then, it will be asked, have the Government and the Municipality jointly agreed to call in an expert, when the information sought was at hand?', the writer asked.[24] Worse, Simpson was proven to be seriously mistaken. On the 'Deaths from Tuberculosis' map, a reader of the *Singapore Free Press* asserted that the shophouses were not residential areas but dying places for tuberculosis sufferers, to which the Chinese would remove the sick from the community.[25] Medical officer David Galloway concurred that the shophouses were 'houses for the dying' a decade later.[26] Whether it was for this glaring error or the financial costs, Simpson's proposals were shelved for two decades. But his name remained a reference point in subsequent calls for sanitary reform. A decade passed before a follow-up study was undertaken in 1917 by the Singapore Housing Commission, which reiterated the issues of overcrowding, sanitation and tuberculosis. Again, the commission saw the problem in socio-environmental terms, lamenting that the town population 'cares nothing for sanitation, ventilation or even bare comfort'.[27]

Echoing Simpson's call for a sanitary service, the commission proposed the creation of a Singapore Improvement Trust (SIT), separate from the Municipal Commission and responsible for improvement schemes and town planning. An important principle guiding its work was to rehouse dwellers before insanitary buildings were demolished. This foreshadowed the work of the Singapore Improvement Trust and its successor, the Housing and Development Board (HDB). Conscious of its lack of expertise, the Housing Commission also proposed a tuberculosis expert to visit Singapore. This did not happen; instead the government appointed a Tuberculosis Committee in 1923, comprising doctors from the colonial civil service. The committee called for improvement works to reduce overcrowding and for housing to be built close to the congested areas to rehouse the displaced – an expensive course of action but one which Singapore took in the 1950s. Rising anger among the educated classes over the 'slums of Singapore' finally brought into existence, in 1927, the sanitary agency Simpson had called for: the SIT. Backed by $10 million government funding, the Trust was mandated to 'provide for the Improvement of the Town and Island of Singapore', including sanitising buildings and building back lanes.[28] Its board consisted of the president of the Municipal Commission (who was chairman of the Trust) and the municipal health officer – the medical representation Simpson had called for.[29] The SIT attempted to cleanse the houses in the town, but acquiring insanitary housing was too costly. Before the outbreak of the Pacific War, the interior of shophouses had 'become warrens of cubicles and form slums of the worst description'.[30] The Trust began to build new housing close to the congested areas, an idea proposed by the Tuberculosis Committee.[31] In 1934, the colonial government lauded the replacement of slums as 'one of the most potent anti-tuberculosis measures we have'.[32] A major fire in a squatter settlement in Tiong Bahru in 1934 gave the Trust the opportunity to begin its rehousing work. The assistant municipal health officer, W.E. Hutchinson, deemed 'general weapons' like housing to be more effective in reforming 'hygiene and social standards' than building sanatoria for tuberculosis.[33] By 1941, the Trust had made a modest start, building 784 flats in Tiong Bahru Estate.

The UN mission of experts and British town planners

After the Second World War, Singapore's public housing development was less influenced by sanitary expertise than by a new set of urban planning ideas. This is not to say that the insanitation had disappeared. On the contrary, persistent overcrowding in the shophouses led bigger families to move out of the town into squatter settlements, or urban kampongs. These kampongs, made of unauthorised, dilapidated housing, presented a new problem of insanitation. The Medical Department wondered why diseases like tuberculosis were not more prevalent 'in view of the many overcrowded cubicle dwellings . . . [and] the many squatter areas, and the thousands of hawkers to be met with in Singapore'.[34] Hutchinson, now deputy municipal health officer, continued to push for the government to build clean housing as an effective public health measure: 'Whatever may be the killing property of overcrowding [in the Central Area] or the ill-health that may result, it has nothing of the urgency that now exists in the creation of these insanitary kampongs'.[35] Such views influenced the 1947 Singapore Housing Committee, the first post-war body to consider a preliminary building plan for Singapore. Notably, the committee tasked the SIT to carry out the building programme, which was outside its role as a sanitary agency. The Trust should have full powers to build, plan ahead of development and to disperse the town population to housing and industrial estates.[36] Only the HDB, formed in 1960, had such powers. Rather, public housing development after the war was driven by the emerging influence of town and urban planning – a body of post-war ideas which superseded the sanitary doctrine. Housing would be planned as part of urban development, following two main ideas. The first was master planning, or long-term, zonal planning for Singapore as a whole. The second was the new town, based on upon British satellite towns encapsulated in the Barlow, Uthwatt and other town planning reports. A central element was the dispersal of the inner city population to 'garden' new towns in the suburbs with green areas.

While still a serious health problem and a major part of colonial health policy, tuberculosis became a lesser theme in the public housing programme. Urban planners supplanted the doctors, because while they continued to warn about disease, they were able to connect housing to broader issues of citizenship, democracy and the free market. Charles Abrams, a familiar name on UN missions, including one on urban renewal in Singapore in the early 1960s, saw squatters as a 'formidable threat to the structure of private rights established through the centuries'.[37] He warned that amid the globalising Cold War, Asia's 'housing famine' could quickly turn 'today's masses' into 'tomorrow's mobs'.[38] The first major intervention of the urban planning expertise in Singapore was the UN Mission of Experts on Tropical Housing, which visited six countries in Southeast and South Asia in 1950–1951. Led by US urban planner Jacob Crane, it studied the possibility of building low-cost housing to combat the problem of 'tropical housing'.[39] The insanitary squatter hut should be replaced by public housing or improved through aided self-help. But above all, 'a planned policy of decentralisation (in the form of detached suburban communities or new townships), based on new urban land policies, is the only solution'.[40] The state would draw up a comprehensive land-use plan, while experts advised on a gamut of technical issues ranging from town and regional planning to housing finance, design, research and legislation. In an early paraphrase of the 'ogre' statement, the mission feared that 'Singapore is losing the war against poverty and disease'.[41] It supported the recommendations of the 1947 Housing Committee, particularly for a 20-year master plan to zone land-use and build low-cost housing for the general population.[42]

Subsequently, British town planner George Pepler was appointed adviser to the SIT between 1950–1954. He was heavily involved in the 1955 Master Plan. Pepler had made his career in Britain, helping to draft the Town and Country Planning Act of 1947. His ideas have become commonplace in Singapore urban planning: the importance of master planning, zonal land-use and green belts to manage urban growth. He arrived in Singapore in 1950, the same year as the UN mission, and also when a great fire razed the squatter settlement of Kampong Bugis, rendering 3,000 people homeless. The disaster was the trigger for a 'diagnostic survey' of the squatter areas between 1952 and 1954, which the government had approved in 1949 but lacked the staff to undertake. Lamenting the shortage of locals, Pepler recruited planners from Britain, including D.H. Komlosay, chief town planner of Lancashire, who became the SIT's planning adviser and the diagnostic survey's chief planning officer. Geography student volunteers from the University of Malaya, like Simpson's inspectors entering the shophouses half a century earlier, visited the unauthorised houses, asking 'all sorts of questions'.[43] After the survey, Komlosay and S.C. Woolmer, the Trust's chief architect, warned the government of 'steps that must be taken AT THIS MOMENT' for a 'firm coordinated policy' of urban development.[44] These views contributed to the rejection of squatter housing in the Master Plan. Pepler's opinion was that 'The Attap Dwelling will not be appropriate within the built-up precincts of a modern City'.[45] The plan accepted that some urban kampongs would be tolerated for a time or cleaned up, but the majority would be demolished, with their dwellers rehoused in new towns.[46]

In a circuitous way, Simpson's sanitary expertise had morphed into a public housing state more than half a century later. The latter initially involved the clearance of urban kampongs, with the HDB building emergency flats on the sites of great fires. This was followed by urban renewal to disperse the population of the inner city to new towns.[47] Singapore did not become a welfare state in the mould of the Beveridge Report, but its early urban development under the PAP owed much to the 1955 Master Plan, itself the product of international planning and sanitary expertise rendered to the colonial regime.

Britain's ex-principals and the Singapore polytechnic

After the Second World War, the Singapore government also recruited international experts to attack the other 'ogres': ignorance (through educational reform), idleness (by creating full-time industrial work) and poverty (by redistributing wealth through such work). As with urban planning and housing, the late-colonial state took the first steps which were later expanded by the PAP government. Technical education in particular was important, being connected to both Singapore's industrialisation programme and, as envisaged by the 10-year Education Plan of 1947, for 'fostering and extending the capacity for self-government, and the ideal of civic loyalty and responsibility'.[48] The first polytechnic, the Singapore Polytechnic, formed in 1958 just before Singapore attained self-government, would produce the skilled manpower. This required a major cultural change, for parents and students to refrain from joining the 'chair-borne brigade' to take up technical or vocational education.[49]

The making of the Singapore Polytechnic was heavily influenced by the Advisory Committee on Colonial Colleges of Arts, Science and Technology (ACCCAST), formed in Britain in 1949. The committee was an autonomous network of current and former principals of British and African institutions which advised the Secretary of State for the Colonies on technical education. Besides Singapore, ACCCAST helped form polytechnics and technical colleges in British colonies and later the Commonwealth. It was renamed the Council for Overseas Colleges of Arts, Science and Technology (COCAST) in 1958, and the Council for Technical Education and Training in Overseas Countries (CTETOC) four years later. ACCCAST and its successors maintained a long relationship with Singapore, bridging the transition from colonial to postcolonial education.

The early Singapore Polytechnic, as conceptualised in the 1953 Dobby report, was a thoroughly British institution. E.H.G. Dobby was a professor of geography at the University of Malaya whose team of 12 endorsed the feasibility of a local polytechnic. The team consulted three British advisers in Singapore at the time:

Alexander Carr-Saunders, Director of the London School of Economics (who had endorsed the formation of the University of Malaya in 1949); D.G. James, Vice-Chancellor of the University of Southampton; and most crucially, F.J. Harlow, assistant adviser on higher and technical education to the Secretary of State for the Colonies.[50] The Dobby report accepted Harlow's proposal that the polytechnic's board should have representatives from industry and commerce. The Dobby team had in mind a 'typical U.K. college catering mainly for technical personnel but also providing a wide range of technical courses in commercial subjects', including Engineering, Architecture, Commerce, and Liberal Arts.[51] On the latter, the report wanted to bring together 'students with widely differing interests'.[52] The polytechnic would have a majority (75 per cent) of part-time students and use the certifications of professional bodies in Britain. Unlike British polytechnics, however, it would be a mid-level institution and would not offer degree courses. It would be autonomous of the government, based on the British 'aided system' where it would receive state funding.

Two aspects of the Dobby report were politically fractious. One was the use of expatriates to initially fill senior staff positions, as there were allegedly no capable locals. This ran counter to the Malayanisation of the colonial service and to nationalist sentiment. The report proposed higher salaries for expatriates and long contracts of five or ten years, even though technical teachers in Britain were not paid above national salary scales. The other controversy was the use of English as the medium of instruction. The polytechnic accepted a lower standard of English than in Britain, but maintained that 'there can be no short-cut to good, well-accepted technical qualifications'.[53]

ACCCAST subsequently arranged for A.W. Gibson, principal of Dudley and Staffordshire Technical College in Britain, to draft a more detailed plan for the polytechnic, which endorsed the earlier recommendations.[54] It also helped recruit the first principal, D.J. Williams, previously principal of the Lancaster and Morecambe College of Further Education. It also helped recruit heads of departments and senior lecturers, while advising on the polytechnic's planning, equipment and construction.[55]

The British-styled system did not sit well when the PAP government was elected into office the following year. In an anti-colonial gesture, the new leadership instituted a pay cut throughout the civil service, including the Singapore Polytechnic, despite its formal autonomy. This divided the polytechnic's board, as a pay cut would break the expatriates' contracts.[56] The board decided to exempt them. In July 1959, as its term expired, the government responded by appointing a new board headed by Toh Chin Chye, the deputy prime minister and chairman of the PAP. Toh laid down a 'first things first' policy: the polytechnic must gear itself to meet the nation's technical needs.[57] Toh announced sweeping changes: the polytechnic would have full-time students from the vernacular schools rather than working adults.[58] English remained the medium of instruction, although a pass, not credit, would suffice. Locals would set the examinations and the polytechnic would award the diplomas. Non-technical courses, including Liberal Studies and Commerce courses like typewriting and stenography, were scrapped. Liberal

Studies at the polytechnic, Toh said, was ridiculous.[59] On these drastic measures, he explained, 'We have got to protect this young plant from worms in the ground and pests in the air'.[60] The principal and many expatriates recruited by ACCCAST resigned, as did many from the SIT and City Council.

This, however, did not dismantle the polytechnic's links to the experts, although H.M. Collins at COCAST called Toh's reforms 'idiotic without exception' and 'a disaster which it would take years to retrieve'.[61] In November, pragmatism prevailed within the PAP and the reforms were scaled back. Toh conceded that external examiners would help locals set and mark the examinations – to ensure high standards – while the polytechnic would seek overseas recognition for its diplomas.[62] COCAST officials dismissed Toh's statements as an attempt at 'face saving'.[63] But the gulf between the Committee and the PAP continued to narrow. In January 1960, C.I.C. Scollay, the new principal of the Singapore Polytechnic, privately asked COCAST to help recruit expatriates.[64] A practical issue brought both sides closer: upgrading the polytechnic to a university, as recommended by a commission of inquiry into technical and vocational education appointed by the PAP in 1961.[65] The recommendation was a modern one, following trends in Britain and Africa, where a few technical colleges were being converted into universities. In October 1962, Scollay wrote to CTETOC, asking for a team of British advisers to visit the Singapore Polytechnic.[66] CTETOC arranged for Dr G.E. Watts, principal of Brighton College of Technology, which had recently been upgraded from a technical college to a college of technology offering higher-level courses, to visit Singapore.[67] After meeting with Toh Chin Chye, Watts reported a 're-orientation towards U.K. policies' on the Singapore government's part. He thought that the PAP had taken the early anti-colonial measures because it 'had been afraid of its own left wing'.[68]

In May 1963, Toh visited technical institutions in Britain and met with Watts and other CTETOC members. Collins felt some of Toh's views to be 'heretical', but agreed that he could be a 'source of benefit to technical education in Singapore'.[69] Subsequently CTETOC agreed to help the polytechnic recruit British staff, repairing the bridges damaged four earlier. Toh admitted the need to learn from Western institutions, declaring, 'It's time we stop boasting about our Polytechnic and technical advances'.[70] There is a final twist to this Singapore-expert narrative. In January 1964, a five-man Colombo Plan team headed by Dr C.A. Hart, principal of the Nigerian College of Technology, supported the expansion of the Singapore Polytechnic into a college of advanced technology (in effect a university), offering degree courses in Engineering, Architecture and Accountancy. This was necessary for the polytechnic to attract good students.[71] CTOTEC subsequently helped recruit Engineering and Architecture lecturers for the polytechnic's degree courses.

But the Singapore Polytechnic never became a university. There were competing plans to form a faculty of advanced technology at the University of Singapore.[72] Another expert study led by B.V. Bowden, principal of the Manchester College of Science and Technology, proposed a merger of degree courses at the polytechnic and university. The polytechnic would remain financially independent with its board of governors, and continue to manage its technical courses; in time it would become a full-fledged technical university.[73] The university would award the degrees. This awkward arrangement, Hart deemed, was an attempt to 'save our face and Dr Toh's too'.[74] For a brief period after 1965, the polytechnic jointly ran degree courses in Engineering and Accountancy with the University of Singapore. But within three years, the unwieldy arrangement was summarily dropped. Britain's announcement in 1968 that it would close its military bases in Singapore earlier than expected meant the need for Singapore to industrialise was more urgent than ever. The degree courses were moved to the university, with the polytechnic left to train technicians. Toh Chin Chye left the polytechnic that year to become Vice-Chancellor of the university.[75] Technician education expanded at the polytechnic in the 1970s. The government had consulted the experts but made its decision based on the country's needs.

Albert Winsemius and the politics of industrialisation

Albert Winsemius is often credited for his role in Singapore's industrialisation. Yet, although he directed the Netherlands' post-war economic recovery and advised other small countries, Singapore was originally unknown to him – it was 'neither an underdeveloped, nor a half-developed or a highly developed country',[76] not one of the 'underdeveloped nations possessing adequate natural resources but lacking capital and managerial know-how'.[77] The UN terms of reference for Winsemius in 1960 were extremely modest, which made the audaciousness of his advice even more jarring. His team was to investigate feasible industries for Singapore, prepare a plan for industrial estates, and propose ways to promote manufacturing.[78] The stakes for Singapore were high. Industrialisation was being pushed not because the long-standing entrepôt trade was floundering but because it would not provide jobs for a population growing at an annual rate of 4.5 per cent. This was perhaps the central problem of post-war Singapore, also worsening overcrowding in the city and fuelling the social discontent which spurred the rise of the left. In a way, Winsemius departed from the typical expert: he did not approve of 'the group [of experts] which Singapore has known for a long time, usually people from more developed countries who come two or three days or a week to Singapore, and then . . . give a press conference or interview, telling the Singaporeans what they do wrong and what they really should do'.[79] He spoke to locals, from policy-makers and bureaucrats to employers and unionists, 'listening at least the first two/three months, listening to others who know more about it'.[80]

The Winsemius report made several logical, if hardly earth-shaking, recommendations. He affirmed the official industrial policy: 'in the long run, only an expansion of manufacturing industry can keep stride with the growing population'.[81] Winsemius rejected contrary arguments supporting the entrepôt trade as derivative of a 'village mentality'.[82] His more substantive proposal was for 'A crash programme . . . to alleviate the immediate unemployment problem before the 10-year industrialisation programme could be expected to create the full impact'.[83] This would create a tenth of the 200,000-odd industrial jobs required in two to three years. Winsemius supported other measures being considered or implemented by the government: the establishment of the Economic Development Board to promote Singapore industry, granting pioneer status (tax holidays for five years) to investors, and the development of Jurong industrial estate, which was endorsed more strongly by a team of Japanese advisers.[84] A more important intervention was for the state to create a conducive environment for industrialists, rather than become one itself in the socialist vein. Winsemius' advice was implemented in the government's first State Development Plan of 1961–1964, authored by Minister for Finance Goh Keng Swee. The plan also endorsed the leading role of private – 'local and foreign' – rather than state capital, as Winsemius proposed.[85] While the EDB received $100 million from the budget to make industrial investments, most of the economic development budget of $508 million went to land and infrastructure.

One of the successes oft-credited to the PAP government is the adoption of an export strategy of industrialisation when most developing countries produced for the domestic market. Winsemius' intervention here was his only piece of advice not implemented in the State Development Plan. He made a nuanced and politically correct proposal, characteristic of his subtle approach to Singaporean matters. He knew that the government was pursuing merger and a common market with the Federation of Malaya. But he was sceptical about the prospects, given the political differences between the two countries. Winsemius was unequivocal that 'the unemployment of Singapore cannot be solved by industries manufacturing for the home market. The solution lies mainly in the establishment and expansion of export industries'.[86] In his report, he deftly sidestepped the question of import substitution and treated the common market as one of a number of export markets Singapore should cultivate, which included the rest of southeast Asia, Europe, the US, the Middle East and Africa. Winsemius' advice for export-led industrialisation was put on hold during the Malaysia years. He was elated about separation in 1965, calling it 'the best day in Singapore we ever had'.[87] Calmly, he assured the PAP leaders that the manufacturing sector had performed well in creating jobs in the first half of the 1960s, while compiling a list of 'emergency measures' to provide further incentives to multinationals.[88] These measures merely extended his recommendations on export markets in the 1961 UN report.

Winsemius' approach to the common market highlights the importance he attached to political matters. Unknown to the UN, when he first arrived in Singapore, 'Overriding was in my opinion at that time the political situation'.[89] He told US and British diplomatic officials in Singapore that the purpose of his mission was political – to help the PAP win the next election. He thought that 'pertinent recommendations with political connotations could be made in a confidential memo to the Government which would accompany the report'.[90] His fixation with politics should not surprise us: his endorsement of private capital would drive a wedge between the government and its left-wing allies. James Puthucheary, a leftist economist, disagreed with Winsemius, arguing that the state should own the strategic heavy industries.[91] Winsemius' political interest though went even further. He was confident about the Singaporean worker: 'The Singaporean worker is industrious and has considerable aptitude to work in manufacturing industries'.[92] But he was worried about the state of industrial relations. Although the UN report attributed part of the problem to local businessmen, it laid the bulk of the blame at the feet of the left-wing trade unions. Winsemius argued that demands for higher wages should wait till worker productivity had risen comparably, as in the case of the Netherlands.[93] Strikes served the short-term interests of workers but placed Singapore's industrialisation in jeopardy. Winsemius took the vantage point of the foreign investor, 'only interested in price and quality, only in what he gets for his money'.[94] As the UN report warned, 'If not, labour will suffer for it. Capital can go to other countries. Enterprise can quiet down or escape. Labour has no escape possibilities. It needs employment here and has no time to wait'.[95]

These were strong words in a technical report, but Winsemius' most intrepid advice did not make it to print. He adjudged industrial relations in Singapore in a bipolar frame: the left-wing unionists he spoke to – Lim Chin Siong, Fong Swee Suan, Sydney Woodhull, S.T. Bani and James Puthucheary – were all dangerous communists. His discussions with them were 'intellectual firework' – stimulating but useless from a practical standpoint.[96] Privately, Winsemius advised Lee Kuan Yew that two things were important above all else: to retain the statue of Raffles as a gesture of Singapore's openness to foreign capital, and to 'eliminate the Communists'.[97] Lee later recalled that he gave a 'mirthless laugh' at the suggestion to take on the left at the height of its power in mid-1961.[98] But whether it was due to Winsemius' advice or political developments in Malaya, Lee changed his stance towards his uneasy allies around this time. In June 1961, Lee 'rather surprisingly' told British officials that 'the moment might well have come to break with Lim and Co.'.[99] This happened quickly the following month. In February 1963, a major crackdown orchestrated by the leaders of Singapore, Malaya and Britain broke the left and helped level industrial relations, as Winsemius had advised.

Whether Winsemius influenced Lee is unclear, but unquestionably Lee had influenced him. The UN mission had admitted that '[w]e would not dare to present ourselves as specialists in the field of industrial relations in Singapore'.[100] Winsemius, who initially knew little about Singapore yet was convinced about his political mission, had learnt about Singapore politics from Lee and other PAP leaders. The adviser had learnt from the advised in a dialogic, circular fashion. Winsemius became the most highly regarded of the plethora of international experts who visited Singapore, being an unofficial economic adviser to the government into the 1980s.

Conclusion

Winsemius' personal success in Singapore belies how adapting advice to the local context was key to what all experts do. As Mitchell surmises in his study of expertise, Winsemius had extended the realm of economics beyond the UN's terms of reference into politics.[101] Other advisers to Singapore had failed because they did not take the context into account. Despite the support of local doctors, Simpson had not appreciated the financial constraints and/or political disinterest of the

Straits government. It was after the war when the SIT's housing work expanded, when both the colonial and PAP governments recognised public housing as a vital plank of decolonisation and citizenship. Similarly, in advising on the Singapore Polytechnic in the 1960s, British ex-principals were able to reconcile with the PAP's developmental agenda for technical education.

On the role of colonialism across 200 years of Singapore history, was technical expertise a form of colonial influence or neo-colonialism? Ronald Robinson has marked the period of decolonisation as one of two defining moments in the history of Britain's informal empire, after the imperialism of free trade in the early nineteenth century; local collaboration, in his view, underpinned both forms of imperialism.[102] In Singapore, there were undoubtedly similarities and continuities between colonial and postcolonial policies. But there was also national and local agency, and the presence of experts as mediators. In the war on ogres, the advisers shaped the development of postcolonial Singapore in crucial ways: ensuring the triumph of public housing over squatter settlements, establishing a planning regime across all major aspects of life, subordinating technical education and industrial relations to the nation's needs and advocating an open policy to foreign trade, capital and expertise. As collaborators, the experts' cumulative historical impact helped ease the transition from colonial to postcolonial governance, never going against the agendas of the governments they advised.

Notes

1 Ministry of Culture, *Democratic Socialism in Action, June 1959-April 1963*, Singapore: Ministry of Culture, 1963, unpaginated.
2 'Towards an Economic Policy,' *Petir*, October 1958.
3 See for instance Joseph Morgan Hodge, *Triumph of the Expert: Agrarian Doctrines of Development and the Legacies of British Colonialism*, Athens: Ohio University Press, 2007; Michael Ashley Havinden and David Meredith, *Colonialism and Development: Britain and Its Tropical Colonies, 1850–1960*, London and New York: Routledge, 1993.
4 National Archives of Singapore (hereafter NAS), SIT 70/41 Report of the Committee Appointed to Make Recommendations for the Redevelopment of Certain Crown Lease Land in Singapore.
5 Hodge, *Triumph of the Expert*.
6 Sarah Stockwell, 'Ends of Empire,' in Sarah Stockwell (ed.), *The British Empire: Themes and Perspectives*, Malden, MA: Blackwell Publishers, 2008, pp. 269–293; Frederick Cooper, *Decolonisation and African Society: The Labour Question in French and British Africa*, Cambridge: Cambridge University Press, 1996.
7 James C. Scott, *Seeing Like a State: How Certain Schemes to Improve the Human Condition have Failed*, New Haven: Yale University Press, 1998.
8 T.N. Harper, 'The Tools of Transition: Education and Development in Modern Southeast Asian History,' in C.A. Bayly, Vijayendra Rao, Simon Szreter, and Michael Woolcock (eds.), *History, Historians and Development Policy: A Necessary Dialogue*, Manchester and New York: Manchester University Press, 2011, pp. 193–212.
9 A.D. King, 'Exporting Planning: The Colonial and Neo-colonial Experience,' in Gordon E. Cherry (ed.), *Shaping an Urban World*, London: Mansell, 1980, pp. 203–226.
10 Timothy Mitchell, *Rule of Experts: Egypt, Techno-politics, Modernity*, Berkeley: University of California Press, 2002.

11 William Easterly, *The Tyranny of Experts: Economists, Dictators, and the Forgotten Rights of the Poor*, New York: Basic Books, 2013.

12 Akira Iriye, *Global Community: The Role of International Organisations in the Making of the Contemporary World*, Berkeley: California University Press, 2004.

13 Easterly, *Tyranny of Experts*.

14 W.G. Huff, *The Economic Growth of Singapore: Trade and Development in the Twentieth Century*, Cambridge and New York: Cambridge University Press, 1994; Garry Rodan, *The Political Economy of Singapore's Industrialisation: National State and International Capital*, Basingstoke: Macmillan, 1989.

15 Hodge, *Triumph of the Expert*, p. 54.

16 The National Archives of the United Kingdom (hereafter TNA), CO 273/310 Letter from Governor John Anderson to Secretary of State for the Colonies Alfred Lyttelton, 12 September 1905.

17 Brenda S.A. Yeoh, *Contesting Space in Colonial Singapore: Power Relations and the Urban Built Environment*, 2nd edn., Singapore: Singapore University Press, 2003.

18 Hodge, *Triumph of the Expert*.

19 TNA, CO 275/107 1922 Straits Settlements Registration of Births and Deaths.

20 W.J. Simpson, *Report of the Sanitary Condition of Singapore*, London: Waterlow & Sons, 1907, p. 14.

21 Ibid., p. 12.

22 Ibid., p. 10.

23 Ibid., p. 29.

24 'Our Health Officer,' *Eastern Daily Mail*, 12 July 1907.

25 'Dr. Simpson and Phthisis Mortality,' *Singapore Free Press and Mercantile Advertiser*, 27 June 1907.

26 D.J. Galloway, 'Notes on Tuberculosis,' 8 November 1917, in Singapore, *Proceedings and Report of the Commission Appointed to Inquire into the Cause of the Present Housing Difficulties in Singapore, and the Steps Which Should be Taken to Remedy Such Difficulties*, Vol. I, Singapore: Government Printing Office, 1918, p. C9.

27 Singapore, *Present Housing Difficulties in Singapore*, Vol. I, p. A6.

28 TNA, CO 273/529 Memo by P.S. Hunter 3 July 1925.

29 Singapore Improvement Trust, *Annual Report 1927–1947*, Singapore: Singapore Improvement Trust, 1948, p. 1.

30 NAS, SIT 70/41 Report of the Committee Appointed to Make Recommendations for the Redevelopment of Certain Crown Lease Land in Singapore.

31 NAS, SIT 662/31 Memo, 21 July 1931.

32 TNA, CO 275/136 1934 Straits Settlements Medical Report, p. 999.

33 W.E. Hutchinson, 'Some Aspects of the Tuberculosis Problem in Singapore,' *Journal of the Malayan Branch of the British Medical Association*, vol. I, no. 3, December 1937, pp. 218–229.

34 Medical Department, *Annual Report 1952*, Singapore: Government Printing Office, 1952, p. 2.

35 NAS, SIT 348/46, Memo by Deputy Municipal Health Officer to Chairman, SIT, 30 October 1946.

36 NAS, SIT 475/47 Notes for Discussion on Housing by Commissioner of Lands, 13 June 1947.

37 Charles Abrams, 'Squatting in the Philippines,' in A.R. Desai and S. Devadas Pillai (eds.), *Slums and Urbanisation*, London: Sangam Books, 1970, p. 143.

38 Charles Abrams, *Housing in the Modern World*, London: Faber, 1966, pp. 287–88, 296.

39 United Nations Mission of Experts, *Low Cost Housing in South and Southeast Asia*, New York: United Nations, 1951.

40 Ibid., p. 19.

41 'Singapore Losing Poverty and Disease War,' *Straits Times*, 11 January 1951.

42 Singapore, *Report of the Housing Committee*, Singapore: Government Printing House, 1948.
43 'Huge Task for 30 Colony Students,' *Straits Times*, 8 June 1952.
44 NAS, SIT 617/54, Memo titled 'Housing Programs and Policy' by Chief Architect, SIT, and Planning Adviser, SIT, 5 July 1954.
45 NAS, SIT 808/50, Report by George Pepler titled 'Attap Dwellings on Land Likely to Be Required for Permanent Forms of Development in the City Area during the Next Five Years,' 26 July 1952.
46 Singapore, *Master Plan: Report of Survey*, Singapore: Printed at Government Printing Office, 1955.
47 Loh Kah Seng, *Squatters into Citizens: The 1961 Bukit Ho Swee Fire and the Making of Modern Singapore*, Singapore: NUS Press, 2013.
48 Singapore, *First Education Triennial Survey: Covering the Years 1955–7 Inclusive*, Singapore: Government Printing Office, 1959.
49 'Parents Told: Avoid This Queue,' *Straits Times*, 28 October 1958.
50 E.H.G. Dobby, *Report of the Committee on a Polytechnic Institute for Singapore*, Singapore: Government Printing Office, 1953.
51 TNA, BW 91/819 Report on Singapore Polytechnic, 10 July 1957.
52 TNA, BW 91/819 Minutes of the special meeting of the Board of Governors, Singapore Polytechnic, 28 March 1958.
53 Dobby, *Polytechnic Institute for Singapore*, p. 23.
54 A.W. Gibson, *The Singapore Polytechnic Report*, Singapore: Singapore Government Printer, 1954.
55 TNA, CO 1030/923 Memo from Sir David Keir to the Undersecretary of State for the Colonies, 14 January 1960.
56 NAS, ME 1326/56 Minutes of the emergency board meeting of the Board of Governors, Singapore Polytechnic, 30 June 1959.
57 Singapore Polytechnic, *Annual Report 1958*, Singapore: Singapore Polytechnic, 1958, p. 1.
58 TNA, BW 91/820 Memo from British High Commissioner to Alan Lennox Boyd, 5 October 1959.
59 'Axe Falls on S'pore Poly,' *Singapore Free Press*, 5 September 1959.
60 'Big Changes at the Polytechnic,' *Straits Times*, 3 September 1959.
61 TNA, BW 91/819 Memo from H.M. Collins to Sir Christopher Cox, 28 September 1959.
62 TNA, CO 1030/923 Memo from H.T. Bourdillon to Secretary of State for the Colonies, 18 February 1960.
63 TNA, CO 1030/923 Secret letter from H.T. Bourdillon to C.Y. Cabstairs, 3 February 1960.
64 TNA, BW 91/820 Memo from Sir David Keir to the Undersecretary of State for the Colonies, 14 January 1960.
65 Singapore Polytechnic, *Annual Report 1963*, Singapore: Singapore Polytechnic, 1963, p. 13.
66 NAS, BW 91/820 Letter from C.I.C. Scollay to H.M. Collins, 19 October 1962.
67 TNA, BW 91/820 Letter from H.M. Collins to C.I.C. Scollay, 31 December 1962.
68 TNA, BW 91/821 Note of a meeting, 24 April 1963.
69 TNA, BW 91/821 Memo by H.M. Collins, 14 May 1963.
70 'Experts Will Help Govt. to Expand Technical Training,' *Straits Times*, 2 June 1963.
71 UK Colombo Plan Team to Singapore Polytechnic, Unpublished Report, Annexure I: Entry Qualifications for Degree Courses, 1964.
72 TNA, BW 91/821 Memo from N. Leach to P.B.C Moore, 30 September 1963.
73 TNA, BW 91/822 Memo from H.I. Baker to H.M. Collins, 10 November 1964.
74 TNA, BW 91/822 Note from the *Straits Times* dictated over the phone by Dr Hart, 3 July 1964.
75 Singapore Polytechnic, *Annual Report 1969*, Singapore: Singapore Polytechnic, 1969.

76 United Nations, *A Proposed Industrialisation Programme for the State of Singapore*, Singapore: United Nations Commissioner for Technical Assistance, Department of Economic and Social Affairs, 1963, p. 195.
77 United Nations S-0175–1798–05 Industrial Survey Singapore Sing (1–2), Press Release, 3 October 1960.
78 United Nations S-0175–1798–05 Industrial Survey Singapore Sing (1–2), Memo, Application by the Government of Singapore for an Industrial Survey Team of Preferably 5 Members, undated.
79 NAS, Albert Winsemius Interview with Singapore Oral History Unit, 30 August-3 September 1982, Reel 1.
80 Ibid., Reel 1.
81 United Nations, *Proposed Industrialisation Programme*, p. xxiii.
82 NAS, Albert Winsemius Interview, Reel 12.
83 United Nations, *Proposed Industrialisation Programme*, p. ii.
84 Loh Kah Seng, 'Imaginaries of Jurong Industrial Estate,' *International Institute of Asian Studies Newsletter*, vol. 81, Autumn 2018, pp. 6–7.
85 Ministry of Finance, *State of Singapore Development Plan*, Singapore: Ministry of Finance, 1961, p. 33.
86 United Nations, *Proposed Industrialisation Programme*, p. 103.
87 NAS, Albert Winsemius Interview, Reel 15.
88 TNA, PREM 13/1833 Dr. A. Winsemius, Memorandum (Revised) to the Government of Singapore on the Economic Situation After Singapore Day, 1965, p. 6.
89 NAS, Albert Winsemius Interview, Reel 1.
90 National Archives of Australia, A1838/318 Item 3024/4/1 Part I, Memo titled 'Singapore: Industrial Development' from Acting Commissioner J.E. Ryan (Australian High Commission) to Secretary, Department of External Affairs, Canberra, ACT, 22 October 1960, p. 2.
91 Seng Guo-quan, 'How I Wished That It Could Have Worked': James Puthucheary's Political-Economic Thought and the Myth of Singapore's Developmental Model,' in Loh Kah Seng, Thum Ping Tjin, and Jack Chia (eds.), *Living with Myths in Singapore*, Singapore: Ethos Books, 2017, pp. 93–102.
92 United Nations, *Proposed Industrialisation Programme*, p. v.
93 Ibid., p. 100.
94 Ibid., p. xxiii.
95 Ibid., p. xxiv.
96 NAS, Albert Winsemius Interview, Reel 3.
97 Ibid., Reel 2.
98 Lee Kuan Yew, 'Tribute to Dr Albert Winsemius,' 6 December 1996.
99 TNA, FO 1091/104, Memo from Moore to Bourdillon and Selkirk, 5 June 1961, p. 2.
100 United Nations, *Proposed Industrialisation Programme*, p. 97.
101 Mitchell, *Rule of Experts*.
102 Ronald Robinson, 'Non-European Foundations of European Imperialism: Sketch for a Theory of Collaboration,' in R. Owen and B. Sutcliffe (eds.), *Studies in the Theory of Imperialism*, London: Longman, 1972, pp. 117–142.

12 'The Gibraltar of the East'? Singapore and other fortress colonies during the Second World War

A. J. Stockwell

A fortress is a seat of military power. Its purpose may be to secure a trade route, a sea lane or a frontier, or to levy taxes, control migration or provide a place of refuge. It might embrace a town or consist of only an inner citadel. It might stand as a 'monument to fear' or instil a sense of false security.[1] All fortresses are pregnable. To claim otherwise is to court defeat as did Richard the Lionheart when he boasted that his Château Gaillard (perched high above the Seine) would defy King Philippe Auguste even if 'its walls were made of butter'. Five years after its completion it was captured by the French king. Walls alone would not secure a fortress when the trebuchet gave way to the cannon, and later when aerial assault supplemented war on land and sea. The more prominent a fortress, the greater the temptation either to attack it (notably the German onslaught upon Verdun which proved to be the costliest engagement of the First World War) or to avoid it altogether (as in May 1940 when the German army bypassed the string of apparently impregnable French forts along the Maginot Line). Furthermore, the longer a fortress managed to withstand a siege, the shorter the odds on its being brought down by enemies within: disease, starvation and treachery. And even if it withstood all such challenges, a fortress might yet prove incapable of fulfilling its principal strategic function, as Churchill feared might be the fate of Gibraltar: 'The Rock', he wrote in November 1940, 'will stand a long siege, but what is the good of that if we cannot use the harbour or pass the Straits?'[2]

Of the many ports and forts that linked and defended the seaborne empire when Britannia ruled the waves and had yet to be threatened by attacks from the air – Aden, Alexandria, Bermuda, Colombo, the Falklands, Freetown, Gibraltar, Halifax, Hong Kong, Malta, Singapore and others too – only three were classified officially as 'Fortress Colonies'.[3] They were Bermuda, Gibraltar and Malta, and their governors were generally senior military officers. Fortresses they might once have been, but in the summer of 1940 the beleaguered British government contemplated using them as diplomatic bargaining chips with which either to mediate peace or to win allies. When Churchill succeeded Neville Chamberlain in May 1940, Britain's prospects were bleak indeed. In Western Europe, French and British forces were in retreat and Belgium was on the point of surrendering to Hitler. The new prime minister could not risk clearing out the appeasers at a stroke. His scope for patronage was further restricted by the need to accommodate

Labour and Liberal members of the coalition. While he was able immediately to banish the appeaser Samuel Hoare to the embassy in Madrid and reward some 'trusties' such as Lord Lloyd (Colonial Office) and Leo Amery (India Office), Churchill had no option but to retain Lord Halifax (another appeaser) as Foreign Secretary, at least until the end of the year. In a last-ditch attempt to buy off the dictators, Halifax proposed the cession of Gibraltar and Malta in exchange for the convention of an international peace conference.[4] His scheme came to nought, however, when in June 1940 Mussolini joined Hitler and declared war on Britain. The prospect of Gibraltar and Malta exchanging their historic role as fortress colonies for that of diplomatic pawns immediately vanished.

Bermuda: the Gibraltar of the West

Meanwhile, Churchill scoured the Atlantic for colonial bait (notably Bermuda) with which to attract American support and possibly a wartime partnership. Fortress Bermuda had been settled by the Virginia Company in the early seventeenth century as a plantation colony and adopted as a crown colony in the 1680s. Thereafter, its strategic importance came to outweigh its commercial value. Bermuda became known as 'the Gibraltar of the West'. A naval base at Hamilton watched over the sea lanes in the western Atlantic during successive wars: the war of American independence, the global conflict with the French and the Anglo-American War of 1812. Although its military role diminished thereafter, forts were maintained to protect Hamilton's harbour. During the First World War, Bermuda resumed a military role, but its significance subsided once again in the 1920s. By the late 1930s its economy depended on tourism while its principal political problem concerned the constitutional claims of white settlers.

President Roosevelt was attracted by Churchill's suggestion of an Anglo-American arrangement that would secure the United States' economic interests in the Caribbean as well as the shipping routes to South America. Indeed, the United States' administration was as ambitious in the West Indies as it was critical of European colonialism there. A preliminary agreement (September 1940) provided for 99-year leases of rent-free land in Bermuda and in seven other British/Commonwealth territories where US bases would be established in return for 50 redundant American destroyers.[5] Subsequent negotiations over precise terms, however, grew increasingly acrimonious. A vociferous lobby in Congress was determined that the United States should not be drawn into another European war, and American negotiators drove increasingly hard bargains. For their part, Bermudans were dismayed by the prospect of United States over-lordship. Britain's secretary of state for the colonies regarded American negotiators as 'gangsters' in their 'high-handed' determination to challenge British colonial sovereignty. King George VI was appalled by Britain's 'humiliating position': 'we are being treated as Panamanians'.[6]

Pouring oil on troubled waters and in order to secure agreement, Churchill appealed personally to Bermuda's elected House of Assembly. He also took care that the colonial governor had appropriate skills to handle the American military.

The incumbent, Lieutenant-General Sir Denis Bernard, was reported to be a good 'mixer' with 'plenty of tact and social aptitude'. However, reports reached London that Bernard 'was not acting in the way best calculated to ensure that the inevitable friction between the Americans and the local inhabitants was brought to an end as soon as possible'. Churchill immediately broke with the long tradition of military governors and appointed a civilian, Lord Knollys, a courtier and a businessman with a reputation for getting on well with Americans. Knollys's two-year term in Bermuda was so successful that Churchill decided to replace him with another civilian, the youthful Lord Burghley, a former Conservative MP and, at the time of his appointment to Bermuda, controller of American Supplies and Repairs at the Ministry of Aircraft.

As a result of the Anglo-American agreement, Caribbean islands became assembly points for transatlantic convoys during the Battle of the Atlantic. Fortress Bermuda also served as the main hub for transatlantic Postal Censorship and Contraband Control, and supplied the Allied intelligence agencies. Bermuda was the lend-lease base where British and Americans learned to coexist as allies of a kind. Bermuda reprised its eighteenth- century role as the 'Gibraltar of the West', though with significant differences: during the Second World War it was more a military base and communications hub than a fortress, and an Anglo-American one at that.[7]

Gibraltar: 'two square miles of concentrated defiance'[8]

Commanding the straits where the Atlantic meets the Mediterranean, Gibraltar had been fought over for centuries by Christians and Muslims, Spanish and Moors. Britain seized it during the War of Spanish Succession and was confirmed in possession by the Treaty of Utrecht (1713). Thereafter, Gibraltar together with Malta (annexed in 1814) had secured the route to Britain's empire in the Middle East, India and beyond. From June 1940, however, this imperial lifeline was gravely jeopardised by Mussolini's Italy and Vichy France, both of which straddled the shores of the Mediterranean. As battle was joined on land, sea and in the air, Gibraltar resumed its historic role as a fortress. Safe passage through the Straits of Gibraltar for British convoys bound for Malta and Alexandria was essential for the campaigns in North Africa and the Middle East. In addition to commanding the gateway to the Mediterranean, Gibraltar acted as a staging post for convoys on the round-Africa route between the United Kingdom and the Far East.

Gibraltar was vital but vulnerable. The Axis targeted it; General Franco laid claim to it; saboteurs infiltrated it. Its defences had been run down after the First World War but from 1939 military governors, notably Generals Ironside and Gort, were tireless in putting the Rock on a war footing. Gort was a compelling leader. He had served with spectacular gallantry during the First World War but, as the unfortunate commander-in-chief of the British Expeditionary Force in northern France in 1940, he took the rap for its failure and was sidelined to this colonial governorship. Here he rose to the challenge of making the Rock impregnable. He supervised the construction of an airstrip to facilitate the passage of east-bound aircraft, he installed anti-aircraft defences and he extended the labyrinth of tunnels within and below the Rock.[9] Furthermore, he reinforced liaison between the armed services and between them and the civil administration and local leaders – crucial measures that would be disastrously neglected during the Malayan campaign. In anticipation of a prolonged siege, almost the whole of the civilian population, including most of the children (*bouches inutiles* or useless mouths) were evacuated across perilous seas, mostly to Britain.[10] Planning for survival alone would not be enough. To repeat Churchill's adage: 'The Rock . . . will stand a long siege, but what is the good of that if we cannot use the harbour or pass the Straits?'

The Straits of Gibraltar were threatened by Italy, Germany and Vichy France, but the fate of the Rock 'hung on the actions of Spain'.[11] 'If Spain should prove hostile', then Gibraltar would be 'untenable'.[12] Gibraltarians relied in very large measure upon Spain for supplies and labour: some 8,000–10,000 workers crossed the isthmus each day, even in wartime. General Franco, like Spanish monarchs of old, was committed to *reconquista*. He had emerged from the civil war (1936–39) as a victorious but impoverished dictator. He sought German assistance but not to the extent of surrendering control to Hitler. Meanwhile, indulging in bribery and cajolery, those arch-appeasers of the late 1930s, Lord Halifax (Foreign Secretary until the end of 1940) and Samuel Hoare (Ambassador to Madrid, 1940–44) managed to dissuade Franco from committing to the Axis cause, and, in effect, to secure Spanish neutrality.[13] The Führer had expected to advance on Gibraltar almost as soon as Franco broached the matter with him, but when negotiations stalled, he abandoned the project in order to focus on Operation Barbarossa, which he launched against the Soviet Union in June 1941. Thus, Gibraltar was spared invasion from the north, but there was little let-up in Axis bombardment, sabotage and espionage, so much so that, in the light of the superstition that Gibraltar would remain British for only as long as its colony of macaques survived, Churchill commanded that their numbers should be monitored regularly and supplemented if necessary.

Notwithstanding Japan's onslaught on Pearl Harbor (7 December 1941), the 'day of infamy' that had brought the United States into the Second World War, Roosevelt and Churchill agreed (Arcadia Conference, December 1941–January 1942) that their priority should be to wage war against Germany, the predominant member of the Triple Axis, and to strike first against Field-Marshal Rommel's forces in North Africa. 'Operation Torch' (November 1942) was an Allied, though largely American, expedition. It was commanded by General Eisenhower who, during the planning stage, established his headquarters on Gibraltar. By this time Gort had been transferred to Malta and succeeded on the Rock by General Sir Noel Mason-Macfarlane. Mason-Mac (as he was known) was an inspirational leader with an unruly temper. He resented the influx of American generals and at first derided Eisenhower as 'the grocer from the Middle West'. No offence was taken and these 'allies of a kind' soon came to respect each other and to work well together as the 'two square miles of concentrated defiance' which constituted Gibraltar was transformed into 'the Clapham Junction of the Allied Nations – a fortified medley of Croydon, Southampton, Hendon, and Portsmouth'.[14] Military matters would continue to take priority over civil administration and it would not be until 1950 that partial self-government was introduced.[15]

Malta – the great siege, 1940–43

Sixty miles from Italy and 180 miles from Africa, Malta was the guardian of Europe's southern flank. Over the centuries it had resisted but succumbed in turn to Phoenicians, Carthagenians, Romans, Byzantines, Vandals, Arabs, Normans, Knights of St. John and the French until it fell to Britain in the Napoleonic Wars. Malta became the headquarters of the Royal Navy's Mediterranean Fleet and remained so until the mid-1930s when its vulnerability was exposed during the Abyssinian crisis. The Committee of Imperial Defence then judged it to be virtually indefensible and withdrew the fleet to Alexandria rather than risk confrontation with Italy.[16]

The priority thereafter was the reinforcement of Malta's defences against aerial bombardment. Even so, this 'fortress colony' was scarcely prepared for the air offensive that accompanied Italy's declaration of war on 10 June 1940, nor did it offer a secure staging post for convoys carrying supplies and armament for campaigns in North Africa and the Middle East. Ramparts may have protected the harbour from the sea, but they were an easy target for the bombers. Furthermore, the fact that many islanders were of Italian origin raised the possibility of their jeopardising the naval dockyard, although the British government recognised that the 'Maltese people are probably more deeply and fundamentally attached by ties of sentiment and interest to the British Empire than the peoples of any other colony'.[17] For the best part of three years the Axis would bomb and blockade Malta, filling the docks with rubble and wrecked ships, and driving the Maltese to the verge of starvation. It seemed unlikely that Malta would prove to be the 'unsinkable aircraft carrier' of Churchill's dreams.

During his term as governor (1936–40) General Sir Charles Bonham-Carter strove to win Maltese cooperation, but by the spring of 1940 his health collapsed and he was replaced by General Sir William Dobbie who was brought out of retirement, his last post having been general officer commanding Malaya and Singapore. Dobbie rallied the Maltese to the island's defence. He imposed strict rationing of food and oil, interned all known Italian sympathizers and urged the inhabitants of Valletta to seek refuge in the countryside until sufficient air-raid shelters had been dug. The siege and constant bombardment reduced civilians to a troglodyte existence but there was no attempt, as in Gibraltar, to evacuate *bouches inutiles*. Dobbie was a devout Christian and exhorted the Maltese to put their trust in 'God's good hand'. Churchill described him as 'a Cromwellian figure' with sword in one hand and the Bible in the other. Although he was a strict Protestant (a Plymouth Brother) while the Maltese were devout Catholics, Dobbie's faith impressed the islanders. They came to believe the governor led a charmed life.

There was no respite from the raids, yet Dobbie's pleas for fighter planes for too long went unheeded. Convoys came under heavy attack. Of the 17 ships that embarked from Alexandria and Gibraltar in June 1941, only two reached Malta. Between December 1941 and February 1942 there was a daily average of 60 air sorties against the island, rising to 173 in April when Malta was subjected to an aerial bombardment more than twice as heavy as that inflicted upon Britain throughout the whole year.[18] In March 1942 an attempt to unload a convoy in Valletta's Grand Harbour was bungled and much of its cargo sunk. Differences between the service chiefs, and between them and the governor became sharper. 'The Boadicea of Malta', Mabel Strickland (editor and proprietor of *The Times of Malta*) intrigued against him. The most serious challenge to Dobbie's position came from Middle East Command (MEC). Based in Cairo, MEC was responsible for the British imperial war effort across North Africa, the Mediterranean, East Africa, Arabia and the Balkans. It unreservedly recommended that Dobbie should be relieved of the governorship as soon as possible on the grounds that 'he is a tired man, has lost grip of situation and is no longer capable of affording higher direction and control which is vital (repeat vital) to present situation.'[19]

The urgency of this recommendation shocked ministers in London. To replace Dobbie at such a 'critical juncture' after presenting him 'as a great national hero' would have an 'exceedingly bad' effect on morale in both Britain and Malta.[20] Notwithstanding his admiration for Dobbie, however, Churchill could not ignore the advice of Middle East Command. Battered but unbowed, Dobbie tendered his resignation in early May and returned to a hero's welcome in England. At the same time, General Gort was transferred from Gibraltar to the governorship of Malta expecting 'to meet what he and many others supposed must be death or captivity'.[21]

Gort brought with him the George Cross awarded by King George VI with the following citation: 'To honour her brave people I award the George Cross to the Island Fortress of Malta to bear witness to a heroism and devotion that will long be famous in history'. Indeed, Malta 'had become as potent a symbol of British determination to stand and fight, as Stalingrad was later to be for the Russian people. The ignominy of Singapore was not to be repeated'.[22] A fortnight after the surrender of Singapore, *The Times* (London) published a letter which Mabel Strickland had cabled from Malta. Under the headline 'Malta the indomitable island – a stepping- stone to the Far East', she wrote:

> For some 80 days in Malta there has been a period of almost continuous alert with few respites. Days and nights have been enlivened by the sound of air battles, anti-aircraft guns in action, and the whistling and crash of bombs. With this we have had to chronicle the wider happenings of the outside world, far-off Singapore and close-up Libya; but the spirit of Malta burns brightly. . . . This is the determination of the three services in Malta as well as the fourth – the civilians. Malta's chief consolation in her trial is that her defence is not static, that she is the target that hits back.[23]

In the same month, Churchill insisted that Malta should be supplied, whatever the costs and no matter the risks that might be incurred elsewhere. After the fall of

Singapore, the War Cabinet placed Malta very high in its global priorities. Without Churchill's powerful advocacy, Malta might well have been lost. Thereafter, the fate of Singapore was constantly in his mind whenever Malta was in peril, and Malta was constantly in peril throughout 1942. Angered and humiliated by the manner of Singapore's surrender, Churchill rounded on General Auchinleck for postponing the Eighth Army's offensive against Field-Marshal Rommel in North Africa. The prime minister was dismayed by the delay since he had been 'looking to the Eighth Army, on which everything has been lavished, to repair the shame of Singapore'.[24]

Lessons from the fall of Singapore were now applied to the defence of Malta. One was to establish a supremo in the colony by investing General Gort with the responsibilities and functions of both governor and commander-in-chief. Another was to ensure the governor complied with directives from Middle East Command regarding the region as a whole. Nevertheless, Lord Cranborne (secretary of state for the colonies) was uneasy about Gort's inexperience in colonial administration, especially as Malta, unlike Gibraltar, was 'an extremely political colony'. When he visited the island in July 1942, Cranborne was disturbed by a lack of liaison between the military and civil authorities, and was apprehensive lest the defence of Malta were to be plagued by the uncoordinated, even haphazard, leadership that had undermined Singapore. Certainly, Gort focused upon military matters rather than civil affairs. His priority was to secure Malta as a base from which to attack Axis convoys and in due course to launch a counteroffensive against Italy. Even though constant bombardment, lack of protection from the air and a dearth of materials and provisions meant that the chances of the colony's survival diminished by the hour, Gort became immensely popular with the Maltese on account of his scrupulous supervision of the daily distribution of food rations and water supplies. Most of all, by personal example he impressed upon the islanders 'his own indomitable fortitude and cheerfulness in adversity'.[25]

And the tide turned. Soon after Gort's arrival in Valletta, a consignment of 60 Spitfires reached Malta. Three months later 'Operation Pedestal' got underway. 'Pedestal' was a convoy of some 50 vessels of which 14 were merchant ships carrying supplies from Britain. During the agonisingly slow voyage across the Mediterranean, Axis bombers and submarines inflicted massive damage. The aircraft carrier, HMS *Eagle* with its complement of aircraft was sunk and only five of the merchant vessels reached Malta. Of those that survived, the most crucial for Malta was the badly damaged USS *Ohio*. Its cargo of aviation fuel would revitalise Malta's air offensive against Axis shipping. When the battered convoy limped into Valletta, only ten days remained before the governor would have had to surrender for lack of supplies.[26]

'Operation Pedestal' marked a turning point. Thereafter, the Allies would challenge the Axis in the air with increasing success while further convoys would complete the trans-Mediterranean passage. Following victory in North Africa, the Allies mustered their forces for the invasion of southern Europe. Just as Gibraltar had been selected as command headquarters for 'Operation Torch', so Malta provided the natural bridgehead for 'Operation Husky' to occupy Sicily and then advance upon the Italian mainland. By July 1943 Malta had mustered some 600 aircraft of which over 500 were fighters and most were Spitfires. The island had been transformed into an enormous aircraft carrier, though at the expense of Singapore. Nearly 20 years later, General Ismay, Churchill's chief military assistant during the war, put it this way: 'The loss of our great base at Singapore had been a bitter blow; but she was far away and historically speaking a comparative upstart. Malta was near at hand, and almost one of our kith and kin. To lose her would be almost as painful as to lose a part of England itself.'[27] More was sacrificed than gained in the battle for Malta which was fought for reputation, honour and as a memorial to Singapore. Malta, indeed, was 'the Verdun of maritime war'.[28]

Singapore: the Gibraltar of the East?[29]

The terms of the Washington Treaty of 1922 so reduced British naval construction that it was no longer possible to maintain fleets simultaneously in the North Sea, the Mediterranean and the Far East. This limitation (together with the demise of the Anglo-Japanese Alliance of 1902 and periodic cuts in defence expenditure) severely exposed British interests in East and Southeast Asia. Consequently, the 'main fleet to Singapore strategy' was devised: in the event of a crisis, the fleet would be despatched to a specially constructed base in Singapore. However, budget restraints and political vicissitudes at home delayed its completion until 1938. By this time the gathering storm over Europe meant that the strategy was wholly unrealistic. In short, Britain lacked the resources simultaneously to defend the empire against three increasingly hostile major powers: Germany, Italy and Japan.

Churchill, within a week of his becoming prime minister, approached Roosevelt in the hope of creating in the East the sort of partnership that in due course they would later conclude with respect to military bases in Bermuda and elsewhere in the Caribbean. He invited the president to make use of the empty naval base: 'I am looking to you to keep that Japanese dog quiet in the Pacific using Singapore in any way convenient.'[30] When in late September 1940, Germany, Italy and Japan formed their tripartite pact. Churchill again approached Roosevelt in the hope of American support in the South China Sea. Since British resources could not be spared from the Mediterranean and North Africa, he asked whether it would 'be possible for you to send an American squadron, the bigger the better, to pay a friendly visit to Singapore'. In December he appealed for an American naval presence to deter Japan from patrolling the seas round Indochina and the Dutch East Indies. By the following autumn he was looking to a British naval force not so much to engage with the Japanese as to deter them. All that could be mustered of any significance was HMS *Prince of Wales* which in due course joined the *Repulse* in Singapore. When on 7 December the Japanese bombed Pearl Harbor Churchill was jubilant: 'To have the United States at our side was to me the greatest joy. . . . Hitler's fate was sealed. Mussolini's fate was sealed. As for the Japanese, they would be ground to powder.' Since, however, the Americans were preoccupied with the Pacific and British Malaya lacked air cover, the Japanese ensured their mastery of the South China Sea by sinking the *Prince of Wales* and *Repulse*.

Without naval protection, the security of Singapore now depended upon the security of the Malayan peninsula. However, initial landings in the northeast soon grew into a full-scale invasion as General Yamashita's battle-hardened army swept aside or outflanked the more numerous British, Indian and Commonwealth troops while Japanese aircraft immobilised Malayan air fields. Singapore now faced an invasion from the north which Gibraltar had escaped. Churchill, whose military priority was the war in the West, assumed that the 'island fortress' had the capacity to withstand a siege of at least two months. General Wavell (Commander-in-Chief, Allied forces in Southeast Asia) was unable to provide this assurance: 'I am sorry to give you depressing picture', he signalled, 'but I do not want you to have false picture of island fortress.' There were, he explained, no permanent fortifications on the landward side of the naval base or of the city. All defences had been constructed to meet a seaward attack. Moreover, much of Singapore's garrison had already been despatched north while those troops that remained on the island were of 'doubtful value'. Churchill was appalled. It had never occurred to him 'that the gorge of the fortress of Singapore, with its splendid moat half-a-mile to a mile wide' was not entirely fortified against such an attack. 'What is the use of having an island for a fortress if it is not to be made into a citadel? Over the last two years I have repeatedly shown that I relied upon the defence of Singapore Island against a formal siege'.[31] A week after the first wave of Japanese crossed the Johor straits, General Yamashita received General Percival's surrender at the Ford Factory.

All fortresses are pregnable, some more so than others, witness the centuries of conflict over Gibraltar and Malta. Singapore had never been such a fortress, at least not in the British era. Raffles had acquired it by treaty, and thereafter it became and remained 'essentially a place of business, a market, a port of call, the Clapham Junction of the Eastern Sea', the region's commercial hub.[32] Although Singapore was hailed as 'the Gibraltar of the East' when the naval base was completed in 1938,[33] British Malaya as a whole continued to be valued principally as a 'dollar arsenal'. It provided 40 per cent of the world's rubber and 60 per cent of the world's tin. Production and profit were the yardsticks by which the colonial regime was judged during the first two years of the Second World War. Thus, Sir Shenton Thomas's term as governor and high commissioner had been extended on account of his record in peacetime, not for his potential as an inspirational leader which he did not aspire to be.

In stark contrast to the defence of Gibraltar and Malta, the Malayan campaign was hobbled first by misplaced confidence, then by irresolution and increasingly by disagreements between service chiefs and civil authorities. In October 1941 Churchill's envoy to Southeast Asia, Alfred Duff Cooper, reported that 'the affairs of the British Empire were being conducted . . . by machinery that had undergone no important change since the days of Queen Victoria'. He identified the need for immediate improvements in civil administration and in civil/military liaison but cautioned against 'drastic reform' as being 'undesirable in time of crisis'.[34] Unlike

Gibraltar and Malta where the command was vested in a single military governor, the leaders of the armed services in Singapore were at sixes and sevens. Generals Percival (Britain), Gordon Bennett (Australia) and Lewis Heath (Indian troops) clashed over tactics. Discord reigned. Air Chief Marshal Brooke-Popham was replaced by General Pownall as commander-in-chief. Fort Canning, which by no stretch of the imagination was a citadel, came to be dubbed 'Confusion Castle'. The Allied Command Far East with its headquarters in Java had been intended, like Middle East Command in Cairo, to impress a coherent strategy upon the region but was established too late to arrest Japan's advances.

As retreating troops (still substantially more numerous than the Japanese army) crossed from mainland to island, Churchill urged a last stand. After all, Japanese troops were also exhausted, and their commanders had their differences. Churchill, who had assured John Curtin (prime minister of Australia) that Singapore would be held 'with utmost tenacity', called for street-by-street resistance just as he had vainly expected of Parisians in June 1940. He urged the conscription of the 'entire male population' and the conversion of 'the city of Singapore' into 'a citadel' to be 'defended to the death'. He insisted that no surrender could be contemplated 'until after protracted fighting among the ruins of Singapore'. His call went unheeded as the island became a refuge for demoralised, leaderless and increasingly unruly soldiers. Singapore was to be their Dunkirk, but a Dunkirk without the prospect of rescue, and *sauve qui peut* would be their watchword. As much as anything, it was the plight of civilians which convinced General Percival that there was no alternative to surrender. However, while the British administration had been reluctant to take any action that might undermine the morale of civilians, it had failed to provide them with clear information or useful direction. In fact, it did not wholly trust local communities and their leaders. Unlike the Rock, whose 'non-essential' civilians had been evacuated from Gibraltar, the population of Singapore – some 500,000 at the start of the campaign – more or less doubled in size as displaced persons and refugees arrived from mainland Malaya. In contrast with Gibraltar, Singapore was large enough to accommodate *bouches inutiles*, but supplies of food and water were running low and could not be guaranteed in the event of prolonged urban warfare. Nor, it must be added, were they guaranteed by Percival's act of surrender.

Ceylon was now a front-line state in the war against Japan, the last refuge in the defence of the Indian Ocean and bastion on the route to Australasia. Churchill was determined to place 'a first-rate soldier in supreme command of all local services including civil government. . . . We do not want to have another Singapore'. Wavell (now commander-in-chief of India) concurred. He was 'profoundly shocked by [the] state of unreadiness and unjustified complacency in nearly all circles in Ceylon'. On 2 March 1942 the War Cabinet approved as a matter of urgency the appointment of a 'Military Governor' of Ceylon who would have control over both the military forces and civil administration. Pre-dating but shaping Gort's appointment to Malta, this was the first time a unified command structure was applied to an operational theatre. Vice-Admiral Sir Geoffrey Layton, who, in Wavell's judgment, had 'more aggressive fighting spirit and drive than any other High Commander in [the] East', was chosen as the new supremo. However, Lord Cranborne (secretary of state for the colonies) voiced dissent. Just as he would fret over what he felt was Gort's neglect of civil affairs in Malta, so he objected to Layton's designation as 'Military Governor'. It would, he argued with good reason, undermine the current governor, Sir Andrew Caldecott, and also relations with Ceylon's Board of Ministers, upon whom civil administration depended. Layton's title was duly amended to commander-in-chief, but his role and powers remained unchanged. On military matters his immediate superior would be the commander-in chief of India; on civil matters he would report to the secretary of state for the colonies and consult with the colonial governor. Caldecott would continue to carry out civil administration but subject to Layton's overriding authority.[35] It seemed an arrangement destined to fail. That it did not was in large measure due to Caldecott's affable temperament and his local popularity which increased partly from sympathy for his unenviable position at the receiving end of a choleric admiral eager to impose 'a military despotism'.[36] In April 1944 Admiral Mountbatten, Supreme Allied Commander South East Asia Command, transferred his headquarters to Kandy in order to prepare for what turned out to be a shambolic reoccupation of Europe's lost colonies.

'We let them down'

The need for a regional authority in Southeast Asia was the prime lesson drawn from the Singapore debacle and was applied by planners when preparing for post-war re-occupation. Following the British return to Singapore, Phoenix Park (Tanglin) became a veritable 'Whitehall of the East'. It accommodated the new office of commissioner-general for Southeast Asia and Far East Command, and continued to grow not so much in accordance with 'Parkinson's Law' but in response to the many problems of peace and the costs associated with decolonisation. Successive British governments were faced, as they had been in the 1930s, with the problem of squaring means with commitments. In January 1968 the Labour government announced that all forces would be withdrawn from Singapore by the end of 1971. For Singaporeans this amounted to a second betrayal. The city-state was heavily dependent on the British base not only for its security but also for its economy. When Lee Kuan Yew responded by threatening to withdraw from the sterling area, disrupt British shipping, hand the dockyard to the Japanese and even hire mercenaries to protect the island state, the British government agreed to postpone the final withdrawal until November 1971 and to grant a generous aid package.[37]

Sir Arthur de la Mare was Britain's high commissioner during this particularly fraught period. In his 'Farewell Despatch' he reviewed Britain's role in Singapore, not least the legacy of 1942:

> Reminders of that shame beset me daily . . . the smell of ignominy still hangs
> in the air . . . the monument erected near the Padang to the local Chinese
> victims of Japanese atrocity is a memorial not only of Japanese savagery but

also of our betrayal of our trust.[38] And it does not relieve me to recall that the military pomp and ostentation – not to say the arrogance – with which we reoccupied Singapore was a sham and a fraud.

In any case, he concluded, the British settlement at Singapore had never been intended as a fortress:

> [W]e, like Singaporeans, must remember Raffles. It was not as a military man but as a trader that he came here, and it is by trade that his vision will be accomplished. It is our traders, our entrepreneurs, our investors and our businessmen who must lead for Britain in Singapore in the 1970s.[39]

Fostering a national identity for post-war Singapore has been a feature of the school curriculum. Two issues have been particularly sensitive: the interdependence of the Chinese majority and multi-ethnic immigrants, and relations between the city-state and its much larger neighbours. 'Lessons to be learned' from the British failure to defend Singapore and from the Japanese occupation were rarely broached until 1984 when 'Total Defence Day' was inaugurated. It has been commemorated ever since in every school on 15 February, the anniversary of Britain's surrender. Its purpose is to convey a sense of common history, common suffering and common purpose. Total Defence, a concept adopted notably from Switzerland and Sweden, has five aspects: military defence, civil defence, economic defence, social defence and psychological defence. The principal lessons from 1942 are: 'You can't depend on others to defend you' and 'all have a part to play in total defence'.[40]

Notes

1 Voltaire's verdict on the Great Wall of China, David Frye, *Walls: A History of Civilization in Blood and Brick*, London: Faber and Faber, 2018, pp. 205–206.
2 Martin Gilbert, *Finest Hour: Winston Churchill 1939–1941*, London: Minerva ed., 1989, p. 921.
3 As political authority was devolved to settlement colonies during the nineteenth century, so they had assumed responsibility for local defence. However, the British government continued to bear the defence costs of Bermuda, Gibraltar and Malta since these territories were crucial to imperial defence. Until the early twentieth century, Halifax (Nova Scotia) had also been a designated fortress colony. After the formation of the self-governing Canadian Confederation (1867), a British military garrison remained in Halifax until 1906 when it was replaced by the Canadian army, and in 1910 the Royal Navy was replaced by the Royal Canadian Navy. During the Second World War, Halifax played a crucial role in the Battle of the Atlantic and as an assembly point for transatlantic convoys.
4 CAB 65/13/24, WM145(40)1, 28 May 1940, The National Archives of the United Kingdom, Kew (hereafter TNA).
5 Forty-one of the 50 destroyers were inoperable at the time of hand-over. The territories were: Newfoundland, the Bahamas, Bermuda, Jamaica, St Lucia, Antigua, Trinidad and British Guiana.
6 See 'United States activities in the West Indies and other British dependencies', memorandum by the Secretary of State for the Colonies, 27 December 1940, WP (40) 485,

CAB 66/14/15; Conclusions of a meeting of the War Cabinet, 30 December 1940, WM 311(40)7, CAB 65/10/31 (TNA); also S.R. Ashton and S.E. Stockwell (eds.), *British Documents on the End of Empire, Imperial Policy and Colonial Practice 1925– 1945*, pt I, London: HMSO, 1996, pp. 158–159. For the terms of the agreement, see *Agreement between the governments of the United Kingdom and the United States of America relating to the bases leased to the United States of America*, Cmd. 6259 (27 March 1941); Sir Gordon Lethem to Lord Moyne, 20 February 1941, reporting conversation with the King, CO 967/133 (TNA).

7   Bermuda (now a self-governing British Overseas Territory) became a site for post-war Cold War summitry: 1953 heads of government of USA, UK and France; 1957 Eisenhower and Macmillan in the wake of the Suez crisis; 1961 Kennedy and Macmillan with respect to nuclear weaponry. The American base was wound down in the 1990s and the lease was terminated in 2002.

8   See Allen Andrews, *Proud Fortress: The Fighting Story of Gibraltar*, London: Evans Brothers Ltd, 1958; E.G. Archer, *Gibraltar, Identity and Empire*, Abingdon: Routledge, 2006; Ewan Butler, *Mason-Mac: The Life of Lieutenant Sir Noel Mason-Macfarlane*, London: Macmillan, 1972; T.J. Finlayson, *The Fortress Came First: The Story of the Civilian Population of Gibraltar during the Second World War*, Grendon, Northants: Gibraltar Books Ltd, 1996; Ashley Jackson, *The British Empire and the Second World War*, London: Hambledon Continuum, 2006; David Lambert, '"As Solid as the Rock"? Belonging and the Local Approbation of Imperial Discourse in Gibraltar,' *Transactions of the Institute of British Geographers*, no, 30, 2 June 2005, pp. 206– 220; Caroline Norrie, 'The Last Rock in the Empire: Evacuation, Identity and Myth in Gibraltar,' *Oral History*, vol. 31, no. 1, Spring 2003, pp. 73–84; D.W. Pike, 'Franco and the Axis Stigma,' *Journal of Contemporary History*, vol. 17, no. 3, July 1982, pp. 369–407; Nicholas Rankin, *Defending the Rock: How Gibraltar Defeated Hitler*, London: Faber & Faber, 2017; Gareth Stockey, *Gibraltar: 'A Dagger in the Spine of Spain?'* Brighton: Sussex Academic Press, 2009.

9   The Rock was three miles long and just under two square miles in area. Malta measured approximately 95 square miles and Singapore some 220 square miles. Within the Rock an existing network of tunnels, including galleries, fire-points and shelters, was extended from 7 miles to 25 miles. (It is currently 34 miles.) In August 1940, German intelligence estimated that the garrison of 10,000 was supplied with sufficient food for 18 months. Rankin, *Defending the Rock*, pp. 276, 292.

10   Both humanitarian and utilitarian in intent, this measure was by no means popular with Gibraltarians and it would not be until February 1951 that the final cohort of evacuees returned to Gibraltar. The Colonial Office's review of *The Colonial Empire (1939– 1947)*, HMSO, Cmd 7267 (July 1947) gives two different figures for 'the wholesale displacement of civil population': 14,500 (paragraph 5) and 16,700 (paragraph 201). The majority were sent to England and the rest to Northern Ireland, Jamaica, Madeira and Tangier.

11   Rankin, *Defending the Rock*, p. 301.

12   'European appreciation, 1939–1940', report by the Chiefs of Staff Sub-Committee of the Committee of Imperial Defence on the broad strategic policy for the conduct of war, Ashton and Stockwell (eds.), *Imperial Policy and Colonial Practice 1925*, pt 1, p. 151.

13   S. Hoare, *Ambassador on Special Mission*, London: Collins, pp. 107–110. See also Dan Smyth, *Diplomacy and Strategy of Survival: British Policy and Franco's Spain, 1940– 41*, Cambridge: Cambridge University Press, 1986; Rankin, *Defending the Rock*, p. 392.

14   Mason-Macfarlane quoted in *The Times*, 27 November 1943, 'New Outlook at Gibraltar: A Fortress Colony Plans for the Future.'

15   Nevertheless, Gibraltarians overwhelmingly preferred British rule to the prospect of Spanish, and in a referendum held on 10 September 1967 (in which less than 3 per cent of Gibraltarians failed to vote) 12,138 voted for British rule while only 44 supported a change to Spanish control. Thereafter 10 September has been celebrated as National

Day. The referendum did not resolve the issue: Franco regarded the British presence as a 'thorn in the heart of Spain' and the United Nations opposed continuing British rule. In a second referendum held in November 2002, 98.9 per cent voted to remain British.

16 Douglas Austin, *Malta and British Strategic Policy, 1925–43*, London: Frank Cass, 2004, p. 20 ff; also Douglas Austin, *Churchill and Malta: A Special Relationship*, Stroud: Spellmount, 2006; Austin, *Churchill and Malta's War, 1939–1943;* Michael J. Budden, 'Defending the Indefensible? The Air Defence of Malta, 1936–1940,' *War in History*, vol. 6, no. 4, November 1999, pp. 447–467.

17 'Political Background: Malta' n.d. [1942], CO 968/95/3 (TNA). The constitution of 1921, which introduced a limited form of self-government, had been suspended following the pro-Italian-Nationalist ministry in November 1933 and subsequently revoked. A constitution re-establishing representative government by way of a partly elected council, was introduced in 1939.

18 Draft parliamentary statement [1942], CO 967/87 (TNA); Budden, 'Defending the Indefensible?' p. 464.

19 Middle East Defence Committee to Air Ministry, tel., 20 April 1942 for the Prime Minister and Chiefs of Staff, PREM 3/266/1 (TNA).

20 Cranborne to prime minister, 21 April 1942, PREM/266/1 (TNA).

21 J.R. Colville, *Man of Valour: The Life of Field Marshal the Viscount Gort, VC, GCB, DSO, MVO, MC*, London: Collins, 1972, pp. 240–246.

22 Austin, *Malta and British Strategic Policy*, p. 149. To this day, the national flag of the republic of Malta retains a representation of the George Cross. In 1943 the secretary of state for the Colonies committed the government to the restoration of responsible government after the war. See Ashton and Stockwell (eds.), *Imperial Policy and Colonial Practice*, pt I, pp. 287–291; Simon C. Smith (ed.), *Malta: British Documents on End of Empire*, London: HMSO, 2006.

23 *The Times*, 28 February 1942.

24 Rommel's two successful campaigns (early 1941 and early 1942) were carried out when Malta had been neutralised by the Luftwaffe, while 'British successes were achieved in periods of greater Malta pressure on stream of Axis supplies.' Austin, *Malta and British Strategic Policy*, pp. 185–189.

25 Cyril Falls, revised Brian Bond, 'Viscount Gort, 1886–1946,' *Oxford Dictionary of National Biography*, online, 2012.

26 Peter Elliott, *The Cross and the Ensign: A Naval History of Malta 1798–1979*, Cambridge: Patrick Stephens, 1980, p. 165. For Operation Pedestal, see James Holland, *Fortress Malta: An Island Under Siege 1940–1943*, London: Phoenix, 2004, pp. 341–369.

27 *The Memoirs of General Lord Ismay*, 1960 cited in Austin, *Churchill and Malta's War*, p. 194.

28 Correlli Barnett, *Engage the Enemy More Closely: The Royal Navy in the Second World War*, London: Classic Penguin, 2000, pp. 491–526. Malta required massive post-war reconstruction. In 1943 the British government promised the restoration of responsible government once the war was over. Debate ranged over the island's future status – independence or union with Britain – and the status of the dockyard which was gradually run down. Malta achieved independence in 1964, acknowledging the Queen as head of state. It subsequently became a republic continuing its membership of the Commonwealth, and also a member of European Economic Community and later European Union. See Ashton and Stockwell (eds.), *Imperial Policy and Colonial Practice*, pt I, pp. 287–291; see Smith, ed., *Malta*.

29 The vast literature on the rise and fall of the naval base – what Blackburn and Hack have called a 'never-ending post-mortem' – includes the following indicative titles: W.D. McIntyre, *The Rise and Fall of the Singapore Naval Base*, London: Macmillan, 1979; Alan Warren, *Singapore 1942: Britain's Greatest Defeat*, London: Hambledon, 2002; Karl Hack and Kevin Blackburn, *Did Singapore Have to Fall? Churchill and the Impregnable Fortress*, London: RoutledgeCurzon, 2004; Brian Farrell, *The Defence*

and Fall of Singapore 1940–1942, Stroud: Tempus Publishing, 2005; Brian Farrell (ed.), *Churchill and the Lion City: Shaping Modern Singapore*, Singapore: National University Singapore Press, 2011.

30 Churchill to Roosevelt, Gilbert, *Finest Hour*, p. 346; see also pp. 825, 959, 1257, 1261 and 1263.

31 Signals between Churchill and Wavell, 19 January 1942, Martin Gilbert, *Road to Victory: Winston Churchill 1941–1945*, London: Minerva, 1989, pp. 45–46.

32 Sir Frank Swettenham's, *British Malaya*, rev ed, 1948. Similarly, Roland Braddell described called Singapore 'a Clapham Junction of the world, served . . . by some eighty lines of steamers!' *The Lights of Singapore*, 5th edn., London: Methuen, 1941, p. 5.

33 C.M. Turnbull, *A History of Modern Singapore 1819–2005*, Singapore: NUS Press, 2009, chapter 5, 'War in the East, 1941–1942,' pp. 169–192.

34 A. Duff Cooper, *Old Men Forget: The Autobiography of Duff Cooper Viscount Norwich*, London: Hart-Davis, 1955, pp. 280–296; 'British Administration in the Far East: Report by the Chancellor of the Duchy of Lancaster,' 29 October 1941, CAB 66/20/9, WP (41)286 (TNA).

35 CAB 65/25/26, WM26(42)2 (TNA); PREM 3/153/1 (TNA); K.M. de Silva, *British Documents on the End of Empire, Sri Lanka*, pt 1, London: HMSO, 1997, pp. 192–198.

36 V.L.B. Mendis, *British Governors and Colonial Policy in Sri Lanka*, The Ceylon Historical Monograph Series, Vol. 9, Dehiwala, Sri Lanka: Tisara Prakasakayo Ltd., 1984.

37 Turnbull, *A History of Modern Singapore 1819–2005*, p. 309. The United Kingdom remained a member of SEATO (South East Asia Treaty Organisation) and, with Australia, Malaysia, New Zealand and Singapore, continues to subscribe to the FPDA (Five Power Defence Arrangements) of 1971.

38 The monument was originally a privately sponsored memorial to the victims of the Sook Ching, the extermination of almost one-fifth of the Chinese adult male population. In the 1960s the Singapore government assumed control to promote nation-building by also commemorating the suffering of Malays, Indians and Eurasians. Kevin Blackburn, 'The Collective Memory of the Sook Ching Massacre and the Civilian War Memorial of Singapore,' *Journal of the Malaysian Branch of the Royal Asiatic Society*, vol. 73, no. 2 2000, pp. 71–90. Similarly Sir William Goode, 'We let them down'. End of Empire transcripts, Granada TV, Mss Brit Emp s 527, Bodleian Library, Oxford. Goode entered the MCS in 1931; prisoner of war 1942–45; last colonial governor of Singapore 1957–59.

39 Sir Arthur de la Mare, British High Commissioner, Singapore, valedictory despatch to Sir Alec Douglas Home (Foreign Secretary), 2 October 1970, S.R. Ashton and Wm Roger Louis (eds.), *British Documents on the End of Empire: East of Suez and the Commonwealth 1964–1971*, London: HMSO, pt 1, pp. 388–393. At the time of writing (January 2019) and as the UK government prepares to leave the European Union, the British Foreign and Defence Secretaries were putting out feelers for both a special trade relationship with Singapore and a military base in the area.

40 See, for example, report on Total Defence Day, 15 February 2017, available at: www.straitstimes.com/singapore/2-bitter-but-valuable-lessons-from-japanese-occupation. See also Goh Chor Boon and Saravanan Gopinathan, 'History Education and the Construction of National Identity in Singapore, 1945–2000,' in Edward Vickers and Alisa Jones (eds.), *History Education and National Identity in East Asia*, London: Routledge, 2005, pp. 203–225.

13 Temasek, Singapore and modern national identity construction

John Miksic

Archaeological research in Singapore began in 1984. In the 30 years that followed, hundreds of thousands of artefacts have been unearthed in excavations there, the majority dating from the pre-Raffles period. The Temasek era (AD 1300–1600) of Singapore's existence lasted more than 100 years longer than the current post-Raffles period of occupation (1819 to present). Historical records on the Temasek period consist of the *Malay Annals* (*Sejarah Malayu*), a chronicle written in 1612; Chinese references in Yuan dynasty records, a provincial gazetteer and early Ming records of the voyages of Admiral Zheng He; a claim to suzerainty by the Javanese kingdom of Majapahit in 1365; and references in Portuguese sources of the sixteenth and seventeenth centuries. A Singaporean source, a long stone inscription probably written in the fourteenth century, once existed but was destroyed in the colonial period.

Archaeological evidence has proven that a thriving and prosperous settlement arose on the island now called Singapore around 1300. The upper strata of sites in Singapore yield remains of the colonial period. For many Singaporeans, these artefacts are more interesting even though they are more recent, because they date from the period when their ancestors arrived here. Interest in the precolonial period has recently increased, ironically in part due to national introspection connected with the discussion about how to commemorate the arrival of Raffles and the East India Company in Singapore in January 1819. For the past 50 years, Sir Thomas Stamford Raffles has been acknowledged as Singapore's founder. This story may change in future; Raffles himself never wished to be considered the father of Singapore, which can be inferred from his own statements about wishing to revive ancient Singapore.

Current attitudes towards heritage in Singapore

Singapore has numerous institutions charged with caring for and developing various aspects of the nation's heritage. These include the National Heritage Board, which oversees several institutions. The National Museum and the Peranakan Museum use artefacts and other media to narrate Singapore's past. The National Library and National Archives display and curate textual sources and documents. The Urban Redevelopment Authority (URA) has the responsibility to coordinate the preservation and conservation of the built environment. The URA endeavours to foster the development of 'a nation with a memory', and quotes the words of S. Rajaratnam, who was speaking in his capacity as the second deputy prime minister (Foreign Affairs): 'A nation must have a memory to give it a sense of cohesion, continuity and identity. *The longer the past, the greater the awareness of a nation's identity*'.[1]

Despite this emphasis on the importance of time depth in forming Singapore's identity, the general attitude toward the past has been that nothing important happened in Singapore before Sir Stamford Raffles arrived in January 1819 and brought life to a sleepy fishing village and pirate lair. Later in the same speech, Rajaratnam said:

> The island of Singapore as such has no long past. When Raffles founded Singapore in 1819 it was the home of a few hundred fishing folk. All we know of its past prior to this are vague hints that it was used as a halting place by mariners, traders and pirates before they moved on to more congenial places. What happened before 1819 – if anything worthwhile happened at all – has been irretrievably lost in the mists of time.
>
> Singapore's knowable past began in 1819.
>
> We could have contrived a more lengthy and eye-boggling lineage by tracing our ancestry back to the lands from which our forefathers emigrated – China, India, Sri Lanka, the Middle East, and Indonesia.
>
> The price we would have to pay for this more impressive genealogical table would be to turn Singapore into a bloody battle-ground for endless racial and communal conflicts and interventionist politics by the more powerful and bigger nations from which Singaporeans had emigrated. So from our point of view to push a Singaporean's historic awareness beyond 1819 would have been a misuse of history. . . . After attaining independence in 1965 there was debate as to who should be declared the founding fathers of Singapore. The debate was brought to an abrupt end when the government fixed responsibility for this on Sir Stamford Raffles and officially declared him the founder of Singapore. Many of our Third World friends are completely mystified that contrary to usual practice a dyed-in-the-wool British imperialist should have been named the founder of modern Singapore. In fact there were some well-meaning patriots in Singapore who were all for casting the Raffles statue situated in front of Victoria Memorial Hall into what was then the revoltingly filthy and smelly Singapore River.
>
> To cut a long story short, there was a reprieve and Raffles was saved.
>
> Our decision to name Raffles the founder of Singapore is an example of the proper use of history; the proper approach to the preservation of historic monuments.
>
> First in nominating Raffles as the founder of modern Singapore, we are accepting a fact of history. To pretend otherwise is to falsify history.
>
> Raffles founded Singapore. This is a fact.[2]

Thus, even after independence, in order to preserve social stability, Singapore textbooks passed off the precolonial period as a period empty of history when nothing of consequence worth recording had taken place on the island. The only nod to the precolonial past was to note that a traditional Malay text usually known in English as the *Malay Annals*, in Malay *Sejarah Melayu*, labelled Singapore as the first great Malay trading port.

O.W. Wolters, a highly regarded British historian who had been a civil servant in Malaya before World War II and later became a professor of history at Cornell University, dedicated a book to the explication of the Singapore section of the *Malay Annals*.[3] He concurred with the conclusion that the Singapore section of the *Annals* was a complete fabrication. He accounted for this by noting evidence that two Malay polities on the east coast of Sumatra had struggled for supremacy during the pre-Islamic period in the fourteenth century: one called Malayu in Jambi, the other Srivijaya in Palembang. Wolters inferred that the Singapore episode was intended to conceal a period when Srivijaya was eclipsed by Malayu. According to the *Malay Annals*, Singapore's first ruler, Sri Tri Buana, was enthroned in Palembang and then migrated to Singapore, where he established a dynasty which lasted for 100 years. The fifth ruler in his line, Iskandar Shah, was attacked by Java and fled to the Malay Peninsula where he established a new kingdom, Melaka. The Singapore period was thus meant to account for the period between Palembang's decline and Melaka's rise, when Malayu/Jambi was assumed to have been in the ascendant.

The *Malay Annals* has been the subject of numerous translations and analyses.[4] Approximately 30 versions or recensions exist. Two important versions of the *Malay Annals* are known as the Raffles MS18 and the Shellabear texts. The Raffles version is the oldest. The actual title of the manuscripts is in Arabic: *Sulalatu'l-salatin*, 'The Genealogy of the Kings'. The oldest manuscript gives a date for a composition of the origins and descent of Malay rajas and the development and significance of court ceremonies 'for the information of my descendants' by a person named Patih Ludang, who was instructed to do so by his sultan, Ala-ud-din Ri'ayat Shah. He gave a date of 1021 Anno Hijra (equivalent to 1612 CE) for the completion of the manuscript, when the Malay capital was located at Batu Sawar, up the Johor River. The Shellabear version was written around 1750, when the capital was on Pulau Penyengat, near Bintan Island, in the Riau archipelago.

A major political shift took place in the Johor-Singapore-Riau heartland of the Malays between 1612 and 1750. The Malay polity gradually came under the control of Bugis refugees from their home island of Sulawesi after the fall of the kingdom of Makassar to the Dutch in 1667. The Malay rulers were puppets of the Bugis. This change of fortune is epitomized by the fact that the great Malay hero Hang Tuah in the Shellabear version had become a Bugis.[5]

The Shellabear version became well known in Singapore in the nineteenth century because it was chosen by a missionary as an exemplar of excellent Malay prose and was printed on one of Singapore's earliest printing presses. This had a significant impact on the perception of Singapore's role in the evolution of the famous port of Melaka, which was one of the greatest ports in Asia in the early sixteenth century. The Portuguese writer Tome Pires famously proclaimed that 'whoever is lord of Melaka has his hands on the throat of Venice'.⁶ The conquest of Melaka in 1511 was the culmination of Portugal's thrust into the Indian Ocean; for a few decades Portugal indeed became wealthy from the spice trade until the port of Banten ('Bantam' in Portuguese) crystallized as the new Indonesian Muslim centre in the archipelago.

The sobriquet 'Raffles MS 18' is entirely justified; it was acquired by Sir Stamford Raffles himself. The precise circumstances by which it came into his hands are not known, but one of Raffles's main interests was the acquisition of Southeast Asian artefacts of all sorts. He actively encouraged people to bring him items for him to choose among. He learned Malay on his voyage to Penang, where he took up his first Southeast Asian position, and was able to read and possibly write Malay in the modified Arabic script used in the early nineteenth century to write the language.

The first chapter of the *Raffles MS 18* begins with the story of Raja Iskandar Dzul-karnein (the Two-Horned), a 'Roman' from Macedonia (Alexander the Great as filtered through Persian sources), who conquers Raja Kida Hindi, who ruled half of India and converted him to Islam. Alexander then married Raja Kida Hindi's daughter and they had a son, Raja Shulan, who succeeded him. In the second chapter, Raja Shulan conquered the rest of India, and ruled in Nagapatam. This city was an important early centre of Buddhism in southeast India. An inscription shows that the rulers of this city and kingdom had close relations with Sumatra; pilgrims from Srivijaya went there to study. Raja Shulan had a son, Raja Chulan, who succeeded to the throne. Frustrated because there was no land left in India to conquer, he set out to attack China.

The Chinese learned of Raja Chulan's plan. They knew they could not defeat him in battle, so they devised a stratagem. They sent an ancient ship crewed by old men to intercept Raja Chulan. They met him in Temasek. Thus Temasek (the future Singapore) served as the place where Indians and Chinese met. There was no reference to any population in Temasek at this time, however. Raja Chulan asked the Chinese how much further he would have to go to get to China. They answered that the distance was so great that when they left China they were young men; he would become old and die before he could reach it.

Raja Chulan abandoned his plan to conquer China and decided instead to get his artisans to make him a glass box so that he could explore the bottom of the sea (by implication the waters of the Singapore Strait). Reaching the seabed, he discovered another kingdom there where he found a beautiful princess. They married and had three sons. After a time, Raja Chulan became homesick and decided to return to India. He mounted a winged horse which carried him to the mouth of the Singapore River; there he had his artisans carve an inscription on a big boulder 'in Hindustani script' which recorded his underwater exploits. Beneath the stone, he hid gold and gems for his sons to find when they came of age; he then returned to India.

Raja Shulan and Raja Chulan were thinly disguised names for real rulers of the Chola kingdom which ruled south India in the early eleventh century. In 1025

Rajaraja Chola launched a naval attack which is recorded in an inscription on a royal temple in Tanjor, India. The inscription records that the attack conquered all the ports of Srivijaya and captured its king, who was taken back to India. It seems that the Cholas set up a viceroyalty at the northern end of the Straits, in the modern state of Kedah. Indian trading guilds set up inscriptions in Sumatra in the later eleventh century; their motive for this invasion seems to have been commercial. The story of Rajas Shulan and Chulan are a somewhat mythologised version of actual events, therefore, to avoid calling attention to the fact that Srivijaya had been conquered by the Cholas of south India.

In Chapter 3, the three sons of Raja Chulan miraculously appear on Seguntang Hill in Palembang. Archaeologists have found evidence that this hill was an important Buddhist sanctuary in the seventh through ninth centuries, in the form of ruined brick sanctuaries and stone statues. The natives decide to send the eldest son to West Sumatra to become their ruler. West Sumatra was an important source of gold. An enormous stone statue which probably portrays a fourteenth-century ruler of that region is now in the Museum Nasional in Jakarta. This statue has an important indirect link to Singapore's archaeology, as we shall see. The second son is sent to Borneo to become king there. The youngest, whose name is Sang Nilatanam, a Malay name, remains in Palembang and becomes the local ruler. The local people make a pact with him: they will be loyal to him no matter how badly he oppresses them, but in return he has to promise never to cause his subjects to feel shame, to lose face. One of the major sources for early Sumatran history is a set of inscriptions erected in Palembang and other areas of Sumatra which records an oath of loyalty to the Srivijayan rulers in the seventh century. Thus the importance of this oath-taking ceremony is also corroborated by archaeological remains. The young prince then receives a new title: Sri Tri Buana, 'Lord of the Three Worlds' in Sanskrit.

The name 'Sri Tri Buana' was important in the fourteenth century in several contexts. In the early fourteenth century Java was ruled by a queen, Tribuvanesvaratunggadevi. According to a fifteenth-century Javanese source, her prime minister, Patih Gajah Mada, swore to conquer the Indonesian archipelago, including Temasek.[7] Another source, a poem entitled *Desawarnana*, written in Java in 1365, records that Temasek was one of the territories of the east Javanese kingdom of Majapahit.[8]

A second fourteenth-century context for the name *Sritribuana* is a Thai text composed around 1345. This source uses the term Sri Tri Buana, 'Lord of the Three Worlds', to refer to a Buddhist doctrine about the law of karma and the importance of resigning oneself to birth in a particular stratum of society as a result of one's actions in previous lives. Thus the name Sri Tri Buana was quite symbolic at the time when the young man was given the name.

Eventually Sri Tri Buana became dissatisfied with Palembang and decided to set off on a search for a new place to establish a kingdom. He first visited the island of Bintan, 45 kilometres southeast of Singapore, where he met a queen, Wan Sri Benian (or Sakidar Shah in some versions), who adopted him as her son and created a coronation ceremony which was handed down to future generations of Malay courtiers. Sri Tri Buana then went hunting and looking across the water saw a beach with sand so white it appeared like a sheet of cloth. His companions informed him that this was Temasek (theoretically he was born under the strait across which he is looking; apparently he does not remember this). He then landed on Temasek and saw a strange animal with a red body, black head, and white breast, somewhat bigger than a goat. The animal then disappeared into the jungle and was never seen again. All were puzzled by the nature of the beast, but after some discussion they decided it must have been a lion, though none of them were quite sure what a lion looked like. Sri Tri Buana decided to build a city there and to call it Singapura, 'Lion City'.

The name Singapura was rather popular in Southeast Asia. According to Indian Buddhist literature, the future Buddha, Gautama, once lived in a city of this name. From the time of Ashoka in the third century BCE the lion had been a popular Buddhist icon. Cities called Singapura are known to have existed in southern Vietnam by the fifth century, the east coast of the area in the Malay Peninsula which is now southern Thailand near the border with Malaysia in the sixth century, and in the part of central Thailand which was under the Khmer empire in the twelfth century (and which is still a Thai city today, known as Singburi). The Sanskrit word *singa* was also used as an element of names for the kingdom of Singasari in east Java in the thirteenth century, and Singaraja, a city on Bali's north coast.

Sri Tri Buana founded a new Singapura, and ruled there for 48 years before he died. 'And Singapura became a great city, to which foreigners resorted in great numbers so that the fame of the city and its greatness spread throughout the world.'[9] Eventually he died and was buried on 'the hill of Singapura', together with his adopted mother, the queen of Bintan, and the chief of his followers from Palembang, Demang Lebar Daun.

It is worth pointing out that the two changes of name, from Sang Nilatanam to Sri Tri Buana and Temasek to Singapura, are both instances of a transition from Malay to Sanskrit; in other words, from a local to an international language. In modern terms, this might be construed as an exercise in rebranding: to signify the ambition of a regional commercial enterprise to become a major internationally known port. This ploy was immediately successful, and for a century Singapore flourished. This excited envy on the part of the Malays' more populous rivals, the Javanese, whose king, Bhatara Majapahit, was upset that the Malays did not pay him tribute. He attacked Singapore, but was repelled. This occurred in Chapter 4.

Chapter 5 tells the story of Singapore's Herculean figure, Badang. He wins a contest of strength with a champion from India by throwing a rock from the hill of Singapore to the mouth of the Singapore River. The 'Hill of Singapore' can be identified with Fort Canning Hill, which was known as the Forbidden Hill, the *Bukit Larangan* in Malay, when Raffles arrived, because the palace of the ancestors was said to be on top of it.

In Chapter 6, Singapore comes to grief. Women of the raja's court, jealous of the beauty of a young consort, spread false rumours that she has been unfaithful to him. As punishment, he forces her to stand naked in the marketplace. The girl's father, a treasury official, in revenge opens the city gates and allows the Javanese to enter. They sack the city but the king, Iskandar Shah, escapes and founds a new city, Melaka. The traitorous official is however turned into stone in the moat of Singapore. Although it is not made explicit, the fate of Singapore clearly has a moral connotation. The ruler broke the ancient covenant not to shame any of his subjects. As a result, he lost his kingdom. The traitorous subject, however, was also punished by fate and became stone. This is one of several occasions in the *Malay Annals* where the chronicler adds the information that this landmark can still be seen in Singapore in his day (i.e. 1612). This is the only section of the entire work in which such statements are made, as if to ensure that the audience for his tale will take it seriously, not as fable. Singapore does not disappear from the text after Melaka is founded. It retains an important role throughout the fifteenth century as the naval base for the kingdom. Singapore is the fief of the *Seri Bija Diraja*, the title conferred on the man who held the office of *laksamana*, the admiral of the fleet. Singapore is described as having 40 three-masted cruisers, a sizeable force for this place and time. Hang Tuah, the foremost hero of the *Malay Annals*, is the *laksamana*.

The *Malay Annals* was not meant to be a literal chronicle of history. It was apparently a written version of an oral composition to be read aloud in public as a means of entertainment, which would have the dual function of perpetuating a particular view of the source of legitimacy of the Malay ruling family. In this it seems to have been successful. When Patih Ludang composed the *Raffles MS 18*, Singapore had probably just been sacked. Patih Ludang may have been a Singaporean himself, which would have explained why he made a special effort to ensure that his audience believed in its veracity. As it turned out, the memory of Singapore's past was preserved for the next 200 years and was still alive when Raffles arrived there in 1819.

Raffles and the Sejarah Melayu

We do not know when Raffles obtained his copy of the *Sejarah Melayu*, but it obviously made a major impact on him. The *Malay Annals* was influential in Raffles's decision to establish a base in Singapore in 1819. As Raffles wrote to Marsden on 31 January 1819, 'Here I am at Singapore, true to my word, and in the enjoyment of all the pleasure which a foot on such classic ground must inspire'.[10] Lady Raffles 'later claimed it was the specific account of the founding of Singapore in the third chapter of the *Annals* which first gave her husband the idea for an 'Eastern Settlement' on the same site'.[11] As he wrote on 12 December 1818 to his friend William Marsden, who had lived for years in Sumatra: '[Y]ou must not be surprised if my next letter to you is dated from the site of the ancient city of Singapura.'[12] After his establishment of a trading station in Singapore, Raffles wrote to his royal patron, the Duchess of Somerset, that

> in Marsden's map of Sumatra you will observe an Island to the north of these straits called Singapura; this is the spot, the site of the ancient maritime capital of the Malays, and within the walls of these fortifications, raised not less than six centuries ago, on which I have planted the British flag.[13]

The historian John Bastin has argued that Raffles's selection of Singapore for a base was governed by more hard-headed considerations: 'That Raffles knew of Singapura from the Sejarah Melayu . . . is obvious; but that it was the prime inspiration for the British settlement on the island overlooks the complex factors that actually led to its foundation.'[14] Certainly these were not absent from his calculations. On the other hand, several other locations could also have been chosen. Col. William Farquhar, who accompanied Raffles on his voyage to the Singapore area, favoured the island of Karimun. In fact, Farquhar had already visited Karimun in July 1818 in a search for a base in the area, and reported that 'there is no place which holds out so many advantages in every way as do the Kariman Islands, which are so situated as to be a compete key to the Straits of Singapore, Dryon, and Soban'.[15] This island lies 40 kilometres west of Singapore, and from some respects is more strategically located. It sits in the exact centre of the southern entrance to the Straits of Melaka, from where no ship can enter or leave the Straits without being seen. An inscription on the northern tip of the island indicates that it has been inhabited by people with an intricate connection to the maritime trading network for 1,000 years.[16] It was certainly a logical location to consider. Raffles, however, seems to have humoured Farquhar by visiting it first and then heading to the place which seems to have been his intended destination all along: the Singapore River.

Raffles was clearly cognisant of the need to find a place with a good source of water and a protected harbour. Karimun does not seem to have satisfied either of these criteria. But there was another merit which Singapore possessed that Karimun did not: a brand name. The population of Singapore and surrounding areas was well acquainted with Singapore's location and its glorious image in legend. But Raffles was convinced that the *Sejarah Melayu* was not purely legendary; he believed that Singapore had been an ancient port. And quickly after his arrival he and his companions discovered evidence that he was correct in his interpretation of the Malay literary source which had inspired him to visit the island in the first place. Raffles was not only looking for a convenient stopover between India and China; he also wanted to tap the spices of the Indonesian archipelago and sell British wares to Java and the thousands of other islands there, by attracting Indonesian ships.[17]

If Raffles considered the *Sejarah Melayu* to be an important historical source, and if he studied it intensively, as seems to be quite true, then he would have been familiar with the details of the Singapore chapters. The salient points of the image of Singapore for him would have been: its antiquity; its prosperity; its cosmopolitan nature; its defensible nature; its location between what is now Fort Canning Hill, the Singapore River, the sea, and its fortification wall and moat; and the importance of Fort Canning Hill, where the palace stood and where the ancient Malay kings were buried. It is quite possible that Raffles planned to write about Singapore's antiquity after he retired. He did note that he planned to write a sequel to his monumental two-volume work *The History of Java*, but unfortunately he did not live long enough after his return to England to fulfil that objective. He may have had important artefacts from the Singapore in his possession when he set sail from Bencoolen (modern-day Bengkulu) for home, but a few hours after leaving port the ship, *Fame*, caught fire and sank, with the loss of all his possessions. An inventory of his lost property exists in a claim for insurance compensation but does not include details of the items.

Raffles himself noted that if he were to die in Singapore, his 'bones would have the honour of mixing with the ashes of the Malay kings'. John Crawford, the captain of one of the ships which brought Raffles's party to Singapore in 1819, mentioned the old earthen embankment on the northeast side of the ancient city:

> Where the tents are pitched, the ground is level above one mile, partly cleared of the jungle, with a transparent fresh water brook or rivulet running through it. . . . This spot of ground is the site of the very ancient city and fort of Singapore. . . . No remnants of its former grandeur exists, not the slightest vestige of it has ever been discovered. As for the strength of the fortifications, no remains are to be seen excepting by those possessing a fertile imagination and can trace the foundation or parts of earthen bastions in a mound of earth that lines the beach and winds round the margins of the creek. . . . Sir Stamford found accounts of it in a very old Malay work.[18]

Obviously, not everyone was able to discern the ruins of ancient Singapore, even in 1819. However, in 1821 John Crawfurd, who became Singapore's second Resident in 1823, passed through Singapore on his way to the courts of Siam and Cochin China (south Vietnam) in the course of a diplomatic mission. Fortunately he was much more conversant with relics of the past than his near-namesake John Crawford.[19] He whiled away a morning by strolling around the boundaries of what he could clearly discern was an ancient city.[20] He noted the size and location of the ancient rampart and the natural stream which flowed next to it for much of its course.[21] This rampart was demolished in 1828 to construct what is now Stamford Road, which runs between the National Museum and the campus of the Singapore Management University. The stream which once ran beside it (and probably formed the *Parit Singapura* or 'Singapore canal' mentioned as the place where the traitorous official was turned into stone in the *Sejarah Melayu*) is no longer visible at this point either. It is now covered by concrete in its lower stretch; it can be seen emerging from underground near Mt. Sophia, where the old Cathay Building, once Singapore's tallest building, once stood at the corner of Stamford and Bras Basah Roads. Near the stream's former mouth, on the north side of Stamford Road opposite the Padang and the Singapore Sports Club, is an iron plaque on a small granite wall. The plaque bears the simple inscription 'Stamford Bridge 1956'. This remnant of a once-significant Singapore landmark now seems quite anomalous given the lack of a bridge or a need for one.

Following the course of the rampart inland, Crawfurd reached the southeast foot of the 'Forbidden Hill'. There he found the remains of an ancient orchard; Munshi Abdullah also mentioned the old garden with shaddock, durian, rambutan, duku, lime, *langsat, petai, jering* (local fruit trees) of great age which no longer bore fruit.[22] He would probably have been familiar with the palace gardens of

Java such as the Taman Sari in Yogyakarta, which the British forces had stormed in a furious battle a few years earlier. Raffles was later to exploit the same patch of ground to set up Singapore's first botanic garden. This is further evidence of Raffles's interest in patterning his new settlement partly according to the remnants of the ancient site.

Crawfurd then ascended the 'Forbidden Hill'. Raffles had not yet built his house on top of the hill, but Col. Farquhar had already had the forest cleared from its slopes, enabling Crawfurd to describe dense remains of structures made of good-quality brick. He interpreted the two largest ruins as a 'sepulchre' and a temple. The largest ruin was 40 feet (12 meters) on a side, on an artificial terrace near the top of the hill. At the location where Raffles later built a house, he found 14 square sandstone blocks which he correctly interpreted as bases for wooden pillars, part of a pavilion, and other structures. At another terrace, he saw what his informants told him was the grave of 'a ruler', but no name was mentioned. 'A rude structure' was quickly built at the site, which became known as the *Keramat Iskandar Shah*. The word *keramat* is used in Singapore and the surrounding region to refer to a spot associated with a pious Muslim, sometimes but not always a tomb. Iskandar Shah is the name of Singapore's last king according to the *Sejarah Melayu*, who was forced to flee and founded Melaka in 1400. Between the ruins he could plainly see pieces of Chinese and local pottery 'in great abundance' as well as Chinese copper coins with dates as early as 967.

Another early visitor to Singapore was Munshi Abdullah, who had taught Raffles Malay. He recorded a feature which Crawfurd neglects to mention: a spring

Figure 13.1 Location of Raffles's Bungalow on Fort Canning Hill.

of water on the west side of the hill which he noted was called the 'Forbidden Spring', and recorded the story that the princesses of Singapore bathed there in ancient times.[23] The spring appears on early nineteenth-century maps of Singapore. The British built an aqueduct to channel water from the spring to a tank on the bank of the river. The Singapore River was not a source of fresh water; it was actually an estuary, and its water was salty. The *Parit Singapura* was a fresh water stream, but the water from the hill was better quality. For the first ten years of British occupation, the water from the Forbidden Spring was sufficient to supply the ships in the harbour.[24] When demand exceeded the spring's supply, wells were dug around the hill, which caused the spring to dry up. The street named Tank Road on the northwest side of Fort Canning preserves a memory of that era. This spring is not mentioned in the *Sejarah Melayu*, but a Chinese visitor to Singapore in the fourteenth century implies that it was an important landmark at that time (see later discussion).

At the mouth of the Singapore River a 'Rocky Point' jutted into the sea. This is the location according to the *Sejarah Melayu* where Raja Chulan had his experts inscribe a boulder with the story of his exploits beneath the Singapore Strait, and where the rock which Badang threw from the hill landed. Crawfurd indeed observed a boulder at that location with an ancient inscription on it. The inscription had been discovered in June 1819 when labourers from Bengal called attention to it while they were clearing the forest and collecting rocks to fill in the swamp which then covered the area known today as Raffles Place. The boulder had been intentionally split in ancient times to create a flat surface suitable for writing, a technique known from other sites in Java. Another stone nearby was called Garfish Head Rock (*Batu Kepala Todak*), which was highly revered by the local Sea Nomad boat-dwellers who lived in the Singapore River estuary; Abdullah observed that there 'they are accustomed to make all their solemn agreements, as they hold it in reverence. They also pay great respect to the rock, decorating it with flags'.[25] When Singapore became independent, a new monument, the Merlion, was erected at the same site.

An official of the East India Company, J. Prinsep, studied a rubbing of the stone but was unable to decipher it.[26] In 1843 the stone was blown up when the site was requisitioned by the army to build quarters for the commander of Fort Fullerton.[27] Col. James Low, who had a considerable interest in antiquities, happened to pass by the site just after the explosion. He collected several fragments of the boulder, and sent three of them to Calcutta.[28] Another piece of the stone was picked up by Col. W.J. Butterworth (governor of Singapore from 1843 to 1855). He first had it moved to his house on Government (later Fort Canning) Hill and later sent it to Calcutta. More pieces seem to have been saved but subsequently disappeared. W.H. Read saw a large fragment of the inscription 'at the corner of Government House, where Fort Canning is now; but during the absence of the Governor at Penang on one occasion the convicts requiring stone to replace the road, chipped up the valuable relic of antiquity'.[29] Tiny fragments of the ancient stone may still be scattered from the river mouth to Fort Canning Hill. A large piece of the Singapore Stone was returned to Singapore in 1918 on indefinite loan from the Trustees of the Indian Museum.[30] Presumably the other pieces are still in Calcutta.

Figure 13.2 Site of the Singapore Stone at the mouth of the Singapore River.

Thus, within 25 years of Raffles's arrival, all major monuments surviving from ancient Singapore had been destroyed: the old rampart, the ruins on Fort Canning, and the Singapore inscription. Once these tangible pieces of evidence that Singapore had been an ancient city vanished, the memory of their existence gradually faded away. By the early twentieth century, the image of ancient Singapore as a reality had declined to the status of a legend told in an old Malay text in which it was associated with a magical beast something like a lion which vanished, an Indian king who explored the sea floor and then returned on a winged horse and a prince who was the son of the underwater princess. One major opportunity for archaeological research presented itself in 1928, when the fort which had been built on top of the hill was demolished and a reservoir covering six acres (three hectares) was excavated. Chinese workers engaged in the project unearthed a buried hoard of gold ornaments, including an armlet with an elaborate design, but even this discovery did not lead to any research on the part of the staff of the Raffles Museum located a few hundred meters away. P.V. van Stein Callenfels, a Dutch archaeologist with much experience in Java, stated that the gold ornaments found on Fort Canning reminded him of the best fourteenth-century Javanese craftsmanship.[31] This dating has since been corroborated by the excavation of a large image from West Sumatra carved in the fourteenth century of a person who is depicted as wearing a very similar ornament.[32]

Since the early 1900s, historians have known that Chinese sources from the Yuan Dynasty (1260–1367) and Ming (1368–1643) also record the name Temasek (*Dan ma xi*), and that a Ming map places it where Singapore is today. Closely associated with Temasek are two other place names: *Long ya men*, 'Dragon's Tooth Strait' and *Ban zu* (a transliteration of the Malay word *pancur*, 'spring of water'. The first reference to *Long ya men* appears in 1320 in the *Yüan shih:* 'In the ninth month of the seventh year of the reign of Yen You [1320], Ma Cha Man and others were sent as envoys to *Zhan-cheng* [Champa], *Zhanla* [Cambodia], and *Longya men*, asking for tame elephants.' Probably as a result of the expression of interest in this region by the Chinese government, a kingdom on the nearby island of Bintan sent a mission to China in 1323. In 1325 *Long ya men* sent its own mission to China with a memorial and tribute.[33] *Long ya men* and Bintan seem to have been rivals at this time, which casts interesting light on the role of Bintan in the *Sejarah Melayu* as a queendom which existed before Sri Tri Buana's arrival. Archaeological research on Bintan has revealed fourteenth-century artefacts at several locations.[34]

In 1349 a Chinese text entitled *Dao yi zhi lue* ['Description of the Barbarians of the Isles', abbreviated DYZL) was incorporated into a gazetteer, *Qing yuan xu zhi*, 'A Continuation of the History and Topography of Quanzhou'. Two-thirds of the text has been translated into English.[35] Wang seems to have made two voyages to Southeast Asia between 1330 and 1339.[36] Wang mentioned two overseas Chinese communities. One of these communities consisted of some Chinese who belonged to a fleet sent to attack Java in 1292. Those who fell ill during the outward voyage were left behind on Goulan Shan (possibly Gelam Island, off west Borneo). In Wang's day, 40 years later, 'over 100' of these men were still alive, 'mixed up with the native families'.[37] Wang's second reference to overseas Chinese implies the existence of a community of merchants at *Long ya men*, which he also characterised as a pirate lair. This is difficult to comprehend, since he also mentions a peaceful, 'honest' settlement of traders on the hill of Temasek, which is only eight kilometres away.[38]

The 'honest' settlement was called *Ban zu*. It was built on a hill behind *Long ya men*. The place afforded one exotic item which was highly valued in China: 'very fine hornbill casques'. The inhabitants of *Ban zu* wore rather elaborate costumes, such as 'turbans of gold-brocaded satin, and red oiled clothes [covering] their bodies',[39] which sounds reminiscent of batik. They also pursued several specialised occupations such as salt-making from sea water and brewing rice wine. They were also militarily adept. In another section of the *DYZL*, on *Xian* ('people of Shan/Siam']; he records that a few years before his visit, 70-odd ships from *Xian* came to attack the city moat:

[The town] resisted for a month, the place having closed the gates and defending itself, and they not daring to assault it. It happened just then that an Imperial envoy was passing by (*Dan-ma-xi*), so the men of *Xian* drew off and hid, after plundering *Xi-li*.[40]

The raid on Temasek was one in a long series of Siamese raids on the Malays. The *History of the Yuan*, quoting the words of the Chinese emperor, says that around 1295,

'since the people of *Sien* and of *Ma-li-yü-erh* have long been killing each other and are all in submission at this moment, an imperial order has been issued telling the people of Sien: do no harm to the *Ma-li-yü-erh* and hold to your promise.'

This is why the *Xian* fled when the Chinese envoy passed by.[41]

Pancur is not an unusual place name in the Singapore area. Knowledge of locations where drinkable water could be obtained was vital for sailors. The Straits of Melaka and the island south of them were lined with broad mangrove fringes; one had to know in advance which ones had fresh water near the shore. Other places named Pancur include a major port of the tenth century on the northwest coast of Sumatra, a sixteenth-century capital of Johor up the Johor River and a modern town on the northeast coast of the island of Lingga. It would not have been unusual for a place with a source of fresh water such as Singapore to have been called Pancur.

Although Chinese sources on Singapore in the fifteenth century are not plentiful, the *Shun feng xiang sung*, 'Fair Winds for Escort', which Joseph Needham dated to about 1430, says that 'after Ch'ang Yao island [now called Sentosa] had been sighted, the ship "on the inside" passed Tan-ma-hsi strait, where passengers could change ship'.[42] It was common practice for traders to move from one ship to another in Southeast Asia.[43] This record indicates that Singapore performed the same function of linking smaller regional ports to a larger network in the fifteenth century that Singapore's harbour and airport still do today. Although Melaka became the main centre of trade after Iskandar Shah was expelled from Singapore in 1396, Singapore did not disappear from the *Sejarah Melayu*. Singapore was still the fiefdom of Melaka's admiral.[44]

Archaeological remains

In the early 1980s, the Singapore government commissioned a plan to develop Fort Canning which would have involved considerable landscaping of the hill. Mr. Kwa Chong Guan, a Singaporean scholar-administrator who had long suspected that the accounts of ancient Singapore in the *Sejarah Melayu* and John Crawfurd were worth investigating, feared that any chance of testing this hypothesis might be lost. He contacted the Singapore National Museum, and a plan was formed to conduct archaeological research on the hill in advance of any such landscaping. With funding from Royal Dutch Shell, approval from the Parks and Recreation Department, and the Singapore Ministry of Defence, which provided some manpower for digging, an excavation was carried out over 10 days in January 1984 under the direction of this author, who was then teaching at Gadjah Mada University in Yogyakarta, Indonesia. This research focused on the area near the Keramat Iskandar Shah, since it seemed that area had not been disturbed by colonial period development.

The excavation succeeded in discovering fourteenth-century Chinese and local artefacts in an undisturbed context. In 1987, it was Singapore's turn to conduct an archaeological workshop as part of a collaborative effort undertaken by the Association of Southeast Asian Nations (ASEAN); I was hired as a lecturer with the Department of History, National University of Singapore, and a part-time consultant with Parks and Recreation, and asked to coordinate further excavations at Fort Canning. Further excavations took place almost annually until 2000. Further excavations were undertaken within the area between Fort Canning Hill, the Singapore River, the Padang and Stamford Road, as well as other areas. This research has resulted in the recovery of over half a million artefacts from the fourteenth century.[45] Most of these consist of ceramics, about half of which in terms of quantity is of probable local production in Malay style, with Chinese ceramics constituting the other half. The local Malay-style pottery is mainly utilitarian, some of which was used for industrial purposes. Copper was worked at the Parliament House Complex site to make hooks and other fishing gear; iron and copper/bronze were worked at the Padang.

Fort Canning Hill seems to have been the site of a palace, and religious structures. Archaeological excavations conducted since 1984 have revealed a palace workshop where specialized craftsmen worked gold and recycled broken Chinese glass vessels to make bangles. Chinese glass beads were also strung or sewn onto textiles there. Fort Canning has yielded numerous unusual artefacts which indicate that the inhabitants of *Ban zu* enjoyed a special relationship with China. These include shards of elaborate glass vessels, fragments of a porcelain pillow in the shape of a theatre, a porcelain compass and hundreds of porcelain bowls and plates. Chinese bowls and plates seem to have been commonly used in all habitation areas of fourteenth-century Singapore. Chinese and Sri Lankan coins demonstrate that the economy was based on money rather than barter. Indian glass bangles and stone beads further demonstrate the links between fourteenth-century Singapore and South Asia. In addition to the gold hoard found in 1928, fragments of gold were also found at St. Andrew's Cathedral, along with a mysterious artefact consisting of a pointed stone peg-like object with a man's head at one end. The latter may have been a touchstone; similarly shaped artefacts have been reported from Scythian sites.[46]

Another significant artefact from the fourteenth century is a lead statue found at Empress Place, very close to the modern Asian Civilisations Museum. The statue portrays a man in a typical Indonesian sarong riding a winged horse. The style is reminiscent of that seen on fourteenth-century Javanese temple reliefs, and still used for shadow puppets, but no other metal statue in this style, or any image of this particular subject, has ever been discovered. It is tempting but speculative to relate this statue to the story of Raja Chulan's return from the underwater world on a winged horse and his landing in the same vicinity where he is supposed to have been dropped off.

In the fifteenth century, Fort Canning was abandoned, a fact which can be explained by reference to the attacks recorded in the *Sejarah Melayu* and in Portuguese accounts of stories they heard in Melaka. The Singapore River, however, continued to see foreign traders. Thai and Vietnamese as well as Chinese pottery from the fifteenth century has been found in excavations as well as in dredging activity at the Kallang Basin just east of the Singapore River. This is what one would expect in view of the record of a harbourmaster still residing at the Singapore River in 1604. The 1984 discovery of fourteenth-century artefacts on Fort Canning was seen as sufficiently important to merit a front-page story in the *Straits Times*, Singapore's main English-language newspaper. In 1996 a display of artefacts from Fort Canning was held in the rotunda of the National Museum. This was later expanded to a new gallery in the rear part of the building. Since that time, archaeological displays have formed a part of the narrative of the National Museum. Exhibitions of archaeological finds from precolonial Singapore are also found in the Asian Civilisations Museum, the museum of the National University of Singapore and at St. Andrew's Cathedral. The National Parks Board (successor to the Parks and Recreation Department) opened an outdoor display in 2001 with informational signs, cases of artefacts and a preserved archaeological excavation which draws many schoolchildren and tour groups.

The National Parks Board has continued to develop Fort Canning as a park that combines nature and heritage. A spice garden commemorating Raffles's original experimental garden and the precolonial palace garden still occupies part of the original site where Crawfurd found the ancient fruit trees. An elaborate series of carved reliefs decorates the staircase leading up the hill at the Hill Street entrance to Fort Canning Park. Two walks of history are laid out on the hill, with signs posted to explain to visitors the role played by the hill in the fourteenth century and during the colonial era. There is, however, no legislation affording protection to potential archaeological sites. In 2004, a three-part television series about Singapore history was made; the story begins with the arrival of Raffles in 1819. Until 2015, the standard depiction of pre-Raffles Singapore in school texts was that of a fishing village and den of pirates, connected with some Malay fables about an undersea fairy princess and an attack by swordfish.

In 2014, a new curriculum was promulgated for Singapore social studies at the Secondary One level. A textbook published in conjunction with this revised curriculum devotes one-third of its more than 200 pages to the precolonial era.[47] The significance of this development was discussed in an article in the *New York Times* education section.[48] This curriculum revision has caused a certain amount of consternation among teachers, since they were not trained to deal with that period or with archaeological remains as a source for Singapore history. The effect of this change will become apparent as children from that cohort reach maturity, with consequences which cannot be clearly envisioned.

In 2017, the National Heritage Board held a series of discussions with focus groups regarding possible new policies regarding archaeology in Singapore. The results of those discussions are expected to result in new official involvement in and support for archaeology. The National Heritage Board has already begun to give grants to support the analysis and publication of research on archaeological materials from Singapore.[49]

Conclusion

Raffles was not aware of the existence of Chinese sources which confirm many details of the *Sejarah Melayu*'s account of Singapore, nor of Portuguese sources of the sixteenth century such as Tomé Pirés or Godinho de Eredia. The latter was born in Melaka in 1563; he was the son of a Bugis princess and a Portuguese member of a diplomatic mission to Sulawesi. In 1600, he became commander of a squadron of 70 Portuguese ships which guarded the south end of the Straits of Melaka. In 1604, he ordered that a fort be built at Singapore, but these plans never came to fruition.[50] A map attributed to him which was printed in 1604 indicates place names on the south coast of Singapore which still exist. The word *Xabandaria* shown on this map at the mouth of the Singapore River is a Malay word for harbourmaster. Singapore must still have had sufficient external trade to make such an appointment worthwhile. A Flemish merchant who spent much time in the region in the early seventeenth century called Singapore 'Island of the Old Xabandaria'.[51]

Raffles was apparently unaware that an English captain had been offered Singapore for free in 1703 by the ruler of Johor.[52] Captain Hamilton regretfully declined the offer due to a lack of capital to develop a port there. Someone, however, seems to have taken the Johor sultan's offer seriously. In 1709, a sketch of 'yᵉ Narrow Straights of Singapura' depicts 'Lotts Wife', the same landmark the Chinese in the fourteenth century called the Dragon's Tooth, which stood at the western entrance to Keppel Harbour between Sentosa and Labrador Point (and which was also blown up during the colonial period to widen the entrance to the harbour).[53] This chart indicates the water depths through the harbour. It is not known who took these soundings, or why. Thus 110 years before Raffles, some British notice was already taken of the potential of this small bay.

Nine years later, in 1718, Raja Kecil ('Little Raja'), a pretender to the throne of Johor, sent a messenger to Singapura to gather support from the *Orang Laut* (Sea People).[54] The leader of the Sea People, who bore the high-sounding title Raja Negara, was still associated with the Singapura area. Fifty years later, during a war between Bugis and Siak princes, Raja Kechil's grandson, Raja Ismail, sailed to Singapura, 'where he treated the sea-people harshly, forcing them to join his side and ordering them to prepare *perahu* and *sampan*.' The Raja Negara led his people in a sea battle against the Bugis off Tanah Merah on Singapore's east coast, in 1767.[55]

During the eighteenth century, British attention was focused on India. Britain's only Southeast Asian base, a little settlement at Bengkulu, southwest Sumatra, was a remote and insignificant outpost. In 1786, the East India Company occupied Penang; a few years later Melaka came into their temporary possession as a result of the Napoleonic Wars. Trade between India and China began to expand. This expansion was followed by Raffles's founding of an East India Company settlement at Singapore, 116 years after Hamilton envisioned exactly that course of action. The reports which Raffles heard when he arrived in 1819 show that the Malays had not forgotten Singapore's ancient history. By the early twentieth century, however, the icon of Raffles as the founder of Singapore was well established. A standard work on Singapore history concludes that '[t]he great trading city of the *Malay Annals* was probably a myth.'[56]

There are thus many new materials with which Singapore's national identity could become deeper and stronger as suggested by Senior Minister Rajaratnam soon after the country became independent. Singapore is 700 years old. It was not isolated before 1819; it was an important connecting point between east and west for 300 years. It was prosperous before the arrival of Europeans. Chinese, Malays, Indians and other Southeast Asians lived there. It had local industries: imported raw materials, finished products of metal, clay, glass. The economy was sophisticated: Singaporeans used money. It had at least a cosmopolitan, possibly hybrid society.

New discoveries about Singapore's pre-Raffles history are becoming integrated into the ongoing process of national identity formation. In 2010, the National Heritage Board sponsored the development of a massive online multiplayer game called *The World of Temasek*. Any visitor could log on to the website and create an avatar who could explore fourteenth-century Singapore. The object of the game was to become wealthy by engaging in various collecting and trading activities. Different layers of information were provided so that visitors who wanted to know more could determine what sources of evidence for the reconstruction of fourteenth-century Temasek were available. The site included elements of dress, architecture, religion, ecology and history. The site was sponsored for seven years; it was taken down in 2017.

On television, Singapore archaeology has been covered in the regular news media on several occasions. One example was broadcast on 10 October 2016 in a show called 'Sherlock at Work'.[57] The compère of the show visited the archaeological site in Fort Canning Park, tried his hand at digging and then visited the laboratory to see how artefacts are transformed into new data. More news stories and interviews about Singapore archaeology can be found by using an internet search engine.

How would Raffles have felt about this development? Would he have objected to being demoted from his status as putative founder of Singapore? It is more logical to infer that he would have felt gratified that his conviction that Singapore was 'classic ground' is gradually returning to occupy a significant position in the ongoing development of a Singaporean identity. Political conditions in Singapore may also have changed sufficiently that any reason to fear that social unrest may ensue from including Singapore's pre-Raffles history in Singapore's identity no longer exists. For many Singaporeans, the identity of being Singaporean now supersedes that of Malay, Chinese, or Indian.

218   *John Miksic*

Notes

Extract from speech by Mr. S. Rajaratnam, Second Deputy Prime Minister (Foreign Affairs), at a seminar on 'Adaptive Reuse: Integrating traditional areas into the modern urban fabric' held at the Shangri-La Hotel on 28 April 1984. In Kwa Chong Guan (ed.), *S. Rajaratnam on Singapore: From Ideas to Reality*, Singapore: World Scientific and Institute of Defence and Strategic Studies, 2006, p. 250. Emphasis added.

Kwa, *S. Rajaratnam*, pp. 251–253.

O.W. Wolters, *The Fall of Srivijaya in Malay History*, Ithaca and London: Cornell University Press, 1970. This in no way diminishes the scholarship of Prof. Wolters, who was the teacher of the author of this chapter. Prof. Wolters was writing before any archaeological data was available.

C.C. Brown (ed. and trans.), *Sejarah Melayu/Malay Annals*, Kuala Lumpur: Oxford University Press, 1970.

W.G. Shellabear (ed. and trans.), *Sejarah Melayu*, Petaling Jaya, Kuala Lumpur: Penerbit Fajar Bakti Sdn. Bhd., p. 86.

A. Cortesao (ed. and trans.), *The Suma Orientale of Tome Pires*, 2nd Series, Vol. 889, London: Hakluyt Society.

N.J. Krom, *Hindoe-Javaansche Geschiedenis* (2nd revised edition), 's-Gravenhage: M. Nijhoff, 1931, p. 36.

T.G. Th. Pigeaud, *Java in the Fourteenth Century: A Study in Cultural History*, Vol. III, The Hague: M. Nijhoff, Koninklijk Instituut voor Taal-, Land- en Volkenkunde, 1960, p. 11, Translation Series number 4.

Brown, *Sejarah Melayu*, p. 21.

10 C.E. Wurtzburg, *Raffles of the Eastern Isles*, Singapore: Oxford University Press, 1984, p. 487.

11 V.M. Hooker and M.B. Hooker, 'Introductory Essay,' in *John Leyden's Malay Annals*, Kuala Lumpur: Malaysian Branch of the Royal Asiatic Society, Reprint No. 20, 2001, pp. 43–45.

12 D. Moore and J. Moore, *The First 150 Years of Singapore*, Singapore: D. Moore, 1969, p. 16.

13 D. Moore and J. Moore, *The First 150 Years of Singapore*, Singapore: D. Moore, 1969, p. 31.

14 John Bastin, 'John Leyden and the Publication of the *Malay Annals*,' *Journal of the Malaysian Branch of the Royal Asiatic Society*, vol. 75, no. 2, 2002, p. 109.

15 Arnold Wright, 'The Straits Settlements,' in Arnold Wright and H.A. Cartwright (eds.), *Twentieth Century Impressions of British Malaya*, Singapore: Reprint Edition (first edition: 1909), Graham Brash (Pte) Ltd, 1989, p. 21.

16 R.C. Majumdar, *Suvarnadvipa*, Vol. II, New Delhi: Gian, 1986, p. 146, footnote 6. See photo in Miksic, *Singapore and the Silk Road of the Sea*, Singapore: NUS Press, 2013, p. 158.

17 Cf. C.A. Trocki, *Prince of Pirates*, Singapore: Singapore University Press, 1979, p. xviii.

18 Moore, *First 150 Years of Singapore*, p. 20.

19 John Crawford was the captain of the ship which carried Raffles to Singapore in 1819; John Crawfurd was a long-serving member of the East India Company, who had served in India and Java before becoming Singapore's second Resident in 1823.

20 John Crawfurd, *Journal of an Embassy from the Governor-General of India to the Courts of Siam and Cochin China*, original edition 1828, reprinted in 1967 by Oxford University Press; also in Paul Wheatley, *The Golden Khersonese*, Kuala Lumpur: University of Malaya Press, 1960, pp. 120-122.

21 It was a substantial earth wall 16 feet (5 metres) wide at its base and 8 or 9 feet (2.5 metres) high, next to which flowed a small brook. This feature, which Raffles and Captain Crawford referred to as a 'fortification' or 'bastion', is clearly labelled on a map drawn in 1822, as the 'Old Lines of Singapore'; the brook is called the Freshwater Stream. British Library IOR: X/3347 reproduced in Miksic, *Singapore and the Silk Road of the Sea*, p. 209.

22 A.H. Hill, *The Hikayat Abdullah*, Kuala Lumpur: Oxford University Press, 1960, p. 168.

23 Ibid., p. 142.
24 *Straits Settlement Records* L15: 284–7, J. Crawfurd to G. Swinton, 9 October 1823; A28: 186, Presgrave to Cracroft, 15 August 1826; A32: 733–736; N1: 49–51, Bonham, Jackson and Scott to Prince, 17 January 1827; I31: 187, Anderson to Prince, 15 February 1827; Cheng Hui Cheng, 'Singapore: Early Town Development 1819–1836,' B.A. Honours Thesis, National University of Singapore, 1981/82, p. 22.
25 J.W. Laidlay, 'Note on the Inscriptions from Singapur and Province Wellesley,' *Journal of the Asiatic Society of Bengal*, vol. 17, no. 2, 1848, p. 70; Hill, *Hikayat Abdullah*, pp. 145, 165–166.
26 In the *Journal of the Asiatic Society of Bengal*, volume 6, 1837, p. 681; cited by G.P. Rouffaer, 'Was Malaka emporium voor 1400 A.D. genaamd Malajoer? En waar lag Woerawari, Ma-Hasin, Langka, Batoesawar?' *Bijdragen tot de Taal-, Land- en Volkenkunde van Nederlandsch-Indie*, vol. 77, no. 1, 1918, p. 36.
27 C.A. Gibson-Hill, 'Singapore Old Strait and New Harbour 1300–1870,' *Memoirs of the Raffles Museum*, vol. 3, 1956, p. 24; Rouffaer, 'Was Malaka emporium voor 1400 A.D. genaamd Malajoer,' p. 35, gives a slightly different account.
28 J. Low, 'An Account of Several Inscriptions Found in Province Wellesley on the Peninsula of Malacca,' *Journal of the Asiatic Society of Bengal*, vol. 17, no. 2, 1848, pp. 65–66.
29 Cited in Rouffaer, 'Was Malaka emporium voor 1400 A.D. genaamd Malajoer,' p. 54.
30 J.C. Moulton, compiler, *The Annual Report on the Raffles Museum and Library for the Year 1919*, Singapore: Government Printing Office, 1921, p. 3.
31 R.O. Winstedt, 'Gold Ornaments Dug Up at Fort Canning Singapore,' *Journal of the Malayan Branch of the Royal Asiatic Society*, vol. 6, no. 4, 1928, pp. 1–4; reprinted in *Journal of the Malaysian Branch of the Royal Asiatic Society*, vol. 42, no. 1, 1969, pp. 49–52.
32 Miksic, *Singapore and the Silk Road of the Sea*, pp. 17–18.
33 Hsü Yün-Ts'iao, 'Singapore in the Remote Past,' *Journal of the Malayan Branch of the Royal Asiatic Society*, vol. 45, no. 1, 1973, pp. 1–9.
34 J.N. Miksic, 'Recently Discovered Chinese Green Glazed Wares of the Thirteenth and Fourteenth Centuries in Singapore and Riau Islands,' in *New Light on Chinese Yue and Longquan Wares: Archaeological Ceramics Found in Eastern and Southern Asia, A.D. 800–1400*, Hong Kong: The University of Hong Kong, 1994, pp. 229–250.
35 W.W. Rockhill, 'Notes on the Relations and Trade of China with the Eastern Archipelago and the Coast of the Indian Ocean During the Fourteenth Century,' *T'oung Pao*, vol. 15, Part 1, 1914, pp. 419–447; Part 2, 61–159, 236–271, 374–392, 435–467, 604–626.
36 R. Ptak, 'Images of Maritime Asia in Two Yuan Texts: Daoyi Zhilue and Yiyu zhi,' *Journal of Song-Yuan Studies*, vol. 25, 1995, pp. 47–47.
37 Rockhill, 'Notes on the Relations and Trade,' p. 261.
38 Wang's account of Singapore has been translated several times, with significant differences between them; the most commonly available translation is that by Paul Wheatley, *The Golden Khersonese*, Kuala Lumpur: University of Malaya, 1961, p. 82. See also Miksic, *Singapore and the Silk Road of the Sea*, pp. 174–178.
39 Wheatley, *Golden Khersonese*, p. 83.
40 Rockhill, 'Notes on the Relations and Trade,' p. 100.
41 George Cœdès, *The Indianized States of Southeast Asia*, ed. Walter F. Vella and trans. Susan Brown Cowing, Honolulu: University of Hawaii, 1968, p. 205.
42 J.V.G. Mills (ed. and trans.), *Ma Huan, Ying-yai Sheng-lan*, Cambridge: Hakluyt Society, 1970, pp. 182, 325.
43 Anthony Reid, *Southeast Asia in the Age of Commerce 1450–1680, Volume Two: Expansion and Crisis'*, New Haven: Yale University Press, 1993, p. 64.
44 Brown, *Sejarah Melayu*, pp. 67, 117–118, 241, note 625.
45 Miksic, *Singapore and the Silk Road of the Sea*, p. 22.

46 Martin Jezek, *Archaeology of Touchstones: An Introduction Based on Finds from Birka, Sweden,* Leiden: Sidestone Press, 2017, Fig. 6, p. 19.

47 Curriculum Planning & Development Division, Ministry of Education, Singapore, *Singapore: The Making of a Nation-State, 1300–1975,* Singapore: Star Publishing Pte. Ltd., 2014.

48 Jane A. Peterson, 'In New Textbook, the Story of Singapore Begins 500 Years Earlier,' available at: http://mobile.nytimes.com/2014/05/12/world/asia/in-new-textbook-the-story-of-singapore-begins-500-years-earlier.html?mwrsm=Facebook&referer=http://m.facebook.com, accessed 15 December 2018.

49 For example, see John N. Miksic, *Southeast Asian Archaeological Site Reports Singapore No. 1: The Singapore Cricket Club Excavation,* 20 February 2018. DOI: https://doi.org/10.25717/7w0e-3n3c, available at: http://epress.nus.edu.sg/sitereports/

50 J.V.G. Mills, *Eredia's Description of Malaca, Meridional India, and Cathay,* Kuala Lumpur: Malaysian Branch of the Royal Asiatic Society Reprint 14, 1997.

51 P. Borschberg, 'The Straits of Singapore: Continuity, Change and Confusion,' in Irene Lim (ed.), *Sketching the Straits: A Compilation of the Lecture Series on the Charles Dyce Collection,* Singapore: NUS Museums, 2004, p. 36. The map is reproduced in Mills, op. cit.; Miksic, *Singapore and the Silk Road of the Sea,* p. 164.

52 Alexander Hamilton, *A New Account of the East Indies,* Vol. II, London: Argonaut Press, 1930, p. 53.

53 British Library, K. 38286, reproduced in Miksic, *Singapore and the Silk Road of the Sea,* p. 145.

54 L.Y. Andaya, *The Kingdom of Johor 1641–1782,* Kuala Lumpur: Oxford University Press, 1975, pp. 250–264, 288.

55 V. Matheson and B.W. Andaya, *Ali al-Haji Riau, The Precious Gift=Tuhfat Al-Nafis,* Kuala Lumpur and New York: Oxford University Press, 1982, folio 169–118c.

56 C.M. Turnbull, *A History of Singapore 1819–1975,* Singapore: Oxford University Press, 1977, p. 4.

57 Archived at http://video.toggle.sg/en/series/sherlock-at-work/ep8/464773, accessed 15 December 2018.

14 Stamford Raffles and James Brooke

Colonial legacies and (post)colonial tourism?

Donna Brunero

Singapore's Bicentennial plans for 2019 include the creation of a new logo which depicts a 700 year history with a tagline 'From Singapore to Singaporean', the discussion of what it means to commemorate 1819, and an exhibition at the National Museum of Singapore that places Raffles within a context of the world of the East India Companies and the broader histories of maritime trade in Southeast Asia.[1] Clearly, Raffles and his legacies remain ongoing topics for discussion in modern Singapore, particularly in 2019. But how have these legacies played out and developed up to this point? Colonialism remains a contested topic; for example, Bruce Gilley's 2017 article, 'The Case for Colonialism', drew heated and vehement responses. Pertinently, in the ensuing debate, Singapore was held up as an exemplar of a modern state that had come to grips with its colonial past. This leads to the question: where does the history of the individual 'empire builder' such as Raffles then stand in modern historical narratives?[2] Arguably, there is no single postcolonial representation of heritage in Singapore, or Southeast Asia, and so too, the treatment of colonial heroes is also complex and nuanced. The legacies of Raffles and James Brooke, first rajah of Sarawak, form a comparative focus for this chapter.[3]

This chapter takes its inspiration from a set of Empire Marketing Board posters (see Figure 14.1) which focus on the builders of empire.[4] This may seem an unfashionable choice, but looking at the array of white, male, imperial heroes, all posed looking into the distance, it does give pause for thought as to imperial legacies and the role of the 'man on the spot' in either furthering the aims of empire or in perpetuating the enthusiasm for empire right into the twentieth century (and, some may argue, into more recent times). In the heyday of empire in the Long Nineteenth Century, and even after the Victorian era as empire waned, these individuals were invested with many properties and qualities that embodied the British imperial spirit; they were credited with truly raising the British empire to its zenith. They were valorised, memorialised and even fictionalised as the need, or public interest, arose. While recent scholarship on the British empire and imperial legacies reveals an empire that was much more contested; uneven in how its rule was guided by notions of race, class and gender; and highly nuanced in the articulation of its 'ideologies', the role of individuals and their place in larger imperial (and postcolonial) narratives is still worthy of further study.[5]

Figure 14.1 'Builders of Empire': Empire Marketing Board Poster, 1927–33.
Source: The National Archives of the United Kingdom, CO 956/227

This chapter interrogates the heroic imagery of the empire builder and traces the links between Stamford Raffles, the founding figure of modern Singapore and a key actor in the building of British interests in Southeast Asia, and James Brooke, who gained his own fame (and notoriety) as founder of a dynasty of White Rajahs in Sarawak. In claiming territorial and political pre-eminence in Sarawak, it is possible to argue that Brooke was consciously building on and fulfilling some of Raffles's unrealized ambitions for an expansion of British influence in the region.[6] What is important here is that Raffles, his knowledge of the region and his actions in Singapore helped to inform Brooke's rationale for his actions. In short, a 'Rafflesian vision' served as the inspiration for the man who became known as the White Rajah. In this way, the figure credited with placing Singapore on a firm footing as an English East India Company (EIC) trading outpost in a manner that was later seen as 'visionary' (particularly once the free-trade port of Singapore emerged as one of the great Asian colonial port cities of the British empire)[7] and the White Rajah have histories that have become intertwined, if for no other reason than that both were seen to share a particular vision of British imperial maritime frontiers in Southeast Asia and the potential for the expansion and consolidation of these frontiers. Unsurprisingly, then, both Raffles and Brooke became linked via Victorian imperial propaganda and promotion of the empire in Asia and beyond. And both figures continue to feature in a commodified form in modern states where the colonial and postcolonial are packaged for a tourist market.

This chapter explores the way in which the histories of Raffles and Brooke became intertwined in imperial narratives and the way this has shaped the historical narratives of British influence in Southeast Asia. Raffles's legacy as a founder, and as a founding figure in the larger 'Singapore Story' is generally well accepted, while Brooke's dynasty was also held up by the public (and scholars) as an example of imperial ideals that exemplified the romantic and impassioned commitment to empire, however misguided.[8] Also, both Raffles and Brooke's legacies still have resonance in postcolonial Asia but to differing extents. Raffles is firmly 'cemented' as a founding figure in Singapore's historical narratives and Singapore's heritage landscape, whereas Brooke remains forever 'the White Rajah' and is linked more to tourist dollars than a narrative of nation building. This may not be too surprising if we remember that even tourist sites change; what's valued as heritage and the significance of particular sites and memorials is constantly reinvented and repackaged from one generation to the next.[9] What follows in this chapter, then, is not so much a study of the lives and deeds of these individuals – as they have been subject to numerous studies – both serious scholarly works and hagiographies – but more a reflection on the resonances these individuals have had and continue to hold in present-day Southeast Asian heritage.[10] Through examining the intertwined histories of Raffles and Brooke and their imperial legacies, I argue that we can find new vigour in early classic works on the British empire in Asia – that of John Galbraith's study of the turbulent frontier and the 'man on the spot' and also John MacKenzie's work on the pervasive nature of imperial propaganda in promoting an ideology of empire.

To develop these ideas, this chapter will do a few things: firstly, it will briefly provide a context for understanding the British empire in Asia, through the use of imperial propaganda. Secondly, it will explore the use of the notion of the 'man on the spot' and the individual in representing the empire in the case of the British in Asia; in doing so, Raffles and Brooke are brought into focus. And thirdly, this chapter examines the extent to which these colonial founders and figures have found 'after lives' first in colonial and then in postcolonial Southeast Asia. These individuals once lauded as builders of empire have become commodified as part of a nostalgia of the 'colonial' experience in the modern day. And contemporary scholars and public interest arguably fuel this demand. It is noteworthy that in the past few years both Raffles and Brooke have been the subject of television documentaries, each dedicated to 'uncovering' the histories of these men and their deeds.[11] Finally, this chapter reflects on the ways in which Raffles and Brooke have come to be harnessed as part of modern-day postcolonial heritage and tourism in Southeast Asia.

The British in Asia: propaganda and empire

It is not too far a stretch to describe empire as partly an ideological exercise; if it was about promoting loyalty to the empire and ensuring compliance in colonial territories, it was equally about inspiring the youth and rallying popular support. An empire had strong ideological foundations; people needed to believe in the

British world system. John Seeley's series of lectures (published as *The Expansion of England* in 1883) exhorted the public to support the empire despite the very disparate nature of the territories the British had come to govern.[12] The British empire in Asia was highly varied in how it was ruled, and very often the imperial project was a collaborative venture. For instance, many local rulers were co-opted into the 'imperial family' – such as the Malay Federated States – while other territories (such as India and Burma) were subdued and their economies harnessed into imperial economic networks. Southeast Asia was no exception. The Straits Settlements were a relatively late addition to the British imperial system, and their early administration was closely tied to India.[13] Sarawak fell outside the formal gambit of empire but was in an area that was still contested – a 'frontier' of empire.

The rallying of support for the empire was demonstrated through the pomp and pageantry of imperial rule, of gunboat diplomacy and even as late as the 1920s, the empire cruise of 1923–24 kept viewers at home engaged as they followed the progress of the world's strongest fleet in their tour of the empire.[14] John Mackenzie's work is influential in this regard as in *Propaganda and Empire* he challenged the common (mis)conception that the British were indifferent to empire and revealed that the complexity of empire meant that the British empire may well mean quite different things to different people all at the same time. This is why figures such a Raffles and Brooke could be regarded as heroes in some narratives, as uncontrolled mavericks in others, as embarrassments or representing the excesses of empire; this all depended on the perspective and the audience.

For the British, in the late Victorian era, there was a convergence of influences, ranging from an increased militarism, the cult of personality built around the heroes of empire, the role of the monarchy and to this was added Social Darwinism.[15] MacKenzie describes this as the 'ideological cluster' that gave rise to the pervasive use of propaganda in the British empire. The transmission of ideas and values could be seen through imperial institutions, parades and pageants, and in school texts, but it could also be found readily in advertising campaigns, collectibles and stories of imperial adventures and colonial territories directed to the youth.[16] And in colonial territories, dominions, dependencies, people were also drawn into the pageantry of empire, its ideologies and its hierarchies of knowledge, race and class. The stories and characters crafted by Kipling and Conrad also served to not only build a literary culture that dealt with the empire but reflected evolving attitudes towards the empire; Kipling's enthusiasm for empire had jingoistic appeal, while Conrad's soul-searching works such as *Heart of Darkness* and *Almayer's Folly* create an impression of a more ambivalent engagement with the empire.[17]

The creation of ephemera relating to empire has a long resonance, cigarette cards relating to the empire can still be found in the hands of collectors. Kensitas cigarette cards (c. 1930s) on the builders of empire is a set of fifty cards featuring mainly men and Raffles and Brooke are both included in this collection (see Figure 14.2). The cards are uncommendable in terms of aesthetics (the images were inspired by National Portrait Gallery artworks) but as collectables,

Figure 14.2 Kensitas cigarette cards (c. 1930s): Raffles and Brooke.

Source: Author's collection.

they were valued, traded and exchanged. The text accompanying each card was highly didactic and allows us to consider terms how such individuals were being promoted to a young audience.[18]

While novels and cigarette cards could be aimed at the individual or classroom setting, posters were designed to have a mass audience and mass appeal. What is particularly striking in the many iconic posters of the Empire Marketing Board (EMB) is a pair of posters which highlight the builders of empire. The EMB came into being in 1926, initiated out of the Imperial Conference of the same year. While short-lived, the Board excelled in producing visual images of empire, in poster form and in moving films that promoted empire, imperial bonds and importantly, the products of empire. In the interwar years, the EMB was prolific in its production of posters, distributing a total of 150 designs, many of which related to products from around the empire.[19] These posters were designed not only as billboards but were reproduced in smaller versions which the public could buy for a small sum.[20] These posters are significant for their representations of empire and exemplify Mackenzie's ideas relating to the cult of personality surrounding some imperial figures. Not all were valorised in this way, but some individuals took on significance in imperial rhetoric, for propaganda, in popular culture, art and literature; an example here being General Charles Gordon and his heroic last stand at Khartoum coming to exemplify the nobility and sacrifice of the imperial cause, (without too much emphasis on the politics and personality of Gordon).[21] Within the posters we see figures of the eighteenth century and Victorian era such as Robert Clive and Cecil Rhodes, and also others from an earlier era, revived as heroes in the Victorian age. These figures are 'transcendent heroes' who could be called on in a more ahistorical sense but were all closely associated with the rise of England as a world power. These include Walter Raleigh, Francis Drake and William Dampier (some may quip that these pirates are perhaps the most respectable of this bunch!). Raffles and Brooke both found their way into such representations, as visionaries and empire builders in the Southeast Asian context. The man on the spot is what is idolised in these posters. For the average Briton (or settler in the colonial dominions), most of the names would be familiar, these are the same figures that had been written into children's adventure stories, collected as cigarette cards or featured in other such ephemera of empire.

Empire builders and the man on the spot

John Galbraith's classic work on the 'Turbulent Frontier' in relation to British expansion is the first in-depth coverage of this idea of the primacy and signifi-cance of the man on the spot.[22] Galbraith argues that while much of imperial expansion was in the hands of men of business and industry, the realities of travel in the early nineteenth century and that of the very shifting nature of frontiers and their instability, meant that for long stretches of time an inordinate amount of authority was vested in those administrators on the ground.[23] For instance, the governor of an Asian territory may wait for months for communication to arrive from the metropole. And inaction on the grounds of waiting for instructions was unthinkable for an administrator:

> His supreme task was the maintenance of order within his area; failure to do so was the one unpardonable sin; and in the prosecution of that objective he was often led to take actions which were not authorized by his instruction, indeed, in many cases in direct violation thereof.[24]

It is this tension between needing to assume authority and then being answerable for actions taken *on the spot* which formed the basis of many disputes between local administrators who were seen to have overstepped the mark, or to have exceeded their initial instructions (arguably much of the history of the expansion of the British empire in Asia can be seen in this light). It is the frontier in particular that is pertinent to this chapter.[25] Southeast Asia was a frontier with a maritime dimension, extending beyond the stronghold of British India, and in the nineteenth century it was contested with the Dutch in particular as a constant rival even after territory was roughly demarcated in 1824. This maritime frontier presented challenges and opportunities to British representatives of both the EIC and the empire more broadly. Tensions were constant throughout the British empire in Asia. In respect of the Indian subcontinent, for instance, the emphasis in London was on creating conditions that were conducive to peace and commerce, whereas in India, with a disintegrating Mughal empire, the emphasis was on quelling dissent, expanding EIC (and later British) control over unstable frontiers, and through this to allow conditions for commerce to flourish.[26] Arguably, it was this same logic that drove the British into a series of Anglo-Burmese wars from the 1820s onwards. Local conditions varied considerably between the Cape, the Indian Subcontinent and Southeast Asia (and later to the treaty ports of East Asia), but some key imperatives remained constant: a perceived need for control; a concern over any actions from rivals or indigenous powers which might undermine or weaken British interests in a particular region; the mentality of how the frontier was viewed (be it terrestrial or maritime); and the pressure from lobby groups, particularly business and shipping interests, the latter frequently leading to tensions between administrators based in these fledgling outposts of empire and those who 'directed' from the comfort and relative distance of the metropole.

 And, importantly, these men on the spot had a shared characteristic of being talented, adventurous and willing to move beyond the 'comforts' of Britain to pursue what they saw as either an adventure and/or an imperial calling.[27] It is in this tradition of the Victorian (although Raffles somewhat precedes it) imperialist adventurer that both Raffles and Brooke find resonance. The Victorian age had great interest in such figures. Galbraith's study is, for instance, prefaced by a much earlier work in George Griffith's popular study *Men Who Made the Empire* (1899). In this Victorian era work the author explains that empire making was an unfinished business, that there was more to be done both at home (with the

United Kingdom) but also across the expanse of the empire. Individuals all had a role to play:

> The man will not always be found of the best, nor the work seemingly, of the noblest, but what I shall seek to show you is that the work *had* to be done in order that a certain end might be accomplished, and that the man who did it was, all things considered, the best and, it may be, the only man to do it.[28]

Here the emphasis is on the 'man on the spot', perhaps an admittedly imperfect individual but one who was called on to act as an empire builder. It is notable that neither Raffles nor Brooke were given mention in this volume, but they very much embodied Griffith's idea of the sometimes-imperfect figure who was called on in remarkable times. Both Raffles and Brooke, through their actions in a Southeast Asian fronter, advanced British interests in the region. A pervasive public interest in the 'man on the spot' is illustrated through literary works. Conrad's *Lord Jim* (1900) and Kipling's cautionary tale *The Man Who Would Be King* (1888) are two examples of white men who emerge as leaders in a foreign land, who push beyond the formal boundaries of empire and are re-created in the process.

Sir Stamford Raffles

The history of Raffles has been dealt with extensively by many scholars and there are numerous biographies of the man, published collections of his papers and Singapore is home to a slew of buildings, institutions (including a hotel and medical group) all named in his honour. The name of Raffles has itself become almost synonymous with Singapore on the world stage.[29] As Singaporean historian Kevin Y.L. Tan reflected:

> Even if the thousands of students force-fed a National Education diet of Raffles are probably quite jaded by the mention of his name, Raffles has worn well. He has not, like some of our more modern heroes, faded like the old history books that detail his story and deeds.[30]

Tan attributes the continued proliferation of interest in Raffles to 'powerful images' which have an uncanny hold on the imagination.[31] How has Raffles been described in such works and why does he capture the imagination? Assessments of his actions in 1819, and his return to London (to answer to his EIC employers in disgrace) are very wide ranging. Raffles's own writings demonstrated his skill for self-promotion.[32] And Raffles's work in Asia was valorised in the labours of his wife, Lady Sophia Raffles, who assembled his memoirs and papers, revealing Raffles as a man who sometime felt his vision was misunderstood and undervalued.[33] By modern scholars he's been dubbed variously as a maverick who wouldn't listen, an ambitious man and a schemer who knew how to utilise his knowledge of the Malay world and political scene to his advantage.

For instance, Syed Hussein Alatas's work of 1971, *Thomas Stamford Raffles: Schemer or Reformer?* is a pivotal study which reassessed Raffles; other scholars have similarly reviewed Raffles as an EIC man and scholar, developing a more nuanced assessment of this individual far beyond Sophia Raffles's account of her husband's life.[34]

A constant in many accounts is Raffles's identity as an EIC man, and undoubtedly, he was an EIC man *par excellence*. What is less understood is the nature of the EICs and their far-reaching powers – going far beyond standard private firms – and the rigours of life in this service. The EIC attracted ambitious and risk-taking individuals, and Raffles was both.[35] Arguably, Raffles demonstrated the political wiles, ambition and expansionist tendencies of which the likes of Clive or Dalhousie would have been most approving, but by the 1800s the EIC was dangerously overstretched on the Indian subcontinent (there had already been a series of financial crises in the late 1700s) and this brought about a more circumspect approach to policies by the EIC, particularly in relation to India's frontiers and neighbours (Burma, for example).[36]

Stamford Raffles, of course, played an important role in the founding of Singapore as a trading post of the EIC. The seemingly straightforward narrative of the story of modern Singapore (and Raffles's role therein) has been re-examined by various scholars. The works of Alatas and Aljunied, among others, have questioned Raffles's scholarship and position vis-à-vis the Malay world.[37] Raffles fashioned himself as an expert on the region, and his writings on Java were influential.[38] It is noteworthy that scholars are constantly revisiting and reappraising Raffles in relation to Singapore's history. One interpretation by Leong Yew places Raffles in the juxtaposition of a 'new-old' framing of Singapore's origins, a place founded by a foreign visionary and therefore *new* but a place that could also lay claims to being very old by virtue of the 'age old civilisations' that Singapura tapped into to via the Chinese, Indian and Malay worlds.[39] In this interpretation of Singapore's origins, Raffles is both the exemplar of human agency (the quintessential 'man on the spot') and at the same time the facilitator for allowing the inheritance of a much longer history. In each instance, 'new' or 'old', the agency of Raffles remains central. Raffles's statue, by Woolner, was erected in 1889 (and now resides in front of the Victoria Concert Hall), while another statue erected in the 1970s graces Raffles's 'landing spot' (at a 'new' or 'old' settlement, depending on how this event is framed) along the Singapore River.[40] Raffles is memorialised in Singapore's heritage landscape via these monuments.

Brooke: a successor to Raffles?

The actions of James Brooke in securing himself the position of Rajah in Sarawak is fairly well known. A brief sketch is outlined here. Like Raffles, Brooke started with a career in the EIC, but he didn't last very long as a Company man. He had something that Raffles may have very much hoped for – the financial means to no longer need to be beholden to the Company.[41] Setting out in a ship he'd purchased from his inheritance (following his father's death) Brooke set forth in the aptly named *Royalist* and resolved to venture to Singapore and from there to Borneo. After a series of negotiations and some adroit political manoeuvring, including assisting the Sultan of Brunei to put down a rebellion, Brooke secured for himself the position of the Rajah and in effect, the unrivalled political ruler of Sarawak. Ironically, Sarawak was not an initial priority for Brooke, but it was his visit to Singapore that galvanised his interest in the region.[42]

At the very least in the eyes of Brooke, his actions in Borneo, and his securing of rule and territory in Sarawak was due in part, to the vision and inspiration provided by Stamford Raffles. In 1838, Brooke wrote of his early plans to venture to Southeast Asia, and one of the experts he cited was Sir Stamford Raffles.[43] It was through the written work of Raffles that much of Brooke's early impressions of the region were shaped. Stamford Raffles was a particular hero of Brooke's, and his biographer, Reece, goes so far as to mention his being driven by a 'Rafflesian' vision for Southeast Asia.[44] Furthermore, his letters reveal his sympathies with what he felt was the way that Raffles's vision (and ambition) for Borneo – and further territories in Southeast Asia beyond Singapore – had been thwarted by a lack of support and imagination on the part not only of the EIC but also the British government. Brooke's letters, written to his friend and confidant John Templer and to his mother, mention Raffles numerous times.[45] They also provide insights into how Brooke believed his own actions were helping to bring British civilisation to Southeast Asia. Brooke saw that he was embarking on a grand experiment, 'which, if it succeeds, will bestow a blessing on these poor people, and their children's children will bless my name.'[46]

Brooke's aims for Kuching (the main township) and Sarawak were ambitious, to say the least. Brooke expressed surprise that so little was known of Borneo and that it attracted so little attention: 'Sir Stamford Raffles remarks that its soil is not only as rich as any in the world, but that its mineral productions rival those of South America.'[47] Brooke goes on to list the wealth of materials abundant in Sarawak: diamonds, gold, tin, iron, antimony, copper as reported and 'these mineral mountains as yet unsearched by any man of intelligence.'[48] This is a good example where Raffles's writings and knowledge of the region is used by Brooke and developed further. It is possible that these references to Raffles were driven by a mixture of admiration and a linking of himself with Raffles in the minds of readers. It seems fairly certain that Brooke knew his letters would be published, and in this he was not unlike Raffles in using his writing to advance his interests and deliberately cultivate a certain public persona.

Like Raffles, Brooke was the subject of biographies, histories and artworks.[49] An early biography of Brooke, written based on his personal letters by Spenser St. John (a long-time friend and confidant), gives us a sense of the cult of personality that Brooke attracted. The second trip to Borneo in 1840 was described by St. John as the 'most romantic even in his romantic career', St. John laments:

> I wish I could render it in his own bright, energetic, and brilliant manner, as I have heard him tell this story during the twenty years of our familiar

intercourse. I know the ground well; there is not a spot that I have not visited, and there have I heard the wondrous story in all its curious details.[50]

This extract underlines the admiration that St. John had for Brooke, perceiving him as a charismatic and compelling individual whose life epitomised the romantic adventurer. It is noteworthy that St. John emphasizes the importance of the location where the story of Brooke's rise to power took place. Ironically, there is no statue on a 'special spot' in Kuching or Sarawak, but in the memoir, the importance of place is emphasised (there are small memorials to the Brooke dynasty in Kuching, Sarawak, but not statues of the man). The portrait of Brooke by Sir Francis Grant (one of the most famous portrait artists of the Victorian era) is perhaps the most striking image and casts Brooke as a Byronesque figure, testifying to the romantic notions attached to the White Rajah. Reaffirming the close connection between St. John and Brooke is the fact that St. John bought the portrait in July 1877 and subsequently donated it to the National Portrait Gallery. The portrait was painted in late 1847 when Brooke made a triumphant visit to London, and it contributed greatly to his popular image as a dashing adventurer and a patriot in the style of Raleigh and Drake (an engraving based on this painting appeared in the *Illustrated London News*.)[51] If disinterested contemporaries were to be believed, it was not a particularly good likeness, as Brooke was in his fifties and had a rather slight build.[52] What we see then, via these writings and artworks was the propaganda of empire in action; Brooke had already become an embodiment of the 'ideal' of empire more than anything else.

But despite the scholarly attention given to the Rajahs of Sarawak, James Brooke has received the least coverage. Critics noted that Spenser St. John, of all writers, knew Brooke the best and yet seems to have steered away from 'less admirable' aspects of his personality or political motives that may have been either controversial or less than 'desirable' in a written history. Further to this, Reece, whose own scholarship on Brooke is extensive, poses the question as to whether it is ever really possible to write a definitive biography of James Brooke because of this scant insight into the thinking of the man. Likewise, Tarling, after reviewing 'hundreds, perhaps thousands of letters' admitted he found Sir James elusive and baffling, as there are many parts of his life which remain obscure.[53]

At this juncture it is worth posing the question: is this why Brooke remains a fascinating character? Why he became an interesting figure in the history of the empire? In some ways, he has become a larger-than-life caricature of the Victorian imperialist. There's much that is unknown about his motivations, personal thoughts and actions, and yet, still an interest in him pervades the popular culture realm. In popular culture, Brooke's actions inspired works like the popular George MacDonald *Flashman* series of novels, in which the central character finds himself in one adventure after another, all taking place against the backdrop of major events, or watersheds of the British empire.[54] Furthermore, he is cast as a villainous figure contrasted against the Malay-prince-turned-pirate-hero in Emilio Salgari's *Sandokan* series of novels (c. 1890s) that were made into a highly successful television series in the 1970s.[55]

Representations and (post) colonial tourism

What then, are the legacies of these two individuals, whose histories have become intertwined, in the Victorian age, then through the Empire Marketing Board, as well as Brooke's own efforts to link his own endeavours with those of Raffles's? While the formal colonial era has ended, one does not need to look very far to realise that its traces are widespread, and its influence runs deep. Former colonies the world over are still grappling with colonial legacies. Both Raffles and Brooke have been the subject of documentaries, aired on Channel News Asia, each seeking to uncover something of the man, but also the more contentious aspects of his past. In 'Re-inventing Southeast Asia', TV host and scholar Farish Noor described Brooke as a 'freelance empire builder' while exploring his ambivalent legacy in Sarawak (credited as useful for tourism by locals who are interviewed). Meanwhile, architectural historian and anthropologist Julian Davison, hosted 'Raffles Revealed', a 2015 production, also aimed at presenting Raffles in a fuller light. This approach to uncovering the colonial past is in keeping with bicentennial plans; a member of the Bicentennial Committee, the historian Tan Tai Yong, reflected that the bicentennial in 2019 was not meant to be a rose-tinted account of events of the last two centuries but rather a way to 'capture the full essence and the full complexities of what happened'.[56]

In the case of Singapore, there's been a clear crafting of the role of Raffles vis-à-vis the history of Singapore as a nation state. Even the decision to retain Raffles as a founding figure after 1965 was not without some political (and geopolitical considerations). Raffles and his representations in popular culture have found interesting parallels with those of Lee Kuan Yew. In his work, Leong Yew points out that most Singaporeans accept three key figures in the history of Singapore (the island) Sang Nila Utama, marking a pre-modern history, Stamford Raffles and the dawning of a modern emporium, and Lee Kuan Yew as the leader of the nation state. In particular, he draws attention to two slim volumes produced by Asiapac Books which provide cartoon histories of Raffles and Lee that have similar narrative devices, allowing the reader to make parallels in the life stories of these founding figures. The themes in these child-friendly volumes include overcoming hardship, unfailing vision and opposition to their plans.[57] These volumes are targeted at a young readership and almost serve a similar role to the posters and collectibles found in the age of empire in terms of their didactic and moral devices.

In the last two decades, scholarship on Singapore's history has moved more clearly to incorporate not only a longer history (known colloquially as the '700-year history') but one that also, crucially, situates Singapore within regional histories, as well as European and imperial histories. In these larger narratives, cast by Kwa Chong Guan, Derek Heng, Peter Borschberg and Tan Tai Yong as a history of Singapore in the longue durée, Raffles's role is fleeting but still recognised as important in marking a period in which the history of the island, and the settlement on Singapore flourished under the 'umbrella' of British colonial presence in Asia.[58] And in a move to reconsider Singapore's history in an even broader sense,

S.R. Joey Long writes of the impetus to create an international history of Singapore, one situating it in international events and currents, far beyond the region.[59] What is significant in both impulses, longer histories and broader histories, is that the emphasis is less on the individual (although not dispensing with this altogether) and more on considering Singapore the settlement, the colony and nation state against the larger backdrop of regional and global events.

In contrast, James Brooke, and his dynasty of White Rajahs with a legacy of a quasi-imperial, then imperial territory has a more mixed history. He and his descendants have been more sensationalised.[60] The White Rajahs and the Brooke legacy seems to have left a deep impression, but one without any substantial foundations. Any visitor to Kuching, Sarawak, in the present day would be hard pressed not to notice the references to Brooke, the Rajah and his legacy. But this is more as a tourist attraction perhaps than any deeper-seated consciousness or awareness of the history of the figure. Notably, within Kuching there are a number of cafés, restaurants and hotels that link to the Brooke name. Heritage (colonial era) buildings have been restored, but this colonial 'backwater' offers a utilitarian use of the Brooke name as and when it suits.[61] This is evident in the façade of the Brooke dockyards, the renovation of Fort Margherita (built under the second Rajah in 1879), and the restoration of the Sarawak Museum. James Brooke, however, has not been harnessed for any narratives of state formation or development; his story is seen as specific to Borneo, not a larger entity.[62] The one notable waterfront locale is that of the James Brooke café and the Royalist pub, both named after the 'founding figure' of the Brooke dynasty. Travellers' blogs write of having a 'sense of history' via the 'colonial/antique' furnishings and pictures on the walls, but aside from cultivating a particular ambience (perhaps none too different from the Raffles Hotel's efforts to keep a sense of 'timelessness' to the interior) there has been until recently, little more of substance to memorialise the first Rajah of Sarawak.[63] In 2010, the grandsons of the last Rajah Muda Anthony Brooke established the Brooke Trust as a charitable organisation to uncover Sarawak's history and to 'inform, enrich and inspire'.[64] This organisation has digitised documents relating to Brooke rule, has organized exhibitions relating to the Brookes in Sarawak's Old Courthouse and also offers education bursaries. One interesting project of the Brooke Trust is a plan to build a replica of *The Royalist*. What remains to be seen is whether this initiative gathers sufficient monetary or public support to fund and sustain this project.

In much of this, hagiography remains apparent, and while seemingly modern, is in fact very much a Victorian construct emphasising the history of the 'rags to riches' individual.[65] Two recent books seek to reveal different angles or interpretations of Raffles and situate him more firmly in popular culture. Tim Hannigan's, *Raffles and the British Invasion of Java*, for instance, includes in its cover blurb discussion that book casts Raffles, 'long celebrated as a hero, a liberal and a visionary – in a shocking new light.' Here the focus is on Raffles in Java and providing an 'alternative' history to the more well-known Singapore connection.[66] And Victoria Glendinnings' *Raffles and the Golden Opportunity 1781–1826* was written with the intention of retrieving the 'reality' of Raffles, one that had been submerged as a brand that was 'exclusive, expensive' and 'uniquely Singaporean'.[67] Glendinning writes to move beyond what she regards as this simplistic 'imagining of Raffles' as both a hero and a villain of the British empire. In the National Museum of Singapore, a copy of the UK National Portrait Gallery's picture of Raffles hangs in place, at a point in the gallery to denote the visitor has reached 1819. Visitors to the museum move through the exhibition which begins with the Temasek era and the early settlement of the island and progresses on to Raffles's portrait and the growing British presence in Asia. The portrait, informally dubbed 'Raffles of Java' is readily recognisable, includes in the background items and accoutrements pointing to Raffles scholarship and interest in ancient civilizations in the Malay world.[68] What is ironic is that there is no portrait of Raffles of Singapore, and there has been no local artist to produce a portrait that has made it to the National Museum (though some have created art installations surrounding Raffles statues).[69] The Victorian representation of Raffles still holds the public imagination, and for the National Day Parade (NDP) of SG50 (50 years of nationhood) spectators were treated to a history of Singapore that spanned some 700 years, in which a float with Stamford Raffles and Lady Sophia Raffles circled the performance area on their ship, greeting the crowd (Major William Farquhar, the first British Resident of Singapore was also featured on the ship). Here (see Figure 14.3) Raffles was represented as part of a larger narrative, rather than the

Figure 14.3 SG50 National Day Parade, August 2015.

Source: Author's Image

'starting point' of modern Singapore.[70] Since the SG50 celebrations, however, Raffles has been largely absent from NDP performances. Even so, this absence does not mean he has been removed from national narratives, his name remains firmly in place in popular consciousness.

As Peggy Teo and T.C. Chang reflect in their study of Singapore's heritage tourism, quite often there is an appeal for travellers in places that represent the global and yet local, and the colonial and yet the modern.[71] Boutique hotels (the subject of Teo and Chang's study) reflect this attempt to refashion the colonial and create a new 'tourism' where sites, and places, are simultaneously 'colonial' and yet postcolonial. Following this idea, we may see that 'selling' the Raffles and Brooke name and history has become very appealing as a way of 'hybridising' the past and the present. Marketed widely in Singapore, and likewise in Sarawak, many areas are conserved, and the Raffles and/or Brooke name is seen as having a certain cachet. These men aren't necessarily being idolised, but what is interesting is the way in which they are seen as useful in allowing visitors to link to a colonial past, to think of the 'colourful characters' who built empire and those who were the risk-takers at the outskirts of formal empire in particular. Just as Singapore has been marketed as a modern Asian destination, the historical is recognised as an important anchor for a richer understanding of the island's value in larger narratives; the colonial can become 'exotic'. Sarawak, is arguably different, with an emphasis on local ethnography, but the Brooke name serves a similar purpose in linking to broader colonial histories in the region.

Both Raffles and Brooke were valorised as Victorian heroes of empire building long into the twentieth century and even when the British empire was being hastily dismantled (or violently cast aside). The legacies of these figures have been stretched further through the ways in which they have shaped popular culture. They have found a way into scholarship, particularly through the idea of the man on the spot, and they have a popular and enduring public interest through their use in the tourist market. This chapter has demonstrated the intertwined histories of these two figures and their actions at the frontier of the British empire in Southeast Asia, and how their legacies can be traced through popular culture, heritage conservation and even tourism to the present day. While any study of empire builders raises uncomfortable questions about their role and increasingly tenuous position in modern national narratives, the appeal of these individuals still holds some sway, if for no other reason than a fascination with the Victorian, the ideals they portrayed and the romance of the personalities who dedicated their energies to shaping an empire.

Notes

1 Melody Zaccheus for *The Straits Times,* 'Bicentennial logo launched, design reflects 700 years of history,' 3 December 2018 and 'Singapore's Rich Pre-colonial History to be Showcased,' 22 October 2018.
2 See Adam Lusher, 'Professor's 'Bring Back Colonialism' Call Sparks Fury and Academic Freedom Debate,' *The Independent*, 12 October 2017, available at: www.independent.co.uk/news/world/americas/colonialism-academic-article-bruce-gilley-threats-violence-published-withdrawn-third-world-quarterly-a7996371.html and in

relation to Singapore, see Jeevan Vasagar, 'Can Colonialism Have Benefits? Look at Singapore,' *The Guardian*, 4 January 2018. In this article the treatment of the 'gleaming white statue of Thomas Stamford Raffles' erected along the Singapore River in 1969 is highlighted by the author as evidence of a state where much of its 'colonial legacy had been left intact.' www.theguardian.com/commentisfree/2018/jan/04/colonialism-work-singapore-postcolonial-british-empire, accessed September 2018.

3   As an example of scholarship relating to heritage tourism in Asia, see Tim Winter, Peggy Teo, and T.C. Chang (eds.), *Asia on Tour: Exploring the Rise of Asian Tourism*, London: Routledge, 2002.

4   'Cook_Rhodes' Poster, Empire Marketing Board 1927–33, artwork by Fred Taylor, The National Archives of the United Kingdom, CO 956/227.

5   Examples here that come to mind include Philippa Levine's work on gender and empire. The entire field of subaltern studies has emerged from a concern over the imperial gaze and the silencing of colonial subjects. Ann McClintocks' iconic *Imperial Leather* examines intersections of race, gender and popular imperial culture.

6   Nicholas Tarling, 'Brooke Rule in Sarawak and Its Principles,' *Journal of the Malayan Branch of the Royal Asiatic Society*, vol. 65, no. 1, 1992, pp. 15–17.

7   See Rhodes Murphey, 'Traditionalism and Colonialism: Changing Urban Roles in Asia,' *Journal of Asian Studies*, vol. 29, no. 1, 1969, pp. 67–84 for a classic examination of the colonial port cities of empire. More recently, see Donna Brunero, 'Maritime Goes Global,' in D. Brunero and B. Farrell (eds.), *Empire in Asia: The Long Nineteenth Century*, London: Bloomsbury Academic, 2018 on the role of Asian port cities in the British empire.

8   An example here is Steven Runciman, *The White Rajahs: A History of Sarawak from 1841 to 1946*, Cambridge: Cambridge University Press, 1960. Runciman describes Brooke as 'undeterred' by the challenges of governing Sarawak in spite of his shortcomings, namely: his lack of administrative experience, his unsuccessful business ventures and weakness in the Malay language. 68–9.

9   Michael Hitchcock, Victor T. King, and Michael Parnwell, 'Heritage Tourism in Southeast Asia,' in Michael Hitchcock, Victor T. King and Michael Parnwell (eds.), *Heritage Tourism in Southeast Asia*, Copenhagen: NIAS Press, 2010, pp. 12–14.

10   See the R.H.W. Reece, 'Brooke, Sir James (1803–1868),' in *Oxford Dictionary of National Biography*, Oxford: Oxford University Press, 2004–2014.

11   'Inventing Southeast Asia' by Dr Farish Noor 2018, Channel News Asia. Episode 2 on 'Kings and Pirates' and in 2015 Dr Julian Davison hosted 'Raffles Revealed' a two-part series exploring the life and times of Stamford Raffles and his rise from an EIC clerk.

12   J.R. Seeley, *The Expansion of England: A Series of Two Lectures 1883*, Cambridge: Cambridge University Press, 1984.

13   See John Darwin, *The Empire Project: The Rise and Fall of the British World System 1830–1970*, Cambridge: Cambridge University Press, 2009, for a discussion of the idea of an 'imperial system' as a term used by the Victorians to denote the empire.

14   V.C. Scott O'Connor, *The Empire Cruise*, London: Riddle, Smith & Duffus, 1925.

15   See David Cannadine, *Ornamentalism: How the British Saw Their Empire*, Oxford: Oxford University Press, 2001, as an example of how the cult of the monarchy was understood and fashioned as part of the larger imperial project.

16   See J.M. MacKenzie, *Propaganda and Empire: The Manipulation of British Public Opinion 1880–1960*, Manchester: Manchester University Press, 1986, Chapter 1 for an introduction to the idea of imperial propaganda. Postcards and photos were soon complemented with moving images – the cinema became another powerful purveyor of images of empire.

17   Bradley Deane, 'Imperial Boyhood: Piracy and the Play Ethic,' *Victorian Studies*, vol. 53, no. 4, 2011, pp. 689–714. See also Rudyard Kipling, *Kim*, Macmillan & Co, 1901; Joseph Conrad, *Heart of Darkness*, London: Penguin, 1902, 1994.

18 Kensitas cards: Raffles's card (no. 23) highlights his foresight and genius in recognising the importance of Singapore (and leading to the rise of British Malaya as a
key economic resource), while Brooke (card no. 36) is credited with subduing piracy
in Southeast Asia, and like many pioneers he suffered criticism at home, but was
exonerated.

19 MacKenzie, *Propaganda and Empire*, p. 183. Also see, Uma Kothari, 'Trade, Consumption and Development Alliances: The Historical Legacy of the Empire Marketing
Board Poster Campaign,' *Third World Quarterly*, vol. 35, no. 1, 2014, pp. 43–64.

20 The public could buy a small poster for 1s 6d and as many as 27,000 schools sub-
scribed to a distribution list. See Karl Hack, 'Selling Empire: Posters,' *Open Learn,
The Open University*, Posted Under World History, available at: www.open.edu/open
learn/history-the-arts/history/world-history/selling-empire, accessed June 2017.

21 For Gordon, see the artwork by George William Joy, entitled 'The Siege of Khartoum'
(1893).

22 John S. Galbraith, 'The Turbulent Frontier' as a Factor in British Expansion,' *Comparative Studies in Society and History*, vol. 2, no. 2, 1960, pp. 150–168.

23 Galbraith's work inspired a collection of essays Roger D. Long (ed.), *The Man on the
Spot: Essays on British Empire History*, London and Westport, CT: Greenwood Press,
1995. In this collection, attention is paid to the controversial governor of Bombay,
Sir Bartle Frere, Cape imperialist Cecil Rhodes, and African conqueror-administrator
Frederick Lugard, among others.

24 Galbraith, 'The Turbulent Frontier,' p. 151.

25 For a recent discussion of the frontier in relation to empire building, see Brian P. Far-
rell, 'Staking Out an Imperial States System: The Imperial Frontier in Asia in the
"Long Nineteenth Century",' in Donna Brunero and Brian P. Farrell (eds.), *Empire in
Asia: A New Global History*, Vol. 2, London: Bloomsbury, 2018, pp. 137–174.

26 Galbraith, 'The Turbulent Frontier,' pp. 152–153.

27 Harry A. Gailety, 'Lugard and Abeokuta,' in Long, *The Man on the Spot*, p. 63.

28 George Griffith, *Men Who Made the Empire*, London: C. Arthur Pearson & Co, 1899,
Foreword, p. xv.

29 Kennie Ting, *Singapore 1819: A Living Legacy*, Singapore: Talisman Publishing,
2019, p. 2.

30 Kevin Y.L. Tan, 'Raffles and the Founding of Singapore: An Exhibition of Raffles's
Letters from the Bute Archive and the National Library,' *Biblioasia*, vol. 8, no. 2, 2012,
p. 5, Singapore: National Library Board.

31 Ibid., p. 5.

32 C.H. Wake, 'Raffles and the Rajas: The Founding of Singapore in Malayan and British
Colonial History,' *Journal of the Malayan Branch of the Royal Asiatic Society*, vol. 48,
no. 1 (227), 1975. Wake (p. 52) argues that Raffles promoted himself as a proconsular
figure. See also John Bastin, *The Founding of Singapore: Based on the Private Letters
of Sir Stamford Raffles to the Governor-General and Commander-in-Chief in India,
the Marquess of Hastings, Preserved in the Bute Collection at Mount Stuart, Isle of
Bute, Scotland*, Singapore: National Library Board, 2012. In this collection of letters,
we can trace Raffles's cultivation of contacts – both inside the EIC and beyond – and
the self-promotion of his efforts in Southeast Asia.

33 Lady Sophia Raffles, *Memoir of the Life and Public Services of Sir Thomas Stamford
Raffles, F.R.S &c,: Particularly in the Government of Java, 1811–1816 and of Bencoolen and Its Dependencies 1817–1824: With Details of the Commerce and Resources
of the Eastern Archipelago, and Selections from His Correspondence by His Widow*,
London: John Murray, 1830.

34 Syed Hussein Alatas, *Thomas Stamford Raffles: Schemer or Reformer?* Singapore:
Angus and Robertson, 1971. A good review of Raffles understanding of the Malay
political world is found in Wake, 'Raffles and the Rajas,' pp. 47–73. More recent

re-assessments of Raffles include Nigel Barley (ed.), *The Golden Sword: Raffles and the East,* London: British Museum Press, 1999; Syed Muhd Khairudin Aljunied, 'Sir Thomas Stamford Raffles' Discourse on the Malay World: A Revisionist Perspective,' *Sojourn,* vol. 20, no. 1, 2005, pp. 1–22.

35 Wake, 'Raffles and the Rajas,' pp. 50–52.

36 Anthony Webster, *The Twilight of the East India Company: The Evolution of Anglo-Asian Commerce and Politics, 1790–1860,* London: Boydell & Brewer, 2009.

37 See scholarship by Syed Hussein Alatas, Syed Muhd Khairudin Aljunied and C.H. Wake. In 'Raffles and Rajas' Wake makes the case that Raffles own writings on Java opened new doors for him in terms of social and career opportunities. Raffles's scholarship was subject to further review at an Asian Civilisations Museum exhibition in Singapore (February–April 2019) on 'Raffles in Southeast Asia.'

38 Sir Thomas Stamford Raffles, *The History of Java,* 3 vols, 2nd edn., London: John Murray, 1830.

39 Leong Yew, *Asianism and the Politics of Regional Consciousness in Singapore,* London: Routledge, 2014, chapter 3 'Singapore, Asia and Their Beginnings,' pp. 49–50.

40 Bonny Tan, 'The Statue of Stamford Raffles,' *Infopedia,* National Library Board of Singapore, available at: http://eresources.nlb.gov.sg/infopedia/articles/SIP_119_2005-01-13.html, accessed November 2018.

41 Alex Middleton, 'Rajah Brooke and the Victorians,' *Historical Journal,* vol. 53, no. 2, 2010, pp. 383–384.

42 Tarling, 'Brooke Rule,' pp. 15–26. See also Steven Runciman, *The White Rajahs: A History of Sarawak from 1841 to 1946,* Cambridge: Cambridge University Press, 1960.

43 Brooke, December 1838–January 1839, pp. 3–4, *The Private Letters of Sir James Brooke K.C.B. Rajah of Sarawak, Narrating the Events of His Life from 1838 to the Present Time.* Edited by John C. Templer, *Esq. Barrister-at-law and Once the Master of her Majesty's Court of Exchequer,* 3 vols, Vol. 1, London: Reichard Bently, 1853.

44 Reece, 'Brooke, Sir James (1803–1868)'. Nicholas Tarling echoes similar sentiments in 'Brooke Rule,' pp. 15–16.

45 See, for example, Brooke to John Temple from Kuching, Sarawak, 10 November 1841, *The Private Letters of Sir James Brooke,* Vol. 1, pp. 129–130.

46 Brooke to his Mother from Kuching, Sarawak, 27 September 1841, *The Private Letters of Sir James Brooke,* Vol. 1, p. 121.

47 Brooke to John C. Templer, Kuching, Sarawak 10 November 1841, *The Private Letters of Sir James Brooke,* Vol. 1, pp. 129–130.

48 Ibid.

49 Scholarship by Tarling and Reece on Brooke is well-regarded. For example: Nicholas Tarling, *The Burthen, the Risk and the Glory: A Biography of James Brooke,* Oxford: Oxford University Press, 1982; R.H.W. Reece, *The Name of Brooke: The End of White Rajah Rule in Sarawak,* Oxford: Oxford University Press, 1982. More recent popular histories include Nigel Barley's, *White Rajah,* London: Abacus, 2003.

50 Spenser St. John, *The Life of Sir James Brooke, Rajah of Sarawak, from His Personal Papers and Correspondence, with an Introduction by R.H.W. Reece,* Kuala Lumpur: Oxford University Press, 1994, p. 27.

51 Ibid, introduction by Reece, xxv and xxvi.

52 Ibid.

53 Ibid., p. xliv.

54 The Flashman series of books are interesting, the first of these novels being published in 1969. Written by George MacDonald Fraser they are stories set against the backdrop of empire but are hyper-masculine tales of adventure, of moral ambiguity (at best) and imperial (mis)adventures of Harry Paget Flashman, a fictitious character derived from the character of Flashman who appears in the classic *Tom Brown's School Days.*

55 Kipling, *Man Who Would Be King.* Emilio Salgari's popular Sandokan series (11 books in total) was published from 1895–1913.

56 Kenneth Cheng, 'Singapore's Bicentennial in 2019 to Recapture Historic Events from 720 Years Ago,' *Today Online*, 31 December 2017, available at: www.todayonline. com/singapore/spore-bicentennial-2019-recapture-historic-events-720-years-ago

57 Leong Yew, *Asianism*, pp. 52–53.

58 Kwa Chong Guan, Derek Heng, Peter Borschberg and Tan Tai Yong, *Seven Hundred Years: A history of Singapore*, National Library Board and Bicentennial Office Singapore: Marshal Cavendish, 2019.

59 S.R. Joey Long, 'Bringing the International and Transnational Back in: Singapore, Decolonisation and Cold War,' in Khairudin Aljunied and Derek Heng Thiam Soon (eds.), *Singapore in Global History*, Amsterdam: Amsterdam University Press, 2014.

60 See Ranee Sylvia Brooke (The wife of the third Rajah), *Queen of the Headhunters: An Autobiography of H.H. the Hon. Sylvia Lady Brooke*, London: Sidgwick & Jackson, 1970, as evidence of a conscious self-fashioning as ruler of an exotic land.

61 Anecdotal observations from a Dayak tour guide who spoke quite frankly about the lucrative aspect of the Brooke name and the mystique that this still engenders. Conversation with the author in September 2016.

62 One exception may be the use of the Brooke coat of arms. This has been used in association with a 'Sarawak for Sarawakians' independence movement c. 2014. The Brooke coat of arms appears as an image on this NGO's Facebook page. There is no appearance of James Brooke or the successive Rajahs, available at: www.facebook.com/pg/ SarawakForSarawakianOfficial/about/?ref=page_internal, accessed December 2018.

63 See, for example, the tourist blog: www.illyariffin.com/2017/05/james-brooke-bistro-cafe-sarawak-review.html

64 www.brooketrust.org. Rebuilding *Royalist* is envisaged as an 'education and outreach programme. The replica would be built in Plymouth.

65 Yew, *Asianism* citing Nadia Wright, 57.

66 Tim Hannigan, *Raffles and the British Invasion of Java*, Singapore: Monsoon Books, 2012. Hannigan writes of Raffles actions in Java as not only humiliating the Javanese court, but of his intention to conquer their past, through his writing of the history of Java, 231–232.

67 Victoria Glendinning, *Raffles and the Golden Opportunity 1781–1826*, London: Profile Books, 2012, Introduction.

68 NPG84, 'Sir Thomas Stamford Bingley Raffles' by George Francis Joseph (oil on canvas, 1817). This portrait was painted when Raffles returned to Britain to oversee the publication of his *History of Java* (1817). The Buddhist sculptures and the distant landscape allude to his study of the ethnography, ancient civilisation and languages of the region.

69 A note of thanks to my colleague Dr. Kelvin Lawrence for our discussion of this issue while on a student fieldtrip to the National Museum in February 2018.

70 Based on the author's observations as a spectator at the SG50 National Day Parade at the Padang, Singapore, 9 August 2015.

71 Peggy Teo and T.C. Chang, 'Singapore's Postcolonial Landscape: Boutique Hotels as Agents,' in Tim Winter, Peggy Teo, and T.C. Chang (eds.), *Asia on Tour: Exploring the Rise of Asian Tourism*, London: Routledge, 2002, pp. 82–84. The focus of this chapter is the creation of boutique colonial hotels, but arguably the authors raise useful ideas that can be effectively applied to the notion of heritage sites and colonial figures as having (post) colonial 'tourist appeal.'

Index

Page numbers in *italics* indicate figures.

Printed in the United States
By Bookmasters